Premier
players
formbook

95-96
Premier players
formbook

The complete statistical guide to every player in the English Premier League

HAMLYN

Jeff Harris

First published in Great Britain in 1995
by Hamlyn an imprint of Reed Consumer Books Limited
Michelin House, 81 Fulham Road, London SW3 6RB
and Auckland, Melbourne, Singapore and Toronto

ISBN 0 600 58733 9

A catalogue record for this book is available from the British Library

Printed in Great Britain

ACKNOWLEDGEMENTS
The author would like to thank Duncan McKay, Barry Hugman, Dave Smith at Shoot Magazine, the Premier League, the Football Association, the Football League, the Irish FA, the Scottish FA, the Welsh FA, Sports Projects, the PFA, John 'Wobbly' Claypole, Rene, Fred and Grace for copy-holding, the staff at Reed Books and Rob Pearce for his computing expertise.

AUTHOR'S NOTE
I would like to apologise to all in the plate room at Benham's for being so boring over the last two years.

EDITOR'S NOTE
The editor would like to thank Bash Ahmed, Stuart Armstrong, Pedro Arnold, Lindsay Johnson, Conor Kilgallon, Martin Topping, Andy Tough, and Carl Ward for their help at various stages of this book's production.

PICTURE ACKNOWLEDGEMENTS
Front cover: Allsport, left; Colorsport, right.

Inside: Allsport 121, 122, 123, 124, 125, 126, 127, 128

contents

FOREWORD
By Alan Shearer
BLACKBURN & ENGLAND

Statistics are important to most players, but even more so to goalscorers like myself. It's good to keep a check on your scoring record, especially when you are enjoying a rich vein of form – and I couldn't be happier right now. Strikers are often judged, and also compared to players from the past, by their goals-per-game records and that is something we take a great deal of pride in. I'm sure goalkeepers feel the same way, albeit for different reasons. From a personal point of view, I'm more than happy with a goal return of something in the region of one every other game and that's a ratio I will be looking to maintain throughout my career . . . and perhaps even as I have done over the past couple of seasons, improve upon.

But it is not just goalscoring statistics which have become such an important part of football, and indeed football banter virtually everywhere you go. The ever-increasing popularity of fantasy football leagues has obviously played its part in that. Suddenly, every player in the Premiership is under scrutiny with our performances on the field being monitored to a remarkable degree. But even though players are under the microscope every week, I think I speak for the majority when I say that fantasy football is very popular among colleagues and opponents alike.

All the different fantasy leagues – not to mention the Fantasy Football League programme on TV – are a bit of fun, but the business of goalscoring is still very much a serious one. And you won't find a better place to keep up with all the facts and figures you need to know about than within the pages of this book. I will certainly be keeping it handy as a source of reference.

INTRODUCTION
David Smith
EDITOR SHOOT MAGAZINE

Just why is Ian Rush in a league of his own when it comes to scoring goals . . . who is top of the stoppers . . . who has the worst disciplinary record in the Premiership? All these questions – and a million others – are answered in this remarkable statistics book. The Premier Players Formbook is the most comprehensive guide to the players who make up the Premiership. Everything you need to know about all the players in the top flight is contained in this reference book which makes all its rivals look positively First Division. The Premiership is the place to be and the Premier Players Formbook is the place to find all the information, facts and stats about every current top flight player.

The 1995-96 season has a hard act to follow after last year's dramatic battle for the Premiership. Forget the sleaze, the scandal, the bribes and even Cantona's kick. Let us, instead, remember the great things which happened on the pitch to make the 1994-95 season one of the most exciting in the history of our national game . . .

* The titanic struggle for the Premiership prize between Manchester United and eventual champions Blackburn . . . and in particular the 32 Alan Shearer goals which ensured Rovers were celebrating a title triumph for the first time in 81 years.

* Matthew Le Tissier, many people's choice for Player of the Year, gave us even more reasons to smile – and the stats' buffs reason to dive into the record books to try and unearth a more prolific goalscoring midfielder than the South Coast genius.

* And what about the wonderful impact made by Liverpool striker Robbie Fowler in his first full season at the highest level. He topped the scoring charts at Anfield where he is already being hailed as the new Ian Rush.

So there you have just three players who illuminated the soccer stage last season and whose names deserve a special place in the record books, and in the hearts of Blackburn, Southampton and Liverpool fans. For the 1995-96 season there will be even more talent on display in the Premiership. Foreign stars like Dennis Bergkamp and Ruud Gullit have chosen to turn their backs on the Italian game and seek their fortune in this country. This recent trend says much about the high standard of football in England, as well as the ambitions of our top clubs. And with Blackburn, Manchester United, Nottingham Forest, Leeds, Liverpool and Everton all competing in Europe in the 1995-96 season, the resurgence of the English game will surely be recognised.

It's a safe bet that names like Le Tissier, Fowler and Shearer were very popular in the many thousands of 'dream' teams created so carefully by football fans everywhere as fantasy football fever swept the country last season.

Almost every national newspaper in the country – and one or two well known football magazines as well – found it impossible to ignore the clamour for this latest type of soccer, side-betting. And the craze is far from over yet. Which is why you need to know as much about the players you are selecting as possible if you want to climb your own fantasy league table. And where is all the necessary information, just a finger tip away? Here, of course, within the fact-packed pages of football's ultimate reference book.

HOW TO USE THIS BOOK

The Premier Players Formbook contains all the facts on all the players in the English premier league – everything from sendings-offs to hat-tricks. But first, a few pointers to help you get the most from the book.

THE PROFILES

The profiles are broken up into five chapters, each dealing with a different position. Each chapter is in turn organised alphabetically by player – making it easy to find the record you want even when players are transferred. Players who play in a number of positions are listed by the position they most commonly play.

Every player in every Premiership squad, as at 23 June 1995, is profiled. Where players were transfered between 23 June and 7 July, their records have been updated.

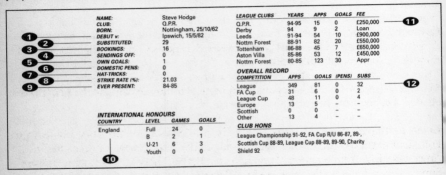

NAME:	Steve Hodge
CLUB:	Q.P.R.
BORN:	Nottingham, 25/10/62
DEBUT v:	Ipswich, 15/5/82
SUBSTITUTED:	29
BOOKINGS:	16
SENDINGS OFF:	0
OWN GOALS:	1
DOMESTIC PENS:	0
HAT-TRICKS:	0
STRIKE RATE (%):	21.03
EVER PRESENT:	84-85

LEAGUE CLUBS	YEARS	APPS	GOALS	FEE
Q.P.R.	94-95	15	0	£250,000
Derby	94	9	2	Loan
Leeds	91-94	54	10	£900,000
Nottm Forest	88-91	82	20	£550,000
Tottenham	86-88	45	7	£650,000
Aston Villa	85-86	53	12	£450,000
Nottm Forest	80-85	123	30	Appr

OVERALL RECORD

COMPETITION	APPS	GOALS	(PENS)	SUBS
League	349	81	0	32
FA Cup	31	6	0	2
League Cup	48	11	0	4
Europe	13	5	–	–
Scottish	0	0	–	–
Other	13	4	–	–

CLUB HONS

League Championship 91-92, FA Cup R/U 86-87, 89-, Scottish Cup 88-89, League Cup 88-89, 89-90, Charity Shield 92

INTERNATIONAL HONOURS

COUNTRY	LEVEL	GAMES	GOALS
England	Full	24	0
	B	2	1
	U-21	6	3
	Youth	0	0

PROFILE HEADINGS (SEE DIAGRAM) – ALL PLAYERS

Debut (1) – The player's first game in the English or Scottish League.

Substituted (2) – The number of League games from which a player has been withdrawn from play.

Bookings (3) – The number of times a player has been shown the yellow card, in domestic and international games, over the last five complete seasons.

Sendings-off (4) – The number of times a player has been shown the red card, in domestic and international games, over the last five complete seasons.

Own goals (5) – The number of times a player has been credited with scoring an own goal in League, FA Cup and League Cup matches.

Ever present (9) – The seasons for which a player appeared in every League game his club played in.

International Honours (10) – The country listed is the country for which the player is registered. Where a player has yet to play an international, this field is left blank.

League Record (11)

League clubs – this is the complete record of each player's League career. Appearances for non-British clubs and non-League clubs are not listed.

Years – these are the years the player was with the club, <u>not</u> the seasons.

Apps – the number of League appearances, including substitute appearances.

Goals – the number of League goals, including penalties.

Fee – transfer fees quoted are from reputable sources, but there is inevitably some disagreement over exact prices. Where fees are not disclosed by the clubs involved in the transfer, 'Undisclosed' appears in the fee column. An abbreviation is also used to indicate where a player has been signed as an apprentice ('Appr'). Where a player is signed on a free transfer or as a trainee, this is also indicated in the fee column.

Overall Record (12)

Competition (European) – figures are for the European Cup, the UEFA Cup and the European Cup Winners' Cup only.

Competition (Scottish) – figures are for the Scottish League, Scottish FA Cup and the Scottish League Cup only.

Competition (Other) – figures are for the English League play-off games, Simod Cup, Full Members Cup, Zenith Data Systems Cup, FA Charity Shield, Sherpa Van Trophy, Anglo-Scottish Trophy, Super Screen Cup, World Club Championship, European Super Cup, Freight Rover/Autoglass Windscreen Trophy, Anglo-Italian Cup, Mercantile Credit and Makita tournament. Appearances made in non-Anglo/Scottish leagues are recorded where possible, as are appearances in the GM Vauxhall Conference.

Appearances – starting appearances, substitute appearances are listed separately.

PROFILE HEADINGS – GOALKEEPERS

Goals conceded (13) – The total number of goals conceded in League matches.

Avg. Goals conceded (14) – The total number of goals conceded in League matches, divided by the number of League appearances (including substitute appearances).

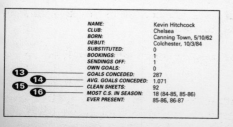

NAME:	Kevin Hitchcock
CLUB:	Chelsea
BORN:	Canning Town, 5/10/62
DEBUT:	Colchester, 10/3/84
SUBSTITUTED:	0
BOOKINGS:	1
SENDINGS OFF:	1
OWN GOALS:	0
GOALS CONCEDED:	287
AVG. GOALS CONCEDED:	1.071
CLEAN SHEETS:	92
MOST C.S. IN SEASON:	18 (84-85, 85-86)
EVER PRESENT:	85-86, 86-87

Clean sheets (15) – The number of League games in which a keeper has played and not conceded any goals.

Most c.s. in season (16) – The most clean sheets a keeper has kept in a single season, and the year it was achieved.

PROFILE HEADINGS – OUTFIELD PLAYERS (SEE DIAGRAM ON PAGE 8)

Dom pens (6) – penalty goals scored in League, FA Cup and League Cup matches.

Hat-tricks (7) – League, FA Cup and League Cup matches only.

Strike rate (8) – calculated by dividing the number of goals scored in the League, FA Cup and League Cup by the number of games played in these competitions. A minimum of 40 games must be played for this figure to be included.

GOALKEEPERS – THE COMPLETE LEAGUE RECORD

The full record of Premiership keepers against Premiership opposition. It shows the League record of each keeper for games played against teams in the 1995-96 English Premiership. Players who have never played against top flight opponents are not listed.

Bartram, Vince – Arsenal	HOME		AWAY		TOTAL	
OPPONENTS	**APPS**	**GC**	**APPS**	**GC**	**APPS**	**GC**
Arsenal	0	0	0	0	0	0
Aston Villa	1	0	0	0	1	0
Blackburn Rovers	0	0	2	4	2	4
Bolton Wanderers	2	4	3	3	5	7
Chelsea	0	0	0	0	0	0
Coventry	0	0	0	0	0	0
Everton	0	0	0	0	0	0
Leeds Utd	1	3	0	0	1	3
Liverpool	0	0	0	0	0	0
Manchester City	0	0	1	1	1	1
Manchester Utd	0	0	1	3	1	3
Middlesbrough	0	0	1	2	1	2
Newcastle	0	0	1	1	1	1
Nottingham Forest	1	1	1	2	2	3
Q.P.R.	1	3	0	0	1	3
Sheffield Wednesday	0	0	0	0	0	0
Southampton	0	0	0	0	0	0
Tottenham	0	0	0	0	0	0
West Ham	1	1	0	0	1	1
Wimbledon	0	0	0	0	0	0

Apps – League appearances, including substitute appearances

GC – goals conceded

SCORERS – THE COMPLETE LEAGUE RECORD:

The goalscoring record of all Premiership players (with a strike rate of 25% or above) against Premiership opposition. It shows the scoring record of each player against teams in the 1995-96 English Premiership.

Campbell, Kevin – Arsenal	HOME		AWAY		TOTAL	
OPPONENTS	**APPS**	**GOALS**	**APPS**	**GOALS**	**APPS**	**GOALS**
Arsenal	0	0	0	0	0	0
Aston Villa	6	2	2	0	8	2
Blackburn Rovers	3	0	3	2	6	2
Bolton Wanderers	0	0	0	0	0	0
Chelsea	6	2	3	0	9	2
Coventry	5	1	5	2	10	3
Everton	5	0	4	0	9	0
Leeds Utd	6	2	4	1	10	3
Liverpool	4	0	4	0	8	0
Manchester City	5	2	4	0	9	2
Manchester Utd	3	0	3	0	6	0
Middlesbrough	1	0	1	0	2	0
Newcastle	1	0	1	1	2	1
Nottingham Forest	4	2	3	0	7	2
Q.P.R.	5	0	3	1	8	1
Sheffield Wednesday	4	2	3	0	7	2
Southampton	4	1	5	1	9	2
Tottenham	2	1	4	0	6	1
West Ham	2	0	2	0	4	0
Wimbledon	3	0	4	0	7	0

GOALKEEPERS – INTRODUCTION

It's obvious that the goals of Alan Shearer were crucial to Blackburn Rovers' Championship triumph. But what about the contribution of their England keeper Tim Flowers? A model of consistency all season, he saved his best almost until last when a faultless display against Newcastle in Rover's penultimate league game kept them in the driving seat. A string of saves earned Blackburn a priceless point in a game they could not afford to lose. Flowers' displays, for both club and country, underline the importance of the man who forms the last line of defence.

One minute, the hero; the next, the villain: there's very little in between for most keepers. You only have to talk to Arsenal's England international David Seaman for confirmation of that. The dying seconds of the 1995 European Cup Winners' Cup final contained every goalkeeper's worst nightmare. Mentally preparing himself for a penalty shoot-out, Seaman was caught out of position as Real Zaragoza's former Spurs star Nayim struck a speculative 50-yard shot goalwards. Seaman back-pedalled, but couldn't prevent the shot crossing the line and the cup was on its way to Spain instead of North London. Never could there have been a more disappointing or cruel way for a season to end.

Not even the dramatic climax to the Premiership campaign experienced by Manchester United keeper Peter Schmeichel could even come close to Seaman's disappointments. The great Dane had been a rock at the back for United all season where his performances were little short of remarkable. He only conceded one goal at home all season! The man with the longest throw-out in football is something of an eccentric and thinks nothing of leaving his goal unguarded to take up a dangerous position in the opposition penalty box in times of crisis. Just as he did in the agonising closing stages of United's final game of the season at West Ham – where the Reds found the Hammers giant Czech keeper Miklosko in fine form.

Another of the game's characters is Bruce Grobbelaar, who was in the news more for his off-the-field activities than his performances on the pitch last season. But whatever you think of the man, there's no arguing with his record. He has won more domestic honours than any other keeper in the game. And it was testimony to his character that in his first game back for Southampton following 'bung' allegations last season he kept a clean sheet. One of many during a remarkable career in England.

And, of course, Schmeichel and Grobbelaar, are not the only overseas keepers to have made an impact in a country which once boasted the best keepers in the world. The days of Banks, Clemence, Shilton and co are long gone, although the likes of Flowers, Seaman and Woods are still proudly flying the English flag in defiance of the foreign invasion. Newcastle, so long in contention for the Premiership title, owed much to the brilliance of their Czech international keeper Pavel Srnicek. Aston Villa too were heavily indebted to the skills of their Australian-born number one Mark Bosnich. Add those names to Ludek Miklosko, Hans Segers, Erik Thorstvedt and Dmitri Kharine and you can judge for yourself the extent of the foreign takeover. But there's still some promising, home grown talent about and, in Spurs' Ian Walker, Sheffield Wednesday's Kevin Pressman and Liverpool's David James, there is ample competition for England regulars Flowers and Seaman.

The styles of every keeper in the Premiership are different . . . as are their career stats.

NAME:	Vince Bartram
CLUB:	Arsenal
BORN:	Birmingham, 7/8/68
DEBUT:	Cambridge, 23/8/86
SUBSTITUTED:	1
BOOKINGS:	0
SENDINGS OFF:	0
OWN GOALS:	0
GOALS CONCEDED:	183
AVG. GOALS CONCEDED:	1.166
CLEAN SHEETS:	48
MOST C.S. IN SEASON:	21 (91-92)
EVER PRESENT:	91-92

LEAGUE CLUBS	YEARS	APPS	GOALS	FEE
Arsenal	94-95	11	0	£250,000
Bournemouth	91-94	132	0	£65,000
Blackpool	89	9	0	Loan
Wolves	85-91	5	0	Appr

OVERALL RECORD

COMPETITION	APPS	GOALS	(PENS)	SUBS
League	157	0	0	0
FA Cup	17	0	0	0
League Cup	12	0	0	0
Europe	0	0	0	0
Scottish	0	0	–	–
Other	8	0	–	–

HONOURS

European Cup Winners' Cup 94-95

INTERNATIONAL APPEARANCES

COUNTRY	LEVEL	GAMES	GOALS
England	Full	0	0
	B	0	0
	U-21	0	0
	Youth	0	0

NAME:	Dave Beasant
CLUB:	Southampton
BORN:	Willesden, 20/3/59
DEBUT:	Blackpool, 12/1/79
SUBSTITUTED:	0
BOOKINGS:	2
SENDINGS OFF:	0
OWN GOALS:	0
GOALS CONCEDED:	721
AVG. GOALS CONCEDED:	1.333
CLEAN SHEETS:	131
MOST C.S. IN SEASON:	18 (85-86)
EVER PRESENT:	81-82, 82-83, 83-84
	84-85, 85-86, 86-87
	87-88, 89-90

LEAGUE CLUBS	YEARS	APPS	GOALS	FEE
Southampton	93-95	38	0	£300,000
Wolves	93	4	0	Loan
Grimsby	92	6	0	Loan
Chelsea	89-93	133	0	£725,000
Newcastle	88-89	20	0	£800,000
Wimbledon	79-88	340	0	£1,000
From: Edgware Town				

OVERALL RECORD

COMPETITION	APPS	GOALS	(PENS)	SUBS
League	540	0	0	1
FA Cup	37	0	0	0
League Cup	34	0	0	0
Europe	0	0	0	0
Scottish	0	0	–	–
Other	21	0	–	–

HONOURS

Division Two Championship 88-89, Division Four
Championship 82-83, FA Cup 87-88

INTERNATIONAL HONOURS

COUNTRY	LEVEL	GAMES	GOALS
England	Full	2	0
	B	6	0
	U-21	0	0
	Youth	0	0

NAME:	Mark Beeney
CLUB:	Leeds United
BORN:	Pembury, 30/12/67
DEBUT:	Walsall, 1/1/87
SUBSTITUTED:	0
BOOKINGS:	0
SENDINGS OFF:	2
OWN GOALS:	0
GOALS CONCEDED:	196
AVG. GOALS CONCEDED:	1.281
CLEAN SHEETS:	37
MOST C.S. IN SEASON:	9 (92-93, 93-94)
EVER PRESENT:	–

LEAGUE CLUBS	YEARS	APPS	GOALS	FEE
Leeds United	93-95	25	0	£350,000
Brighton	91-93	69	0	£30,000
Aldershot	90	7	0	Loan
Maidstone	87-90	50	0	Free
Gillingham	86-87	2	0	Appr

OVERALL RECORD

COMPETITION	APPS	GOALS	(PENS)	SUBS
League	152	0	0	1
FA Cup	21	0	0	0
League Cup	11	0	0	0
Europe	0	0	0	0
Scottish	0	0	–	–
Other	12	0	–	–

HONOURS

GMV Championship 88-89

INTERNATIONAL HONOURS

COUNTRY	LEVEL	GAMES	GOALS
England	Full	0	0
	B	0	0
	U-21	0	0
	Youth	0	0

NAME:	Mark Bosnich
CLUB:	Aston Villa
BORN:	Fairfield, Aust, 13/1/72
DEBUT:	Luton Town, 24/4/92
SUBSTITUTED:	1
BOOKINGS:	5
SENDINGS OFF:	1
OWN GOALS:	1
GOALS CONCEDED:	90
AVG. GOALS CONCEDED:	1.139
CLEAN SHEETS:	23
MOST C.S. IN SEASON:	9 (93-94)
EVER PRESENT:	—

LEAGUE CLUBS	YEARS	APPS	GOALS	FEE
Aston Villa	92-95	76	0	Free
Manchester Utd	89-91	3	0	Free
From: Crotia Sydney				

OVERALL RECORD

COMPETITION	APPS	GOALS	(PENS)	SUBS
League	79	0	0	0
FA Cup	5	0	0	0
League Cup	11	0	0	0
Europe	2	0	—	—
Scottish	0	0	—	—

HONOURS

League Cup 93-94

INTERNATIONAL APPEARANCES

COUNTRY	LEVEL	GAMES	GOALS
Australia	Full	7	0
	B	0	0
	U-21	0	0
	Youth	0	0

NAME:	Keith Branagan
CLUB:	Bolton
BORN:	Fulham, 10/7/66
DEBUT:	Carlisle, 14/1/84
SUBSTITUTED:	2
BOOKINGS:	1
SENDINGS OFF:	1
OWN GOALS:	0
GOALS CONCEDED:	299
AVG. GOALS CONCEDED:	1.159
CLEAN SHEETS:	83
MOST C.S. IN SEASON:	19 (94-95)
EVER PRESENT:	86-87, 92-93

LEAGUE CLUBS	YEARS	APPS	GOALS	FEE
Bolton	92-95	99	0	Free
Gillingham	91	1	0	Loan
Brentford	89	2	0	Loan
Millwall	88-92	46	0	£100,000
Cambridge	83-88	110	0	Appr

OVERALL RECORD

COMPETITION	APPS	GOALS	(PENS)	SUBS
League	258	0	0	0
FA Cup	19	0	0	0
League Cup	29	0	0	0
Europe	0	0	0	0
Scottish	0	0	—	—
Other	16	0	—	—

HONOURS

League Cup r/u 94-95

INTERNATIONAL APPEARANCES

COUNTRY	LEVEL	GAMES	GOALS
Eire	Full	0	0
	B	1	0
	U-21	0	0
	Youth	0	0

NAME:	John Burridge
CLUB:	Manchester City
BORN:	Workington, 3/12/51
DEBUT:	Bradford P.A., 19/4/69
SUBSTITUTED:	0
BOOKINGS:	6
SENDINGS OFF:	2
OWN GOALS:	2
GOALS CONCEDED:	865
AVG. GOALS CONCEDED:	1.144
CLEAN SHEETS:	251
MOST C.S. IN SEASON:	21 (78-79)
EVER PRESENT:	78-79, 82-83, 85-86

INTERNATIONAL APPEARANCES

COUNTRY	LEVEL	GAMES	GOALS
	Full	0	0
	B	0	0
	U-21	0	0
	Youth	0	0

LEAGUE CLUBS	YEARS	APPS	GOALS	FEE
Manchester City	95	4	0	Free
Falkirk	95	3	0	Loan
Aberdeen	94	3	0	Loan
Newcastle	94	0	0	Free
Lincoln	93-94	4	0	Free
Scarborough	93	3	0	Loan
Newcastle	93	0	0	Free
Hibernian	91-93	65	0	Free
Newcastle	89-91	67	0	Free
Southampton	87-89	62	0	£10,000
Sheffield Utd	84-87	109	0	£10,000
Derby	84	6	0	Loan
Wolverhampton	82-84	74	0	£80,000
Q.P.R.	80-82	39	0	£200,000
Crystal Palace	78-80	88	0	£50,000
Southend	77	6	0	Loan
Aston Villa	75-78	65	0	£100,000
Blackpool	71-75	134	0	£10,000
Workington	68-71	27	0	Appr

OVERALL RECORD

COMPETITION	APPS	GOALS	(PENS)	SUBS
League	687	0	0	1
FA Cup	45	0	0	0
League Cup	53	0	0	0
Europe	2	0	0	0
Scottish	82	0	–	–
Other	24	0	–	–

HONOURS

Division Two Championship 78-79, League Cup 76-77, Anglo-Italian Cup Winners 70-71, Anglo-Italian Cup r/u 71-72, PFA Team Award Div 2. 83

NAME:	Tony Coton
CLUB:	Manchester City
BORN:	Tamworth, 19/5/61
DEBUT:	Sunderland, 27/12/80
SUBSTITUTED:	2
BOOKINGS:	6
SENDINGS OFF:	1
OWN GOALS:	2
GOALS CONCEDED:	613
AVG. GOALS CONCEDED:	1.251
CLEAN SHEETS:	132
MOST C.S. IN SEASON:	18 (88-89)
EVER PRESENT:	88-89, 89-90

INTERNATIONAL APPEARANCES

COUNTRY	LEVEL	GAMES	GOALS
England	Full	0	0
	B	1	0
	U-21	0	0
	Youth	0	0

LEAGUE CLUBS	YEARS	APPS	GOALS	FEE
Manchester City	90-95	163	0	£1m
Watford	84-90	233	0	£300,000
Birmingham	78-84	94	0	Free

OVERALL RECORD

COMPETITION	APPS	GOALS	(PENS)	SUBS
League	489	0	0	1
FA Cup	54	0	0	0
League Cup	44	0	0	0
Europe	0	0	–	–
Scottish	0	0	–	–
Other	11	0	–	–

HONOURS

PFA Team Awards: Div 2. 89-90; Div 1. 91-92

NAME:	Mark Crossley
CLUB:	Nottm Forest
BORN:	Barnsley, 16/6/69
DEBUT:	Liverpool, 26/10/88
SUBSTITUTED:	0
BOOKINGS:	3
SENDINGS OFF:	0
OWN GOALS:	1
GOALS CONCEDED:	245
AVG. GOALS CONCEDED:	1.225
CLEAN SHEETS:	55
MOST C.S. IN SEASON:	13 (94-95)
EVER PRESENT:	90-91, 94-95

LEAGUE CLUBS	YEARS	APPS	GOALS	FEE
Nottm Forest	87-95	200	0	Appr

OVERALL RECORD

COMPETITION	APPS	GOALS	(PENS)	SUBS
League	199	0	0	1
FA Cup	23	0	0	0
League Cup	29	0	0	0
Europe	0	0	–	–
Scottish	0	0	–	–
Other	11	0	–	–

HONOURS

FA Cup r/u 90-91

INTERNATIONAL APPEARANCES

COUNTRY	LEVEL	GAMES	GOALS
England	Full	0	0
	B	0	0
	U-21	3	0
	Youth	0	0

NAME:	Aidan Davison
CLUB:	Bolton
BORN:	Sedgefield, 15/5/68
DEBUT:	Preston, 15/4/89
SUBSTITUTED:	1
BOOKINGS:	0
SENDINGS OFF:	2
OWN GOALS:	0
GOALS CONCEDED:	106
AVG. GOALS CONCEDED:	1.514
CLEAN SHEETS:	16
MOST C.S. IN SEASON:	10 (91-92)
EVER PRESENT:	–

LEAGUE CLUBS	YEARS	APPS	GOALS	FEE
Bolton	93-95	35	0	£25,000
Millwall	91-93	34	0	Free
Bury	89-91	0	0	£6,000
Notts County	88-89	1	0	Appr

OVERALL RECORD

COMPETITION	APPS	GOALS	(PENS)	SUBS
League	68	0	0	2
FA Cup	13	0	0	0
League Cup	3	0	0	0
Europe	0	0	–	–
Scottish	0	0	–	–
Other	6	0	–	–

HONOURS

League Cup r/u 94-95

INTERNATIONAL APPEARANCES

COUNTRY	LEVEL	GAMES	GOALS
	Full	0	0
	B	0	0
	U-21	0	0
	Youth	0	0

NAME:	Chris Day
CLUB:	Tottenham
BORN:	Whipps Cross, 28/7/75
DEBUT:	–
SUBSTITUTED:	0
BOOKINGS:	0
SENDINGS OFF:	0
OWN GOALS:	0
GOALS CONCEDED:	0
AVG. GOALS CONCEDED:	–
CLEAN SHEETS:	0
MOST C.S. IN SEASON:	0
EVER PRESENT:	–

LEAGUE CLUBS	YEARS	APPS	GOALS	FEE
Tottenham	93-95	0	0	Trainee

OVERALL RECORD

COMPETITION	APPS	GOALS	(PENS)	SUBS
League	0	0	0	0
FA Cup	0	0	0	0
League Cup	0	0	0	0
Europe	0	0	–	–
Scottish	0	0	–	–

HONOURS

None

INTERNATIONAL APPEARANCES

COUNTRY	LEVEL	GAMES	GOALS
England	Full	0	0
	B	0	0
	U-21	0	0
	Youth	3	0

NAME:	Andy Dibble
CLUB:	Manchester City
BORN:	Cwmbran, 8/5/65
DEBUT:	Crystal Palace, 8/5/82
SUBSTITUTED:	3
BOOKINGS:	2
SENDINGS OFF:	1
OWN GOALS:	1
GOALS CONCEDED:	338
AVG. GOALS CONCEDED:	1.310
CLEAN SHEETS:	66
MOST C.S. IN SEASON:	13 (88-89)
EVER PRESENT:	–

LEAGUE CLUBS	YEARS	APPS	GOALS	FEE
Manchester City	88-95	103	0	£240,000
West Brom	92	9	0	Loan
Bolton	91	13	0	Loan
Middlesborough	91	19	0	Loan
Aberdeen	90	5	0	Loan
Huddersfield	87	5	0	Loan
Sunderland	86	12	0	Loan
Luton	84-88	30	0	£125,000
Cardiff	82-84	62	0	Appr

OVERALL RECORD

COMPETITION	APPS	GOALS	(PENS)	SUBS
League	251	0	0	2
FA Cup	13	0	0	1
League Cup	20	0	0	0
Europe	0	0	–	–
Scottish	5	0	–	–
Other	6	0	–	–

HONOURS

League Cup 87-88

INTERNATIONAL APPEARANCES

COUNTRY	LEVEL	GAMES	GOALS
Wales	Full	3	0
	B	0	0
	U-21	3	0
	Youth	0	0

NAME:	Sieb Dykstra
CLUB:	Q.P.R.
BORN:	Kerkrade, 20/10/66
DEBUT:	Airdrie, 24/8/91
SUBSTITUTED:	0
BOOKINGS:	5
SENDINGS OFF:	0
OWN GOALS:	0
GOALS CONCEDED:	108
AVG. GOALS CONCEDED:	1.187
CLEAN SHEETS:	31
MOST C.S. IN SEASON:	17 (93-94)
EVER PRESENT:	93-94

LEAGUE CLUBS	YEARS	APPS	GOALS	FEE
Q.P.R.	94-95	11	0	£250,000
Motherwell	91-94	80	0	Undisclosed
From: Roda				

OVERALL RECORD

COMPETITION	APPS	GOALS	(PENS)	SUBS
League	11	0	0	0
FA Cup	0	0	0	0
League Cup	1	0	0	0
Europe	0	0	–	–
Scottish	87	0	–	–

HONOURS

None

INTERNATIONAL APPEARANCES

COUNTRY	LEVEL	GAMES	GOALS
Holland	Full	0	0
	B	0	0
	U-21	0	0
	Youth	0	0

NAME:	Ian Feur
CLUB:	West Ham
BORN:	Las Vegas, 20/5/71
DEBUT:	Brighton, 21/2/95
SUBSTITUTED:	0
BOOKINGS:	1
SENDINGS OFF:	0
OWN GOALS:	0
GOALS CONCEDED:	15
AVG. GOALS CONCEDED:	0.93
CLEAN SHEETS:	4
MOST C.S. IN SEASON:	4 (94-95)
EVER PRESENT:	–

LEAGUE CLUBS	YEARS	APPS	GOALS	FEE
West Ham	94-95	0	0	£70,000
Peterborough	95	16	0	Loan
From: U.S.A. Soccer Federation				

OVERALL RECORD

COMPETITION	APPS	GOALS	(PENS)	SUBS
League	16	0	0	0
FA Cup	0	0	0	0
League Cup	0	0	0	0
Europe	0	0	–	–
Scottish	0	0	–	–

HONOURS

None

INTERNATIONAL APPEARANCES

COUNTRY	LEVEL	GAMES	GOALS
	Full	0	0
	B	0	0
	U-21	0	0
	Youth	0	0

NAME:	John Filan
CLUB:	Coventry
BORN:	Sydney, 8/2/70
DEBUT:	Newcastle, 3/4/93
SUBSTITUTED:	0
BOOKINGS:	2
SENDINGS OFF:	0
OWN GOALS:	0
GOALS CONCEDED:	108
AVG. GOALS CONCEDED:	1.543
CLEAN SHEETS:	15
MOST C.S. IN SEASON:	11 (93-94)
EVER PRESENT:	93-94

LEAGUE CLUBS	YEARS	APPS	GOALS	FEE
Coventry	95	2	0	£200,000
Nottm Forest	95	0	0	Loan
Cambridge	93-95	68	0	£40,000
From: Budapest St. George				

OVERALL RECORD

COMPETITION	APPS	GOALS	(PENS)	SUBS
League	70	0	0	0
FA Cup	3	0	0	0
League Cup	6	0	0	0
Europe	0	0	–	–
Scottish	0	0	–	–
Other	3	0	–	–

HONOURS

None

INTERNATIONAL APPEARANCES

COUNTRY	LEVEL	GAMES	GOALS
	Full	0	0
	B	0	0
	U-21	0	0
	Youth	0	0

NAME:	Tim Flowers
CLUB:	Blackburn
BORN:	Kenilworth, 3/2/67
DEBUT:	Sheffield Utd, 25/8/84
SUBSTITUTED:	1
BOOKINGS:	4
SENDINGS OFF:	1
OWN GOALS:	2
GOALS CONCEDED:	529
AVG. GOALS CONCEDED:	1.603
CLEAN SHEETS:	78
MOST C.S. IN SEASON:	16 (94-95)
EVER PRESENT:	92-93

LEAGUE CLUBS	YEARS	APPS	GOALS	FEE
Blackburn	93-95	68	0	£2.3m
Swindon	87	7	0	Loan
Southampton	86-93	192	0	£70,000
Wolves	84-86	63	0	Appr

OVERALL RECORD

COMPETITION	APPS	GOALS	(PENS)	SUBS
League	330	0	0	0
FA Cup	24	0	0	0
League Cup	35	0	0	0
Europe	2	0	0	0
Scottish	0	0	–	–
Other	11	0	–	–

HONOURS

Premier League Championship 94-95, Charity Shield medal 94, PFA Team Award Premier League 95

INTERNATIONAL APPEARANCES

COUNTRY	LEVEL	GAMES	GOALS
England	Full	7	0
	B	0	0
	U-21	3	0
	Youth	3	0

NAME:	Seamus Given
CLUB:	Blackburn
BORN:	Lifford, Eire, 20/4/76
DEBUT:	–
SUBSTITUTED:	0
BOOKINGS:	0
SENDINGS OFF:	0
OWN GOALS:	0
GOALS CONCEDED:	0
AVG. GOALS CONCEDED:	–
CLEAN SHEETS:	0
MOST C.S. IN SEASON:	0
EVER PRESENT:	–

LEAGUE CLUBS	YEARS	APPS	GOALS	FEE
Blackburn	93-95	0	0	Appr

OVERALL RECORD

COMPETITION	APPS	GOALS	(PENS)	SUBS
League	0	0	0	0
FA Cup	0	0	0	0
League Cup	0	0	0	0
Europe	0	0	–	–
Scottish	0	0	–	–

HONOURS

None

INTERNATIONAL APPEARANCES

COUNTRY	LEVEL	GAMES	GOALS
Eire	Full	0	0
	B	0	0
	U-21	2	0
	Youth	0	0

NAME:	Jon Gould
CLUB:	Coventry
BORN:	Paddington, 18/7/68
DEBUT:	Blackpool, 27/10/90
SUBSTITUTED:	1
BOOKINGS:	0
SENDINGS OFF:	0
OWN GOALS:	1
GOALS CONCEDED:	98
AVG. GOALS CONCEDED:	1.719
CLEAN SHEETS:	13
MOST C.S. IN SEASON:	3 (93-94)
EVER PRESENT:	–

LEAGUE CLUBS	YEARS	APPS	GOALS	FEE
Coventry	92-95	25	0	Free
West Brom	92	0	0	Free
Halifax	90-92	32	0	Free

OVERALL RECORD

COMPETITION	APPS	GOALS	(PENS)	SUBS
League	57	0	0	0
FA Cup	5	0	0	0
League Cup	2	0	0	0
Europe	0	0	–	–
Scottish	0	0	–	–
Other	5	0	–	–

HONOURS

None

INTERNATIONAL APPEARANCES

COUNTRY	LEVEL	GAMES	GOALS
England	Full	0	0
	B	0	0
	U-21	0	0
	Youth	0	0

NAME:	Bruce Grobbelaar
CLUB:	Southampton
BORN:	Durban, 6/10/57
DEBUT:	Wigan, 21/12/79
SUBSTITUTED:	2
BOOKINGS:	3
SENDINGS OFF:	1
OWN GOALS:	0
GOALS CONCEDED:	457
AVG. GOALS CONCEDED:	0.918
CLEAN SHEETS:	199
MOST C.S. IN SEASON:	20 (81-82, 83-84)
EVER PRESENT:	81-82, 82-83, 83-84 84-85, 85-86, 89-90

LEAGUE CLUBS	YEARS	APPS	GOALS	FEE
Southampton	94-95	30	0	Free
Stoke	93	4	0	Loan
Liverpool	81-94	440	0	£250,000
From: Vancouver				
Crewe	79-80	24	1	Free
From: Vancouver				

OVERALL RECORD

COMPETITION	APPS	GOALS	(PENS)	SUBS
League	498	1	0	0
FA Cup	67	0	0	0
League Cup	73	0	0	0
Europe	37	0	–	–
Scottish	0	0	–	–
Other	23	0	–	–

HONOURS

League Championship 81-82, 82-83, 83-84, 85-86, 87-88, 89-90, FA Cup 85-86, 88-89, 91-92, FA Cup r/u 87-88, League Cup 81-82, 82-83, 83-84, r/u 86-87, Charity Shield medal 82, 86, 88, 89, 83, 84, 92, European Cup 83-84, European Cup r/u 84-85

INTERNATIONAL APPEARANCES

COUNTRY	LEVEL	GAMES	GOALS
Zimbawbe	Full	20	0
	B	2	0
	U-21	0	0
	Youth	0	0

NAME:	Lee Harper
CLUB:	Arsenal
BORN:	Chelsea, 30/10/71
DEBUT:	–
SUBSTITUTED:	0
BOOKINGS:	0
SENDINGS OFF:	0
OWN GOALS:	0
GOALS CONCEDED:	0
AVG. GOALS CONCEDED:	–
CLEAN SHEETS:	0
MOST C.S. IN SEASON:	0
EVER PRESENT:	–

LEAGUE CLUBS	YEARS	APPS	GOALS	FEE
Arsenal	94-95	0	0	£150,000
Sittingbourne	93-94	0	0	Appr

OVERALL RECORD

COMPETITION	APPS	GOALS	(PENS)	SUBS
League	0	0	0	0
FA Cup	0	0	0	0
League Cup	0	0	0	0
Europe	0	0	–	–
Scottish	0	0	–	–

HONOURS

None

INTERNATIONAL APPEARANCES

COUNTRY	LEVEL	GAMES	GOALS
	Full	0	0
	B	0	0
	U-21	0	0
	Youth	0	0

NAME:	Kevin Hitchcock
CLUB:	Chelsea
BORN:	Custom House 5/10/62
DEBUT:	Colchester, 10/3/84
SUBSTITUTED:	0
BOOKINGS:	1
SENDINGS OFF:	1
OWN GOALS:	0
GOALS CONCEDED:	287
AVG. GOALS CONCEDED:	1.071
CLEAN SHEETS:	92
MOST C.S. IN SEASON:	18 (84-85, 85-86)
EVER PRESENT:	85-86, 86-87

LEAGUE CLUBS	YEARS	APPS	GOALS	FEE
Chelsea	88-95	69	0	£250,000
Northampton	90	17	0	Loan
Mansfield	84-88	182	0	£40,000
Nottm Forest	83-84	0	0	£15,000
From: Barking				

OVERALL RECORD

COMPETITION	APPS	GOALS	(PENS)	SUBS
League	267	0	0	1
FA Cup	15	0	0	0
League Cup	20	0	0	0
Europe	4	0	–	–
Scottish	0	0	–	–
Other	32	0	–	–

HONOURS

PFA Team Award Div 3. 88

INTERNATIONAL APPEARANCES

COUNTRY	LEVEL	GAMES	GOALS
	Full	0	0
	B	0	0
	U-21	0	0
	Youth	0	0

NAME:	Mike Hooper
CLUB:	Newcastle
BORN:	Bristol, 10/2/64
DEBUT:	Lincoln, 1/12/84
SUBSTITUTED:	0
BOOKINGS:	0
SENDINGS OFF:	1
OWN GOALS:	2
GOALS CONCEDED:	169
AVG. GOALS CONCEDED:	1.363
CLEAN SHEETS:	38
MOST C.S. IN SEASON:	8 (84-85)
EVER PRESENT:	–

LEAGUE CLUBS	YEARS	APPS	GOALS	FEE
Newcastle	93-95	24	0	£550,000
Leicester	90	14	0	Loan
Liverpool	85-93	51	0	£40,000
Wrexham	85	34	0	Free
Bristol City	83-85	1	0	Free

OVERALL RECORD

COMPETITION	APPS	GOALS	(PENS)	SUBS
League	122	0	0	2
FA Cup	9	0	0	0
League Cup	16	0	0	0
Europe	7	0	–	–
Scottish	0	0	–	–
Other	3	0	–	–

HONOURS

Charity Shield medal 86

INTERNATIONAL APPEARANCES

COUNTRY	LEVEL	GAMES	GOALS
	Full	0	0
	B	0	0
	U-21	0	0
	Youth	0	0

NAME:	David James
CLUB:	Liverpool
BORN:	Welwyn, Herts, 1/8/70
DEBUT:	Millwall, 25/8/90
SUBSTITUTED:	0
BOOKINGS:	3
SENDINGS OFF:	1
OWN GOALS:	0
GOALS CONCEDED:	189
AVG. GOALS CONCEDED:	1.086
CLEAN SHEETS:	55
MOST C.S. IN SEASON:	17 (91-92, 94-95)
EVER PRESENT:	90-91, 94-95

LEAGUE CLUBS	YEARS	APPS	GOALS	FEE
Liverpool	92-95	85	0	£1m
Watford	88-92	89	0	Trainee

OVERALL RECORD

COMPETITION	APPS	GOALS	(PENS)	SUBS
League	173	0	0	1
FA Cup	9	0	0	0
League Cup	15	0	0	0
Europe	1	0	–	–
Scottish	0	0	–	–
Other	1	0	–	–

HONOURS

FA Youth Cup 88-89, League Cup 94-95, PFA Team Award Div 2. 92

INTERNATIONAL APPEARANCES

COUNTRY	LEVEL	GAMES	GOALS
England	Full	0	0
	B	1	0
	U-21	10	0
	Youth	0	0

NAME: Alan Judge
CLUB: Chelsea
BORN: Kingsbury, 14/5/60
DEBUT: Newcastle, 3/5/80
SUBSTITUTED: 2
BOOKINGS: 1
SENDINGS OFF: 0
OWN GOALS: 2
GOALS CONCEDED: 429
AVG. GOALS CONCEDED: 1.516
CLEAN SHEETS: 56
MOST C.S. IN SEASON: 13 (83-84)
EVER PRESENT: 92-93

LEAGUE CLUBS	YEARS	APPS	GOALS	FEE
Chelsea	94-95	0	0	Free
Hereford	91-94	105	0	Free
Cardiff	87	8	0	Loan
Lincoln	85	2	0	Loan
Oxford	84-91	80	0	£10,000
Reading	82-84	77	0	Free
Luton	78-82	11	0	Appr

OVERALL RECORD

COMPETITION	APPS	GOALS	(PENS)	SUBS
League	283	0	0	0
FA Cup	17	0	0	0
League Cup	21	0	0	0
Europe	0	0	–	–
Scottish	0	0	–	–
Other	14	0	–	–

HONOURS

League Cup 85-86

INTERNATIONAL APPEARANCES

COUNTRY	LEVEL	GAMES	GOALS
	Full	0	0
	B	0	0
	U-21	0	0
	Youth	0	0

NAME: Jason Kearton
CLUB: Everton
BORN: Ipswich Australia, 9/7/69
DEBUT: Bradford, 17/8/91
SUBSTITUTED: 0
BOOKINGS: 1
SENDINGS OFF: 0
OWN GOALS: 0
GOALS CONCEDED: 53
AVG. GOALS CONCEDED: 1.152
CLEAN SHEETS: 10
MOST C.S. IN SEASON: 8 (91-92)
EVER PRESENT: –

LEAGUE CLUBS	YEARS	APPS	GOALS	FEE
Everton	88-95	6	0	Free
Notts County	95	10	0	Loan
Blackpool	92	14	0	Loan
Stoke	91	16	0	Loan

OVERALL RECORD

COMPETITION	APPS	GOALS	(PENS)	SUBS
League	43	0	0	3
FA Cup	1	0	0	0
League Cup	1	0	0	0
Europe	0	0	–	–
Scottish	0	0	–	–
Other	2	0	–	–

HONOURS

FA Cup 94-95

INTERNATIONAL APPEARANCES

COUNTRY	LEVEL	GAMES	GOALS
	Full	0	0
	B	0	0
	U-21	0	0
	Youth	0	0

NAME: Lance Key
CLUB: Sheffield Wed
BORN: Kettering, 13/5/68
DEBUT: Chelsea, 30/10/93
SUBSTITUTED: 0
BOOKINGS: 0
SENDINGS OFF: 0
OWN GOALS: 0
GOALS CONCEDED: 10
AVG. GOALS CONCEDED: –
CLEAN SHEETS: 2
MOST C.S. IN SEASON: 1
EVER PRESENT: –

LEAGUE CLUBS	YEARS	APPS	GOALS	FEE
Sheffield Wed	90-95	0	0	£10,000
Oxford	95	6	0	Loan
Oldham	93	2	0	Loan

OVERALL RECORD

COMPETITION	APPS	GOALS	(PENS)	SUBS
League	8	0	0	0
FA Cup	0	0	0	0
League Cup	0	0	0	0
Europe	0	0	–	–
Scottish	0	0	–	–

HONOURS

None

INTERNATIONAL APPEARANCES

COUNTRY	LEVEL	GAMES	GOALS
	Full	0	0
	B	0	0
	U-21	0	0
	Youth	0	0

NAME:	Dmitri Kharine
CLUB:	Chelsea
BORN:	Moscow, 16/8/68
DEBUT:	Q.P.R., 27/1/93
SUBSTITUTED:	2
BOOKINGS:	4
SENDINGS OFF:	0
OWN GOALS:	0
GOALS CONCEDED:	98
AVG. GOALS CONCEDED:	1.289
CLEAN SHEETS:	22
MOST C.S. IN SEASON:	11 (93-94, 94-95)
EVER PRESENT:	–

LEAGUE CLUBS	YEARS	APPS	GOALS	FEE
Chelsea	92-95	76	0	£200,000
From: C.S.K.A Moscow				

OVERALL RECORD

COMPETITION	APPS	GOALS	(PENS)	SUBS
League	76	0	0	0
FA Cup	11	0	0	0
League Cup	6	0	0	0
Europe	4	0	–	–
Scottish	0	0	–	–
Other	2	0	–	–

HONOURS

FA Cup r/u 93-94

INTERNATIONAL APPEARANCES

COUNTRY	LEVEL	GAMES	GOALS
Russia	Full	27	0
	B	0	0
	U-21	0	0
	Youth	0	0

NAME:	John Lukic
CLUB:	Leeds
BORN:	Chesterfield, 11/12/60
DEBUT:	Brighton, 13/10/79
SUBSTITUTED:	0
BOOKINGS:	2
SENDINGS OFF:	0
OWN GOALS:	0
GOALS CONCEDED:	591
AVG. GOALS CONCEDED:	1.075
CLEAN SHEETS:	210
MOST C.S. IN SEASON:	20 (80-81, 91-92)
EVER PRESENT:	80-81, 81-82, 87-88
	88-89, 89-90, 90-91
	91-92, 94-95

LEAGUE CLUBS	YEARS	APPS	GOALS	FEE
Leeds	90-95	181	0	£1m
Arsenal	83-90	223	0	£75,000
Leeds	78-83	146	0	Appr

OVERALL RECORD

COMPETITION	APPS	GOALS	(PENS)	SUBS
League	550	0	0	0
FA Cup	44	0	0	0
League Cup	55	0	0	0
Europe	8	0	–	–
Scottish	0	0	–	–
Other	18	0	–	–

HONOURS

League Championship 88-89, 91-92, League Cup 86-87, League Cup r/u 87-88, Charity Shield medal 90, 92, 89

INTERNATIONAL APPEARANCES

COUNTRY	LEVEL	GAMES	GOALS
England	Full	0	0
	B	1	0
	U-21	7	0
	Youth	10	0

NAME:	Martyn Margetson
CLUB:	Manchester City
BORN:	West Glamorgan, 8/9/71
DEBUT:	Manchester Utd, 4/5/91
SUBSTITUTED:	0
BOOKINGS:	0
SENDINGS OFF:	0
OWN GOALS:	0
GOALS CONCEDED:	16
AVG. GOALS CONCEDED:	–
CLEAN SHEETS:	1
MOST C.S. IN SEASON:	0
EVER PRESENT:	–

LEAGUE CLUBS	YEARS	APPS	GOALS	FEE
Manchester City	90-95	6	0	Trainee
Bristol Rovers	93	3	0	Loan

OVERALL RECORD

COMPETITION	APPS	GOALS	(PENS)	SUBS
League	7	0	0	2
FA Cup	0	0	0	0
League Cup	1	0	0	1
Europe	0	0	–	–
Scottish	0	0	–	–
Other	1	0	–	–

HONOURS

FA Youth Cup r/u 88-89

INTERNATIONAL APPEARANCES

COUNTRY	LEVEL	GAMES	GOALS
Wales	Full	0	0
	B	2	0
	U-21	7	0
	Youth	0	0

NAME:	Ludo Miklosko
CLUB:	West Ham
BORN:	Ostrava, 9/12/61
DEBUT:	Swindon, 18/2/90
SUBSTITUTED:	0
BOOKINGS:	2
SENDINGS OFF:	0
OWN GOALS:	1
GOALS CONCEDED:	258
AVG. GOALS CONCEDED:	1.122
CLEAN SHEETS:	79
MOST C.S. IN SEASON:	21 (90-91)
EVER PRESENT:	90-91, 92-93, 93-94, 94-95

INTERNATIONAL APPEARANCES

COUNTRY	LEVEL	GAMES	GOALS
R.C.S.	Full	40	0
	B	0	0
	U-21/Youth	0	0

LEAGUE CLUBS	YEARS	APPS	GOALS	FEE
West Ham	90-95	230	0	£300,000
From: Banik Ostrava				

OVERALL RECORD

COMPETITION	APPS	GOALS	(PENS)	SUBS
League	230	0	0	0
FA Cup	20	0	0	0
League Cup	17	0	0	0
Europe	0	0	–	–
Scottish	0	0	–	–
Other	10	0	–	–

HONOURS

PFA Team Awards: Div 2. 91; Div 1. 93

NAME:	Allan Miller
CLUB:	Middlesbrough
BORN:	Epping, 29/3/70
DEBUT:	Oldham, 26/11/88
SUBSTITUTED:	0
BOOKINGS:	0
SENDINGS OFF:	0
OWN GOALS:	0
GOALS CONCEDED:	77
AVG. GOALS CONCEDED:	0.975
CLEAN SHEETS:	27
MOST C.S. IN SEASON:	16 (94-95)
EVER PRESENT:	–

INTERNATIONAL APPEARANCES

COUNTRY	LEVEL	GAMES	GOALS
England	Full	0	0
	B	0	0
	U-21	4	0
	Youth	0	0

LEAGUE CLUBS	YEARS	APPS	GOALS	FEE
Middlesbrough	94-95	41	0	£500,000
Birmingham	91-92	15	0	Loan
West Brom	91	3	0	Loan
Plymouth	88	13	0	Loan
Arsenal	88-94	8	0	Trainee

OVERALL RECORD

COMPETITION	APPS	GOALS	(PENS)	SUBS
League	77	0	0	2
FA Cup	4	0	0	0
League Cup	1	0	0	0
Europe	0	0	–	–
Scottish	0	0	–	–
Other	3	0	–	–

HONOURS

Division One Championship 94-95, FA Cup 92-93, League Cup 92-93, European Cup Winners' Cup 93-94

NAME:	Bobby Mimms
CLUB:	Blackburn
BORN:	York, 12/10/63
DEBUT:	Blackburn, 8/5/82
SUBSTITUTED:	0
BOOKINGS:	1
SENDINGS OFF:	0
OWN GOALS:	0
GOALS CONCEDED:	355
AVG. GOALS CONCEDED:	1.199
CLEAN SHEETS:	96
MOST C.S. IN SEASON:	19 (92-93)
EVER PRESENT:	84-85, 92-93

INTERNATIONAL APPEARANCES

COUNTRY	LEVEL	GAMES	GOALS
England	Full	0	0
	B	1	0
	U-21	3	0
	Youth	0	0

LEAGUE CLUBS	YEARS	APPS	GOALS	FEE
Blackburn	90-95	126	0	£250,000
Aberdeen	90	6	0	Loan
Tottenham	88-90	37	0	£325,000
Manchester City	87	3	0	Loan
Blackburn	87	6	0	Loan
Sunderland	86	4	0	Loan
Notts County	86	2	0	Loan
Everton	85-88	29	0	£150,000
Rotherham	81-85	83	0	£15,000
Halifax	81	0	0	Appr

OVERALL RECORD

COMPETITION	APPS	GOALS	(PENS)	SUBS
League	289	0	0	1
FA Cup	16	0	0	0
League Cup	29	0	0	0
Europe	0	0	–	–
Scottish	8	0	–	–
Other	12	0	–	–

HONOURS

League Championship 86-87, FA Cup r/u 85-86, Charity Shield medal 86, 87, 94

NAME:	Michael Oakes
CLUB:	Aston Villa
BORN:	Northwich, 30/10/73
DEBUT:	Torquay, 27/11/93
SUBSTITUTED:	0
BOOKINGS:	0
SENDINGS OFF:	0
OWN GOALS:	0
GOALS CONCEDED:	2
AVG. GOALS CONCEDED:	0
CLEAN SHEETS:	0
MOST C.S. IN SEASON:	0
EVER PRESENT:	–

LEAGUE CLUBS	YEARS	APPS	GOALS	FEE
Aston Villa	92-95	0	0	Trainee
Scarborough	94	1	0	Loan

OVERALL RECORD

COMPETITION	APPS	GOALS	(PENS)	SUBS
League	1	0	0	0
FA Cup	0	0	0	0
League Cup	1	0	0	0
Europe	0	0	–	–
Scottish	0	0	–	–

HONOURS

None

INTERNATIONAL APPEARANCES

COUNTRY	LEVEL	GAMES	GOALS
England	Full	0	0
	B	0	0
	U-21	5	0
	Youth	0	0

NAME:	Steve Ogrizovic
CLUB:	Coventry
BORN:	Mansfield, 12/9/57
DEBUT:	Port Vale, 20/8/77
SUBSTITUTED:	1
BOOKINGS:	1
SENDINGS OFF:	0
OWN GOALS:	0
GOALS CONCEDED:	665
AVG. GOALS CONCEDED:	1.281
CLEAN SHEETS:	165
MOST C.S. IN SEASON:	15 (87-88)
EVER PRESENT:	82-83, 83-84, 84-85
	85-86, 86-87, 87-88
	88-89

LEAGUE CLUBS	YEARS	APPS	GOALS	FEE
Coventry	84-95	415	1	£72,000
Shrewsbury	82-84	84	0	£70,000
Liverpool	77-82	4	0	£70,000
Chesterfield	77	16	0	Appr

OVERALL RECORD

COMPETITION	APPS	GOALS	(PENS)	SUBS
League	519	1	0	0
FA Cup	30	0	0	0
League Cup	49	0	0	0
Europe	0	0	–	–
Scottish	0	0	–	–
Other	16	0	–	–

HONOURS

FA Cup 86-87, Charity Shield medal 87

INTERNATIONAL APPEARANCES

COUNTRY	LEVEL	GAMES	GOALS
England	Full	0	0
	B	1	0
	U-21/Youth	0	0

NAME:	Paul Pettinger
CLUB:	Leeds
BORN:	Sheffield, 1/10/75
DEBUT:	Hartlepool, 27/12/94
SUBSTITUTED:	0
BOOKINGS:	0
SENDINGS OFF:	0
OWN GOALS:	0
GOALS CONCEDED:	4
AVG. GOALS CONCEDED:	–
CLEAN SHEETS:	1
MOST C.S. IN SEASON:	0
EVER PRESENT:	–

LEAGUE CLUBS	YEARS	APPS	GOALS	FEE
Leeds	92-95	0	0	Appr
Torquay	94-95	3	0	Loan

OVERALL RECORD

COMPETITION	APPS	GOALS	(PENS)	SUBS
League	3	0	0	0
FA Cup	0	0	0	0
League Cup	0	0	0	0
Europe	0	0	–	–
Scottish	0	0	–	–

HONOURS

FA Youth Cup 92-93

INTERNATIONAL APPEARANCES

COUNTRY	LEVEL	GAMES	GOALS
England	Full	0	0
	B	0	0
	U-21	0	0
	Youth	5	0

NAME:	Kevin Pilkington
CLUB:	Manchester Utd
BORN:	Hitchin, 5/3/74
DEBUT:	Crystal Palace, 19/11/94
SUBSTITUTED:	0
BOOKINGS:	0
SENDINGS OFF:	0
OWN GOALS:	0
GOALS CONCEDED:	0
AVG. GOALS CONCEDED:	–
CLEAN SHEETS:	1
MOST C.S. IN SEASON:	1
EVER PRESENT:	–

LEAGUE CLUBS	YEARS	APPS	GOALS	FEE
Manchester Utd	92-95	1	0	Trainee

OVERALL RECORD

COMPETITION	APPS	GOALS	(PENS)	SUBS
League	0	0	0	1
FA Cup	0	0	0	0
League Cup	0	0	0	0
Europe	0	0	–	–
Scottish	0	0	–	–

HONOURS

FA Youth Cup 91-92

INTERNATIONAL APPEARANCES

COUNTRY	LEVEL	GAMES	GOALS
	Full	0	0
	B	0	0
	U-21	0	0
	Youth	0	0

NAME:	Kevin Pressman
CLUB:	Sheffield Wed
BORN:	Fareham, 6/11/67
DEBUT:	Southampton, 5/9/87
SUBSTITUTED:	1
BOOKINGS:	1
SENDINGS OFF:	2
OWN GOALS:	0
GOALS CONCEDED:	181
AVG. GOALS CONCEDED:	1.371
CLEAN SHEETS:	39
MOST C.S. IN SEASON:	10 (94-95)
EVER PRESENT:	–

LEAGUE CLUBS	YEARS	APPS	GOALS	FEE
Sheffield Wed	85-95	128	0	Appr
Stoke	92	4	0	Loan

OVERALL RECORD

COMPETITION	APPS	GOALS	(PENS)	SUBS
League	132	0	0	0
FA Cup	7	0	0	0
League Cup	21	0	0	0
Europe	1	0	–	–
Scottish	0	0	–	–
Other	5	0	–	–

HONOURS

League Cup 90-91, League Cup r/u 92-93

INTERNATIONAL APPEARANCES

COUNTRY	LEVEL	GAMES	GOALS
England	Full	0	0
	B	2	0
	U-21	1	0
	Youth	10	0

NAME:	Malcolm Rigby
CLUB:	Nottm Forest
BORN:	Nottingham, 13/3/76
DEBUT:	–
SUBSTITUTED:	0
BOOKINGS:	0
SENDINGS OFF:	0
OWN GOALS:	0
GOALS CONCEDED:	0
AVG. GOALS CONCEDED:	–
CLEAN SHEETS:	0
MOST C.S. IN SEASON:	0
EVER PRESENT:	–

LEAGUE CLUBS	YEARS	APPS	GOALS	FEE
Nottm Forest	94-95	0	0	£50,000
Notts County	93-94	0	0	Appr

OVERALL RECORD

COMPETITION	APPS	GOALS	(PENS)	SUBS
League	0	0	0	0
FA Cup	0	0	0	0
League Cup	0	0	0	0
Europe	0	0	–	–
Scottish	0	0	–	–

HONOURS

None

INTERNATIONAL APPEARANCES

COUNTRY	LEVEL	GAMES	GOALS
	Full	0	0
	B	0	0
	U-21	0	0
	Youth	0	0

NAME:	Tony Roberts
CLUB:	Q.P.R.
BORN:	Bangor, 4/8/69
DEBUT:	Coventry, 18/12/87
SUBSTITUTED:	1
BOOKINGS:	1
SENDINGS OFF:	0
OWN GOALS:	0
GOALS CONCEDED:	136
AVG. GOALS CONCEDED:	1.447
CLEAN SHEETS:	18
MOST C.S. IN SEASON:	7 (94-95)
EVER PRESENT:	

LEAGUE CLUBS	YEARS	APPS	GOALS	FEE
Q.P.R.	87-95	94	0	Trainee

OVERALL RECORD

COMPETITION	APPS	GOALS	(PENS)	SUBS
League	94	0	0	0
FA Cup	6	0	0	1
League Cup	7	0	0	0
Europe	0	0	–	–
Scottish	0	0	–	–
Other	2	0	–	–

HONOURS

None

INTERNATIONAL APPEARANCES

COUNTRY	LEVEL	GAMES	GOALS
Wales	Full	1	0
	B	2	0
	U-21	2	0
	Youth	0	0

NAME:	Peter Schmeichel
CLUB:	Manchester Utd
BORN:	Glodsone, 18/11/63
DEBUT:	Notts County, 17/8/91
SUBSTITUTED:	2
BOOKINGS:	2
SENDINGS OFF:	1
OWN GOALS:	0
GOALS CONCEDED:	116
AVG. GOALS CONCEDED:	0.753
CLEAN SHEETS:	71
MOST C.S. IN SEASON:	21 (94-95)
EVER PRESENT:	92-93

LEAGUE CLUBS	YEARS	APPS	GOALS	FEE
Manchester Utd. From: Brondby	91-95	154	0	£550,000

OVERALL RECORD

COMPETITION	APPS	GOALS	(PENS)	SUBS
League	154	0	0	0
FA Cup	20	0	0	0
League Cup	16	0	0	0
Europe	29	0	–	–
Scottish	0	0	–	–
Other	3	0	–	–

HONOURS

League Championship 92-93, 93-94, FA Cup 93-94, FA Cup r/u 94-95, League Cup 91-92, League Cup r/u 93-94, Charity Shield medal 93, 94, PFA Team Award Premier League 93, Danish League 86-87, 87-88, 88-89, European Nations Cup 92

INTERNATIONAL APPEARANCES

COUNTRY	LEVEL	GAMES	GOALS
Denmark	Full	73	0
	B	0	0
	U-21	0	0
	Youth	0	0

NAME:	Les Sealey
CLUB:	West Ham
BORN:	Bethnal Green, 29/9/57
DEBUT:	Q.P.R., 11/4/77
SUBSTITUTED:	0
BOOKINGS:	1
SENDINGS OFF:	0
OWN GOALS:	0
GOALS CONCEDED:	601
AVG. GOALS CONCEDED:	1.357
CLEAN SHEETS:	130
MOST C.S. IN SEASON:	17 (86-87)
EVER PRESENT:	83-84

LEAGUE CLUBS	YEARS	APPS	GOALS	FEE
West Ham	94-95	0	0	Free
Blackpool	94	7	0	Free
Birmingham	92	12	0	Loan
Coventry	92	2	0	Loan
Aston Villa	91-93	18	0	Free
Manchester Utd	90-91	33	0	Free
Plymouth	84	6	0	Loan
Luton	83-90	207	0	£100,000
Coventry	76-83	158	0	Appr

OVERALL RECORD

COMPETITION	APPS	GOALS	(PENS)	SUBS
League	443	0	0	0
FA Cup	45	0	0	0
League Cup	41	0	0	0
Europe	8	0	–	–
Scottish	0	0	–	–
Other	11	0	–	–

HONOURS

FA Cup 89-90, League Cup 87-88, League Cup r/u 88-89, 90-91, 93-94, European Cup Winners' Cup 91, Charity Shield medal 90

INTERNATIONAL APPEARANCES

COUNTRY	LEVEL	GAMES	GOALS
	Full	0	0
	B	0	0
	U-21	0	0
	Youth	0	0

NAME:	David Seaman
CLUB:	Arsenal
BORN:	Rotherham, 19/9/63
DEBUT:	Stockport, 28/8/82
SUBSTITUTED:	2
BOOKINGS:	4
SENDINGS OFF:	1
OWN GOALS:	1
GOALS CONCEDED:	485
AVG. GOALS CONCEDED:	0.978
CLEAN SHEETS:	182
MOST C.S. IN SEASON:	24 (90-91)
EVER PRESENT:	85-86, 90-91, 91-92

LEAGUE CLUBS	YEARS	APPS	GOALS	FEE
Arsenal	90-95	189	0	£1.3m
Q.P.R.	86-90	141	0	£225,000
Birmingham	84-86	75	0	£100,000
Peterborough	82-84	91	0	£4,000
Leeds	81-82	0	0	Appr

OVERALL RECORD

COMPETITION	APPS	GOALS	(PENS)	SUBS
League	496	0	0	0
FA Cup	49	0	0	0
League Cup	54	0	0	0
Europe	22	0	–	–
Scottish	0	0	–	–
Other	14	0	–	–

INTERNATIONAL APPEARANCES

COUNTRY	LEVEL	GAMES	GOALS
England	Full	17	0
	B	7	0
	U-21	10	0
	Youth	0	0

HONOURS

League Championship 90-91, FA Cup 92-93, League Cup 92-93, Charity Shield medal 91, 93, European Cup Winners' Cup 93-94, European Cup Winners' Cup r/u 94-95, PFA Team Award Div 1. 91

NAME:	Hans Segers
CLUB:	Wimbledon
BORN:	Eindhoven, 30/10/61
DEBUT:	Coventry, 17/11/84
SUBSTITUTED:	2
BOOKINGS:	10
SENDINGS OFF:	0
OWN GOALS:	1
GOALS CONCEDED:	430
AVG. GOALS CONCEDED:	1.280
CLEAN SHEETS:	100
MOST C.S. IN SEASON:	14 (91-92)
EVER PRESENT:	89-90

LEAGUE CLUBS	YEARS	APPS	GOALS	FEE
Wimbledon	88-95	263	0	£180,000
Dunfermline	88	4	0	Loan
Sheffield Utd	87-88	10	0	Loan
Stoke	87	1	0	Loan
Nottm Forest	84-88	58	0	£50,000
From: PSV Eindhoven				

OVERALL RECORD

COMPETITION	APPS	GOALS	(PENS)	SUBS
League	331	0	0	1
FA Cup	27	0	0	0
League Cup	30	0	0	0
Europe	0	0	–	–
Scottish	4	0	–	–
Other	10	0	–	–

INTERNATIONAL APPEARANCES

COUNTRY	LEVEL	GAMES	GOALS
	Full	0	0
	B	0	0
	U-21/Youth	0	0

HONOURS

None

NAME:	Peter Shilton
CLUB:	Bolton
BORN:	Leicester, 18/9/49
DEBUT:	Everton, 4/5/66
SUBSTITUTED:	0
BOOKINGS:	0
SENDINGS OFF:	1
OWN GOALS:	2
GOALS CONCEDED:	1105
AVG. GOALS CONCEDED:	1.109
CLEAN SHEETS:	330
MOST C.S. IN SEASON:	24 (77-78)
EVER PRESENT:	68-89, 73-74, 75-76
	78-79, 79-80, 83-84
	87-88, 88-89

LEAGUE CLUBS	YEARS	APPS	GOALS	FEE
Bolton	95	1	0	Non-contract
Wimbledon	95	0	0	Non-contract
Plymouth	92-95	34	0	Free
Derby	87-92	175	0	£90,000
Southampton	82-87	188	0	£325,000
Nottm Forest	77-82	202	0	£270,000
Stoke	74-77	110	0	£300,000
Leicester	66-74	286	1	Appr

OVERALL RECORD

COMPETITION	APPS	GOALS	(PENS)	SUBS
League	995	0	0	1
FA Cup	83	0	0	0
League Cup	102	0	0	0
Europe	24	0	–	–
Scottish	0	0	–	–
Other	34	0	–	–

INTERNATIONAL APPEARANCES

COUNTRY	LEVEL	GAMES	GOALS
England	Full	125	0
	B	4	0
	U-23	13	0
	Youth	12	0

HONOURS

League Championship 77-78, Division Two Championship 70-71, FA Cup r/u 68-69, League Cup 77-78, 78-79, League Cup r/u 79-80, Charity Shield medal 71, 78, European Cup 79, 80, PFA Player of the Year 78, PFA Merit Award 90, PFA Team Awards Div 1. 74, 77, 78, 79, 80, 81, 82, 83, 84

NAME:	Neville Southall
CLUB:	Everton
BORN:	Llandudno, 16/9/58
DEBUT:	Wigan, 20/9/80
SUBSTITUTED:	4
BOOKINGS:	6
SENDINGS OFF:	3
OWN GOALS:	0
GOALS CONCEDED:	615
AVG. GOALS CONCEDED:	1.135
CLEAN SHEETS:	192
MOST C.S. IN SEASON:	18 (84-85)
EVER PRESENT:	84-85, 88-89, 89-90 90-91, 91-92, 93-94

LEAGUE CLUBS	YEARS	APPS	GOALS	FEE
Everton	81-95	494	0	£150,000
Port Vale	83	9	0	Loan
Bury	80-81	39	0	£6,000
From: Winsford				

OVERALL RECORD

COMPETITION	APPS	GOALS	(PENS)	SUBS
League	542	0	0	0
FA Cup	69	0	0	0
League Cup	60	0	0	0
Europe	9	0	–	–
Scottish	0	0	–	–
Other	25	0	–	–

HONOURS

League Championship 84-85, 86-87, FA Cup 83-84, 94-95, FA Cup r/u 84-85, 85-86, 88-89, League Cup r/u 83-84, Charity Shield medal 84, 85, European Cup Winners' Cup 84-85, Footballer of the Year 84-85, PFA Team Award Div 1. 87, 88, 89, 90

INTERNATIONAL APPEARANCES

COUNTRY	LEVEL	GAMES	GOALS
Wales	Full	81	0
	B	1	0
	U-21	1	0
	Youth	0	0

NAME:	Nigel Spink
CLUB:	Aston Villa
BORN:	Chelmsford, 8/8/58
DEBUT:	Nottm Forest, 26/12/79
SUBSTITUTED:	2
BOOKINGS:	5
SENDINGS OFF:	0
OWN GOALS:	0
GOALS CONCEDED:	467
AVG. GOALS CONCEDED:	1.308
CLEAN SHEETS:	100
MOST C.S. IN SEASON:	15 (89-90)
EVER PRESENT:	87-88, 89-90

LEAGUE CLUBS	YEARS	APPS	GOALS	FEE
Aston Villa	77-95	359	0	£4,000
From: Chelmsford City				

OVERALL RECORD

COMPETITION	APPS	GOALS	(PENS)	SUBS
League	357	0	0	2
FA Cup	28	0	0	0
League Cup	45	0	0	0
Europe	17	0	–	–
Scottish	0	0	–	–
Other	9	0	–	–

HONOURS

League Cup 93-94, Charity Shield medal 81, European Cup 81-82

INTERNATIONAL APPEARANCES

COUNTRY	LEVEL	GAMES	GOALS
England	Full	1	0
	B	3	0
	U-21/Youth	0	0

NAME:	Pavel Srnicek
CLUB:	Newcastle
BORN:	Ostrava, 10/3/68
DEBUT:	Sheffield Wed, 17/4/91
SUBSTITUTED:	1
BOOKINGS:	2
SENDINGS OFF:	3
OWN GOALS:	0
GOALS CONCEDED:	116
AVG. GOALS CONCEDED:	1.045
CLEAN SHEETS:	36
MOST C.S. IN SEASON:	13 (92-93)
EVER PRESENT:	–

LEAGUE CLUBS	YEARS	APPS	GOALS	FEE
Newcastle	91-95	111	0	£350,000
From: Banik Ostrava				

OVERALL RECORD

COMPETITION	APPS	GOALS	(PENS)	SUBS
League	111	0	0	0
FA Cup	9	0	0	0
League Cup	8	0	0	0
Europe	4	0	–	–
Scottish	0	0	–	–
Other	6	0	–	–

HONOURS

First Division Championship 92-93

INTERNATIONAL APPEARANCES

COUNTRY	LEVEL	GAMES	GOALS
R.C.S.	Full	3	0
	B	0	0
	U-21	0	0
	Youth	0	0

NAME:	Neil Sullivan
CLUB:	Wimbledon
BORN:	Sutton, 24/2/70
DEBUT:	Aston Villa, 20/4/91
SUBSTITUTED:	1
BOOKINGS:	0
SENDINGS OFF:	0
OWN GOALS:	0
GOALS CONCEDED:	18
AVG. GOALS CONCEDED:	12
CLEAN SHEETS:	7
MOST C.S. IN SEASON:	0
EVER PRESENT:	–

LEAGUE CLUBS	YEARS	APPS	GOALS	FEE
Wimbledon	88-95	17	0	Trainee
Crystal Palace	92	1	0	Loan

OVERALL RECORD

COMPETITION	APPS	GOALS	(PENS)	SUBS
League	16	0	0	2
FA Cup	0	0	0	0
League Cup	0	0	0	0
Europe	0	0	–	–
Scottish	0	0	–	–

HONOURS

None

INTERNATIONAL APPEARANCES

COUNTRY	LEVEL	GAMES	GOALS
	Full	0	0
	B	0	0
	U-21	0	0
	Youth	0	0

NAME:	Erik Thorstvedt
CLUB:	Tottenham
BORN:	Stavanger, 28/10/62
DEBUT:	Nottm Forest, 15/1/89
SUBSTITUTED:	2
BOOKINGS:	0
SENDINGS OFF:	0
OWN GOALS:	0
GOALS CONCEDED:	216
AVG. GOALS CONCEDED:	1.249
CLEAN SHEETS:	42
MOST C.S. IN SEASON:	12 (90-91)
EVER PRESENT:	–

LEAGUE CLUBS	YEARS	APPS	GOALS	FEE
Tottenham	88-95	173	0	£400,000
From: IFK Gothenburg				

OVERALL RECORD

COMPETITION	APPS	GOALS	(PENS)	SUBS
League	171	0	0	2
FA Cup	14	0	0	0
League Cup	25	0	0	0
Europe	6	0	–	–
Scottish	0	0	–	–
Other	2	0	–	–

HONOURS

FA Cup 90-91, Charity Shield medal 91

INTERNATIONAL APPEARANCES

COUNTRY	LEVEL	GAMES	GOALS
Norway	Full	88	0
	B	0	0
	U-21	0	0
	Youth	0	0

NAME:	Ian Walker
CLUB:	Tottenham
BORN:	Watford, 31/10/71
DEBUT:	Wolves, 29/9/90
SUBSTITUTED:	1
BOOKINGS:	0
SENDINGS OFF:	0
OWN GOALS:	0
GOALS CONCEDED:	136
AVG. GOALS CONCEDED:	1.511
CLEAN SHEETS:	20
MOST C.S. IN SEASON:	11 (94-95)
RATING:	–
EVER PRESENT:	

LEAGUE CLUBS	YEARS	APPS	GOALS	FEE
Tottenham	89-95	88	0	Trainee
Oxford	90	2	0	Loan

OVERALL RECORD

COMPETITION	APPS	GOALS	(PENS)	SUBS
League	89	0	0	1
FA Cup	8	0	0	0
League Cup	8	0	0	0
Europe	2	0	–	–
Scottish	0	0	–	–
Other	1	0	–	–

HONOURS

FA Youth Cup 89-90, Charity Shield medal 91

INTERNATIONAL APPEARANCES

COUNTRY	LEVEL	GAMES	GOALS
England	Full	0	0
	B	0	0
	U-21	9	0
	Youth	16	0

NAME:	Gary Walsh
CLUB:	Manchester Utd
BORN:	Wigan, 21/3/68
DEBUT:	Aston Villa, 13/12/86
SUBSTITUTED:	0
BOOKINGS:	0
SENDINGS OFF:	0
OWN GOALS:	0
GOALS CONCEDED:	67
AVG. GOALS CONCEDED:	1.136
CLEAN SHEETS:	20
MOST C.S. IN SEASON:	5 (86-87)
EVER PRESENT:	–

LEAGUE CLUBS	YEARS	APPS	GOALS	FEE
Manchester Utd	85-95	50	0	Appr
Oldham	94	6	0	Loan
Airdrie	88	3	0	Loan

OVERALL RECORD

COMPETITION	APPS	GOALS	(PENS)	SUBS
League	55	0	0	1
FA Cup	0	0	0	0
League Cup	7	0	0	0
Europe	6	0	–	–
Scottish	4	0	–	–

HONOURS

FA Cup 93-94, FA Cup r/u 94-95, League Cup 93-94, Charity Shield medal 94, European Cup Winners' Cup 90-91, FA Youth Cup 85-86

INTERNATIONAL APPEARANCES

COUNTRY	LEVEL	GAMES	GOALS
England	Full	0	0
	B	0	0
	U-21	2	0
	Youth	0	0

NAME:	Chris Woods
CLUB:	Sheffield Wed
BORN:	Boston, 14/11/59
DEBUT:	Bristol Rovers, 18/8/79
SUBSTITUTED:	2
BOOKINGS:	1
SENDINGS OFF:	0
OWN GOALS:	0
GOALS CONCEDED:	564
AVG. GOALS CONCEDED:	1.024
CLEAN SHEETS:	214
MOST C.S. IN SEASON:	25 (86-87)
EVER PRESENT:	81-82, 82-83, 83-84 85-86, 90-91

LEAGUE CLUBS	YEARS	APPS	GOALS	FEE
Sheffield Wed	91-95	99	0	£1.2m
Glasgow Rangers	86-91	173	0	£600,000
Norwich	81-86	216	0	£225,000
Q.P.R.	79-81	63	0	£250,000
Nottm Forest	76-79	0	0	Appr

OVERALL RECORD

COMPETITION	APPS	GOALS	(PENS)	SUBS
League	377	0	0	1
FA Cup	31	0	0	0
League Cup	54	0	0	0
Europe	23	0	–	–
Scottish	209	0	–	–
Other	15	0	–	–

HONOURS

Division Two Championship 85-86, FA Cup r/u 92-93, League Cup 77-78, 84-85, League Cup r/u 92-93, Scottish Premier League 86-87, 88-89, 89-90, 90-91, Scottish FA Cup r/u 88-89, Scottish League Cup 86-87, 88-89, 90-91, Scottish League Cup r/u 89-90, PFA Team Award Div 2. 86

INTERNATIONAL APPEARANCES

COUNTRY	LEVEL	GAMES	GOALS
England	Full	43	0
	B	4	0
	U-21	6	0
	Youth	0	0

NAME:	Tommy Wright
CLUB:	Nottm Forest
BORN:	Belfast, 29/8/63
DEBUT:	Aston Villa, 14/1/89
SUBSTITUTED:	2
BOOKINGS:	0
SENDINGS OFF:	0
OWN GOALS:	0
GOALS CONCEDED:	124
AVG. GOALS CONCEDED:	1.393
CLEAN SHEETS:	21
MOST C.S. IN SEASON:	7 (91-92)
EVER PRESENT:	–

LEAGUE CLUBS	YEARS	APPS	GOALS	FEE
Nottm Forest	93-95	10	0	£450,000
Hull City	91	6	0	Loan
Newcastle	88-93	73	0	£30,000
From: Linfield				

OVERALL RECORD

COMPETITION	APPS	GOALS	(PENS)	SUBS
League	88	0	0	1
FA Cup	4	0	0	0
League Cup	8	0	0	0
Europe	4	0	–	–
Scottish	0	0	–	–
Other	1	0	–	–

HONOURS

First Division Championship 92-93

INTERNATIONAL APPEARANCES

COUNTRY	LEVEL	GAMES	GOALS
N. Ireland	Full	22	0
	B	1	0
	U-21	0	0
	Youth	0	0

INTRODUCTION – FULL-BACKS

Full-backs are so often the unsung heroes of any successful side, yet their role in the modern game has taken on a new importance in recent years. With so many teams operating a five-man backline, incorporating a sweeper, the onus on full-backs to get forward in support of the midfield and strikers is greater than ever.

And there can be little doubt that the Premiership contains some of the best attacking full-backs in Europe. One of the best in the business is Manchester United's Republic of Ireland international Denis Irwin who is perfectly at home in either half of the field and looks equally comfortable at right or left back. Irwin combines well with his forward players.

A young man not too far behind is Liverpool's Rob Jones who, but for a cruel bout of injuries, would have been an England regular since bursting onto the scene with a confident and assured debut against France in 1991. He is another player who loves to get forward, but who has the pace and timing in the tackle to recover his ground when a move breaks down. Jones has proved a great buy for Liverpool since he joined the club from Crewe - a great breeding ground for young talent - for just £300,000 in 1990. His transfer value now must be ten times the price Liverpool forked out, although it is unlikely he will be allowed to leave Anfield in the foreseeable future. When fit, Jones' position in a Liverpool defence which boasts £20m worth of talent in Babbs, Scales, Ruddock, and Byornebye, is unquestioned.

But Liverpool's number 2 now finds his international spot under threat following the emergence of former Wimbledon defender Warren Barton who joined Newcastle in the summer for a Dons record £4m. The transfer fee of Barton alone is the clearest indication that full-backs are now rated as valuable as their central defensive counterparts. Yet another multi-million pound player to roll off the Wimbledon production line, Barton made his England debut in the ill-fated 'friendly' with Ireland in Dublin, a game brought to a sad halt by mindless idiots. But there are sure to be more caps in the offing for Barton, particularly as he is now playing for one of the so-called 'bigger clubs' in Newcastle.

But it is at left back that England, in particular, are blessed with such a brilliant array of talent. West Ham hard man Julian Dicks, having lost that lunatic edge somewhat, would be considered by some international managers an absolute must. His goalscoring record is exceptional and, though many have come from free-kicks and penalties he also gets his fair share from open-play. If things go well for the Hammers in 95-96 Dicks could be adding a full cap to the B caps he won under Graham Taylor. But for the 93-94 season the West Ham left-back was probably no higher than fourth in the pecking order for an international place, coming in behind Graeme Le Saux, Stuart Pearce and Tony Dorigo.

The man in the number 3 shirt in Terry Venables' current England squad is Blackburn's le Saux – one of only a few Channel Islanders to hit the big time in this country. Le Saux has improved greatly since he quit Chelsea to join Blackburn for a cut price fee in 1993. There's little doubting the wisdom of that move now. He was a key player in Kenny Dalglish's title-winning side, much to the dismay of Stuart Pearce and Leeds' flyer Dorigo who are both keen to add to their international caps.

NAME:	Viv Anderson
CLUB:	Middlesbrough
BORN:	Nottingham, 29/8/56
DEBUT v:	Sheffield Wed, 21/9/74
SUBSTITUTED:	17
BOOKINGS:	11
SENDINGS OFF:	1
OWN GOALS:	1
DOMESTIC PENS:	0
HAT-TRICKS:	0
STRIKE RATE (%):	7.61
EVER PRESENT:	–

INTERNATIONAL APPEARANCES

COUNTRY	LEVEL	GAMES	GOALS
England	Full	30	2
	B	1	0
	U-21	9	0
	Youth	0	0

LEAGUE CLUBS	YEARS	APPS	GOALS	FEE
Middlesbrough	94-95	2	0	Free
Barnsley	93-94	20	3	Free
Sheffield Wed	91-93	70	8	Free
Manchester Utd	87-91	54	2	£250,000
Arsenal	84-87	120	9	£250,000
Nottm Forest	74-84	328	15	Appr

OVERALL RECORD

COMPETITION	APPS	GOALS	(PENS)	SUBS
League	575	37	0	19
FA Cup	50	7	0	3
League Cup	74	10	0	1
Europe	32	3	–	–
Scottish	0	0	–	–
Other	15	0	–	–

HONOURS

League Championship 77-78, FA Cup 89-90, FA Cup r/u 92-93, League Cup 77-78, 78-79, 86-87, League Cup r/u 79-80, 92-93, Charity Shield medal 78, European Cup 78-79, 79-80, European Super Cup 80, European Super Cup r/u 81, European Cup Winners' Cup 91, World Club Cup finalist 80, Anglo-Scottish Cup 76-77, PFA Team Award Div 1. 79, 80, 82, 87

NAME:	Craig Armstrong
CLUB:	Nottm Forest
BORN:	South Shields, 23/5/75
DEBUT v:	Southend, 31/12/94
SUBSTITUTED:	2
BOOKINGS:	0
SENDINGS OFF:	0
OWN GOALS:	0
DOMESTIC PENS:	0
HAT-TRICKS:	0
STRIKE RATE (%):	–
EVER PRESENT:	–

INTERNATIONAL APPEARANCES

COUNTRY	LEVEL	GAMES	GOALS
	Full	0	0
	B	0	0
	U-21	0	0
	Youth	0	0

LEAGUE CLUBS	YEARS	APPS	GOALS	FEE
Nottm Forest	93-95	0	0	Trainee
Burnley	94-95	4	0	Loan

OVERALL RECORD

COMPETITION	APPS	GOALS	(PENS)	SUBS
League	4	0	0	0
FA Cup	0	0	0	0
League Cup	0	0	0	0
Europe	0	0	–	–
Scottish	0	0	–	–

CLUB HONOURS

None

NAME:	Peter Atherton
CLUB:	Sheffield Wed
BORN:	Orrell, 6/4/70
DEBUT v:	Blackpool, 24/10/87
SUBSTITUTED:	7
BOOKINGS:	12
SENDINGS OFF:	0
OWN GOALS:	1
DOMESTIC PENS:	0
HAT-TRICKS:	0
STRIKE RATE (%):	0.65
EVER PRESENT:	89-90, 90-91

INTERNATIONAL APPEARANCES

COUNTRY	LEVEL	GAMES	GOALS
England	Full	0	0
	B	0	0
	U-21	1	0
	Youth	0	0

LEAGUE CLUBS	YEARS	APPS	GOALS	FEE
Sheffield Wed	94-95	41	1	£800,000
Coventry	91-94	114	0	£300,000
Wigan	87-91	149	1	Appr

OVERALL RECORD

COMPETITION	APPS	GOALS	(PENS)	SUBS
League	299	2	0	5
FA Cup	12	0	0	0
League Cup	16	0	0	0
Europe	0	0	–	–
Scottish	0	0	–	–
Other	13	0	–	–

HONOURS

PFA Team Award Div 3. 91

NAME:	Dean Austin
CLUB:	Tottenham
BORN:	Hemel Hempstead, 6/4/70
DEBUT v:	Burnley, 10/4/90
SUBSTITUTED:	9
BOOKINGS:	22
SENDINGS OFF:	0
OWN GOALS:	0
DOMESTIC PENS:	1
HAT-TRICKS:	0
STRIKE RATE (%):	1.48
EVER PRESENT:	–

LEAGUE CLUBS	YEARS	APPS	GOALS	FEE
Tottenham	92-95	81	0	£375,000
Southend	90-92	96	2	£12,000
From: St Albans City				

OVERALL RECORD

COMPETITION	APPS	GOALS	(PENS)	SUBS
League	172	2	1	5
FA Cup	14	0	0	1
League Cup	8	1	0	2
Europe	0	0	–	–
Scottish	0	0	–	–
Other	9	0	–	–

HONOURS

None

INTERNATIONAL APPEARANCES

COUNTRY	LEVEL	GAMES	GOALS
	Full	0	0
	B	0	0
	U-21	0	0
	Youth	0	0

NAME:	David Bardsley
CLUB:	Q.P.R.
BORN:	Manchester, 11/9/64
DEBUT v:	Bury, 18/5/82
SUBSTITUTED:	13
BOOKINGS:	20
SENDINGS OFF:	0
OWN GOALS:	2
DOMESTIC PENS:	2
HAT-TRICKS:	0
STRIKE RATE (%):	4.33
EVER PRESENT:	90-91

LEAGUE CLUBS	YEARS	APPS	GOALS	FEE
Q.P.R.	89-95	212	4	£500,000
Oxford	87-89	74	7	£265,000
Watford	83-87	100	7	£150,000
Blackpool	82-83	45	0	Appr

OVERALL RECORD

COMPETITION	APPS	GOALS	(PENS)	SUBS
League	428	18	2	3
FA Cup	38	1	0	1
League Cup	38	3	0	0
Europe	0	0	–	–
Scottish	0	0	–	–
Other	7	1	–	–

HONOURS

FA Cup r/u 83-84, PFA Team Awards: Div 2. 89; Premier League 93

INTERNATIONAL APPEARANCES

COUNTRY	LEVEL	GAMES	GOALS
England	Full	2	0
	B	0	0
	U-21	0	0
	Youth	1	0

NAME:	Tony Barness
CLUB:	Chelsea
BORN:	Lewisham, 25/3/73
DEBUT v:	Sunderland, 17/9/91
SUBSTITUTED:	5
BOOKINGS:	2
SENDINGS OFF:	0
OWN GOALS:	1
DOMESTIC PENS:	0
HAT-TRICKS:	0
STRIKE RATE (%):	2.13
EVER PRESENT:	0

LEAGUE CLUBS	YEARS	APPS	GOALS	FEE
Chelsea	92-95	14	0	£350,000
Charlton	91-92	27	1	Trainee

OVERALL RECORD

COMPETITION	APPS	GOALS	(PENS)	SUBS
League	33	1	0	8
FA Cup	3	0	0	0
League Cup	3	0	0	0
Europe	3	0	–	–
Scottish	0	0	–	–
Other	4	0	–	–

HONOURS

None

INTERNATIONAL APPEARANCES

COUNTRY	LEVEL	GAMES	GOALS
	Full	0	0
	B	0	0
	U-21	0	0
	Youth	0	0

NAME:	Earl Barrett
CLUB:	Everton
BORN:	Rochdale, 28/4/67
DEBUT v:	Mansfield, 4/3/86
SUBSTITUTED:	1
BOOKINGS:	12
SENDINGS OFF:	1
OWN GOALS:	0
DOMESTIC PENS:	0
HAT-TRICKS:	0
STRIKE RATE (%):	2.80
EVER PRESENT:	89-90, 90-91, 91-92
	92-93, 94-95

LEAGUE CLUBS	YEARS	APPS	GOALS	FEE
Everton	95	17	0	£1.25m
Aston Villa	92-95	119	1	£1.7m
Oldham	87-92	183	7	£35,000
Chester	86	12	0	Loan
Manchester City	85-87	3	0	Appr

OVERALL RECORD

COMPETITION	APPS	GOALS	(PENS)	SUBS
League	330	8	0	4
FA Cup	23	1	0	0
League Cup	36	2	0	0
Europe	7	0	–	–
Scottish	0	0	–	–
Other	4	0	–	–

INTERNATIONAL APPEARANCES

COUNTRY	LEVEL	GAMES	GOALS
England	Full	3	0
	B	5	0
	U-21	4	0
	Youth	0	0

HONOURS

Second Division Championship 91-92, League Cup 93-94, League Cup r/u 89-90, PFA Team Award Div 2. 90, 91

NAME:	Warren Barton
CLUB:	Newcastle
BORN:	London, 19/3/69
DEBUT v:	Peterborough, 19/8/89
SUBSTITUTED:	15
BOOKINGS:	16
SENDINGS OFF:	0
OWN GOALS:	3
DOMESTIC PENS:	1
HAT-TRICKS:	0
STRIKE RATE (%):	4.72
EVER PRESENT:	91-92

LEAGUE CLUBS	YEARS	APPS	GOALS	FEE
Newcastle	1995	0	0	£4m
Wimbledon	90-95	180	10	£300,000
Maidstone	89-90	42	0	£30,000
From: Leytonstone/Ilford				

OVERALL RECORD

COMPETITION	APPS	GOALS	(PENS)	SUBS
League	219	10	1	3
FA Cup	14	1	0	0
League Cup	16	1	0	2
Europe	0	0	–	–
Scottish	0	0	–	–
Other	9	0	–	–

INTERNATIONAL APPEARANCES

COUNTRY	LEVEL	GAMES	GOALS
England	Full	3	0
	B	3	0
	U-21	0	0
	Youth	0	0

HONOURS

None

NAME:	Francis Benali
CLUB:	Southampton
BORN:	Southampton, 30/12/68
DEBUT v:	Derby, 1/10/88
SUBSTITUTED:	13
BOOKINGS:	31
SENDINGS OFF:	2
OWN GOALS:	1
DOMESTIC PENS:	0
HAT-TRICKS:	0
STRIKE RATE (%):	–
EVER PRESENT:	–

LEAGUE CLUBS	YEARS	APPS	GOALS	FEE
Southampton	87-95	173	0	Appr

OVERALL RECORD

COMPETITION	APPS	GOALS	(PENS)	SUBS
League	151	0	0	22
FA Cup	17	0	0	0
League Cup	13	0	0	6
Europe	0	0	–	–
Scottish	0	0	–	–
Other	4	0	–	–

HONOURS

None

INTERNATIONAL APPEARANCES

COUNTRY	LEVEL	GAMES	GOALS
	Full	0	0
	B	0	0
	U-21	0	0
	Youth	0	0

NAME:	John Beresford
CLUB:	Newcastle
BORN:	Sheffield, 4/9/66
DEBUT v:	Crystal Palace, 23/8/86
SUBSTITUTED:	24
BOOKINGS:	24
SENDINGS OFF:	0
OWN GOALS:	0
DOMESTIC PENS:	6
HAT-TRICKS:	0
STRIKE RATE (%):	5.54
EVER PRESENT:	–

LEAGUE CLUBS	YEARS	APPS	GOALS	FEE
Newcastle	92-95	109	1	£650,000
Portsmouth	89-92	107	8	£300,000
Barnsley	86-89	87	5	Free
Manchester City	83-86	0	0	Appr

OVERALL RECORD

COMPETITION	APPS	GOALS	(PENS)	SUBS
League	289	14	5	14
FA Cup	25	2	0	2
League Cup	31	4	1	0
Europe	4	0	–	–
Scottish	0	0	–	–
Other	4	0	–	–

HONOURS

First Division Championship 92-93, PFA Team Awards: Div 2. 92; Div 1. 93

INTERNATIONAL APPEARANCES

COUNTRY	LEVEL	GAMES	GOALS
England	Full	0	0
	B	2	0
	U-21	0	0
	Youth	26	3

NAME:	Henning Berg
CLUB:	Blackburn
BORN:	Eidsvell,Norway, 1/9/69
DEBUT v:	Crystal Palace, 2/2/93
SUBSTITUTED:	0
BOOKINGS:	4
SENDINGS OFF:	1
OWN GOALS:	0
DOMESTIC PENS:	0
HAT-TRICKS:	0
STRIKE RATE (%):	2.00
EVER PRESENT:	–

LEAGUE CLUBS	YEARS	APPS	GOALS	FEE
Blackburn	92-95	85	2	£400,000
From: Lillestrom-Sk				

OVERALL RECORD

COMPETITION	APPS	GOALS	(PENS)	SUBS
League	80	2	0	5
FA Cup	6	0	0	0
League Cup	9	0	0	0
Europe	2	0	–	–
Scottish	0	0	–	–
Other	1	0	–	–

HONOURS

League Championship 94-95, Charity Shield medal 94

INTERNATIONAL APPEARANCES

COUNTRY	LEVEL	GAMES	GOALS
Norway	Full	24	1
	B	0	0
	U-21	0	0
	Youth	0	0

NAME:	Gudni Bergsson
CLUB:	Bolton
BORN:	Iceland, 21/7/65
DEBUT v:	Luton, 26/12/88
SUBSTITUTED:	8
BOOKINGS:	4
SENDINGS OFF:	0
OWN GOALS:	1
DOMESTIC PENS:	0
HAT-TRICKS:	0
STRIKE RATE (%):	2.22
EVER PRESENT:	–

LEAGUE CLUBS	YEARS	APPS	GOALS	FEE
Bolton	95	8	0	£80,000
Tottenham	88-95	71	2	£100,000
From: Valur				

OVERALL RECORD

COMPETITION	APPS	GOALS	(PENS)	SUBS
League	59	2	0	20
FA Cup	2	0	0	2
League Cup	4	0	0	3
Europe	6	0	–	–
Scottish	0	0	–	–

HONOURS

League Cup r/u 94-95, Icelandic League Championship 85, 87

INTERNATIONAL APPEARANCES

COUNTRY	LEVEL	GAMES	GOALS
Iceland	Full	62	1
	B	0	0
	U-21	0	0
	Youth	0	0

NAME:	Stig Bjornebye
CLUB:	Liverpool
BORN:	Norway, 11/12/69
DEBUT v:	Coventry, 19/12/92
SUBSTITUTED:	12
BOOKINGS:	8
SENDINGS OFF:	0
OWN GOALS:	0
DOMESTIC PENS:	0
HAT-TRICKS:	0
STRIKE RATE (%):	–
EVER PRESENT:	–

LEAGUE CLUBS	YEARS	APPS	GOALS	FEE
Liverpool	92-95	51	0	£600,000
From: Rosenborg-Bk				

OVERALL RECORD

COMPETITION	APPS	GOALS	(PENS)	SUBS
League	48	0	0	3
FA Cup	7	0	0	2
League Cup	7	0	0	0
Europe	0	0	–	–
Scottish	0	0	–	–

HONOURS

League Cup 94-95

INTERNATIONAL APPEARANCES

COUNTRY	LEVEL	GAMES	GOALS
Norway	Full	39	1
	B	0	0
	U-21	0	0
	Youth	0	0

NAME:	Clayton Blackmore
CLUB:	Middlesbrough
BORN:	Neath, 23/9/64
DEBUT v:	Nottm Forest, 16/5/84
SUBSTITUTED:	33
BOOKINGS:	18
SENDINGS OFF:	0
OWN GOALS:	0
DOMESTIC PENS:	2
HAT-TRICKS:	0
STRIKE RATE (%):	9.50
EVER PRESENT:	–

LEAGUE CLUBS	YEARS	APPS	GOALS	FEE
Middlesbrough	94-95	30	2	Free
Manchester Utd	82-94	186	19	Appr

OVERALL RECORD

COMPETITION	APPS	GOALS	(PENS)	SUBS
League	176	21	2	40
FA Cup	15	1	0	6
League Cup	24	3	0	2
Europe	11	3		
Scottish	0	0		
Other	9	1		

HONOURS

League Championship 92-93, First Division Championship 94-95, FA Cup 89-90, League Cup r/u 90-91, Charity Shield medal 90, European Cup Winners' Cup 90-91

INTERNATIONAL APPEARANCES

COUNTRY	LEVEL	GAMES	GOALS
Wales	Full	38	1
	B	0	0
	U-21	4	1
	Youth	0	0

NAME:	Brian Borrows
CLUB:	Coventry
BORN:	Liverpool, 20/12/60
DEBUT v:	Stoke, 13/2/82
SUBSTITUTED:	11
BOOKINGS:	18
SENDINGS OFF:	0
OWN GOALS:	1
DOMESTIC PENS:	9
HAT-TRICKS:	0
STRIKE RATE (%):	2.31
EVER PRESENT:	88-89, 90-91

LEAGUE CLUBS	YEARS	APPS	GOALS	FEE
Coventry	85-95	365	11	£80,000
Bristol City	93	6	0	Loan
Bolton	83-85	95	0	£10,000
Everton	80-83	27	0	Amateur

OVERALL RECORD

COMPETITION	APPS	GOALS	(PENS)	SUBS
League	487	11	7	6
FA Cup	26	1	1	0
League Cup	44	1	1	0
Europe	0	0	–	–
Scottish	0	0	–	–
Other	17	0	–	–

HONOURS

Charity Shield medal 87

INTERNATIONAL APPEARANCES

COUNTRY	LEVEL	GAMES	GOALS
England	Full	0	0
	B	1	0
	U-21	0	0
	Youth	0	0

NAME:	Tim Breacker
CLUB:	West Ham
BORN:	Bicester, 2/7/65
DEBUT v:	Ipswich, 31/3/84
SUBSTITUTED:	8
BOOKINGS:	23
SENDINGS OFF:	2
OWN GOALS:	0
DOMESTIC PENS:	0
HAT-TRICKS:	0
STRIKE RATE (%):	2.41
EVER PRESENT:	87-88, 89-90

LEAGUE CLUBS	YEARS	APPS	GOALS	FEE
West Ham	90-95	170	8	£600,000
Luton	83-90	210	3	Appr

OVERALL RECORD

COMPETITION	APPS	GOALS	(PENS)	SUBS
League	372	11	0	8
FA Cup	43	0	0	0
League Cup	33	0	0	2
Europe	0	0	–	–
Scottish	0	0	–	–
Other	16	0	–	–

HONOURS

League Cup 87-88, League Cup r/u 88-89

INTERNATIONAL APPEARANCES

COUNTRY	LEVEL	GAMES	GOALS
England	Full	0	0
	B	0	0
	U-21	2	0
	Youth	0	0

NAME:	Rufus Brevett
CLUB:	Q.P.R.
BORN:	Derby, 24/9/69
DEBUT v:	Sunderland, 28/8/87
SUBSTITUTED:	8
BOOKINGS:	11
SENDINGS OFF:	0
OWN GOALS:	1
DOMESTIC PENS:	1
HAT-TRICKS:	0
STRIKE RATE (%):	1.65
EVER PRESENT:	–

LEAGUE CLUBS	YEARS	APPS	GOALS	FEE
Q.P.R.	91-95	58	0	£250,000
Doncaster	87-91	109	3	Trainee

OVERALL RECORD

COMPETITION	APPS	GOALS	(PENS)	SUBS
League	156	3	1	11
FA Cup	7	0	0	0
League Cup	7	0	0	1
Europe	0	0	–	–
Scottish	0	0	–	–
Other	11	0	–	–

HONOURS

None

INTERNATIONAL APPEARANCES

COUNTRY	LEVEL	GAMES	GOALS
	Full	0	0
	B	0	0
	U-21	0	0
	Youth	0	0

NAME:	Kenny Brown
CLUB:	West Ham
BORN:	Barking, 11/7/67
DEBUT v:	Oxford, 29/11/86
SUBSTITUTED:	6
BOOKINGS:	5
SENDINGS OFF:	0
OWN GOALS:	1
DOMESTIC PENS:	1
HAT-TRICKS:	0
STRIKE RATE (%):	4.20
EVER PRESENT:	–

LEAGUE CLUBS	YEARS	APPS	GOALS	FEE
West Ham	91-95	60	5	£175,000
Plymouth	88-91	126	4	Free
Norwich	85-88	25	0	Appr

OVERALL RECORD

COMPETITION	APPS	GOALS	(PENS)	SUBS
League	202	9	1	9
FA Cup	13	1	0	2
League Cup	11	0	0	1
Europe	0	0	–	–
Scottish	0	0	–	–
Other	11	0	–	–

HONOURS

None

INTERNATIONAL APPEARANCES

COUNTRY	LEVEL	GAMES	GOALS
	Full	0	0
	B	0	0
	U-21	0	0
	Youth	0	0

NAME:	David Burrows
CLUB:	Coventry
BORN:	Dudley, 25/10/68
DEBUT v:	Sheffield Wed, 22/4/86
SUBSTITUTED:	12
BOOKINGS:	42
SENDINGS OFF:	0
OWN GOALS:	1
DOMESTIC PENS:	0
HAT-TRICKS:	0
STRIKE RATE (%):	2.00
EVER PRESENT:	–

LEAGUE CLUBS	YEARS	APPS	GOALS	FEE
Coventry	95	11	0	£1.1m
Everton	94-95	19	0	£1.1m
West Ham	93-94	29	1	Undisclosed
Liverpool	88-93	146	3	£550,000
West Brom	86-88	46	1	Appr

OVERALL RECORD

COMPETITION	APPS	GOALS	(PENS)	SUBS
League	231	5	0	20
FA Cup	23	0	0	1
League Cup	24	1	0	1
Europe	10	0	–	–
Scottish	0	0	–	–
Other	6	0	–	–

INTERNATIONAL APPEARANCES

COUNTRY	LEVEL	GAMES	GOALS
England	Full	0	0
	B	4	0
	U-21	7	0
	Youth	0	0

HONOURS

League Championship 89-90, FA Cup 91-92, Charity Shield medal 89, 90, 92

NAME:	Sol Campbell
CLUB:	Tottenham
BORN:	Newham, 18/9/74
DEBUT v:	Chelsea, 5/12/92
SUBSTITUTED:	11
BOOKINGS:	3
SENDINGS OFF:	0
OWN GOALS:	0
DOMESTIC PENS:	0
HAT-TRICKS:	0
STRIKE RATE (%):	2.53
EVER PRESENT:	–

LEAGUE CLUBS	YEARS	APPS	GOALS	FEE
Tottenham	92-95	65	1	Trainee

OVERALL RECORD

COMPETITION	APPS	GOALS	(PENS)	SUBS
League	56	1	0	9
FA Cup	5	0	0	1
League Cup	8	1	0	0
Europe	0	0	–	–
Scottish	0	0	–	–
Other	1	0	–	–

HONOURS

None

INTERNATIONAL APPEARANCES

COUNTRY	LEVEL	GAMES	GOALS
England	Full	0	0
	B	1	0
	U-21	9	1
	Youth	3	0

NAME:	Steve Carr
CLUB:	Tottenham
BORN:	Dublin, 29/8/76
DEBUT v:	–
SUBSTITUTED:	0
BOOKINGS:	0
SENDINGS OFF:	0
OWN GOALS:	0
DOMESTIC PENS:	0
HAT-TRICKS:	0
STRIKE RATE (%):	–
EVER PRESENT:	–

LEAGUE CLUBS	YEARS	APPS	GOALS	FEE
Tottenham	93-95	0	0	Trainee

OVERALL RECORD

COMPETITION	APPS	GOALS	(PENS)	SUBS
League	0	0	0	0
FA Cup	0	0	0	0
League Cup	0	0	0	0
Europe	0	0	–	–
Scottish	0	0	–	–

HONOURS

None

INTERNATIONAL APPEARANCES

COUNTRY	LEVEL	GAMES	GOALS
Eire	Full	0	0
	B	0	0
	U-21	3	0
	Youth	0	0

NAME: Chris Casper
CLUB: Manchester Utd
BORN: Burnley, 28/4/75
DEBUT v: –
SUBSTITUTED: 0
BOOKINGS: 0
SENDINGS OFF: 0
OWN GOALS: 0
DOMESTIC PENS: 0
HAT-TRICKS: 0
STRIKE RATE (%): –
EVER PRESENT: –

LEAGUE CLUBS	YEARS	APPS	GOALS	FEE
Manchester Utd	93-95	0	0	Trainee

OVERALL RECORD

COMPETITION	APPS	GOALS	(PENS)	SUBS
League	0	0	0	0
FA Cup	0	0	0	0
League Cup	1	0	0	0
Europe	0	0	–	–
Scottish	0	0	–	–

HONOURS

FA Youth Cup 91-92, FA Youth Cup Finalist medal 92-93, Charity Shield medal 94

INTERNATIONAL APPEARANCES

COUNTRY	LEVEL	GAMES	GOALS
England	Full	0	0
	B	0	0
	U-21	1	0
	Youth	4	0

NAME: Gary Charles
CLUB: Aston Villa
BORN: Newham, 13/4/70
DEBUT v: Arsenal, 6/11/88
SUBSTITUTED: 9
BOOKINGS: 5
SENDINGS OFF: 1
OWN GOALS: 0
DOMESTIC PENS: 0
HAT-TRICKS: 0
STRIKE RATE (%): 2.99
EVER PRESENT: –

LEAGUE CLUBS	YEARS	APPS	GOALS	FEE
Aston Villa	95	16	0	£1.25m
Derby	93-95	61	3	£750,000
Leicester	89	8	0	Loan
Nottm Forest	87-93	56	1	Appr

OVERALL RECORD

COMPETITION	APPS	GOALS	(PENS)	SUBS
League	134	4	0	7
FA Cup	9	1	0	2
League Cup	14	0	0	1
Europe	0	0	–	–
Scottish	0	0	–	–
Other	15	0	–	–

HONOURS

FA Cup r/u 91, League Cup r/u 91-92, PFA Team Award Div 1. 94

INTERNATIONAL APPEARANCES

COUNTRY	LEVEL	GAMES	GOALS
England	Full	2	0
	B	0	0
	U-21	4	0
	Youth	0	0

NAME: Simon Charlton
CLUB: Southampton
BORN: Huddersfield, 25/10/71
DEBUT v: Crewe, 3/3/90
SUBSTITUTED: 10
BOOKINGS: 7
SENDINGS OFF: 1
OWN GOALS: 0
DOMESTIC PENS: 0
HAT-TRICKS: 0
STRIKE RATE (%): 1.93
EVER PRESENT: 92-93

LEAGUE CLUBS	YEARS	APPS	GOALS	FEE
Southampton	93-95	58	2	£350,000
Huddersfield	89-93	124	1	Trainee

OVERALL RECORD

COMPETITION	APPS	GOALS	(PENS)	SUBS
League	175	3	0	7
FA Cup	12	0	0	0
League Cup	12	1	0	1
Europe	0	0	–	–
Scottish	0	0	–	–
Other	14	0	–	–

HONOURS

PFA Team Awards: Div 3. 91-92; Div 2. 92

INTERNATIONAL APPEARANCES

COUNTRY	LEVEL	GAMES	GOALS
	Full	0	0
	B	0	0
	U-21	0	0
	Youth	0	0

NAME:	Steve Clarke
CLUB:	Chelsea
BORN:	Saltcoats, 29/8/63
DEBUT v:	Hibernian, 4/9/82
SUBSTITUTED:	17
BOOKINGS:	12
SENDINGS OFF:	1
OWN GOALS:	1
DOMESTIC PENS:	0
HAT-TRICKS:	0
STRIKE RATE (%):	2.79
EVER PRESENT:	–

LEAGUE CLUBS	YEARS	APPS	GOALS	FEE
Chelsea	87-95	251	6	£422,000
St. Mirren	81-87	151	6	Appr

OVERALL RECORD

COMPETITION	APPS	GOALS	(PENS)	SUBS
League	247	6	0	4
FA Cup	20	1	0	0
League Cup	16	1	0	0
Europe	5	0	–	–
Scottish	197	5	–	–
Other	25	1	–	–

HONOURS

Division Two Championship 88-89, FA Cup r/u 93-94

INTERNATIONAL APPEARANCES

COUNTRY	LEVEL	GAMES	GOALS
Scotland	Full	6	0
	B	3	0
	U-21	8	0
	Youth	0	0

NAME:	Andrew Couzens
CLUB:	Leeds
BORN:	Shipley, 4/6/75
DEBUT v:	Coventry, 18/3/95
SUBSTITUTED:	0
BOOKINGS:	1
SENDINGS OFF:	0
OWN GOALS:	0
DOMESTIC PENS:	0
HAT-TRICKS:	0
STRIKE RATE (%):	–
EVER PRESENT:	–

LEAGUE CLUBS	YEARS	APPS	GOALS	FEE
Leeds	93-95	4	0	Appr

OVERALL RECORD

COMPETITION	APPS	GOALS	(PENS)	SUBS
League	2	0	0	2
FA Cup	0	0	0	0
League Cup	0	0	0	0
Europe	0	0	–	–
Scottish	0	0	–	–

HONOURS

FA Youth Cup 92-93

INTERNATIONAL APPEARANCES

COUNTRY	LEVEL	GAMES	GOALS
England	Full	0	0
	B	0	0
	U-21	3	0
	Youth	0	0

NAME:	Neil Cox
CLUB:	Middlesbrough
BORN:	Scunthorpe, 8/10/71
DEBUT v:	Halifax, 6/10/90
SUBSTITUTED:	4
BOOKINGS:	12
SENDINGS OFF:	0
OWN GOALS:	0
DOMESTIC PENS:	0
HAT-TRICKS:	0
STRIKE RATE (%):	5.08
EVER PRESENT:	–

LEAGUE CLUBS	YEARS	APPS	GOALS	FEE
Middlesbrough	94-95	40	1	£1m
Aston Villa	91-94	42	3	£400,000
Scunthorpe	90-91	17	1	Trainee

OVERALL RECORD

COMPETITION	APPS	GOALS	(PENS)	SUBS
League	82	5	0	17
FA Cup	8	1	0	2
League Cup	7	0	0	2
Europe	1	0	–	–
Scottish	0	0	–	–
Other	8	0	–	–

HONOURS

First Division Championship 94-95, League Cup 93-94, PFA Team Award Div 1. 95

INTERNATIONAL APPEARANCES

COUNTRY	LEVEL	GAMES	GOALS
England	Full	0	0
	B	0	0
	U-21	6	0
	Youth	0	0

NAME:	Ken Cunningham
CLUB:	Wimbledon
BORN:	Dublin, 28/6/71
DEBUT v:	Norwich, 17/3/90
SUBSTITUTED:	7
BOOKINGS:	5
SENDINGS OFF:	0
OWN GOALS:	1
DOMESTIC PENS:	0
HAT-TRICKS:	0
STRIKE RATE (%):	0.56
EVER PRESENT:	–

LEAGUE CLUBS	YEARS	APPS	GOALS	FEE
Wimbledon	94-95	28	0	£600,000
Millwall	89-94	136	1	Appr

OVERALL RECORD

COMPETITION	APPS	GOALS	(PENS)	SUBS
League	160	1	0	4
FA Cup	5	0	0	0
League Cup	10	0	0	0
Europe	0	0	–	–
Scottish	0	0	–	–
Other	6	1	–	–

HONOURS

None

INTERNATIONAL APPEARANCES

COUNTRY	LEVEL	GAMES	GOALS
Eire	Full	0	0
	B	2	0
	U-21	4	0
	Youth	0	0

NAME:	Julian Dicks
CLUB:	West Ham
BORN:	Bristol, 8/8/68
DEBUT v:	Chelsea, 24/8/85
SUBSTITUTED:	11
BOOKINGS:	36
SENDINGS OFF:	3
OWN GOALS:	1
DOMESTIC PENS:	25
HAT-TRICKS:	0
STRIKE RATE (%):	12.75
EVER PRESENT:	–

LEAGUE CLUBS	YEARS	APPS	GOALS	FEE
West Ham	94-95	29	5	£500,000
Liverpool	93-94	24	3	£1.6m
West Ham	88-93	159	29	£300,000
Birmingham	85-88	89	1	Appr

OVERALL RECORD

COMPETITION	APPS	GOALS	(PENS)	SUBS
League	295	38	23	6
FA Cup	22	2	0	0
League Cup	29	5	2	1
Europe	0	0	–	–
Scottish	0	0	–	–
Other	13	4	–	–

HONOURS

PFA Team Awards Div 2. 87, 90

INTERNATIONAL APPEARANCES

COUNTRY	LEVEL	GAMES	GOALS
England	Full	0	0
	B	2	0
	U-21	4	0
	Youth	0	0

NAME:	Lee Dixon
CLUB:	Arsenal
BORN:	Manchester, 17/3/64
DEBUT v:	Q.P.R., 10/5/83
SUBSTITUTED:	13
BOOKINGS:	18
SENDINGS OFF:	1
OWN GOALS:	5
DOMESTIC PENS:	11
HAT-TRICKS:	0
STRIKE RATE (%):	5.79
EVER PRESENT:	86-87, 89-90, 90-91

LEAGUE CLUBS	YEARS	APPS	GOALS	FEE
Arsenal	88-95	254	16	£400,000
Stoke	86-88	71	5	£40,000
Bury	85-86	45	6	Free
Chester	84-85	57	1	Free
Burnley	82-84	4	0	Appr

OVERALL RECORD

COMPETITION	APPS	GOALS	(PENS)	SUBS
League	427	28	11	4
FA Cup	42	2	0	0
League Cup	45	0	0	0
Europe	21	0	–	–
Scottish	0	0	–	–
Other	30	1	–	–

HONOURS

League Championship 88-89, 90-91, FA Cup 92-93, Charity Shield medal 89, 91, 93, European Cup Winners' Cup 93-94, European Cup Winners Cup r/u 94-95

INTERNATIONAL APPEARANCES

COUNTRY	LEVEL	GAMES	GOALS
England	Full	21	1
	B	6	0
	U-21	0	0
	Youth	0	0

NAME:	Tony Dorigo
CLUB:	Leeds
BORN:	Melbourne, 31/12/65
DEBUT v:	Ipswich, 12/5/84
SUBSTITUTED:	13
BOOKINGS:	9
SENDINGS OFF:	0
OWN GOALS:	0
DOMESTIC PENS:	1
HAT-TRICKS:	0
STRIKE RATE (%):	3.55
EVER PRESENT:	87-88

LEAGUE CLUBS	YEARS	APPS	GOALS	FEE
Leeds	91-95	136	4	£1.3m
Chelsea	87-91	146	11	£475,000
Aston Villa	83-87	111	1	Appr •

OVERALL RECORD

COMPETITION	APPS	GOALS	(PENS)	SUBS
League	388	16	1	5
FA Cup	20	0	0	0
League Cup	36	0	0	2
Europe	5	0	–	–
Scottish	0	0	–	–
Other	23	2	–	–

HONOURS

League Championship 91-92, Division Two Championship 88-89, Charity Shield medal 92, PFA Team Awards: Div 2. 89; Premier League 93

INTERNATIONAL APPEARANCES

COUNTRY	LEVEL	GAMES	GOALS
England	Full	16	0
	B	6	0
	U-21	11	0
	Youth	0	0

NAME:	Andy Dow
CLUB:	Chelsea
BORN:	Dundee, 7/2/73
DEBUT v:	Partick T, 5/10/91
SUBSTITUTED:	6
BOOKINGS:	0
SENDINGS OFF:	0
OWN GOALS:	0
DOMESTIC PENS:	0
HAT-TRICKS:	0
STRIKE RATE (%):	–
EVER PRESENT:	–

LEAGUE CLUBS	YEARS	APPS	GOALS	FEE
Chelsea	93-95	13	0	£300,000
Bradford	94	5	0	Loan
Dundee	90-93	18	1	Appr

OVERALL RECORD

COMPETITION	APPS	GOALS	(PENS)	SUBS
League	17	0	0	1
FA Cup	1	0	0	0
League Cup	2	0	0	0
Europe	0	0	–	–
Scottish	20	1	–	–
Other	2	0	–	–

HONOURS

None

INTERNATIONAL APPEARANCES

COUNTRY	LEVEL	GAMES	GOALS
Scotland	Full	0	0
	B	0	0
	U-21	4	0
	Youth	0	0

NAME:	Richard Edghill
CLUB:	Manchester City
BORN:	Oldham, 23/9/74
DEBUT v:	Wimbledon, 18/9/93
SUBSTITUTED:	0
BOOKINGS:	6
SENDINGS OFF:	1
OWN GOALS:	0
DOMESTIC PENS:	0
HAT-TRICKS:	0
STRIKE RATE (%):	–
EVER PRESENT:	–

LEAGUE CLUBS	YEARS	APPS	GOALS	FEE
Manchester City	92-95	36	0	Trainee

OVERALL RECORD

COMPETITION	APPS	GOALS	(PENS)	SUBS
League	35	0	0	1
FA Cup	1	0	0	0
League Cup	7	0	0	0
Europe	0	0	–	–
Scottish	0	0	–	–

HONOURS

None

INTERNATIONAL APPEARANCES

COUNTRY	LEVEL	GAMES	GOALS
England	Full	0	0
	B	1	0
	U-21	3	0
	Youth	0	0

NAME:	Justin Edinburgh
CLUB:	Tottenham
BORN:	Brentwood, 18/12/69
DEBUT v:	Cardiff, 23/9/88
SUBSTITUTED:	11
BOOKINGS:	23
SENDINGS OFF:	0
OWN GOALS:	0
DOMESTIC PENS:	0
HAT-TRICKS:	0
STRIKE RATE (%):	0.49
EVER PRESENT:	–

LEAGUE CLUBS	YEARS	APPS	GOALS	FEE
Tottenham	90-95	127	1	£150,000
Southend	88-90	37	0	Trainee

OVERALL RECORD

COMPETITION	APPS	GOALS	(PENS)	SUBS
League	156	1	0	8
FA Cup	19	0	0	0
League Cup	16	0	0	4
Europe	3	0	–	–
Scottish	0	0	–	–
Other	5	1	–	–

HONOURS

FA Cup 90-91

INTERNATIONAL APPEARANCES

COUNTRY	LEVEL	GAMES	GOALS
	Full	0	0
	B	0	0
	U-21	0	0
	Youth	0	0

NAME:	Gary Elkins
CLUB:	Wimbledon
BORN:	Wallingford, 4/5/66
DEBUT v:	Middlesbrough, 22/9/84
SUBSTITUTED:	18
BOOKINGS:	18
SENDINGS OFF:	0
OWN GOALS:	2
DOMESTIC PENS:	0
HAT-TRICKS:	0
STRIKE RATE (%):	2.58
EVER PRESENT:	–

LEAGUE CLUBS	YEARS	APPS	GOALS	FEE
Wimbledon	90-95	100	3	£20,000
Exeter	89-90	5	0	Loan
Fulham	83-90	104	2	Appr

OVERALL RECORD

COMPETITION	APPS	GOALS	(PENS)	SUBS
League	198	5	0	11
FA Cup	9	1	0	2
League Cup	13	0	0	0
Europe	0	0	–	–
Scottish	0	0	–	–
Other	10	0	–	–

HONOURS

None

INTERNATIONAL APPEARANCES

COUNTRY	LEVEL	GAMES	GOALS
England	Full	0	0
	B	0	0
	U-21	0	0
	Youth	11	0

NAME:	Curtis Fleming
CLUB:	Middlesbrough
BORN:	Manchester, 8/10/68
DEBUT v:	Ipswich, 24/8/91
SUBSTITUTED:	6
BOOKINGS:	13
SENDINGS OFF:	1
OWN GOALS:	0
DOMESTIC PENS:	0
HAT-TRICKS:	0
STRIKE RATE (%):	–
EVER PRESENT:	–

LEAGUE CLUBS	YEARS	APPS	GOALS	FEE
Middlesbrough	91-95	113	0	£50,000
St. Patricks	89-91	0	0	No Fee
Swindon	88-89	0	0	Appr

OVERALL RECORD

COMPETITION	APPS	GOALS	(PENS)	SUBS
League	101	0	0	12
FA Cup	7	0	0	0
League Cup	7	0	0	2
Europe	4	0	–	–
Scottish	0	0	–	–
Other	7	0	–	–

HONOURS

First Division Championship 94-95, Eire League
Championship 89-90

INTERNATIONAL APPEARANCES

COUNTRY	LEVEL	GAMES	GOALS
Eire	Full	0	0
	B	1	0
	U-21	6	0
	Youth	0	0

NAME:	Scott Green
CLUB:	Bolton
BORN:	Walsall, 15/1/70
DEBUT v:	Shrewsbury, 21/4/90
SUBSTITUTED:	26
BOOKINGS:	5
SENDINGS OFF:	0
OWN GOALS:	0
DOMESTIC PENS:	0
HAT-TRICKS:	0
STRIKE RATE (%):	10.85
EVER PRESENT:	–

LEAGUE CLUBS	YEARS	APPS	GOALS	FEE
Bolton	90-95	177	20	£50,000
Derby	88-90	0	0	Trainee

OVERALL RECORD

COMPETITION	APPS	GOALS	(PENS)	SUBS
League	133	20	0	44
FA Cup	16	2	0	2
League Cup	16	1	0	1
Europe	0	0	–	–
Scottish	0	0	–	–
Other	20	1	–	–

HONOURS

League Cup r/u 94-95

INTERNATIONAL APPEARANCES

COUNTRY	LEVEL	GAMES	GOALS
	Full	0	0
	B	0	0
	U-21	0	0
	Youth	0	0

NAME:	Gareth Hall
CLUB:	Chelsea
BORN:	Croydon, 20/3/69
DEBUT v:	Wimbledon, 5/5/87
SUBSTITUTED:	9
BOOKINGS:	14
SENDINGS OFF:	0
OWN GOALS:	0
DOMESTIC PENS:	0
HAT-TRICKS:	0
STRIKE RATE (%):	1.95
EVER PRESENT:	–

LEAGUE CLUBS	YEARS	APPS	GOALS	FEE
Chelsea	86-95	135	3	Appr

OVERALL RECORD

COMPETITION	APPS	GOALS	(PENS)	SUBS
League	117	3	0	18
FA Cup	6	0	0	0
League Cup	12	0	0	1
Europe	2	0	–	–
Scottish	0	0	–	–
Other	13	2	–	–

HONOURS

Division Two Championship 88-89

INTERNATIONAL APPEARANCES

COUNTRY	LEVEL	GAMES	GOALS
Wales	Full	9	0
	B	0	0
	U-21	1	0
	Youth	0	0

NAME:	Steve Harkness
CLUB:	Liverpool
BORN:	Carlisle, 27/8/71
DEBUT v:	Hereford, 18/2/89
SUBSTITUTED:	5
BOOKINGS:	10
SENDINGS OFF:	0
OWN GOALS:	0
DOMESTIC PENS:	0
HAT-TRICKS:	0
STRIKE RATE (%):	2.78
EVER PRESENT:	–

LEAGUE CLUBS	YEARS	APPS	GOALS	FEE
Liverpool	89-95	40	2	£75,000
Southend	95	6	0	Loan
Huddersfield	93	5	0	Loan
Carlisle	89	13	0	Trainee

OVERALL RECORD

COMPETITION	APPS	GOALS	(PENS)	SUBS
League	57	2	0	7
FA Cup	2	0	0	0
League Cup	4	0	0	2
Europe	6	0	–	–
Scottish	0	0	–	–
Other	1	0	–	–

HONOURS

None

INTERNATIONAL APPEARANCES

COUNTRY	LEVEL	GAMES	GOALS
England	Full	0	0
	B	0	0
	U-21	0	0
	Youth	13	2

NAME:	Andy Hill
CLUB:	Manchester City
BORN:	Maltby, 20/1/65
DEBUT v:	Darlington, 25/8/84
SUBSTITUTED:	26
BOOKINGS:	5
SENDINGS OFF:	0
OWN GOALS:	1
DOMESTIC PENS:	0
HAT-TRICKS:	0
STRIKE RATE (%):	4.15
EVER PRESENT:	89-90

LEAGUE CLUBS	YEARS	APPS	GOALS	FEE
Manchester City	90-95	98	6	£200,000
Bury	84-90	264	10	Free
Manchester Utd	83-84	0	0	Appr

OVERALL RECORD

COMPETITION	APPS	GOALS	(PENS)	SUBS
League	355	16	0	7
FA Cup	14	0	0	1
League Cup	33	1	0	0
Europe	0	0	–	–
Scottish	0	0	–	–
Other	20	2	–	–

HONOURS

None

INTERNATIONAL APPEARANCES

COUNTRY	LEVEL	GAMES	GOALS
England	Full	0	0
	B	0	0
	U-21	0	0
	Youth	2	0

NAME:	Andy Hinchcliffe
CLUB:	Everton
BORN:	Manchester, 5/2/69
DEBUT v:	Plymouth, 15/8/87
SUBSTITUTED:	7
BOOKINGS:	7
SENDINGS OFF:	0
OWN GOALS:	2
DOMESTIC PENS:	3
HAT-TRICKS:	0
STRIKE RATE (%):	5.34
EVER PRESENT:	–

LEAGUE CLUBS	YEARS	APPS	GOALS	FEE
Everton	90-95	119	4	£800,000
Manchester City	86-90	112	8	Appr

OVERALL RECORD

COMPETITION	APPS	GOALS	(PENS)	SUBS
League	221	12	3	10
FA Cup	23	2	0	0
League Cup	25	1	0	2
Europe	0	0	–	–
Scottish	0	0	–	–
Other	8	1	–	–

HONOURS

FA Cup 94-95, PFA Team Award Div 2. 88

INTERNATIONAL APPEARANCES

COUNTRY	LEVEL	GAMES	GOALS
England	Full	0	0
	B	0	0
	U-21	1	0
	Youth	8	1

NAME:	Marc Hottiger
CLUB:	Newcastle
BORN:	Lausanne, 7/11/67
DEBUT v:	Leicester, 21/8/94
SUBSTITUTED:	2
BOOKINGS:	5
SENDINGS OFF:	0
OWN GOALS:	0
DOMESTIC PENS:	0
HAT-TRICKS:	0
STRIKE RATE (%):	4.26
EVER PRESENT:	–

LEAGUE CLUBS	YEARS	APPS	GOALS	FEE
Newcastle	94-95	38	1	£600,000
From: F.C. Zion				

OVERALL RECORD

COMPETITION	APPS	GOALS	(PENS)	SUBS
League	38	1	0	0
FA Cup	4	1	0	0
League Cup	5	0	0	0
Europe	4	0	–	–
Scottish	0	0	–	–

HONOURS

None

INTERNATIONAL APPEARANCES

COUNTRY	LEVEL	GAMES	GOALS
Switzerland	Full	49	5
	B	0	0
	U-21	0	0
	Youth	0	0

NAME:	Dennis Irwin
CLUB:	Manchester Utd
BORN:	Cork, 31/10/65
DEBUT v:	Fulham, 21/1/84
SUBSTITUTED:	21
BOOKINGS:	9
SENDINGS OFF:	0
OWN GOALS:	1
DOMESTIC PENS:	2
HAT-TRICKS:	0
STRIKE RATE (%):	5.14
EVER PRESENT:	93-94

LEAGUE CLUBS	YEARS	APPS	GOALS	FEE
Manchester Utd	90-95	194	13	£625,000
Oldham	86-90	167	4	Free
Leeds	83-86	72	1	Appr

OVERALL RECORD

COMPETITION	APPS	GOALS	(PENS)	SUBS
League	430	18	1	3
FA Cup	39	6	1	0
League Cup	52	3	0	1
Europe	18	0	–	–
Scottish	0	0	–	–
Other	10	0	–	–

HONOURS

League Championship 92-93, 93-94, FA Cup 93-94, FA Cup r/u 94-95, League Cup 91-92, League Cup r/u 89-90, 90-91, 93-94, Charity Shield medal 90, 93, European Cup Winners' Cup 90-91, PFA Team Awards: Div 2. 90; Premier League 94

INTERNATIONAL APPEARANCES

COUNTRY	LEVEL	GAMES	GOALS
Eire	Full	36	1
	B	1	0
	U-21	4	0
	Youth	0	0

NAME:	Matt Jackson
CLUB:	Everton
BORN:	Leeds, 19/10/71
DEBUT v:	Crewe, 30/3/91
SUBSTITUTED:	13
BOOKINGS:	12
SENDINGS OFF:	0
OWN GOALS:	0
DOMESTIC PENS:	0
HAT-TRICKS:	0
STRIKE RATE (%):	3.75
EVER PRESENT:	–

LEAGUE CLUBS	YEARS	APPS	GOALS	FEE
Everton	91-95	125	4	£600,000
Preston	91	4	0	Loan
Luton	90-91	9	0	School

OVERALL RECORD

COMPETITION	APPS	GOALS	(PENS)	SUBS
League	129	4	0	9
FA Cup	12	2	0	0
League Cup	10	0	0	0
Europe	0	0	–	–
Scottish	0	0	–	–
Other	3	0	–	–

HONOURS

FA Cup 94-95

INTERNATIONAL APPEARANCES

COUNTRY	LEVEL	GAMES	GOALS
England	Full	0	0
	B	0	0
	U-21	11	0
	Youth	1	0

NAME:	Rob Jones
CLUB:	Liverpool
BORN:	Wrexham, 5/11/71
DEBUT v:	Darlington, 9/4/88
SUBSTITUTED:	20
BOOKINGS:	16
SENDINGS OFF:	1
OWN GOALS:	0
DOMESTIC PENS:	0
HAT-TRICKS:	0
STRIKE RATE (%):	0.8
EVER PRESENT:	–

LEAGUE CLUBS	YEARS	APPS	GOALS	FEE
Liverpool	91-95	127	0	£300,000
Crewe	88-91	75	2	Trainee

OVERALL RECORD

COMPETITION	APPS	GOALS	(PENS)	SUBS
League	186	2	0	16
FA Cup	20	0	0	3
League Cup	24	0	0	1
Europe	4	0	–	–
Scottish	0	0	–	–
Other	3	0	–	–

HONOURS

FA Cup 91-92, League Cup 94-95, PFA Team Awards: Div 1. 92; Premier League 95

INTERNATIONAL APPEARANCES

COUNTRY	LEVEL	GAMES	GOALS
England	Full	10	0
	B	0	0
	U-21	2	0
	Youth	2	1

NAME:	Roger Joseph
CLUB:	Wimbledon
BORN:	Paddington, 24/12/65
DEBUT v:	Millwall, 19/5/85
SUBSTITUTED:	20
BOOKINGS:	9
SENDINGS OFF:	1
OWN GOALS:	0
DOMESTIC PENS:	0
HAT-TRICKS:	0
STRIKE RATE (%):	0.65
EVER PRESENT:	90-91

LEAGUE CLUBS	YEARS	APPS	GOALS	FEE
Wimbledon	88-95	162	0	£150,000
Millwall	95	5	0	Loan
Brentford	84-88	104	2	Juniors

OVERALL RECORD

COMPETITION	APPS	GOALS	(PENS)	SUBS
League	263	2	0	8
FA Cup	12	0	0	1
League Cup	24	0	0	2
Europe	0	0	–	–
Scottish	0	0	–	–
Other	14	0	–	–

HONOURS

PFA Team Award Div 3. 88

INTERNATIONAL APPEARANCES

COUNTRY	LEVEL	GAMES	GOALS
England	Full	0	0
	B	2	0
	U-21	0	0
	Youth	0	0

NAME:	Garry Kelly
CLUB:	Leeds
BORN:	Drogheda, 9/7/74
DEBUT v:	Nottm Forest, 22/12/91
SUBSTITUTED:	3
BOOKINGS:	9
SENDINGS OFF:	0
OWN GOALS:	0
DOMESTIC PENS:	0
HAT-TRICKS:	0
STRIKE RATE (%):	–
EVER PRESENT:	93-94, 94-95

LEAGUE CLUBS	YEARS	APPS	GOALS	FEE
Leeds	91-95	86	0	Appr

OVERALL RECORD

COMPETITION	APPS	GOALS	(PENS)	SUBS
League	84	0	0	2
FA Cup	7	0	0	0
League Cup	4	0	0	0
Europe	0	0	–	–
Scottish	0	0	–	–

HONOURS

PFA Team Award Premier League 94

INTERNATIONAL APPEARANCES

COUNTRY	LEVEL	GAMES	GOALS
Eire	Full	14	1
	B	0	0
	U-21	4	0
	Youth	0	0

NAME:	Jeff Kenna
CLUB:	Blackburn
BORN:	Dublin, 27/8/70
DEBUT v:	Derby, 4/5/91
SUBSTITUTED:	3
BOOKINGS:	8
SENDINGS OFF:	0
OWN GOALS:	0
DOMESTIC PENS:	0
HAT-TRICKS:	0
STRIKE RATE (%):	2.92
EVER PRESENT:	–

LEAGUE CLUBS	YEARS	APPS	GOALS	FEE
Blackburn	95	9	1	£1.5m
Southampton	89-95	114	3	Trainee

OVERALL RECORD

COMPETITION	APPS	GOALS	(PENS)	SUBS
League	119	4	0	4
FA Cup	10	0	0	1
League Cup	3	0	0	0
Europe	0	0	–	–
Scottish	0	0	–	–
Other	3	0	–	–

HONOURS

None

INTERNATIONAL APPEARANCES

COUNTRY	LEVEL	GAMES	GOALS
Eire	Full	3	0
	B	1	0
	U-21	8	0
	Youth	0	0

NAME:	David Kerslake
CLUB:	Tottenham
BORN:	Stepney, 19/6/66
DEBUT v:	Newcastle, 13/4/85
SUBSTITUTED:	25
BOOKINGS:	9
SENDINGS OFF:	0
OWN GOALS:	0
DOMESTIC PENS:	2
HAT-TRICKS:	0
STRIKE RATE (%):	4.38
EVER PRESENT:	–

LEAGUE CLUBS	YEARS	APPS	GOALS	FEE
Tottenham	93-95	34	0	£650,000
Leeds	93	8	0	£500,000
Swindon	89-93	135	2	£110,000
Q.P.R.	83-89	58	6	Appr

OVERALL RECORD

COMPETITION	APPS	GOALS	(PENS)	SUBS
League	211	8	2	24
FA Cup	11	0	0	3
League Cup	23	4	0	2
Europe	0	0	–	–
Scottish	0	0	–	–
Other	15	0	–	–

HONOURS

PFA Team Awards: Div 2. 91-92; Div 1. 93

INTERNATIONAL APPEARANCES

COUNTRY	LEVEL	GAMES	GOALS
England	Full	0	0
	B	2	0
	U-21	1	0
	Youth	27	8

NAME:	Alan Kimble
CLUB:	Wimbledon
BORN:	Dagenham, 6/8/66
DEBUT v:	Sheffield Utd, 16/4/85
SUBSTITUTED:	10
BOOKINGS:	20
SENDINGS OFF:	1
OWN GOALS:	1
DOMESTIC PENS:	20
HAT-TRICKS:	0
STRIKE RATE (%):	6.13
EVER PRESENT:	92-93

LEAGUE CLUBS	YEARS	APPS	GOALS	FEE
Wimbledon	93-95	40	0	£175,000
Cambridge	86-93	299	24	Free
Exeter	85	1	0	Loan
Charlton	84-86	6	0	Appr

OVERALL RECORD

COMPETITION	APPS	GOALS	(PENS)	SUBS
League	342	24	19	4
FA Cup	32	1	1	0
League Cup	29	0	0	1
Europe	0	0	–	–
Scottish	0	0	–	–
Other	22	0	–	–

HONOURS

Division Three Championship 90-91

INTERNATIONAL APPEARANCES

COUNTRY	LEVEL	GAMES	GOALS
	Full	0	0
	B	0	0
	U-21	0	0
	Youth	0	0

NAME:	Phil King
CLUB:	Aston Villa
BORN:	Bristol, 28/12/67
DEBUT v:	Halifax, 23/2/85
SUBSTITUTED:	29
BOOKINGS:	7
SENDINGS OFF:	0
OWN GOALS:	3
DOMESTIC PENS:	0
HAT-TRICKS:	0
STRIKE RATE (%):	2.46
EVER PRESENT:	87-88

LEAGUE CLUBS	YEARS	APPS	GOALS	FEE
Aston Villa	94-95	16	0	£200,000
Notts County	93	6	0	Loan
Sheffield Wed	89-94	129	2	£400,000
Swindon	87-89	116	4	£155,000
Torquay	86-87	24	3	£3,000
Exeter	85-86	27	0	Appr

OVERALL RECORD

COMPETITION	APPS	GOALS	(PENS)	SUBS
League	302	9	0	16
FA Cup	15	0	0	0
League Cup	33	0	0	0
Europe	4	0	–	–
Scottish	0	0	–	–
Other	24	0	–	–

HONOURS

League Cup 90-91, League Cup r/u 92-93, FA Cup r/u 92-93

INTERNATIONAL APPEARANCES

COUNTRY	LEVEL	GAMES	GOALS
England	Full	0	0
	B	1	0
	U-21	0	0
	Youth	0	0

Graeme Le Saux

NAME:	Graeme Le Saux
CLUB:	Blackburn
BORN:	Jersey, 17/10/68
DEBUT v:	Portsmouth, 13/5/89
SUBSTITUTED:	20
BOOKINGS:	30
SENDINGS OFF:	1
OWN GOALS:	0
DOMESTIC PENS:	0
HAT-TRICKS:	0
STRIKE RATE (%):	6.57
EVER PRESENT:	–

LEAGUE CLUBS	YEARS	APPS	GOALS	FEE
Blackburn	93-95	89	5	£750,000
Chelsea	87-93	90	8	Appr

OVERALL RECORD

COMPETITION	APPS	GOALS	(PENS)	SUBS
League	165	13	0	14
FA Cup	12	0	0	1
League Cup	15	1	0	6
Europe	2	0	–	–
Scottish	0	0	–	–
Other	10	0	–	–

HONOURS

League Championship 94-95, Charity Shield medal 94
PFA Team Award Premier League 95

INTERNATIONAL APPEARANCES

COUNTRY	LEVEL	GAMES	GOALS
England	Full	10	1
	B	2	0
	U-21	4	0
	Youth	0	0

Steve Lomas

NAME:	Steve Lomas
CLUB:	Manchester City
BORN:	Germany, 18/1/74
DEBUT v:	Sheffield Utd, 25/9/93
SUBSTITUTED:	3
BOOKINGS:	6
SENDINGS OFF:	0
OWN GOALS:	0
DOMESTIC PENS:	0
HAT-TRICKS:	0
STRIKE RATE (%):	7.14
EVER PRESENT:	–

LEAGUE CLUBS	YEARS	APPS	GOALS	FEE
Manchester City	91-95	43	2	Appr

OVERALL RECORD

COMPETITION	APPS	GOALS	(PENS)	SUBS
League	35	2	0	8
FA Cup	2	0	0	1
League Cup	10	2	0	0
Europe	0	0	–	–
Scottish	0	0	–	–

HONOURS

None

INTERNATIONAL APPEARANCES

COUNTRY	LEVEL	GAMES	GOALS
Northern Ireland	Full	6	1
	B	1	0
	U-21	0	0
	Youth	0	0

Des Lyttle

NAME:	Des Lyttle
CLUB:	Nottm Forest
BORN:	Wolverhampton, 24/9/71
DEBUT v:	Burnley, 15/8/92
SUBSTITUTED:	3
BOOKINGS:	16
SENDINGS OFF:	1
OWN GOALS:	0
DOMESTIC PENS:	0
HAT-TRICKS:	0
STRIKE RATE (%):	1.37
EVER PRESENT:	92-93

LEAGUE CLUBS	YEARS	APPS	GOALS	FEE
Nottm Forest	93-95	75	1	£375,000
Swansea	92-93	46	1	£12,500
From: Worcester City				

OVERALL RECORD

COMPETITION	APPS	GOALS	(PENS)	SUBS
League	121	2	0	0
FA Cup	13	0	0	0
League Cup	12	0	0	0
Europe	0	0	–	–
Scottish	0	0	–	–
Other	3	0	–	–

HONOURS

None

INTERNATIONAL APPEARANCES

COUNTRY	LEVEL	GAMES	GOALS
	Full	0	0
	B	0	0
	U-21	0	0
	Youth	0	0

NAME:	Gavin McGowan
CLUB:	Arsenal
BORN:	Blackheath, 16/1/76
DEBUT v:	Sheffield Wed, 6/5/93
SUBSTITUTED:	1
BOOKINGS:	0
SENDINGS OFF:	0
OWN GOALS:	0
DOMESTIC PENS:	0
HAT-TRICKS:	0
STRIKE RATE (%):	–
EVER PRESENT:	–

LEAGUE CLUBS	YEARS	APPS	GOALS	FEE
Arsenal	93-95	3	0	Trainee

OVERALL RECORD

COMPETITION	APPS	GOALS	(PENS)	SUBS
League	1	0	0	2
FA Cup	0	0	0	0
League Cup	0	0	0	0
Europe	0	0	–	–
Scottish	0	0	–	–

HONOURS

FA Youth Cup 93-94

INTERNATIONAL APPEARANCES

COUNTRY	LEVEL	GAMES	GOALS
England	Full	0	0
	B	0	0
	U-21	0	0
	Youth	2	0

NAME:	Lee Makel
CLUB:	Blackburn
BORN:	Sunderland, 11/1/73
DEBUT v:	West Brom, 4/5/91
SUBSTITUTED:	2
BOOKINGS:	0
SENDINGS OFF:	0
OWN GOALS:	0
DOMESTIC PENS:	0
HAT-TRICKS:	0
STRIKE RATE (%):	–
EVER PRESENT:	–

LEAGUE CLUBS	YEARS	APPS	GOALS	FEE
Blackburn	92-95	3	0	£160,000
Newcastle	91-92	12	1	Appr

OVERALL RECORD

COMPETITION	APPS	GOALS	(PENS)	SUBS
League	7	1	0	8
FA Cup	0	0	0	0
League Cup	1	0	0	2
Europe	0	0	–	–
Scottish	0	0	–	–
Other	1	0	–	–

HONOURS

None

INTERNATIONAL APPEARANCES

COUNTRY	LEVEL	GAMES	GOALS
	Full	0	0
	B	0	0
	U-21	0	0
	Youth	0	0

NAME:	Scott Minto
CLUB:	Chelsea
BORN:	Heswall, 6/8/71
DEBUT v:	Q.P.R., 10/12/88
SUBSTITUTED:	12
BOOKINGS:	22
SENDINGS OFF:	0
OWN GOALS:	1
DOMESTIC PENS:	0
HAT-TRICKS:	0
STRIKE RATE (%):	3.18
EVER PRESENT:	–

LEAGUE CLUBS	YEARS	APPS	GOALS	FEE
Chelsea	94-95	19	0	£775,000
Charlton	88-94	180	6	Trainee

OVERALL RECORD

COMPETITION	APPS	GOALS	(PENS)	SUBS
League	190	6	0	9
FA Cup	11	0	0	2
League Cup	8	1	0	0
Europe	6	0	–	–
Scottish	0	0	–	–
Other	7	2	–	–

HONOURS

PFA Team Award Div 1. 94

INTERNATIONAL APPEARANCES

COUNTRY	LEVEL	GAMES	GOALS
England	Full	0	0
	B	0	0
	U-21	5	0
	Youth	8	0

NAME:	Paul Mitchell
CLUB:	West Ham
BORN:	Bournemouth, 20/10/71
DEBUT v:	Brentford, 25/8/90
SUBSTITUTED:	1
BOOKINGS:	0
SENDINGS OFF:	0
OWN GOALS:	0
DOMESTIC PENS:	0
HAT-TRICKS:	0
STRIKE RATE (%):	–
EVER PRESENT:	–

LEAGUE CLUBS	YEARS	APPS	GOALS	FEE
West Ham	93-95	1	0	£40,000
Bournemouth	89-93	12	0	Trainee

OVERALL RECORD

COMPETITION	APPS	GOALS	(PENS)	SUBS
League	6	0	0	7
FA Cup	0	0	0	0
League Cup	0	0	0	0
Europe	0	0	–	–
Scottish	0	0	–	–
Other	2	0	–	–

HONOURS

None

INTERNATIONAL APPEARANCES

COUNTRY	LEVEL	GAMES	GOALS
England	Full	0	0
	B	0	0
	U-21	0	0
	Youth	3	0

NAME:	Chris Morris
CLUB:	Middlesbrough
BORN:	Newquay, 24/12/63
DEBUT v:	Swansea, 27/8/83
SUBSTITUTED:	8
BOOKINGS:	8
SENDINGS OFF:	0
OWN GOALS:	2
DOMESTIC PENS:	0
HAT-TRICKS:	0
STRIKE RATE (%):	1.875
EVER PRESENT:	–

LEAGUE CLUBS	YEARS	APPS	GOALS	FEE
Middlesbrough	92-95	55	1	£500,000
Celtic	87-92	163	8	£125,000
Sheffield Wed	82-87	74	1	Appr

OVERALL RECORD

COMPETITION	APPS	GOALS	(PENS)	SUBS
League	111	2	0	18
FA Cup	11	0	0	5
League Cup	11	1	0	4
Europe	9	0	–	–
Scottish	200	9	–	–
Other	4	1	–	–

HONOURS

First Division Championship 94-95, Scottish Premier
League Championship 87-88, Scottish Cup 87-88, Scottish
Cup r/u 88-89, Scottish League Cup r/u 90-91

INTERNATIONAL APPEARANCES

COUNTRY	LEVEL	GAMES	GOALS
Eire	Full	35	0
	B	2	0
	U-21	0	0
	Youth	0	0

NAME:	Steve Morrow
CLUB:	Arsenal
BORN:	Bangor, 2/7/70
DEBUT v:	Exeter, 19/1/91
SUBSTITUTED:	4
BOOKINGS:	2
SENDINGS OFF:	0
OWN GOALS:	0
DOMESTIC PENS:	0
HAT-TRICKS:	0
STRIKE RATE (%):	3.80
EVER PRESENT:	–

LEAGUE CLUBS	YEARS	APPS	GOALS	FEE
Arsenal	88-95	44	1	Trainee
Barnet	92	1	0	Loan
Reading	91	3	0	Loan
Watford	91	8	0	Loan
Reading	91	10	0	Loan

OVERALL RECORD

COMPETITION	APPS	GOALS	(PENS)	SUBS
League	52	1	0	14
FA Cup	3	0	0	2
League Cup	6	2	0	2
Europe	5	0	–	–
Scottish	0	0	–	–
Other	2	0	–	–

HONOURS

FA Youth Cup 87-88, League Cup 92-93, European Cup
Winners' Cup 93-94, European Cup Winners Cup r/u 94-95

INTERNATIONAL APPEARANCES

COUNTRY	LEVEL	GAMES	GOALS
N. Ireland	Full	17	1
	B	1	0
	U-21	3	0
	Youth	0	0

NAME:	Andy Myers
CLUB:	Chelsea
BORN:	Hounslow, 3/11/73
DEBUT v:	Luton, 6/4/91
SUBSTITUTED:	4
BOOKINGS:	3
SENDINGS OFF:	0
OWN GOALS:	0
DOMESTIC PENS:	0
HAT-TRICKS:	0
STRIKE RATE (%):	2.44
EVER PRESENT:	–

LEAGUE CLUBS	YEARS	APPS	GOALS	FEE
Chelsea	91-95	33	1	Trainee

OVERALL RECORD

COMPETITION	APPS	GOALS	(PENS)	SUBS
League	27	1	0	6
FA Cup	6	0	0	0
League Cup	1	0	0	1
Europe	2	0	–	–
Scottish	0	0	–	–
Other	2	0	–	–

HONOURS

None

INTERNATIONAL APPEARANCES

COUNTRY	LEVEL	GAMES	GOALS
England	Full	0	0
	B	0	0
	U-21	4	1
	Youth	11	1

NAME:	Alan Neilson
CLUB:	Southampton
BORN:	Wegberg, Ger, 26/9/72
DEBUT v:	Watford, 9/3/91
SUBSTITUTED:	2
BOOKINGS:	3
SENDINGS OFF:	0
OWN GOALS:	0
DOMESTIC PENS:	0
HAT-TRICKS:	0
STRIKE RATE (%):	2.17
EVER PRESENT:	–

LEAGUE CLUBS	YEARS	APPS	GOALS	FEE
Southampton	95	0	0	£500,000
Newcastle	91-95	42	1	Trainee

OVERALL RECORD

COMPETITION	APPS	GOALS	(PENS)	SUBS
League	36	1	0	6
FA Cup	0	0	0	0
League Cup	4	0	0	0
Europe	0	0	–	–
Scottish	0	0	–	–
Other	4	0	–	–

HONOURS

None

INTERNATIONAL APPEARANCES

COUNTRY	LEVEL	GAMES	GOALS
Wales	Full	4	0
	B	2	0
	U-21	7	0
	Youth	0	0

NAME:	Gary Neville
CLUB:	Manchester Utd
BORN:	Bury, 18/2/75
DEBUT v:	Coventry, 7/5/94
SUBSTITUTED:	3
BOOKINGS:	8
SENDINGS OFF:	0
OWN GOALS:	0
DOMESTIC PENS:	0
HAT-TRICKS:	0
STRIKE RATE (%):	–
EVER PRESENT:	–

LEAGUE CLUBS	YEARS	APPS	GOALS	FEE
Manchester Utd	93-95	20	0	Trainee

OVERALL RECORD

COMPETITION	APPS	GOALS	(PENS)	SUBS
League	18	0	0	2
FA Cup	5	0	0	0
League Cup	2	0	0	1
Europe	3	0	–	–
Scottish	0	0	–	–

HONOURS

FA Cup r/u 94-95, FA Youth Cup 91-92, FA Youth Cup r/u 92-93

INTERNATIONAL APPEARANCES

COUNTRY	LEVEL	GAMES	GOALS
England	Full	2	0
	B	0	0
	U-21	0	0
	Youth	10	0

NAME:	Ian Nolan
CLUB:	Sheffield Wed
BORN:	Liverpool, 9/7/70
DEBUT v:	Wolves, 26/10/91
SUBSTITUTED:	3
BOOKINGS:	11
SENDINGS OFF:	1
OWN GOALS:	0
DOMESTIC PENS:	0
HAT-TRICKS:	0
STRIKE RATE (%):	3.21
EVER PRESENT:	94-95

LEAGUE CLUBS	YEARS	APPS	GOALS	FEE
Sheffield Wed	94-95	42	3	£1.5m
Tranmere	91-94	88	1	£10,000
From: Marine				

OVERALL RECORD

COMPETITION	APPS	GOALS	(PENS)	SUBS
League	129	4	0	1
FA Cup	12	0	0	0
League Cup	14	1	0	0
Europe	0	0	–	–
Scottish	0	0	–	–
Other	8	0	–	–

HONOURS

None

INTERNATIONAL APPEARANCES

COUNTRY	LEVEL	GAMES	GOALS
	Full	0	0
	B	0	0
	U-21	0	0
	Youth	0	0

NAME:	Keith O'Hallaron
CLUB:	Middlesbrough
BORN:	Eire, 10/11/75
DEBUT v:	Derby, 18/3/95
SUBSTITUTED:	1
BOOKINGS:	0
SENDINGS OFF:	0
OWN GOALS:	0
DOMESTIC PENS:	0
HAT-TRICKS:	0
STRIKE RATE (%):	–
EVER PRESENT:	–

LEAGUE CLUBS	YEARS	APPS	GOALS	FEE
Middlesbrough	94-95	1	0	Appr

OVERALL RECORD

COMPETITION	APPS	GOALS	(PENS)	SUBS
League	1	0	0	0
FA Cup	0	0	0	0
League Cup	0	0	0	0
Europe	0	0	–	–
Scottish	0	0	–	–
Other	1	0	–	–

HONOURS

None

INTERNATIONAL APPEARANCES

COUNTRY	LEVEL	GAMES	GOALS
	Full	0	0
	B	0	0
	U-21	0	0
	Youth	0	0

NAME:	Paul Parker
CLUB:	Manchester Utd
BORN:	West Ham, 4/4/64
DEBUT v:	Reading, 25/4/81
SUBSTITUTED:	14
BOOKINGS:	5
SENDINGS OFF:	1
OWN GOALS:	5
DOMESTIC PENS:	0
HAT-TRICKS:	0
STRIKE RATE (%):	1.08
EVER PRESENT:	87-88

LEAGUE CLUBS	YEARS	APPS	GOALS	FEE
Manchester Utd	91-95	99	1	£2m
Q.P.R.	87-91	125	1	£300,000
Fulham	81-87	153	2	Appr

OVERALL RECORD

COMPETITION	APPS	GOALS	(PENS)	SUBS
League	356	4	0	21
FA Cup	40	0	0	0
League Cup	44	1	0	0
Europe	9	0	–	–
Scottish	0	0	–	–
Other	8	0	–	–

HONOURS

League Championship 92-93, 93-94, FA Cup 93-94, League Cup 91-92, League Cup r/u 93-94, Charity Shield medal 93 PFA Team Awards: Div 2. 85-86; Div 3. 87; Div 1. 89

INTERNATIONAL APPEARANCES

COUNTRY	LEVEL	GAMES	GOALS
England	Full	18	0
	B	3	0
	U-21	8	1
	Youth	3	0

NAME: Joe Parkinson
CLUB: Everton
BORN: Eccles, 11/6/71
DEBUT v: Blackpool, 30/9/88
SUBSTITUTED: 14
BOOKINGS: 18
SENDINGS OFF: 0
OWN GOALS: 1
DOMESTIC PENS: 0
HAT-TRICKS: 0
STRIKE RATE (%): 4.52
EVER PRESENT: –

LEAGUE CLUBS	YEARS	APPS	GOALS	FEE
Everton	94-95	34	0	£700,000
Bournemouth	93-94	32	1	£35,000
Wigan	88-93	119	6	Trainee

OVERALL RECORD

COMPETITION	APPS	GOALS	(PENS)	SUBS
League	179	7	0	6
FA Cup	19	1	0	0
League Cup	17	2	0	0
Europe	0	0	–	–
Scottish	0	0	–	–
Other	8	0	–	–

HONOURS

FA Cup 94-95

INTERNATIONAL APPEARANCES

COUNTRY	LEVEL	GAMES	GOALS
	Full	0	0
	B	0	0
	U-21	0	0
	Youth	0	0

NAME: Stuart Pearce
CLUB: Nottm Forest
BORN: Hammersmith, 24/4/62
DEBUT v: Q.P.R., 12/11/83
SUBSTITUTED: 6
BOOKINGS: 24
SENDINGS OFF: 1
OWN GOALS: 2
DOMESTIC PENS: 22
HAT-TRICKS: 0
STRIKE RATE (%): 15.63
EVER PRESENT: –

LEAGUE CLUBS	YEARS	APPS	GOALS	FEE
Nottm Forest	85-95	337	55	£200,000
Coventry	83-85	51	4	£25,000
From: Wealdstone				

OVERALL RECORD

COMPETITION	APPS	GOALS	(PENS)	SUBS
League	388	59	20	0
FA Cup	35	7	0	0
League Cup	57	9	2	0
Europe	0	0	–	–
Scottish	0	0	–	–
Other	17	1	–	–

HONOURS

FA Cup r/u 90-91, League Cup 88-89, 89-90, PFA Team
Awards Div 1. 88, 89, 90, 91, 92

INTERNATIONAL APPEARANCES

COUNTRY	LEVEL	GAMES	GOALS
England	Full	59	4
	B	0	0
	U-21	1	0
	Youth	0	0

NAME: John Pemberton
CLUB: Leeds
BORN: Oldham, 18/11/64
DEBUT v: Aldershot, 2/10/84
SUBSTITUTED: 10
BOOKINGS: 28
SENDINGS OFF: 0
OWN GOALS: 2
DOMESTIC PENS: 0
HAT-TRICKS: 0
STRIKE RATE (%): 1.17
EVER PRESENT: –

LEAGUE CLUBS	YEARS	APPS	GOALS	FEE
Leeds	93-95	36	0	£500,000
Sheffield Utd	90-93	68	0	£300,000
Crystal Palace	88-90	78	2	£80,000
Crewe	85-88	121	1	Free
Rochdale	84-85	1	0	Non-contract

OVERALL RECORD

COMPETITION	APPS	GOALS	(PENS)	SUBS
League	288	3	0	16
FA Cup	20	0	0	0
League Cup	17	1	0	2
Europe	0	0	–	–
Scottish	0	0	–	–
Other	19	0	–	–

HONOURS

FA Cup r/u 89-90

INTERNATIONAL APPEARANCES

COUNTRY	LEVEL	GAMES	GOALS
	Full	0	0
	B	0	0
	U-21	0	0
	Youth	0	0

NAME:	Terry Phelan
CLUB:	Manchester City
BORN:	Manchester, 16/3/67
DEBUT v:	Shrewsbury, 7/9/85
SUBSTITUTED:	12
BOOKINGS:	21
SENDINGS OFF:	1
OWN GOALS:	3
DOMESTIC PENS:	0
HAT-TRICKS:	0
STRIKE RATE (%):	1.34
EVER PRESENT:	–

LEAGUE CLUBS	YEARS	APPS	GOALS	FEE
Manchester City	92-95	94	1	£2.5m
Wimbledon	87-92	159	1	£100,000
Swansea	86-87	45	0	Free
Leeds	84-86	14	0	Appr

OVERALL RECORD

COMPETITION	APPS	GOALS	(PENS)	SUBS
League	305	2	0	7
FA Cup	29	3	0	0
League Cup	30	0	0	2
Europe	0	0	–	–
Scottish	0	0	–	–
Other	13	0	–	–

HONOURS

FA Cup 87-88, Charity Shield medal 88, PFA Team Award Div 4. 87

INTERNATIONAL APPEARANCES

COUNTRY	LEVEL	GAMES	GOALS
Eire	Full	26	0
	B	0	0
	U-21	1	0
	Youth	0	0

NAME:	Jimmy Phillips
CLUB:	Bolton
BORN:	Bolton, 8/2/66
DEBUT v:	Gillingham, 7/4/84
SUBSTITUTED:	8
BOOKINGS:	18
SENDINGS OFF:	1
OWN GOALS:	2
DOMESTIC PENS:	4
HAT-TRICKS:	0
STRIKE RATE (%):	3.11
EVER PRESENT:	89-90, 94-95

LEAGUE CLUBS	YEARS	APPS	GOALS	FEE
Bolton	93-95	88	1	£250,000
Middlesbrough	90-93	139	6	£250,000
Oxford	88-90	79	7	£110,000
Rangers	86-88	25	0	£95,000
Bolton	83-86	108	2	Appr

OVERALL RECORD

COMPETITION	APPS	GOALS	(PENS)	SUBS
League	408	15	4	6
FA Cup	29	0	0	0
League Cup	39	0	0	0
Europe	4	0	–	–
Scottish	29	0	–	–
Other	30	5	–	–

HONOURS

League Cup r/u 94-95

INTERNATIONAL APPEARANCES

COUNTRY	LEVEL	GAMES	GOALS
	Full	0	0
	B	0	0
	U-21	0	0
	Youth	0	0

NAME:	Karl Ready
CLUB:	Q.P.R.
BORN:	Neath, 14/8/72
DEBUT v:	Wimbledon, 1/2/92
SUBSTITUTED:	1
BOOKINGS:	5
SENDINGS OFF:	1
OWN GOALS:	0
DOMESTIC PENS:	0
HAT-TRICKS:	0
STRIKE RATE (%):	4.88
EVER PRESENT:	–

LEAGUE CLUBS	YEARS	APPS	GOALS	FEE
Q.P.R.	90-95	39	2	Appr

OVERALL RECORD

COMPETITION	APPS	GOALS	(PENS)	SUBS
League	33	2	0	6
FA Cup	0	0	0	0
League Cup	0	0	0	2
Europe	0	0	–	–
Scottish	0	0	–	–

HONOURS

None

INTERNATIONAL APPEARANCES

COUNTRY	LEVEL	GAMES	GOALS
Wales	Full	0	0
	B	2	0
	U-21	5	1
	Youth	0	0

NAME:	Alex Robertson
CLUB:	Coventry
BORN:	Edinburgh, 26/4/71
DEBUT v:	Dundee, 6/5/89
SUBSTITUTED:	0
BOOKINGS:	0
SENDINGS OFF:	0
OWN GOALS:	0
DOMESTIC PENS:	0
HAT-TRICKS:	0
STRIKE RATE (%):	3.23
EVER PRESENT:	–

LEAGUE CLUBS	YEARS	APPS	GOALS	FEE
Coventry	94-95	5	0	£650,000
Rangers	88-94	27	1	Appr

OVERALL RECORD

COMPETITION	APPS	GOALS	(PENS)	SUBS
League	1	0	0	4
FA Cup	0	0	0	0
League Cup	0	0	0	0
Europe	2	0	–	–
Scottish	29	1	–	–

HONOURS

Scottish Premier League 90-91

INTERNATIONAL APPEARANCES

COUNTRY	LEVEL	GAMES	GOALS
Scotland	Full	0	0
	B	0	0
	U-21	3	0
	Youth	0	0

NAME:	Kevin Sharp
CLUB:	Leeds
BORN:	Ontario, Canada, 19/9/74
DEBUT v:	Crystal Palace, 17/4/93
SUBSTITUTED:	4
BOOKINGS:	1
SENDINGS OFF:	0
OWN GOALS:	0
DOMESTIC PENS:	0
HAT-TRICKS:	0
STRIKE RATE (%):	–
EVER PRESENT:	–

LEAGUE CLUBS	YEARS	APPS	GOALS	FEE
Leeds	92-95	16	0	£60,000
From: Auxerre				

OVERALL RECORD

COMPETITION	APPS	GOALS	(PENS)	SUBS
League	11	0	0	5
FA Cup	0	0	0	0
League Cup	0	0	0	0
Europe	0	0	–	–
Scottish	0	0	–	–

HONOURS

FA Youth Cup 92-93

INTERNATIONAL APPEARANCES

COUNTRY	LEVEL	GAMES	GOALS
England	Full	0	0
	B	0	0
	U-21	0	0
	Youth	8	3

NAME:	Frank Sinclair
CLUB:	Chelsea
BORN:	Lambeth, 3/12/71
DEBUT v:	Luton, 6/4/91
SUBSTITUTED:	5
BOOKINGS:	29
SENDINGS OFF:	2
OWN GOALS:	2
DOMESTIC PENS:	0
HAT-TRICKS:	0
STRIKE RATE (%):	4.93
EVER PRESENT:	–

LEAGUE CLUBS	YEARS	APPS	GOALS	FEE
Chelsea	90-95	113	4	Trainee
West Brom	91-92	6	1	Loan

OVERALL RECORD

COMPETITION	APPS	GOALS	(PENS)	SUBS
League	119	5	0	0
FA Cup	12	1	0	0
League Cup	11	1	0	0
Europe	7	2	–	–
Scottish	0	0	–	–
Other	1	0	–	–

HONOURS

FA Cup r/u 93-94

INTERNATIONAL APPEARANCES

COUNTRY	LEVEL	GAMES	GOALS
England	Full	0	0
	B	0	0
	U-21	0	0
	Youth	1	0

NAME:	Justin Skinner
CLUB:	Wimbledon
BORN:	Dorking, 17/9/72
DEBUT v:	Liverpool, 26/9/92
SUBSTITUTED:	1
BOOKINGS:	3
SENDINGS OFF:	0
OWN GOALS:	0
DOMESTIC PENS:	0
HAT-TRICKS:	0
STRIKE RATE (%):	–
EVER PRESENT:	–

LEAGUE CLUBS	YEARS	APPS	GOALS	FEE
Wimbledon	91-95	1	0	Appr
Wycombe	94	5	0	Loan
Bournemouth	94	16	0	Loan

OVERALL RECORD

COMPETITION	APPS	GOALS	(PENS)	SUBS
League	21	0	0	1
FA Cup	0	0	0	0
League Cup	0	0	0	0
Europe	0	0	–	–
Scottish	0	0	–	–

HONOURS

None

INTERNATIONAL APPEARANCES

COUNTRY	LEVEL	GAMES	GOALS
	Full	0	0
	B	0	0
	U-21	0	0
	Youth	0	0

NAME:	Bryan Small
CLUB:	Aston Villa
BORN:	Birmingham, 15/11/71
DEBUT v:	Everton, 19/10/91
SUBSTITUTED:	8
BOOKINGS:	3
SENDINGS OFF:	0
OWN GOALS:	0
DOMESTIC PENS:	0
HAT-TRICKS:	0
STRIKE RATE (%):	–
EVER PRESENT:	–

LEAGUE CLUBS	YEARS	APPS	GOALS	FEE
Aston Villa	90-95	36	0	Trainee
Birmingham	94	3	0	Loan

OVERALL RECORD

COMPETITION	APPS	GOALS	(PENS)	SUBS
League	34	0	0	5
FA Cup	2	0	0	1
League Cup	2	0	0	0
Europe	2	0	–	–
Scottish	0	0	–	–
Other	2	0	–	–

HONOURS

None

INTERNATIONAL APPEARANCES

COUNTRY	LEVEL	GAMES	GOALS
England	Full	0	0
	B	0	0
	U-21	12	0
	Youth	4	0

NAME:	Nicky Spooner
CLUB:	Bolton
BORN:	Manchester, 5/6/71
DEBUT v:	Fulham, 1/2/91
SUBSTITUTED:	2
BOOKINGS:	2
SENDINGS OFF:	0
OWN GOALS:	0
DOMESTIC PENS:	0
HAT-TRICKS:	0
STRIKE RATE (%):	–
EVER PRESENT:	–

LEAGUE CLUBS	YEARS	APPS	GOALS	FEE
Bolton	89-95	23	2	Appr

OVERALL RECORD

COMPETITION	APPS	GOALS	(PENS)	SUBS
League	22	2	0	1
FA Cup	3	0	0	0
League Cup	3	0	0	0
Europe	0	0	–	–
Scottish	0	0	–	–
Other	1	0	–	–

HONOURS

None

INTERNATIONAL APPEARANCES

COUNTRY	LEVEL	GAMES	GOALS
	Full	0	0
	B	0	0
	U-21	0	0
	Youth	0	0

NAME:	Steve Staunton
CLUB:	Aston Villa
BORN:	Drogheda, 19/1/69
DEBUT v:	Sheffield Utd, 14/11/87
SUBSTITUTED:	29
BOOKINGS:	15
SENDINGS OFF:	0
OWN GOALS:	1
DOMESTIC PENS:	2
HAT-TRICKS:	1
STRIKE RATE (%):	6.84
EVER PRESENT:	92-93

LEAGUE CLUBS	YEARS	APPS	GOALS	FEE
Aston Villa	91-95	138	13	£1.1m
Bradford	87	8	0	Loan
Liverpool	86-91	65	0	£20,000
From: Dundalk				

OVERALL RECORD

COMPETITION	APPS	GOALS	(PENS)	SUBS
League	199	13	2	12
FA Cup	26	1	0	2
League Cup	22	4	0	2
Europe	6	0	–	–
Scottish	0	0	–	–
Other	2	1	–	–

HONOURS

League Championship 89-90, FA Cup 88-89, League Cup 93-94

INTERNATIONAL APPEARANCES

COUNTRY	LEVEL	GAMES	GOALS
Eire	Full	59	5
	B	1	0
	U-21	3	0
	Youth	0	0

NAME:	Vance Warner
CLUB:	Nottm Forest
BORN:	Leeds, 3/9/74
DEBUT v:	Luton, 28/8/93
SUBSTITUTED:	0
BOOKINGS:	0
SENDINGS OFF:	0
OWN GOALS:	0
DOMESTIC PENS:	0
HAT-TRICKS:	0
STRIKE RATE (%):	–
EVER PRESENT:	–

LEAGUE CLUBS	YEARS	APPS	GOALS	FEE
Nottm Forest	93-95	2	0	Trainee

OVERALL RECORD

COMPETITION	APPS	GOALS	(PENS)	SUBS
League	2	0	0	0
FA Cup	0	0	0	0
League Cup	0	0	0	0
Europe	0	0	–	–
Scottish	0	0	–	–

HONOURS

None

INTERNATIONAL APPEARANCES

COUNTRY	LEVEL	GAMES	GOALS
England	Full	0	0
	B	0	0
	U-21	0	0
	Youth	0	0

NAME:	Clive Wilson
CLUB:	Tottenham
BORN:	Manchester, 13/11/61
DEBUT v:	Wolves, 28/12/81
SUBSTITUTED:	17
BOOKINGS:	8
SENDINGS OFF:	1
OWN GOALS:	0
DOMESTIC PENS:	10
HAT-TRICKS:	0
STRIKE RATE (%):	7.46
EVER PRESENT:	86-87, 93-94

LEAGUE CLUBS	YEARS	APPS	GOALS	FEE
Tottenham	95	0	0	Free
Q.P.R.	90-95	172	12	£450,000
Chelsea	87-90	81	5	£250,000
Chester	82-83	21	2	Loan
Manchester City	79-87	109	9	Appr

OVERALL RECORD

COMPETITION	APPS	GOALS	(PENS)	SUBS
League	366	28	8	17
FA Cup	14	1	1	0
League Cup	29	3	1	3
Europe	0	0	–	–
Scottish	0	0	–	–
Other	20	0	–	–

HONOURS

Division Two Championship 88-89, PFA Team Award Div 2. 85

INTERNATIONAL APPEARANCES

COUNTRY	LEVEL	GAMES	GOALS
	Full	0	0
	B	0	0
	U-21	0	0
	Youth	0	0

NAME: Nigel Winterburn
CLUB: Arsenal
BORN: Nuneaton, 11/12/63
DEBUT v: Bolton, 27/8/83
SUBSTITUTED: 21
BOOKINGS: 27
SENDINGS OFF: 1
OWN GOALS: 0
DOMESTIC PENS: 0
HAT-TRICKS: 0
STRIKE RATE (%): 3.04
EVER PRESENT: 86-87, 88-89, 90-91

LEAGUE CLUBS	YEARS	APPS	GOALS	FEE
Arsenal	87-95	272	5	£400,000
Wimbledon	83-87	165	8	Free
Birmingham	81-83	0	0	Appr

OVERALL RECORD

COMPETITION	APPS	GOALS	(PENS)	SUBS
League	435	13	0	2
FA Cup	42	0	0	0
League Cup	48	3	0	0
Europe	22	0	–	–
Scottish	0	0	–	–
Other	22	1	–	–

HONOURS

League Championship 88-89, 90-91, FA Cup 92-93, League Cup 92-93, League Cup r/u 87-88, Charity Shield medal 89, 91, 93, European Cup Winners' Cup 93-94, European Cup Winners Cup r/u 94-95

INTERNATIONAL APPEARANCES

COUNTRY	LEVEL	GAMES	GOALS
England	Full	2	0
	B	4	0
	U-21	1	0
	Youth	1	0

NAME: Nigel Worthington
CLUB: Leeds
BORN: Ballymena, 4/11/61
DEBUT v: Wolves, 26/9/81
SUBSTITUTED: 30
BOOKINGS: 19
SENDINGS OFF: 2
OWN GOALS: 1
DOMESTIC PENS: 0
HAT-TRICKS: 0
STRIKE RATE (%): 3.63
EVER PRESENT: –

LEAGUE CLUBS	YEARS	APPS	GOALS	FEE
Leeds	94-95	27	1	£2.2m
Sheffield Wed	84-94	338	12	£125,000
Notts County	81-84	67	4	£10,000
From: Ballymena United				

OVERALL RECORD

COMPETITION	APPS	GOALS	(PENS)	SUBS
League	423	17	0	9
FA Cup	36	1	0	1
League Cup	54	1	0	0
Europe	5	1	–	–
Scottish	0	0	–	–
Other	6	0	–	–

HONOURS

FA Cup r/u 92-93, League Cup 90-91, League Cup r/u 92-93

INTERNATIONAL APPEARANCES

COUNTRY	LEVEL	GAMES	GOALS
N. Ireland	Full	58	0
	B	2	0
	U-21	1	0
	Youth	0	0

NAME: Alan Wright
CLUB: Aston Villa
BORN: Aston-under-Lyme,28/9/71
DEBUT v: Chesterfield, 2/5/88
SUBSTITUTED: 13
BOOKINGS: 6
SENDINGS OFF: 0
OWN GOALS: 0
DOMESTIC PENS: 0
HAT-TRICKS: 0
STRIKE RATE (%): 0.5
EVER PRESENT: –

LEAGUE CLUBS	YEARS	APPS	GOALS	FEE
Aston Villa	95	8	0	£800,000
Blackburn	91-95	73	1	£500,000
Blackpool	88-91	98	0	Trainee

OVERALL RECORD

COMPETITION	APPS	GOALS	(PENS)	SUBS
League	165	1	0	14
FA Cup	13	0	0	1
League Cup	18	0	0	2
Europe	0	0	–	–
Scottish	0	0	–	–
Other	15	0	–	–

HONOURS

Charity Shield medal 94

INTERNATIONAL APPEARANCES

COUNTRY	LEVEL	GAMES	GOALS
England	Full	0	0
	B	0	0
	U-21	2	0
	Youth	10	0

INTRODUCTION – CENTRE-BACKS

If, at the start of the 94-95 season, you had asked any so-called soccer expert which centre-backs would be the most valuable in the Premiership, the name Colin Hendry is unlikely to have been amongst them. Liverpool's expensive trio of Ruddock, Scales and Babb, possibly; Arsenal's influential skipper Tony Adams, perhaps; Manchester United's man-mountain Gary Pallister, definitely. But, incredibly, the most expensive defenders in the game were forced to take a back seat because of the staggering performances of Championship winner Colin Hendry. The Blackburn defender provided the cornerstone of the Rovers defence . . . marshalling and dominating at the back; threatening and often scoring at key times in the opposite box.

Hendry was a man amongst men for Rovers. His performances in the centre of Rovers' defence also earned him more international recognition for Scotland where he is now considered his country's most important defender.

The same could arguably be said of Arsenal skipper Tony Adams who, together with Tim Flowers, David Platt and Alan Shearer, provides the backbone of the England side Terry Venables hopes will lead the country to European Championship glory in 1996. He has become the most successful skipper in Arsenal's history, leading them to two Championships, two domestic cups and one European Cup Winners' Cup triumph. He rarely misses a game and, when he does, his club suffers.

The red half of Manchester also owes much to its men at the back, most notably Gary Pallister, a £2.3m signing from Middlesbrough, who has formed a dominant defensive partnership with Steve Bruce in recent seasons. Of course, the flair of Cantona, the brilliance of Giggs and the goals of Hughes have been major factors in United's belated return to the top of English football. But the contribution of Pallister and Bruce should not be overlooked. Together with super stopper Peter Schmeichel they have made United one of the most difficult teams to score against.

It is considered important in the modern game for central defenders to be able to play rather than simply 'hoof'. And both Adams and Pallister have become more accomplished in this department. But it is not just skill that a central defender needs to be successful. The pace of the game has increased so much that athleticism has become more important than ever. And there is no stronger or quicker defender than Manchester City's £2.5m defender Keith Curle. His massive transfer tag weighed heavily on his shoulders when he went to Maine Road in 1991. But Curle has since become a model of consistency and City owe him a huge debt of gratitude for helping them retain their Premiership status . . . for another year at least.

No such worries these days for Liverpool, whose defence became something of a standing joke during the ill-fated Graeme Souness era when the club's reputation, once the biggest in Europe, sank faster than the Titanic. And now they can smile again thanks to the formation of the most expensive defence in the country. Ahead of David James in the Liverpool goal now stand three formidable figures in the shape of hard man Neil Ruddock, Mr Reliable John Scales and the elegant Phil Babb. The Red Army is already on the march after a lengthy spell in the trenches and, with those three men ready to tackle the strongest of opposition, Liverpool have their best chance for years of recapturing former Championship glories.

NAME:	Gary Ablett
CLUB:	Everton
BORN:	Liverpool, 19/11/65
DEBUT v:	Bournemouth, 30/1/85
SUBSTITUTED:	7
BOOKINGS:	20
SENDINGS OFF:	1
OWN GOALS:	0
DOMESTIC PENS:	0
HAT-TRICKS:	0
STRIKE RATE (%):	2.11
EVER PRESENT:	–

INTERNATIONAL APPEARANCES

COUNTRY	LEVEL	GAMES	GOALS
England	Full	0	0
	B	1	0
	U-21	1	0
	Youth	0	0

LEAGUE CLUBS	YEARS	APPS	GOALS	FEE
Everton	92-95	115	5	£750,000
Hull City	86	5	0	Loan
Derby	85	6	0	Loan
Liverpool	83-92	109	1	Appr

OVERALL RECORD

COMPETITION	APPS	GOALS	(PENS)	SUBS
League	226	6	0	9
FA Cup	25	0	0	2
League Cup	21	0	0	1
Europe	6	0	–	–
Scottish	0	0	–	–
Other	5	0	–	–

HONOURS

League Championship 87-88, 89-90, FA Cup 88-89, 94-95, FA Cup r/u 87-88, Charity Shield medal 88, 90

NAME:	Tony Adams
CLUB:	Arsenal
BORN:	Romford, 10/10/66
DEBUT v:	Sunderland, 5/11/83
SUBSTITUTED:	16
BOOKINGS:	30
SENDINGS OFF:	2
OWN GOALS:	2
DOMESTIC PENS:	0
HAT-TRICKS:	0
STRIKE RATE (%):	7.277
EVER PRESENT:	86-87, 89-90

INTERNATIONAL HONOURS

COUNTRY	LEVEL	GAMES	GOALS
England	Full	35	4
	B	4	1
	U-21	5	1
	Youth	18	6

LEAGUE CLUB	YEARS	APPS	GOALS	FEE
Arsenal	83-95	346	23	Appr

OVERALL RECORD

COMPETITION	APPS	GOALS	(PENS)	SUBS
League	343	23	0	3
FA Cup	29	5	0	1
League Cup	49	3	0	1
Europe	20	2	–	–
Scottish	0	0	–	–
Other	20	1	–	–

HONOURS

League Championship 88-89, 90-91, FA Cup 92-93, League Cup 86-87, 92-93, League Cup r/u 87-88, Charity Shield medal 91, 89, 93, European Cup Winners' Cup 93-94, European Cup Winners' Cup r/u 94-95, PFA Young Player of the Year 86-87, PFA Team Awards: Div 1. 87; Premier League 94

NAME:	Philippe Albert
CLUB:	Newcastle
BORN:	Belgium, 10/8/67
DEBUT v:	Leicester, 21/8/94
SUBSTITUTED:	1
BOOKINGS:	4
SENDINGS OFF:	1
OWN GOALS:	0
DOMESTIC PENS:	0
HAT-TRICKS:	0
STRIKE RATE (%):	–
EVER PRESENT:	–

INTERNATIONAL HONOURS

COUNTRY	LEVEL	GAMES	GOALS
Belgium	Full	35	5
	B	0	0
	U-21	0	0
	Youth	0	0

LEAGUE CLUBS	YEARS	APPS	GOALS	FEE
Newcastle	94-95	17	2	£2.65m
From: Anderlecht				

OVERALL RECORD

COMPETITION	APPS	GOALS	(PENS)	SUBS
League	17	2	0	0
FA Cup	0	0	0	0
League Cup	4	1	0	0
Europe	4	0	–	–
Scottish	0	0	–	–

HONOURS

Belgian League Championship 88-89, 92-93, 93-94, Belgian Cup 93-94, Belgian Cup r/u 90-91, 91-92, Belgian Player of the Year 91-92

NAME: Derek Allan
CLUB: Southampton
BORN: Irving, 24/12/74
DEBUT v: Morton, 9/2/93
SUBSTITUTED: 0
BOOKINGS: 0
SENDINGS OFF: 0
OWN GOALS: 0
DOMESTIC PENS: 0
HAT-TRICKS: 0
STRIKE RATE (%): –
EVER PRESENT: –

LEAGUE CLUBS	YEARS	APPS	GOALS	FEE
Southampton	92-95	1	0	£75,000
Ayr	92	5	0	Appr

OVERALL RECORD

COMPETITION	APPS	GOALS	(PENS)	SUBS
League	1	0	0	0
FA Cup	0	0	0	0
League Cup	0	0	0	0
Europe	0	0	–	–
Scottish	5	0	–	–

HONOURS

None

INTERNATIONAL APPEARANCES

COUNTRY	LEVEL	GAMES	GOALS
	Full	0	0
	B	0	0
	U-21	0	0
	Youth	0	0

NAME: Phil Babb
CLUB: Liverpool
BORN: Lambeth, 30/11/70
DEBUT v: Reading, 8/9/90
SUBSTITUTED: 9
BOOKINGS: 15
SENDINGS OFF: 1
OWN GOALS: 0
DOMESTIC PENS: 0
HAT-TRICKS: 0
STRIKE RATE (%): 8.219
EVER PRESENT: 91-92

LEAGUE CLUBS	YEARS	APPS	GOALS	FEE
Liverpool	94-95	33	0	£2.8m
Coventry	92-94	77	3	£500,000
Bradford	90-92	80	14	Free
Millwall	89-90	0	0	Appr

OVERALL RECORD

COMPETITION	APPS	GOALS	(PENS)	SUBS
League	175	17	0	15
FA Cup	11	0	0	0
League Cup	17	1	0	1
Europe	0	0	–	–
Scottish	0	0	–	–
Other	4	0	–	–

HONOURS

League Cup 94-95

INTERNATIONAL APPEARANCES

COUNTRY	LEVEL	GAMES	GOALS
Eire	Full	16	0
	B	2	0
	U-21	0	0
	Youth	0	0

NAME: Dean Blackwell
CLUB: Wimbledon
BORN: Camden, 5/12/69
DEBUT v: Man City, 16/9/89
SUBSTITUTED: 6
BOOKINGS: 11
SENDINGS OFF: 0
OWN GOALS: 0
DOMESTIC PENS: 0
HAT-TRICKS: 0
STRIKE RATE (%): 0.96
EVER PRESENT: –

LEAGUE CLUBS	YEARS	APPS	GOALS	FEE
Wimbledon	88-95	76	1	Appr
Plymouth	90	7	0	Loan

OVERALL RECORD

COMPETITION	APPS	GOALS	(PENS)	SUBS
League	67	1	0	16
FA Cup	7	0	0	1
League Cup	3	0	0	0
Europe	0	0	–	–
Scottish	0	0	–	–
Other	1	0	–	–

HONOURS

None

INTERNATIONAL APPEARANCES

COUNTRY	LEVEL	GAMES	GOALS
England	Full	0	0
	B	0	0
	U-21	6	0
	Youth	0	0

NAME:	Steve Bould
CLUB:	Arsenal
BORN:	Stoke, 16/11/62
DEBUT v:	Middlesbrough, 26/9/81
SUBSTITUTED:	15
BOOKINGS:	23
SENDINGS OFF:	0
OWN GOALS:	4
DOMESTIC PENS:	0
HAT-TRICKS:	0
STRIKE RATE (%):	2.46
EVER PRESENT:	90-91

LEAGUE CLUBS	YEARS	APPS	GOALS	FEE
Arsenal	88-95	192	4	£390,000
Torquay	82	9	0	Loan
Stoke	80-88	183	6	Appr

OVERALL RECORD

COMPETITION	APPS	GOALS	(PENS)	SUBS
League	372	10	0	12
FA Cup	29	0	0	0
League Cup	35	1	0	0
Europe	13	2	–	–
Scottish	0	0	–	–
Other	15	1	–	–

HONOURS

League Championship 88-89, 90-91, European Cup Winners' Cup 93-94

INTERNATIONAL APPEARANCES

COUNTRY	LEVEL	GAMES	GOALS
England	Full	2	0
	B	1	1
	U-21	0	0
	Youth	0	0

NAME:	Steve Bruce
CLUB:	Manchester Utd
BORN:	Newcastle, 31/12/60
DEBUT v:	Blackpool, 18/8/79
SUBSTITUTED:	23
BOOKINGS:	24
SENDINGS OFF:	0
OWN GOALS:	4
DOMESTIC PENS:	19
HAT-TRICKS:	0
STRIKE RATE (%):	13.45
EVER PRESENT:	85-86, 88-89, 92-93 93-94

LEAGUE CLUBS	YEARS	APPS	GOALS	FEE
Manchester Utd	87-95	280	36	£800,000
Norwich	84-87	141	14	£125,000
Gillingham	78-84	205	29	Appr

OVERALL RECORD

COMPETITION	APPS	GOALS	(PENS)	SUBS
League	624	79	17	2
FA Cup	59	5	0	0
League Cup	65	17	2	1
Europe	24	6	–	–
Scottish	0	0	–	–
Other	19	2	–	–

HONOURS

League Championship 92-93, 93-94, Division Two Championship 85-86, FA Cup 89-90, 93-94, FA Cup r/u 94-95, League Cup 84-85, 91-92, League Cup r/u 90-91, 93-94, Charity Shield medal 90, 93, 94, European Cup Winners' Cup 90-91, PFA Team Awards: Div 3. 83, 84; Div 2. 86

INTERNATIONAL APPEARANCES

COUNTRY	LEVEL	GAMES	GOALS
England	Full	0	0
	B	1	0
	U-21	0	0
	Youth	7	1

NAME:	David Busst
CLUB:	Coventry
BORN:	Birmingham, 30/6/67
DEBUT v:	Norwich, 16/1/93
SUBSTITUTED:	3
BOOKINGS:	2
SENDINGS OFF:	0
OWN GOALS:	0
DOMESTIC PENS:	0
HAT-TRICKS:	0
STRIKE RATE (%):	–
EVER PRESENT:	–

LEAGUE CLUBS	YEARS	APPS	GOALS	FEE
Coventry	92-95	33	2	–
From: Moor Green				

OVERALL RECORD

COMPETITION	APPS	GOALS	(PENS)	SUBS
League	32	2	0	1
FA Cup	0	0	0	1
League Cup	3	0	0	1
Europe	0	0	–	–
Scottish	0	0	–	–

HONOURS

None

INTERNATIONAL APPEARANCES

COUNTRY	LEVEL	GAMES	GOALS
	Full	0	0
	B	0	0
	U-21	0	0
	Youth	0	0

NAME: Colin Calderwood
CLUB: Tottenham
BORN: Stranraer, 20/1/65
DEBUT v: Crewe, 13/3/82
SUBSTITUTED: 8
BOOKINGS: 15
SENDINGS OFF: 4
OWN GOALS: 2
DOMESTIC PENS: 0
HAT-TRICKS: 0
STRIKE RATE (%): 4.48
EVER PRESENT: 85-86, 86-87, 89-90
91-92, 92-93

LEAGUE CLUBS	YEARS	APPS	GOALS	FEE
Tottenham	93-95	62	2	£1.2m
Swindon	85-93	320	20	£30,000
Mansfield	82-85	100	1	Amateur

OVERALL RECORD

COMPETITION	APPS	GOALS	(PENS)	SUBS
League	476	23	0	6
FA Cup	31	2	0	0
League Cup	45	0	0	0
Europe	0	0	–	–
Scottish	0	0	–	–
Other	41	0	–	–

HONOURS

Division Four Championship 85-86, PFA Team Award
Div 2. 92

INTERNATIONAL APPEARANCES

COUNTRY	LEVEL	GAMES	GOALS
Scotland	Full	5	1
	B	2	0
	U-21	0	0
	Youth	0	0

NAME: Steve Chettle
CLUB: Nottm Forest
BORN: Nottingham, 27/9/68
DEBUT v: Chelsea, 5/9/87
SUBSTITUTED: 6
BOOKINGS: 13
SENDINGS OFF: 1
OWN GOALS: 1
DOMESTIC PENS: 0
HAT-TRICKS: 0
STRIKE RATE (%): 2.5
EVER PRESENT: –

LEAGUE CLUBS	YEARS	APPS	GOALS	FEE
Nottm Forest	86-95	255	7	Appr

OVERALL RECORD

COMPETITION	APPS	GOALS	(PENS)	SUBS
League	242	7	0	13
FA Cup	25	0	0	1
League Cup	36	1	0	3
Europe	0	0	–	–
Scottish	0	0	–	–
Other	16	1	–	–

HONOURS

FA Cup r/u 90-91, League Cup 89-90

INTERNATIONAL APPEARANCES

COUNTRY	LEVEL	GAMES	GOALS
England	Full	0	0
	B	0	0
	U-21	12	0
	Youth	0	0

NAME: Simon Coleman
CLUB: Bolton
BORN: Worksop, 13/3/68
DEBUT v: Port Vale, 18/4/87
SUBSTITUTED: 4
BOOKINGS: 13
SENDINGS OFF: 1
OWN GOALS: 5
DOMESTIC PENS: 0
HAT-TRICKS: 0
STRIKE RATE (%): 5.33
EVER PRESENT: –

LEAGUE CLUBS	YEARS	APPS	GOALS	FEE
Bolton	94-95	22	4	£200,000
Sheffield Wed	93-94	16	1	£250,000
Derby	91-93	70	2	£300,000
Middlesbrough	89-91	55	2	£400,000
Mansfield	85-89	96	7	Appr

OVERALL RECORD

COMPETITION	APPS	GOALS	(PENS)	SUBS
League	242	16	0	17
FA Cup	20	0	0	0
League Cup	20	0	0	1
Europe	0	0	–	–
Scottish	0	0	–	–
Other	29	2	–	–

HONOURS

None

INTERNATIONAL APPEARANCES

COUNTRY	LEVEL	GAMES	GOALS
England	Full	0	0
	B	1	0
	U-21	0	0
	Youth	0	0

NAME:	Colin Cooper
CLUB:	Nottm Forest
BORN:	Nottingham, 28/2/67
DEBUT v:	Crystal Palace, 8/3/86
SUBSTITUTED:	10
BOOKINGS:	36
SENDINGS OFF:	2
OWN GOALS:	0
DOMESTIC PENS:	0
HAT-TRICKS:	0
STRIKE RATE (%):	5.64
EVER PRESENT:	86-87

LEAGUE CLUBS	YEARS	APPS	GOALS	FEE
Nottm Forest	93-95	74	8	£1.7m
Millwall	91-93	77	6	£300,000
Middlesbrough	84-91	188	6	Appr

OVERALL RECORD

COMPETITION	APPS	GOALS	(PENS)	SUBS
League	333	20	0	6
FA Cup	19	1	0	0
League Cup	32	1	0	0
Europe	0	0	–	–
Scottish	0	0	–	–
Other	22	2	–	–

HONOURS

PFA Team Award Div 1. 94

INTERNATIONAL APPEARANCES

COUNTRY	LEVEL	GAMES	GOALS
England	Full	2	0
	B	0	0
	U-21	8	0
	Youth	0	0

NAME:	Jason Cundy
CLUB:	Tottenham
BORN:	Wimbledon, 12/11/69
DEBUT v:	Q.P.R., 1/9/90
SUBSTITUTED:	2
BOOKINGS:	5
SENDINGS OFF:	1
OWN GOALS:	2
DOMESTIC PENS:	0
HAT-TRICKS:	0
STRIKE RATE (%):	3.75
EVER PRESENT:	–

LEAGUE CLUBS	YEARS	APPS	GOALS	FEE
Tottenham	92-95	25	1	£750,000
Chelsea	88-92	41	2	Trainee

OVERALL RECORD

COMPETITION	APPS	GOALS	(PENS)	SUBS
League	63	3	0	3
FA Cup	6	0	0	0
League Cup	8	0	0	0
Europe	0	0	–	–
Scottish	0	0	–	–
Other	5	0	–	–

HONOURS

None

INTERNATIONAL APPEARANCES

COUNTRY	LEVEL	GAMES	GOALS
England	Full	0	0
	B	0	0
	U-21	3	1
	Youth	0	0

NAME:	Keith Curle
CLUB:	Manchester City
BORN:	Bristol, 14/11/63
DEBUT v:	Chester, 29/8/81
SUBSTITUTED:	12
BOOKINGS:	23
SENDINGS OFF:	1
OWN GOALS:	1
DOMESTIC PENS:	13
HAT-TRICKS:	0
STRIKE RATE (%):	5.17
EVER PRESENT:	89-90

LEAGUE CLUBS	YEARS	APPS	GOALS	FEE
Manchester City	91-95	139	11	£2.5m
Wimbledon	88-91	93	3	£500,000
Reading	87-88	40	0	£150,000
Bristol City	84-87	121	1	£10,000
Torquay	83-84	16	5	£5,000
Bristol Rovers	81-83	32	4	Appr

OVERALL RECORD

COMPETITION	APPS	GOALS	(PENS)	SUBS
League	420	24	12	21
FA Cup	21	1	0	0
League Cup	40	1	1	1
Europe	0	0	–	–
Scottish	0	0	–	–
Other	28	1	–	–

HONOURS

None

INTERNATIONAL APPEARANCES

COUNTRY	LEVEL	GAMES	GOALS
England	Full	3	0
	B	5	0
	U-21	0	0
	Youth	0	0

NAME:	Jason Dodd
CLUB:	Southampton
BORN:	Bath, 2/11/70
DEBUT v:	Q.P.R., 14/10/89
SUBSTITUTED:	8
BOOKINGS:	11
SENDINGS OFF:	0
OWN GOALS:	0
DOMESTIC PENS:	0
HAT-TRICKS:	0
STRIKE RATE (%):	1.76
EVER PRESENT:	–

LEAGUE CLUBS	YEARS	APPS	GOALS	FEE
Southampton	89-94	135	3	£50,000
Bath City	88-89	0	0	Appr

OVERALL RECORD

COMPETITION	APPS	GOALS	(PENS)	SUBS
League	119	3	0	16
FA Cup	16	0	0	0
League Cup	18	0	0	1
Europe	0	0	–	–
Scottish	0	0	–	–
Other	5	0	–	–

HONOURS

None

INTERNATIONAL APPEARANCES

COUNTRY	LEVEL	GAMES	GOALS
England	Full	0	0
	B	0	0
	U-21	8	0
	Youth	0	0

NAME:	Michael Duberry
CLUB:	Chelsea
BORN:	Enfield, 14/10/75
DEBUT v:	Coventry, 12/3/94
SUBSTITUTED:	0
BOOKINGS:	0
SENDINGS OFF:	0
OWN GOALS:	0
DOMESTIC PENS:	0
HAT-TRICKS:	0
STRIKE RATE (%):	–
EVER PRESENT:	–

LEAGUE CLUBS	YEARS	APPS	GOALS	FEE
Chelsea	93-95	1	0	Trainee

OVERALL RECORD

COMPETITION	APPS	GOALS	(PENS)	SUBS
League	1	0	0	0
FA Cup	0	0	0	0
League Cup	0	0	0	0
Europe	0	0	–	–
Scottish	0	0	–	–

HONOURS

None

INTERNATIONAL APPEARANCES

COUNTRY	LEVEL	GAMES	GOALS
	Full	0	0
	B	0	0
	U-21	0	0
	Youth	0	0

NAME:	Ngochuku Ehiogu
CLUB:	Aston Villa
BORN:	Hackney, 3/11/72
DEBUT v:	Hull, 22/9/90
SUBSTITUTED:	1
BOOKINGS:	8
SENDINGS OFF:	1
OWN GOALS:	0
DOMESTIC PENS:	0
HAT-TRICKS:	0
STRIKE RATE (%):	3.8
EVER PRESENT:	–

LEAGUE CLUBS	YEARS	APPS	GOALS	FEE
Aston Villa	91-95	68	3	£40,000
West Brom	89-91	2	0	Trainee

OVERALL RECORD

COMPETITION	APPS	GOALS	(PENS)	SUBS
League	57	3	0	13
FA Cup	2	0	0	2
League Cup	4	0	0	1
Europe	4	1	–	–
Scottish	0	0	–	–
Other	1	0	–	–

HONOURS

League Cup 93-94

INTERNATIONAL APPEARANCES

COUNTRY	LEVEL	GAMES	GOALS
England	Full	0	0
	B	1	0
	U-21	15	1
	Youth	0	0

NAME:	Chris Fairclough
CLUB:	Leeds
BORN:	Nottingham, 12/4/64
DEBUT v:	Liverpool, 4/9/82
SUBSTITUTED:	9
BOOKINGS:	14
SENDINGS OFF:	1
OWN GOALS:	1
DOMESTIC PENS:	0
HAT-TRICKS:	0
STRIKE RATE (%):	7.38
EVER PRESENT:	87-88

LEAGUE CLUBS	YEARS	APPS	GOALS	FEE
Leeds	89-95	193	23	£500,000
Tottenham	87-89	60	5	£387,000
Nottm Forest	81-87	107	1	Appr

OVERALL RECORD

COMPETITION	APPS	GOALS	(PENS)	SUBS
League	349	29	0	11
FA Cup	23	0	0	1
League Cup	33	3	0	3
Europe	16	0	–	–
Scottish	0	0	–	–
Other	11	0	–	–

HONOURS

League Championship 91-92, Division Two Championship 89-90, Charity Shield medal92, PFA Team Award Div 2. 90

INTERNATIONAL APPEARANCES

COUNTRY	LEVEL	GAMES	GOALS
England	Full	0	0
	B	1	0
	U-21	7	2
	Youth	0	0

NAME:	Scott Fitzgerald
CLUB:	Wimbledon
BORN:	Westminster, 13/8/69
DEBUT v:	Tottenham, 28/4/90
SUBSTITUTED:	6
BOOKINGS:	10
SENDINGS OFF:	0
OWN GOALS:	0
DOMESTIC PENS:	0
HAT-TRICKS:	0
STRIKE RATE (%):	0.83
EVER PRESENT:	–

LEAGUE CLUBS	YEARS	APPS	GOALS	FEE
Wimbledon	87-95	102	1	Trainee

OVERALL RECORD

COMPETITION	APPS	GOALS	(PENS)	SUBS
League	93	1	0	9
FA Cup	5	0	0	0
League Cup	13	0	0	0
Europe	0	0	–	–
Scottish	0	0	–	–
Other	1	0	–	–

HONOURS

None

INTERNATIONAL APPEARANCES

COUNTRY	LEVEL	GAMES	GOALS
Eire	Full	0	0
	B	1	0
	U-21	7	1
	Youth	0	0

NAME:	John Foster
CLUB:	Manchester City
BORN:	Manchester, 19/9/73
DEBUT v:	Newcastle, 1/1/94
SUBSTITUTED:	1
BOOKINGS:	0
SENDINGS OFF:	0
OWN GOALS:	0
DOMESTIC PENS:	0
HAT-TRICKS:	0
STRIKE RATE (%):	–
EVER PRESENT:	–

LEAGUE CLUBS	YEARS	APPS	GOALS	FEE
Manchester City	92-95	12	0	Trainee

OVERALL RECORD

COMPETITION	APPS	GOALS	(PENS)	SUBS
League	10	0	0	2
FA Cup	2	0	0	1
League Cup	1	0	0	1
Europe	0	0	–	–
Scottish	0	0	–	–

HONOURS

None

INTERNATIONAL APPEARANCES

COUNTRY	LEVEL	GAMES	GOALS
	Full	0	0
	B	0	0
	U-21	0	0
	Youth	0	0

NAME:	Gary Gillespie
CLUB:	Coventry
BORN:	Stirling, 5/7/60
DEBUT v:	Berwick, 20/8/77
SUBSTITUTED:	19
BOOKINGS:	2
SENDINGS OFF:	2
OWN GOALS:	2
DOMESTIC PENS:	0
HAT-TRICKS:	0
STRIKE RATE (%):	5.17
EVER PRESENT:	82-83

LEAGUE CLUBS	YEARS	APPS	GOALS	FEE
Coventry	94-95	3	0	Free
Celtic	91-94	69	2	£925,000
Liverpool	83-91	156	14	£325,000
Coventry	78-83	172	6	£75,000
Falkirk	77-78	22	0	School

OVERALL RECORD

COMPETITION	APPS	GOALS	(PENS)	SUBS
League	325	20	0	6
FA Cup	34	0	0	2
League Cup	39	1	0	0
Europe	10	0	–	–
Scottish	104	2	–	–
Other	15	0	–	–

HONOURS

European Cup r/u 84-85, League Championship 85-86, 87-88, FA Cup r/u 87-88, League Cup r/u 86-87, Charity Shield medal 88, PFA Team Award Div 1. 88

INTERNATIONAL APPEARANCES

COUNTRY	LEVEL	GAMES	GOALS
Scotland	Full	13	0
	B	0	0
	U-21	8	0
	Youth	0	0

NAME:	Richard Hall
CLUB:	Southampton
BORN:	Ipswich, 14/3/72
DEBUT v:	Grimsby, 26/12/89
SUBSTITUTED:	5
BOOKINGS:	20
SENDINGS OFF:	1
OWN GOALS:	0
DOMESTIC PENS:	0
HAT-TRICKS:	0
STRIKE RATE (%):	11.19
EVER PRESENT:	–

LEAGUE CLUBS	YEARS	APPS	GOALS	FEE
Southampton	91-95	96	11	£200,000
Scunthorpe	90-91	22	3	Trainee

OVERALL RECORD

COMPETITION	APPS	GOALS	(PENS)	SUBS
League	111	14	0	7
FA Cup	13	2	0	0
League Cup	11	0	0	1
Europe	0	0	–	–
Scottish	0	0	–	–
Other	7	0	–	–

HONOURS

None

INTERNATIONAL APPEARANCES

COUNTRY	LEVEL	GAMES	GOALS
England	Full	0	0
	B	0	0
	U-21	11	2
	Youth	0	0

NAME:	Paul Harford
CLUB:	Blackburn
BORN:	Chelmsford, 21/10/74
DEBUT v:	Cardiff, 26/12/94
SUBSTITUTED:	1
BOOKINGS:	1
SENDINGS OFF:	0
OWN GOALS:	0
DOMESTIC PENS:	0
HAT-TRICKS:	0
STRIKE RATE (%):	–
EVER PRESENT:	–

LEAGUE CLUBS	YEARS	APPS	GOALS	FEE
Blackburn	93-95	0	0	Free
Shrewsbury	94-95	6	0	Loan
Arsenal	93	0	0	Trainee

OVERALL RECORD

COMPETITION	APPS	GOALS	(PENS)	SUBS
League	3	0	0	3
FA Cup	0	0	0	0
League Cup	0	0	0	0
Europe	0	0	–	–
Scottish	0	0	–	–

HONOURS

None

INTERNATIONAL APPEARANCES

COUNTRY	LEVEL	GAMES	GOALS
	Full	0	0
	B	0	0
	U-21	0	0
	Youth	0	0

NAME:	Colin Hendry
CLUB:	Blackburn
BORN:	Keith, 7/12/65
DEBUT v:	Hearts, 7/1/84
SUBSTITUTED:	13
BOOKINGS:	20
SENDINGS OFF:	0
OWN GOALS:	4
DOMESTIC PENS:	0
HAT-TRICKS:	0
STRIKE RATE (%):	11.47
EVER PRESENT:	87-88

LEAGUE CLUBS	YEARS	APPS	GOALS	FEE
Blackburn	91-95	132	9	£700,000
Manchester City	89-91	63	5	£700,000
Blackburn	87-89	102	22	£30,000
Dundee	83-87	41	2	–

OVERALL RECORD

COMPETITION	APPS	GOALS	(PENS)	SUBS
League	283	36	0	14
FA Cup	18	2	0	1
League Cup	23	1	0	1
Europe	2	0	–	–
Scottish	48	3	–	–
Other	22	3	–	–

HONOURS

League Championship 94-95, Charity Shield medal 94, PFA Team Awards: Div 2. 89; Premier League 95

INTERNATIONAL APPEARANCES

COUNTRY	LEVEL	GAMES	GOALS
Scotland	Full	11	1
	B	1	0
	U-21	1	0
	Youth	0	0

NAME:	Steve Howey
CLUB:	Newcastle
BORN:	Sunderland, 26/10/71
DEBUT v:	Man Utd, 13/5/89
SUBSTITUTED:	7
BOOKINGS:	13
SENDINGS OFF:	1
OWN GOALS:	0
DOMESTIC PENS:	0
HAT-TRICKS:	0
STRIKE RATE (%):	3.55
RATING:	0
EVER PRESENT:	

LEAGUE CLUBS	YEARS	APPS	GOALS	FEE
Newcastle	89-95	118	4	Trainee

OVERALL RECORD

COMPETITION	APPS	GOALS	(PENS)	SUBS
League	99	4	0	19
FA Cup	10	0	0	2
League Cup	9	1	0	2
Europe	3	0	–	–
Scottish	0	0	–	–
Other	5	0	–	–

HONOURS

First Division Championship 92-93

INTERNATIONAL APPEARANCES

COUNTRY	LEVEL	GAMES	GOALS
England	Full	1	0
	B	0	0
	U-21	0	0
	Youth	0	0

NAME:	Lee Hurst
CLUB:	Coventry
BORN:	Nuneaton, 21/9/70
DEBUT v:	Wimbledon, 2/2/91
SUBSTITUTED:	3
BOOKINGS:	4
SENDINGS OFF:	0
OWN GOALS:	0
DOMESTIC PENS:	0
HAT-TRICKS:	0
STRIKE RATE (%):	3.64
RATING:	–
EVER PRESENT:	

LEAGUE CLUBS	YEARS	APPS	GOALS	FEE
Coventry	89-95	49	2	Trainee

OVERALL RECORD

COMPETITION	APPS	GOALS	(PENS)	SUBS
League	46	2	0	3
FA Cup	1	0	0	1
League Cup	3	0	0	1
Europe	0	0	–	–
Scottish	0	0	–	–

HONOURS

None

INTERNATIONAL APPEARANCES

COUNTRY	LEVEL	GAMES	GOALS
	Full	0	0
	B	0	0
	U-21	0	0
	Youth	0	0

NAME:	Erland Johnsen
CLUB:	Chelsea
BORN:	Fredrikstad, 5/4/67
DEBUT v:	Q.P.R., 9/12/89
SUBSTITUTED:	4
BOOKINGS:	18
SENDINGS OFF:	1
OWN GOALS:	1
DOMESTIC PENS:	0
HAT-TRICKS:	0
STRIKE RATE (%):	0.81
EVER PRESENT:	–

LEAGUE CLUBS	YEARS	APPS	GOALS	FEE
Chelsea	89-95	105	1	£306,000
From: Bayern Munich				

OVERALL RECORD

COMPETITION	APPS	GOALS	(PENS)	SUBS
League	103	1	0	2
FA Cup	14	0	0	0
League Cup	4	0	0	0
Europe	8	0	–	–
Scottish	0	0	–	–
Other	8	0	–	–

HONOURS

FA Cup r/u 93-94, Bundesliga 88-89

INTERNATIONAL APPEARANCES

COUNTRY	LEVEL	GAMES	GOALS
Norway	Full	27	2
	B	0	0
	U-21	0	0
	Youth	0	0

NAME:	Martin Keown
CLUB:	Arsenal
BORN:	Oxford, 24/7/66
DEBUT v:	Man City, 23/2/85
SUBSTITUTED:	15
BOOKINGS:	24
SENDINGS OFF:	3
OWN GOALS:	5
DOMESTIC PENS:	0
HAT-TRICKS:	0
STRIKE RATE (%):	1.52
EVER PRESENT:	–

LEAGUE CLUBS	YEARS	APPS	GOALS	FEE
Arsenal	93-95	79	1	£2m
Everton	89-93	96	0	£750,000
Aston Villa	86-89	112	3	£200,000
Brighton	85	23	1	Loan
Arsenal	84-86	22	0	Appr

OVERALL RECORD

COMPETITION	APPS	GOALS	(PENS)	SUBS
League	306	5	0	26
FA Cup	26	0	0	3
League Cup	31	1	0	3
Europe	12	0	–	–
Scottish	0	0	–	–
Other	12	1	–	–

HONOURS

Charity Shield medal 93, European Cup Winners Cup r/u 94-95

INTERNATIONAL APPEARANCES

COUNTRY	LEVEL	GAMES	GOALS
England	Full	11	1
	B	1	0
	U-21	8	0
	Youth	4	0

NAME:	Alan Kernaghan
CLUB:	Manchester City
BORN:	Otley, 25/4/67
DEBUT v:	Notts County, 9/2/85
SUBSTITUTED:	23
BOOKINGS:	25
SENDINGS OFF:	0
OWN GOALS:	1
DOMESTIC PENS:	0
HAT-TRICKS:	1
STRIKE RATE (%):	6.89
EVER PRESENT:	–

LEAGUE CLUBS	YEARS	APPS	GOALS	FEE
Manchester City	93-95	46	1	£1.6m
Bolton	94	11	0	Loan
Charlton	91	13	0	Loan
Middlesbrough	85-93	212	16	Appr

OVERALL RECORD

COMPETITION	APPS	GOALS	(PENS)	SUBS
League	235	18	0	47
FA Cup	12	4	0	4
League Cup	29	1	0	7
Europe	0	0	–	–
Scottish	0	0	–	–
Other	17	2	–	–

HONOURS

None

INTERNATIONAL APPEARANCES

COUNTRY	LEVEL	GAMES	GOALS
Eire	Full	12	1
	B	1	0
	U-21	0	0
	Youth	0	0

NAME:	Jakob Kjeldbjerg
CLUB:	Chelsea
BORN:	Denmark, 21/10/69
DEBUT v:	Wimbledon, 17/8/93
SUBSTITUTED:	2
BOOKINGS:	5
SENDINGS OFF:	0
OWN GOALS:	0
DOMESTIC PENS:	0
HAT-TRICKS:	0
STRIKE RATE (%):	3.08
EVER PRESENT:	–

LEAGUE CLUBS	YEARS	APPS	GOALS	FEE
Chelsea	93-95	52	2	£400,000
From: Silkeborg				

OVERALL RECORD

COMPETITION	APPS	GOALS	(PENS)	SUBS
League	52	2	0	0
FA Cup	6	0	0	1
League Cup	6	0	0	0
Europe	1	0	–	–
Scottish	0	0	–	–
Other	2	0	–	–

HONOURS

FA Cup r/u 93-94

INTERNATIONAL APPEARANCES

COUNTRY	LEVEL	GAMES	GOALS
Denmark	Full	15	1
	B	0	0
	U-21	0	0
	Youth	0	0

NAME:	David Lee
CLUB:	Chelsea
BORN:	Kingswood, 26/11/69
DEBUT v:	Leicester, 1/10/88
SUBSTITUTED:	7
BOOKINGS:	5
SENDINGS OFF:	1
OWN GOALS:	0
DOMESTIC PENS:	0
HAT-TRICKS:	0
STRIKE RATE (%):	9.94
EVER PRESENT:	–

LEAGUE CLUBS	YEARS	APPS	GOALS	FEE
Chelsea	88-95	119	9	Trainee
Portsmouth	94	5	0	Loan
Plymouth	92	9	1	Loan
Reading	92	5	5	Loan

OVERALL RECORD

COMPETITION	APPS	GOALS	(PENS)	SUBS
League	108	15	0	30
FA Cup	3	0	0	4
League Cup	12	1	0	4
Europe	2	0	–	–
Scottish	0	0	–	–
Other	8	0	–	–

HONOURS

Division Two Championship 88-89

INTERNATIONAL APPEARANCES

COUNTRY	LEVEL	GAMES	GOALS
England	Full	0	0
	B	0	0
	U-21	10	0
	Youth	1	0

NAME:	Andy Linighan
CLUB:	Arsenal
BORN:	Hartlepool, 18/6/62
DEBUT v:	Stockport, 28/3/81
SUBSTITUTED:	11
BOOKINGS:	6
SENDINGS OFF:	0
OWN GOALS:	3
DOMESTIC PENS:	0
HAT-TRICKS:	0
STRIKE RATE (%):	6.03
EVER PRESENT:	84-85, 87-88

LEAGUE CLUBS	YEARS	APPS	GOALS	FEE
Arsenal	90-95	89	4	£1.25m
Norwich	88-90	86	8	£350,000
Oldham	86-88	87	6	£65,000
Leeds	84-86	66	3	£200,000
Hartlepool	80-84	110	4	–

OVERALL RECORD

COMPETITION	APPS	GOALS	(PENS)	SUBS
League	423	25	0	15
FA Cup	35	1	0	1
League Cup	38	5	0	2
Europe	7	1	–	–
Scottish	0	0	–	–
Other	14	1	–	–

HONOURS

FA Cup 92-93, League Cup 92-93, Charity Shield medal 93, European Cup Winners' Cup 93-94, European Cup Winners' Cup r/u 94-95

INTERNATIONAL APPEARANCES

COUNTRY	LEVEL	GAMES	GOALS
England	Full	0	0
	B	4	0
	U-21	0	0
	Youth	0	0

NAME: Brian Linighan
CLUB: Sheffield Wed
BORN: Hartlepool, 2/11/73
DEBUT v: Wimbledon, 15/1/94
SUBSTITUTED: 1
BOOKINGS: 0
SENDINGS OFF: 0
OWN GOALS: 0
DOMESTIC PENS: 0
HAT-TRICKS: 0
STRIKE RATE (%): –
EVER PRESENT: –

LEAGUE CLUBS	YEARS	APPS	GOALS	FEE
Sheffield Wed	92-95	1	0	Trainee

OVERALL RECORD

COMPETITION	APPS	GOALS	(PENS)	SUBS
League	1	0	0	0
FA Cup	1	0	0	0
League Cup	1	0	0	0
Europe	0	0	–	–
Scottish	0	0	–	–

HONOURS

FA Youth Cup r/u 90-91

INTERNATIONAL APPEARANCES

COUNTRY	LEVEL	GAMES	GOALS
	Full	0	0
	B	0	0
	U-21	0	0
	Youth	0	0

NAME: Brian McAllister
CLUB: Wimbledon
BORN: Glasgow, 30/11/70
DEBUT v: Arsenal, 13/1/90
SUBSTITUTED: 5
BOOKINGS: 11
SENDINGS OFF: 1
OWN GOALS: 0
DOMESTIC PENS: 0
HAT-TRICKS: 0
STRIKE RATE (%): –
EVER PRESENT: –

LEAGUE CLUBS	YEARS	APPS	GOALS	FEE
Wimbledon	89-95	53	0	Trainee
Plymouth	90-91	8	0	Loan

OVERALL RECORD

COMPETITION	APPS	GOALS	(PENS)	SUBS
League	56	0	0	5
FA Cup	3	0	0	0
League Cup	5	0	0	0
Europe	0	0	–	–
Scottish	0	0	–	–
Other	1	0	–	–

HONOURS

None

INTERNATIONAL APPEARANCES

COUNTRY	LEVEL	GAMES	GOALS
	Full	0	0
	B	0	0
	U-21	0	0
	Youth	0	0

NAME: Alan McCarthy
CLUB: Q.P.R.
BORN: Wandsworth, 11/1/72
DEBUT v: Arsenal, 24/11/90
SUBSTITUTED: 1
BOOKINGS: 1
SENDINGS OFF: 0
OWN GOALS: 1
DOMESTIC PENS: 0
HAT-TRICKS: 0
STRIKE RATE (%): –
EVER PRESENT: –

LEAGUE CLUBS	YEARS	APPS	GOALS	FEE
Q.P.R.	89-95	11	0	Appr
Plymouth	94	2	0	Loan
Watford	94	9	0	Loan

OVERALL RECORD

COMPETITION	APPS	GOALS	(PENS)	SUBS
League	17	0	0	5
FA Cup	1	0	0	1
League Cup	0	0	0	0
Europe	0	0	–	–
Scottish	0	0	–	–
Other	1	0	–	–

HONOURS

None

INTERNATIONAL APPEARANCES

COUNTRY	LEVEL	GAMES	GOALS
N. Ireland	Full	0	0
	B	1	0
	U-21	3	0
	Youth	1	0

NAME:	Alan McDonald
CLUB:	Q.P.R.
BORN:	Belfast, 12/10/63
DEBUT v:	Crystal Palace, 4/4/83
SUBSTITUTED:	9
BOOKINGS:	27
SENDINGS OFF:	1
OWN GOALS:	3
DOMESTIC PENS:	0
HAT-TRICKS:	0
STRIKE RATE (%):	2.93
EVER PRESENT:	85-86

LEAGUE CLUBS	YEARS	APPS	GOALS	FEE
Q.P.R.	81-95	336	9	Appr
Charlton	83	9	0	Loan

OVERALL RECORD

COMPETITION	APPS	GOALS	(PENS)	SUBS
League	340	9	0	5
FA Cup	27	1	0	0
League Cup	38	2	0	0
Europe	0	0	–	–
Scottish	0	0	–	–
Other	5	0	–	–

HONOURS

League Cup r/u 85-86

INTERNATIONAL APPEARANCES

COUNTRY	LEVEL	GAMES	GOALS
N. Ireland	Full	49	3
	B	0	0
	U-21	0	0
	Youth	0	0

NAME:	Paul McGrath
CLUB:	Aston Villa
BORN:	Greenford, 4/12/59
DEBUT v:	Tottenham, 13/11/82
SUBSTITUTED:	13
BOOKINGS:	18
SENDINGS OFF:	0
OWN GOALS:	5
DOMESTIC PENS:	0
HAT-TRICKS:	0
STRIKE RATE (%):	5.22
EVER PRESENT:	92-93

LEAGUE CLUBS	YEARS	APPS	GOALS	FEE
Aston Villa	89-95	223	7	£400,000
Manchester Utd	82-89	163	12	£30,000
From: St Patricks Ath				

OVERALL RECORD

COMPETITION	APPS	GOALS	(PENS)	SUBS
League	378	19	0	8
FA Cup	35	2	0	2
League Cup	37	3	0	0
Europe	15	0	–	–
Scottish	0	0	–	–
Other	11	0	–	–

HONOURS

FA Cup 84-85, League Cup 93-94, Charity Shield medal 85, PFA Player of the Year 92-93, PFA Team Awards: Div 1. 86; Premier League 93

INTERNATIONAL APPEARANCES

COUNTRY	LEVEL	GAMES	GOALS
Eire	Full	76	6
	B	1	0
	U-21	1	0
	Youth	0	0

NAME:	Gary Mabbutt
CLUB:	Tottenham
BORN:	Bristol, 23/8/61
DEBUT v:	Burnley, 16/12/78
SUBSTITUTED:	10
BOOKINGS:	3
SENDINGS OFF:	0
OWN GOALS:	4
DOMESTIC PENS:	0
HAT-TRICKS:	0
STRIKE RATE (%):	6.63
EVER PRESENT:	80-81, 88-89

LEAGUE CLUBS	YEARS	APPS	GOALS	FEE
Tottenham	82-95	433	27	£105,000
Bristol Rovers	78-82	131	10	Appr

OVERALL RECORD

COMPETITION	APPS	GOALS	(PENS)	SUBS
League	539	37	0	25
FA Cup	44	5	0	3
League Cup	66	3	0	2
Europe	26	4	–	–
Scottish	0	0	–	–
Other	16	0	–	–

HONOURS

FA Cup 90-91, FA Cup r/u 86-87, Charity Shield medal 82, 91, UEFA Cup 83-84

INTERNATIONAL APPEARANCES

COUNTRY	LEVEL	GAMES	GOALS
England	Full	16	1
	B	10	0
	U-21	5	0
	Youth	11	2

NAME:	Danny Maddix
CLUB:	Q.P.R.
BORN:	Ashford, 11/10/67
DEBUT v:	Scunthorpe, 4/11/86
SUBSTITUTED:	10
BOOKINGS:	12
SENDINGS OFF:	0
OWN GOALS:	2
DOMESTIC PENS:	0
HAT-TRICKS:	0
STRIKE RATE (%):	5.45
EVER PRESENT:	–

LEAGUE CLUBS	YEARS	APPS	GOALS	FEE
Q.P.R.	87-95	167	7	Free
Southend	86	2	0	Loan
Tottenham	85-87	0	0	Appr

OVERALL RECORD

COMPETITION	APPS	GOALS	(PENS)	SUBS
League	146	7	0	23
FA Cup	18	2	0	0
League Cup	15	2	0	0
Europe	0	0	–	–
Scottish	0	0	–	–
Other	5	0	–	–

HONOURS

None

INTERNATIONAL APPEARANCES

COUNTRY	LEVEL	GAMES	GOALS
	Full	0	0
	B	0	0
	U-21	0	0
	Youth	0	0

NAME:	Paul Mahorn
CLUB:	Tottenham
BORN:	Whipps Cross, 13/8/73
DEBUT v:	Huddersfield, 25/9/93
SUBSTITUTED:	0
BOOKINGS:	0
SENDINGS OFF:	0
OWN GOALS:	0
DOMESTIC PENS:	0
HAT-TRICKS:	0
STRIKE RATE (%):	–
EVER PRESENT:	–

LEAGUE CLUBS	YEARS	APPS	GOALS	FEE
Tottenham	92–95	1	0	Trainee
Fulham	93	3	0	Loan

OVERALL RECORD

COMPETITION	APPS	GOALS	(PENS)	SUBS
League	2	0	0	2
FA Cup	0	0	0	0
League Cup	0	0	0	0
Europe	0	0	–	–
Scottish	0	0	–	–
Other	1	0	–	–

HONOURS

None

INTERNATIONAL APPEARANCES

COUNTRY	LEVEL	GAMES	GOALS
	Full	0	0
	B	0	0
	U-21	0	0
	Youth	0	0

NAME:	Nicky Marker
CLUB:	Blackburn
BORN:	Exeter, 3/5/65
DEBUT v:	Burnley, 17/10/81
SUBSTITUTED:	13
BOOKINGS:	20
SENDINGS OFF:	1
OWN GOALS:	3
DOMESTIC PENS:	2
HAT-TRICKS:	0
STRIKE RATE (%):	4.29
EVER PRESENT:	–

LEAGUE CLUBS	YEARS	APPS	GOALS	FEE
Blackburn	92-95	36	0	£250,000
Plymouth	87-92	202	13	£95,000
Exeter	81-87	202	3	Appr

OVERALL RECORD

COMPETITION	APPS	GOALS	(PENS)	SUBS
League	424	16	1	16
FA Cup	21	1	1	0
League Cup	29	4	0	0
Europe	0	0	–	–
Scottish	0	0	–	–
Other	16	3	–	–

HONOURS

None

INTERNATIONAL APPEARANCES

COUNTRY	LEVEL	GAMES	GOALS
	Full	0	0
	B	0	0
	U-21	0	0
	Youth	0	0

NAME:	Scott Marshall
CLUB:	Arsenal
BORN:	Edinburgh, 1/5/73
DEBUT v:	Sheffield Wed, 6/5/93
SUBSTITUTED:	0
BOOKINGS:	5
SENDINGS OFF:	0
OWN GOALS:	0
DOMESTIC PENS:	0
HAT-TRICKS:	0
STRIKE RATE (%):	–
EVER PRESENT:	–

LEAGUE CLUBS	YEARS	APPS	GOALS	FEE
Arsenal	91-95	2	0	Trainee
Sheffield Utd	94	16	0	Loan
Rotherham	94	10	1	Loan

OVERALL RECORD

COMPETITION	APPS	GOALS	(PENS)	SUBS
League	28	1	0	0
FA Cup	0	0	0	0
League Cup	0	0	0	0
Europe	0	0	–	–
Scottish	0	0	–	–
Other	1	0	–	–

HONOURS

None

INTERNATIONAL APPEARANCES

COUNTRY	LEVEL	GAMES	GOALS
Scotland	Full	0	0
	B	0	0
	U-21	2	0
	Youth	3	0

NAME:	Alvin Martin
CLUB:	West Ham
BORN:	Bootle, 29/7/58
DEBUT v:	Aston Villa, 18/3/78
SUBSTITUTED:	11
BOOKINGS:	9
SENDINGS OFF:	0
OWN GOALS:	1
DOMESTIC PENS:	1
HAT-TRICKS:	1
STRIKE RATE (%):	5.85
EVER PRESENT:	–

LEAGUE CLUBS	YEARS	APPS	GOALS	FEE
West Ham	76-95	455	27	Appr

OVERALL RECORD

COMPETITION	APPS	GOALS	(PENS)	SUBS
League	452	27	1	3
FA Cup	39	0	0	0
League Cup	70	6	0	0
Europe	6	0	–	–
Scottish	0	0	–	–
Other	11	1	–	–

HONOURS

Division Two Championship 80-81, FA Cup 79-80, League Cup r/u 80-81, Charity Shield medal 80, PFA Team Award Div 2. 81

INTERNATIONAL APPEARANCES

COUNTRY	LEVEL	GAMES	GOALS
England	Full	17	0
	B	2	0
	U-21	0	0
	Youth	1	0

NAME:	David May
CLUB:	Manchester Utd
BORN:	Oldham, 24/6/70
DEBUT v:	Swindon, 1/4/89
SUBSTITUTED:	8
BOOKINGS:	17
SENDINGS OFF:	0
OWN GOALS:	2
DOMESTIC PENS:	0
HAT-TRICKS:	0
STRIKE RATE (%):	5.36
EVER PRESENT:	–

LEAGUE CLUBS	YEARS	APPS	GOALS	FEE
Manchester Utd	94-95	19	2	£1.5m
Blackburn	88-94	123	3	Trainee

OVERALL RECORD

COMPETITION	APPS	GOALS	(PENS)	SUBS
League	138	5	0	4
FA Cup	11	1	0	0
League Cup	14	3	0	1
Europe	4	0	–	–
Scottish	0	0	–	–
Other	6	0	–	–

HONOURS

Charity Shield medal 94

INTERNATIONAL APPEARANCES

COUNTRY	LEVEL	GAMES	GOALS
	Full	0	0
	B	0	0
	U-21	0	0
	Youth	0	0

NAME:	Ken Monkou
CLUB:	Southampton
BORN:	Surinam, 29/11/64
DEBUT v:	Stoke, 1/5/89
SUBSTITUTED:	13
BOOKINGS:	24
SENDINGS OFF:	2
OWN GOALS:	3
DOMESTIC PENS:	0
HAT-TRICKS:	0
STRIKE RATE (%):	4.07
EVER PRESENT:	–

LEAGUE CLUBS	YEARS	APPS	GOALS	FEE
Southampton	92-95	99	6	£750,000
Chelsea	89-92	94	2	£100,000
From: Feyenoord				

OVERALL RECORD

COMPETITION	APPS	GOALS	(PENS)	SUBS
League	191	8	0	2
FA Cup	10	1	0	0
League Cup	18	0	0	0
Europe	0	0	–	–
Scottish	0	0	–	–
Other	10	0	–	–

HONOURS

None

INTERNATIONAL APPEARANCES

COUNTRY	LEVEL	GAMES	GOALS
Holland	Full	0	0
	B	0	0
	U-21	2	0
	Youth	0	0

NAME:	Neil Moore
CLUB:	Everton
BORN:	Liverpool, 21/9/72
DEBUT v:	Sheffield Utd, 4/5/93
SUBSTITUTED:	1
BOOKINGS:	1
SENDINGS OFF:	0
OWN GOALS:	0
DOMESTIC PENS:	0
HAT-TRICKS:	0
STRIKE RATE (%):	–
EVER PRESENT:	–

LEAGUE CLUBS	YEARS	APPS	GOALS	FEE
Everton	91-95	5	0	Trainee
Oldham	95	5	0	Loan
Blackpool	94	7	0	Loan

OVERALL RECORD

COMPETITION	APPS	GOALS	(PENS)	SUBS
League	16	0	0	1
FA Cup	0	0	0	0
League Cup	0	0	0	1
Europe	0	0	–	–
Scottish	0	0	–	–
Other	1	0	–	–

HONOURS

None

INTERNATIONAL APPEARANCES

COUNTRY	LEVEL	GAMES	GOALS
	Full	0	0
	B	0	0
	U-21	0	0
	Youth	0	0

NAME:	Steve Morgan
CLUB:	Coventry
BORN:	Oldham, 19/9/68
DEBUT v:	Bristol Rovers, 12/4/86
SUBSTITUTED:	27
BOOKINGS:	22
SENDINGS OFF:	0
OWN GOALS:	2
DOMESTIC PENS:	0
HAT-TRICKS:	0
STRIKE RATE (%):	6.23
EVER PRESENT:	87-88

LEAGUE CLUBS	YEARS	APPS	GOALS	FEE
Coventry	93-95	68	2	£150,000
Plymouth	90-93	121	6	£115,000
Blackpool	86-90	144	10	Appr

OVERALL RECORD

COMPETITION	APPS	GOALS	(PENS)	SUBS
League	320	18	0	13
FA Cup	27	1	0	0
League Cup	25	5	0	0
Europe	0	0	–	–
Scottish	0	0	–	–
Other	16	1	–	–

HONOURS

None

INTERNATIONAL APPEARANCES

COUNTRY	LEVEL	GAMES	GOALS
	Full	0	0
	B	0	0
	U-21	0	0
	Youth	2	0

NAME:	Stuart Nethercott
CLUB:	Tottenham
BORN:	Chadwell Heath, 21/3/73
DEBUT v:	Scunthorpe, 7/9/91
SUBSTITUTED:	6
BOOKINGS:	1
SENDINGS OFF:	0
OWN GOALS:	0
DOMESTIC PENS:	0
HAT-TRICKS:	0
STRIKE RATE (%):	3.70
EVER PRESENT:	–

LEAGUE CLUBS	YEARS	APPS	GOALS	FEE
Tottenham	91-95	33	0	Appr
Barnet	92	3	0	Loan
Maidstone	91	13	1	Loan

OVERALL RECORD

COMPETITION	APPS	GOALS	(PENS)	SUBS
League	37	1	0	12
FA Cup	3	1	0	2
League Cup	0	0	0	0
Europe	0	0	–	–
Scottish	0	0	–	–
Other	1	0	–	–

HONOURS

FA Youth Cup 89-90

INTERNATIONAL APPEARANCES

COUNTRY	LEVEL	GAMES	GOALS
England	Full	0	0
	B	0	0
	U-21	8	0
	Youth	0	0

NAME:	Phil Neville
CLUB:	Manchester Utd
BORN:	Bury, 21/1/77
DEBUT v:	Sheffield Wed, 7/5/95
SUBSTITUTED:	0
BOOKINGS:	0
SENDINGS OFF:	0
OWN GOALS:	0
DOMESTIC PENS:	0
HAT-TRICKS:	0
STRIKE RATE (%):	–
EVER PRESENT:	–

LEAGUE CLUBS	YEARS	APPS	GOALS	FEE
Manchester Utd	94-95	1	0	Trainee

OVERALL RECORD

COMPETITION	APPS	GOALS	(PENS)	SUBS
League	0	0	0	1
FA Cup	0	0	0	0
League Cup	0	0	0	0
Europe	0	0	–	–
Scottish	0	0	–	–

HONOURS

FA Youth Cup r/u 92-93

INTERNATIONAL APPEARANCES

COUNTRY	LEVEL	GAMES	GOALS
	Full	0	0
	B	0	0
	U-21	4	0
	Youth	3	0

NAME:	John O'Kane
CLUB:	Manchester Utd
BORN:	Nottingham, 15/11/74
DEBUT v:	–
SUBSTITUTED:	0
BOOKINGS:	0
SENDINGS OFF:	0
OWN GOALS:	0
DOMESTIC PENS:	0
HAT-TRICKS:	0
STRIKE RATE (%):	–
EVER PRESENT:	–

LEAGUE CLUBS	YEARS	APPS	GOALS	FEE
Manchester Utd	93-95	0	0	Trainee

OVERALL RECORD

COMPETITION	APPS	GOALS	(PENS)	SUBS
League	0	0	0	0
FA Cup	1	0	0	0
League Cup	2	0	0	0
Europe	0	0	–	–
Scottish	0	0	–	–

HONOURS

FA Youth Cup 91-92, FA Youth Cup r/u 92-93

INTERNATIONAL APPEARANCES

COUNTRY	LEVEL	GAMES	GOALS
	Full	0	0
	B	0	0
	U-21	0	0
	Youth	0	0

NAME:	David O'Leary
CLUB:	Leeds
BORN:	London, 2/5/58
DEBUT v:	Burnley, 16/8/75
SUBSTITUTED:	38
BOOKINGS:	1
SENDINGS OFF:	0
OWN GOALS:	1
DOMESTIC PENS:	0
HAT-TRICKS:	0
STRIKE RATE (%):	1.98
EVER PRESENT:	0

LEAGUE CLUBS	YEARS	APPS	GOALS	FEE
Leeds	93-95	10	0	Free
Arsenal	74-93	558	10	

OVERALL RECORD

COMPETITION	APPS	GOALS	(PENS)	SUBS
League	533	11	0	35
FA Cup	66	1	0	4
League Cup	68	2	0	2
Europe	21	0	–	–
Scottish	0	0	–	–
Other	10	0	–	–

HONOURS

League Championship 88-89, 90-91, FA Cup 78-79, 92-93, FA Cup r/u 77-78, 79-80, League Cup 86-87, 92-93, Charity Shield medal 79, 89, PFA Team Awards Div 1. 79, 80

INTERNATIONAL APPEARANCES

COUNTRY	LEVEL	GAMES	GOALS
Eire	Full	67	1
	B	1	0
	U-21	0	0
	Youth	0	0

NAME:	Gary Pallister
CLUB:	Manchester Utd
BORN:	Ramsgate, 30/6/65
DEBUT v:	Wimbledon, 17/8/85
SUBSTITUTED:	5
BOOKINGS:	13
SENDINGS OFF:	0
OWN GOALS:	5
DOMESTIC PENS:	0
HAT-TRICKS:	0
STRIKE RATE (%):	3.31
EVER PRESENT:	87-88, 89-90, 92-93 94-95

LEAGUE CLUBS	YEARS	APPS	GOALS	FEE
Manchester Utd	89-95	236	8	£2.3m
Darlington	85	7	0	Loan
Middlesbrough	84-89	156	5	Appr

OVERALL RECORD

COMPETITION	APPS	GOALS	(PENS)	SUBS
League	396	13	0	3
FA Cup	41	3	0	0
League Cup	44	0	0	0
Europe	24	1	–	–
Scottish	0	0	–	–
Other	17	0	–	–

HONOURS

League Championship 92-93, 93-94, FA Cup 89-90, 93-94, FA Cup r/u 94-95, League Cup 91-92, League Cup r/u 90-91, 93-94, Charity Shield medal 90, 93, 94, European Cup Winners' Cup 90-91, PFA Player of the Year 91-92, PFA Team Awards: Div 3. 87; Div 2. 88; Div 1. 92; Premier League 93, 94, 95

INTERNATIONAL APPEARANCES

COUNTRY	LEVEL	GAMES	GOALS
England	Full	18	0
	B	10	0
	U-21	0	0
	Youth	0	0

NAME:	Carlton Palmer
CLUB:	Leeds
BORN:	West Bromich, 5/12/65
DEBUT v:	Newcastle, 16/9/85
SUBSTITUTED:	8
BOOKINGS:	30
SENDINGS OFF:	2
OWN GOALS:	2
DOMESTIC PENS:	0
HAT-TRICKS:	0
STRIKE RATE (%):	6.03
EVER PRESENT:	91-92

LEAGUE CLUBS	YEARS	APPS	GOALS	FEE
Leeds	94-95	39	3	£2.6m
Sheffield Wed	89-94	205	14	£750,000
West Brom	84-89	121	4	Trainee

OVERALL RECORD

COMPETITION	APPS	GOALS	(PENS)	SUBS
League	357	21	0	8
FA Cup	25	1	0	1
League Cup	39	4	0	1
Europe	4	0	–	–
Scottish	0	0	–	–
Other	11	1	–	–

HONOURS

FA Cup r/u 92-93, League Cup r/u 92-93, PFA Team Award Div 2. 91

INTERNATIONAL APPEARANCES

COUNTRY	LEVEL	GAMES	GOALS
England	Full	17	0
	B	5	0
	U-21	4	1
	Youth	0	0

NAME:	Darren Peacock
CLUB:	Newcastle
BORN:	Bristol, 3/2/68
DEBUT v:	Plymouth, 14/9/85
SUBSTITUTED:	6
BOOKINGS:	23
SENDINGS OFF:	0
OWN GOALS:	0
DOMESTIC PENS:	0
HAT-TRICKS:	0
STRIKE RATE (%):	4.73
EVER PRESENT:	–

LEAGUE CLUBS	YEARS	APPS	GOALS	FEE
Newcastle	94-95	44	1	£2.7m
Q.P.R.	90-94	126	6	£200,000
Hereford	89-90	59	4	Free
Newport	85-89	28	0	Appr

OVERALL RECORD

COMPETITION	APPS	GOALS	(PENS)	SUBS
League	247	12	0	10
FA Cup	15	1	0	0
League Cup	24	1	0	0
Europe	4	0	–	–
Scottish	0	0	–	–
Other	10	0	–	–

HONOURS

None

INTERNATIONAL APPEARANCES

COUNTRY	LEVEL	GAMES	GOALS
	Full	0	0
	B	0	0
	U-21	0	0
	Youth	0	0

NAME:	Andy Pearce
CLUB:	Sheffield Wed
BORN:	Bradford, 20/4/66
DEBUT v:	Leeds, 9/3/91
SUBSTITUTED:	3
BOOKINGS:	29
SENDINGS OFF:	1
OWN GOALS:	2
DOMESTIC PENS:	0
HAT-TRICKS:	0
STRIKE RATE (%):	4.24
EVER PRESENT:	–

LEAGUE CLUBS	YEARS	APPS	GOALS	FEE
Sheffield Wed	93-95	66	3	£500,000
Coventry	90-93	71	4	£15,000
From: Halesowen				

OVERALL RECORD

COMPETITION	APPS	GOALS	(PENS)	SUBS
League	131	7	0	6
FA Cup	9	0	0	1
League Cup	17	0	0	1
Europe	0	0	–	–
Scottish	0	0	–	–
Other	1	0	–	–

HONOURS

None

INTERNATIONAL APPEARANCES

COUNTRY	LEVEL	GAMES	GOALS
	Full	0	0
	B	0	0
	U-21	0	0
	Youth	0	0

NAME:	Ian Pearce
CLUB:	Blackburn
BORN:	Bury St Edmonds
DEBUT v:	7/5/74
SUBSTITUTED:	Aston Villa, 11/5/91
BOOKINGS:	1
SENDINGS OFF:	3
OWN GOALS:	0
DOMESTIC PENS:	0
HAT-TRICKS:	0
STRIKE RATE (%):	0
EVER PRESENT:	4.65

LEAGUE CLUBS	YEARS	APPS	GOALS	FEE
Blackburn	93-95	34	1	£300,000
Chelsea	91-93	4	0	Trainee

OVERALL RECORD

COMPETITION	APPS	GOALS	(PENS)	SUBS
League	24	1	0	14
FA Cup	1	0	0	2
League Cup	0	1	0	2
Europe	1	0	–	–
Scottish	0	0	–	–
Other	2	0	–	–

HONOURS

League Championship 94-95, Charity Shield medal 94

INTERNATIONAL APPEARANCES

COUNTRY	LEVEL	GAMES	GOALS
England	Full	0	0
	B	0	0
	U-21	2	0
	Youth	10	1

NAME:	Nigel Pearson
CLUB:	Middlesbrough
BORN:	Nottingham, 21/8/63
DEBUT v:	Oldham, 28/8/82
SUBSTITUTED:	18
BOOKINGS:	13
SENDINGS OFF:	0
OWN GOALS:	1
DOMESTIC PENS:	0
HAT-TRICKS:	0
STRIKE RATE (%):	6.56
EVER PRESENT:	86-87

LEAGUE CLUBS	YEARS	APPS	GOALS	FEE
Middlesbrough	94-95	33	3	£750,000
Sheffield Wed	87-94	180	14	£250,000
Shrewsbury	81-87	153	5	£5,000
From: Heanor Town				

OVERALL RECORD

COMPETITION	APPS	GOALS	(PENS)	SUBS
League	362	22	0	4
FA Cup	23	1	0	0
League Cup	36	5	0	2
Europe	3	0		
Scottish	0	0		
Other	10	0		

HONOURS

Division One Championship 94-95, League Cup 90-91, PFA Team Award Div 2. 91

INTERNATIONAL APPEARANCES

COUNTRY	LEVEL	GAMES	GOALS
	Full	0	0
	B	0	0
	U-21	0	0
	Youth	0	0

NAME:	Chris Perry
CLUB:	Wimbledon
BORN:	Sutton, 26/4/73
DEBUT v:	Liverpool, 4/4/94
SUBSTITUTED:	1
BOOKINGS:	4
SENDINGS OFF:	0
OWN GOALS:	0
DOMESTIC PENS:	0
HAT-TRICKS:	0
STRIKE RATE (%):	–
EVER PRESENT:	–

LEAGUE CLUBS	YEARS	APPS	GOALS	FEE
Wimbledon	91-95	24	0	Trainee

OVERALL RECORD

COMPETITION	APPS	GOALS	(PENS)	SUBS
League	17	0	0	7
FA Cup	3	0	0	0
League Cup	1	0	0	0
Europe	0	0	–	–
Scottish	0	0	–	–

HONOURS

None

INTERNATIONAL APPEARANCES

COUNTRY	LEVEL	GAMES	GOALS
	Full	0	0
	B	0	0
	U-21	0	0
	Youth	0	0

NAME:	Ally Pickering
CLUB:	Coventry
BORN:	Manchester, 22/6/67
DEBUT v:	Cardiff, 6/3/90
SUBSTITUTED:	5
BOOKINGS:	11
SENDINGS OFF:	0
OWN GOALS:	0
DOMESTIC PENS:	0
HAT-TRICKS:	0
STRIKE RATE (%):	1.41
EVER PRESENT:	–

LEAGUE CLUBS	YEARS	APPS	GOALS	FEE
Coventry	93-95	34	0	£85,000
Rotherham	90-93	88	2	£18,500
From: Buxton				

OVERALL RECORD

COMPETITION	APPS	GOALS	(PENS)	SUBS
League	115	2	0	7
FA Cup	11	0	0	0
League Cup	9	0	0	0
Europe	0	0	–	–
Scottish	0	0	–	–
Other	7	0	–	–

HONOURS

None

INTERNATIONAL APPEARANCES

COUNTRY	LEVEL	GAMES	GOALS
	Full	0	0
	B	0	0
	U-21	0	0
	Youth	0	0

NAME:	Steve Potts
CLUB:	West Ham
BORN:	Hartford, U.S.A., 7/5/67
DEBUT v:	Q.P.R., 1/1/85
SUBSTITUTED:	8
BOOKINGS:	13
SENDINGS OFF:	0
OWN GOALS:	2
DOMESTIC PENS:	0
HAT-TRICKS:	0
STRIKE RATE (%):	0.29
EVER PRESENT:	92-93, 94-95

LEAGUE CLUBS	YEARS	APPS	GOALS	FEE
West Ham	84-95	278	1	Appr

OVERALL RECORD

COMPETITION	APPS	GOALS	(PENS)	SUBS
League	268	1	0	10
FA Cup	31	0	0	0
League Cup	27	0	0	1
Europe	0	0	–	–
Scottish	0	0	–	–
Other	15	0	–	–

HONOURS

None

INTERNATIONAL APPEARANCES

COUNTRY	LEVEL	GAMES	GOALS
England	Full	0	0
	B	0	0
	U-21	0	0
	Youth	20	0

NAME:	Steven Pressley
CLUB:	Coventry
BORN:	Elgin, 11/10/73
DEBUT v:	Motherwell, 23/4/92
SUBSTITUTED:	1
BOOKINGS:	9
SENDINGS OFF:	1
OWN GOALS:	1
DOMESTIC PENS:	0
HAT-TRICKS:	0
STRIKE RATE (%):	3.23
EVER PRESENT:	–

LEAGUE CLUBS	YEARS	APPS	GOALS	FEE
Coventry	94-95	19	1	£600,000
Rangers	91-94	34	1	Appr

OVERALL RECORD

COMPETITION	APPS	GOALS	(PENS)	SUBS
League	18	1	0	1
FA Cup	3	0	0	0
League Cup	0	0	0	0
Europe	3	0	–	–
Scottish	40	1	–	–

HONOURS

Scottish Premier League 93-94, Scottish FA Cup 92-93

INTERNATIONAL APPEARANCES

COUNTRY	LEVEL	GAMES	GOALS
Scotland	Full	0	0
	B	0	0
	U-21	19	0
	Youth	0	0

NAME:	Alan Reeves
CLUB:	Wimbledon
BORN:	Birkenhead, 19/11/67
DEBUT v:	Bristol City, 11/2/89
SUBSTITUTED:	8
BOOKINGS:	29
SENDINGS OFF:	1
OWN GOALS:	2
DOMESTIC PENS:	0
HAT-TRICKS:	0
STRIKE RATE (%):	6.38
EVER PRESENT:	–

LEAGUE CLUBS	YEARS	APPS	GOALS	FEE
Wimbledon	94-95	31	3	£300,000
Rochdale	91-94	121	9	Free
Chester	89-91	40	2	£10,000
Gillingham	89	18	0	Loan
Norwich	88-89	0	0	Free

OVERALL RECORD

COMPETITION	APPS	GOALS	(PENS)	SUBS
League	199	14	0	11
FA Cup	11	0	0	0
League Cup	13	1	0	1
Europe	0	0	–	–
Scotland	0	0	–	–
Other	8	0	–	–

HONOURS

PFA Team Award Div 3. 94

INTERNATIONAL APPEARANCES

COUNTRY	LEVEL	GAMES	GOALS
	Full	0	0
	B	0	0
	U-21	0	0
	Youth	0	0

NAME:	David Rennie
CLUB:	Coventry
BORN:	Edinburgh, 29/8/64
DEBUT v:	West Brom, 3/9/83
SUBSTITUTED:	29
BOOKINGS:	6
SENDINGS OFF:	0
OWN GOALS:	3
DOMESTIC PENS:	0
HAT-TRICKS:	0
STRIKE RATE (%):	5.35
EVER PRESENT:	–

LEAGUE CLUBS	YEARS	APPS	GOALS	FEE
Coventry	93-95	70	1	£100,000
Birmingham	92-93	35	4	£120,000
Bristol City	89-92	104	8	£175,000
Leeds	86-89	101	5	£50,000
Leicester	82-86	21	1	Appr

OVERALL RECORD

COMPETITION	APPS	GOALS	(PENS)	SUBS
League	319	19	0	12
FA Cup	19	1	0	1
League Cup	23	0	0	0
Europe	0	0	–	–
Scotland	0	0	–	–
Other	10	1	–	–

HONOURS

None

INTERNATIONAL APPEARANCES

COUNTRY	LEVEL	GAMES	GOALS
Scotland	Full	0	0
	B	0	0
	U-21	0	0
	Youth	4	0

NAME:	Marc Rieper
CLUB:	West Ham
BORN:	Denmark, 5/6/68
DEBUT v:	Leeds, 10/12/94
SUBSTITUTED:	1
BOOKINGS:	0
SENDINGS OFF:	0
OWN GOALS:	0
DOMESTIC PENS:	0
HAT-TRICKS:	0
STRIKE RATE (%):	–
EVER PRESENT:	–

LEAGUE CLUBS	YEARS	APPS	GOALS	FEE
West Ham	94-95	21	1	£1.1m
From: Brondby				

OVERALL RECORD

COMPETITION	APPS	GOALS	(PENS)	SUBS
League	17	1	0	4
FA Cup	0	0	0	0
League Cup	0	0	0	0
Europe	8	0	–	–
Scotland	0	0	–	–

HONOURS

Danish Champions 90-91, 91-92, Danish Cup 93-94

INTERNATIONAL APPEARANCES

COUNTRY	LEVEL	GAMES	GOALS
Denmark	Full	21	0
	B	0	0
	U-21	0	0
	Youth	0	0

NAME:	Neil Ruddock
CLUB:	Liverpool
BORN:	Wandsworth, 9/5/68
DEBUT v:	Charlton, 18/4/87
SUBSTITUTED:	8
BOOKINGS:	42
SENDINGS OFF:	4
OWN GOALS:	4
DOMESTIC PENS:	0
HAT-TRICKS:	0
STRIKE RATE (%):	9.59
EVER PRESENT:	–

LEAGUE CLUBS	YEARS	APPS	GOALS	FEE
Liverpool	93-95	76	6	£2.5m
Tottenham	92-93	38	3	£750,000
Southampton	89-92	107	9	£250,000
Millwall	88-89	2	1	£300,000
Tottenham	86-88	9	0	£50,000
Millwall	86	0	0	Appr

OVERALL RECORD

COMPETITION	APPS	GOALS	(PENS)	SUBS
League	221	19	0	11
FA Cup	25	4	0	1
League Cup	33	5	0	1
Europe	0	0	–	–
Scotland	0	0	–	–
Other	12	1	–	–

HONOURS

League Cup 94-95

INTERNATIONAL APPEARANCES

COUNTRY	LEVEL	GAMES	GOALS
England	Full	1	0
	B	1	0
	U-21	4	0
	Youth	10	2

NAME:	John Scales
CLUB:	Liverpool
BORN:	Harrogate, 4/7/66
DEBUT v:	Newport, 7/9/85
SUBSTITUTED:	7
BOOKINGS:	13
SENDINGS OFF:	1
OWN GOALS:	1
DOMESTIC PENS:	0
HAT-TRICKS:	0
STRIKE RATE (%):	4.14
EVER PRESENT:	88-89

LEAGUE CLUBS	YEARS	APPS	GOALS	FEE
Liverpool	94-95	36	2	£3m
Wimbledon	87-94	240	11	£70,000
Bristol Rovers	85-87	72	2	Free

OVERALL RECORD

COMPETITION	APPS	GOALS	(PENS)	SUBS
League	339	15	0	9
FA Cup	33	1	0	1
League Cup	28	1	0	1
Europe	0	0	–	–
Scotland	0	0	–	–
Other	12	3	–	–

HONOURS

FA Cup 87-88, League Cup 94-95, Charity Shield medal 88

INTERNATIONAL APPEARANCES

COUNTRY	LEVEL	GAMES	GOALS
England	Full	3	0
	B	2	0
	U-21	0	0
	Youth	0	0

NAME:	Kevin Scott
CLUB:	Tottenham
BORN:	Easington, 17/12/66
DEBUT v:	Sheffield Wed., 6/9/86
SUBSTITUTED:	6
BOOKINGS:	27
SENDINGS OFF:	2
OWN GOALS:	1
DOMESTIC PENS:	0
HAT-TRICKS:	0
STRIKE RATE (%):	3.73
EVER PRESENT:	–

LEAGUE CLUBS	YEARS	APPS	GOALS	FEE
Tottenham	94-95	17	1	£750,000
Port Vale	95	17	1	Loan
Newcastle	84-94	227	8	Appr

OVERALL RECORD

COMPETITION	APPS	GOALS	(PENS)	SUBS
League	261	10	0	0
FA Cup	16	1	0	0
League Cup	18	0	0	0
Europe	0	0	–	–
Scotland	0	0	–	–
Other	13	2	–	–

HONOURS

First Division Championship 92-93, FA Youth Cup 84-85

INTERNATIONAL APPEARANCES

COUNTRY	LEVEL	GAMES	GOALS
	Full	0	0
	B	0	0
	U-21	0	0
	Youth	0	0

NAME:	Terry Skiverton
CLUB:	Chelsea
BORN:	Mile End, 26/6/75
DEBUT v:	Cardiff, 21/2/95
SUBSTITUTED:	0
BOOKINGS:	0
SENDINGS OFF:	0
OWN GOALS:	0
DOMESTIC PENS:	0
HAT-TRICKS:	0
STRIKE RATE (%):	–
EVER PRESENT:	–

LEAGUE CLUBS	YEARS	APPS	GOALS	FEE
Chelsea	92-95	0	0	Trainee
Wycombe	95	9	0	Loan

OVERALL RECORD

COMPETITION	APPS	GOALS	(PENS)	SUBS
League	7	0	0	2
FA Cup	0	0	0	0
League Cup	0	0	0	0
Europe	0	0	–	–
Scotland	0	0	–	–

HONOURS

None

INTERNATIONAL APPEARANCES

COUNTRY	LEVEL	GAMES	GOALS
	Full	0	0
	B	0	0
	U-21	0	0
	Youth	0	0

NAME:	Simon Stewart
CLUB:	Sheffield Wed
BORN:	Leeds, 1/11/73
DEBUT v:	Ipswich, 10/3/93
SUBSTITUTED:	2
BOOKINGS:	1
SENDINGS OFF:	0
OWN GOALS:	0
DOMESTIC PENS:	0
HAT-TRICKS:	0
STRIKE RATE (%):	–
EVER PRESENT:	–

LEAGUE CLUBS	YEARS	APPS	GOALS	FEE
Sheffield Wed	92-95	6	0	Trainee

OVERALL RECORD

COMPETITION	APPS	GOALS	(PENS)	SUBS
League	6	0	0	0
FA Cup	0	0	0	0
League Cup	1	0	0	1
Europe	0	0	–	–
Scotland	0	0	–	–

HONOURS

None

INTERNATIONAL APPEARANCES

COUNTRY	LEVEL	GAMES	GOALS
	Full	0	0
	B	0	0
	U-21	0	0
	Youth	0	0

NAME:	Alan Stubbs
CLUB:	Bolton
BORN:	Kirkby, 6/10/71
DEBUT v:	Bradford, 1/9/90
SUBSTITUTED:	4
BOOKINGS:	21
SENDINGS OFF:	2
OWN GOALS:	1
DOMESTIC PENS:	0
HAT-TRICKS:	0
STRIKE RATE (%):	5.14
EVER PRESENT:	–

LEAGUE CLUBS	YEARS	APPS	GOALS	FEE
Bolton	90-95	177	5	Trainee

OVERALL RECORD

COMPETITION	APPS	GOALS	(PENS)	SUBS
League	157	5	0	20
FA Cup	14	2	0	3
League Cup	20	4	0	0
Europe	0	0	–	–
Scotland	0	0	–	–
Other	13	0	–	–

HONOURS

League Cup r/u 94-95, PFA Team Award Div 1. 95

INTERNATIONAL APPEARANCES

COUNTRY	LEVEL	GAMES	GOALS
England	Full	0	0
	B	1	0
	U-21	0	0
	Youth	0	0

NAME:	Shaun Teale
CLUB:	Aston Villa
BORN:	Southport, 10/3/64
DEBUT v:	West Brom, 4/2/89
SUBSTITUTED:	5
BOOKINGS:	23
SENDINGS OFF:	1
OWN GOALS:	4
DOMESTIC PENS:	0
HAT-TRICKS:	0
STRIKE RATE (%):	3.48
EVER PRESENT:	90-91, 91-92

LEAGUE CLUBS	YEARS	APPS	GOALS	FEE
Aston Villa	91-95	146	2	£300,000
Bournemouth	89-91	100	4	£50,000
From: Weymouth				

OVERALL RECORD

COMPETITION	APPS	GOALS	(PENS)	SUBS
League	245	6	0	1
FA Cup	18	1	0	0
League Cup	23	3	0	0
Europe	4	0	–	–
Scotland	0	0	–	–
Other	5	0	–	–

HONOURS

League Cup 93-94

INTERNATIONAL APPEARANCES

COUNTRY	LEVEL	GAMES	GOALS
	Full	0	0
	B	0	0
	U-21	0	0
	Youth	0	0

NAME:	Andy Thorn
CLUB:	Wimbledon
BORN:	Carshalton, 12/11/66
DEBUT v:	Notts County, 6/4/85
SUBSTITUTED:	15
BOOKINGS:	26
SENDINGS OFF:	3
OWN GOALS:	4
DOMESTIC PENS:	0
HAT-TRICKS:	0
STRIKE RATE (%):	3.75
EVER PRESENT:	–

LEAGUE CLUBS	YEARS	APPS	GOALS	FEE
Wimbledon	94-95	23	1	Free
Crystal Palace	89-94	128	3	£650,000
Newcastle	88-89	36	2	£850,000
Wimbledon	84-88	107	2	Appr

OVERALL RECORD

COMPETITION	APPS	GOALS	(PENS)	SUBS
League	292	8	0	2
FA Cup	22	1	0	0
League Cup	31	4	0	0
Europe	0	0	–	–
Scotland	0	0	–	–
Other	15	0	–	–

HONOURS

FA Cup 87-88, FA Cup r/u 89-90

INTERNATIONAL APPEARANCES

COUNTRY	LEVEL	GAMES	GOALS
England	Full	0	0
	B	0	0
	U-21	5	0
	Youth	0	0

NAME:	Carl Tiler
CLUB:	Nottm Forest
BORN:	Sheffield, 11/2/70
DEBUT v:	West Brom, 7/5/88
SUBSTITUTED:	2
BOOKINGS:	14
SENDINGS OFF:	1
OWN GOALS:	1
DOMESTIC PENS:	0
HAT-TRICKS:	0
STRIKE RATE (%):	2.40
EVER PRESENT:	–

LEAGUE CLUBS	YEARS	APPS	GOALS	FEE
Nottm Forest	91-95	69	1	£1.4m
Swindon	94	2	0	Loan
Barnsley	88-91	71	3	Trainee

OVERALL RECORD

COMPETITION	APPS	GOALS	(PENS)	SUBS
League	136	4	0	6
FA Cup	9	0	0	1
League Cup	14	0	0	1
Europe	0	0	–	–
Scotland	0	0	–	–
Other	5	0	–	–

HONOURS

None

INTERNATIONAL APPEARANCES

COUNTRY	LEVEL	GAMES	GOALS
England	Full	0	0
	B	0	0
	U-21	13	0
	Youth	0	0

NAME:	Andrew Todd
CLUB:	Middlesbrough
BORN:	Derby, 21/9/74
DEBUT v:	Notts County, 18/12/93
SUBSTITUTED:	3
BOOKINGS:	4
SENDINGS OFF:	0
OWN GOALS:	0
DOMESTIC PENS:	0
HAT-TRICKS:	0
STRIKE RATE (%):	–
EVER PRESENT:	–

LEAGUE CLUBS	YEARS	APPS	GOALS	FEE
Middlesbrough	92-95	8	0	Trainee
Swindon	95	13	0	Loan

OVERALL RECORD

COMPETITION	APPS	GOALS	(PENS)	SUBS
League	20	0	0	1
FA Cup	0	0	0	0
League Cup	1	0	0	1
Europe	0	0	–	–
Scotland	0	0	–	–
Other	5	0	–	–

HONOURS

None

INTERNATIONAL APPEARANCES

COUNTRY	LEVEL	GAMES	GOALS
	Full	0	0
	B	0	0
	U-21	0	0
	Youth	0	0

NAME:	David Unsworth
CLUB:	Everton
BORN:	Preston, 16/10/73
DEBUT v:	Tottenham, 25/4/92
SUBSTITUTED:	5
BOOKINGS:	9
SENDINGS OFF:	0
OWN GOALS:	0
DOMESTIC PENS:	2
HAT-TRICKS:	0
STRIKE RATE (%):	6.67
EVER PRESENT:	–

LEAGUE CLUBS	YEARS	APPS	GOALS	FEE
Everton	92-95	51	4	Appr

OVERALL RECORD

COMPETITION	APPS	GOALS	(PENS)	SUBS
League	48	4	2	3
FA Cup	5	0	0	0
League Cup	3	0	0	1
Europe	0	0	–	–
Scotland	0	0	–	–

HONOURS

FA Cup 94-95

INTERNATIONAL APPEARANCES

COUNTRY	LEVEL	GAMES	GOALS
England	Full	1	0
	B	0	0
	U-21	5	0
	Youth	14	3

NAME:	Steve Vickers
CLUB:	Middlesbrough
BORN:	Bishop Auckland, 13/10/67
DEBUT v:	Northampton, 4/4/86
SUBSTITUTED:	10
BOOKINGS:	14
SENDINGS OFF:	0
OWN GOALS:	2
DOMESTIC PENS:	0
HAT-TRICKS:	0
STRIKE RATE (%):	5.84
EVER PRESENT:	87-88, 88-89

LEAGUE CLUBS	YEARS	APPS	GOALS	FEE
Middlesbrough	93-95	70	6	£700,000
Tranmere	85-93	311	11	Free
From: Spennymoor United				

OVERALL RECORD

COMPETITION	APPS	GOALS	(PENS)	SUBS
League	379	17	0	2
FA Cup	23	3	0	0
League Cup	23	5	0	1
Europe	0	0		
Scotland	0	0		
Other	38	1		

HONOURS

First Division Championship 94-95

INTERNATIONAL APPEARANCES

COUNTRY	LEVEL	GAMES	GOALS
	Full	0	0
	B	0	0
	U-21	0	0
	Youth	0	0

NAME:	Michael Vonk
CLUB:	Manchester City
BORN:	Alkmaar, Holland, 28/10/68
DEBUT v:	Nottm Forest, 21/3/92
SUBSTITUTED:	6
BOOKINGS:	12
SENDINGS OFF:	0
OWN GOALS:	1
DOMESTIC PENS:	0
HAT-TRICKS:	0
STRIKE RATE (%):	5.83
EVER PRESENT:	–

LEAGUE CLUBS	YEARS	APPS	GOALS	FEE
Manchester City	92-95	91	4	£500,000
From: Dordrecht				

OVERALL RECORD

COMPETITION	APPS	GOALS	(PENS)	SUBS
League	87	4	0	4
FA Cup	6	1	0	1
League Cup	3	1	0	2
Europe	0	0	–	–
Scotland	0	0	–	–

HONOURS

None

INTERNATIONAL APPEARANCES

COUNTRY	LEVEL	GAMES	GOALS
Holland	Full	0	0
	B	0	0
	U-21	4	0
	Youth	0	0

NAME:	Des Walker
CLUB:	Sheffield Wed
BORN:	Hackney, 26/11/65
DEBUT v:	Everton, 14/3/84
SUBSTITUTED:	10
BOOKINGS:	4
SENDINGS OFF:	1
OWN GOALS:	4
DOMESTIC PENS:	0
HAT-TRICKS:	0
STRIKE RATE (%):	0.02
EVER PRESENT:	89-90, 93-94

LEAGUE CLUBS	YEARS	APPS	GOALS	FEE
Sheffield Wed	93-95	80	0	£2.7m
Sampdoria	92-93	30	0	£1.5m
Nottm Forest	83-92	264	1	Appr

OVERALL RECORD

COMPETITION	APPS	GOALS	(PENS)	SUBS
League	339	1	0	5
FA Cup	35	0	0	0
League Cup	48	0	0	0
Europe	2	0	–	–
Scotland	0	0	–	–
Other	14	0	–	–

HONOURS

FA Cup r/u 90-91, League Cup 88-89, 89-90, League Cup r/u 91-92, PFA Team Awards Div 1. 89, 90, 91, 92

INTERNATIONAL APPEARANCES

COUNTRY	LEVEL	GAMES	GOALS
England	Full	59	0
	B	0	0
	U-21	7	0
	Youth	0	0

NAME:	Dave Watson
CLUB:	Everton
BORN:	Liverpool, 20/11/61
DEBUT v:	Ipswich, 26/12/80
SUBSTITUTED:	20
BOOKINGS:	13
SENDINGS OFF:	1
OWN GOALS:	2
DOMESTIC PENS:	0
HAT-TRICKS:	0
STRIKE RATE (%):	7.32
EVER PRESENT:	85-86

LEAGUE CLUBS	YEARS	APPS	GOALS	FEE
Everton	86-95	305	20	£900,000
Norwich	80-86	212	11	£100,000
Liverpool	79-80	0	0	Amateur

OVERALL RECORD

COMPETITION	APPS	GOALS	(PENS)	SUBS
League	516	31	0	1
FA Cup	56	6	0	0
League Cup	55	9	0	0
Europe	0	0	–	–
Scotland	0	0	–	–
Other	25	4	–	–

HONOURS

League Championship 86-87, Division Two Championship 85-86, FA Cup 94-95, FA Cup r/u 88-89, League Cup 84-85, Charity Shield medal 87, PFA Team Award Div 2. 86

INTERNATIONAL APPEARANCES

COUNTRY	LEVEL	GAMES	GOALS
England	Full	12	0
	B	0	0
	U-21	7	0
	Youth	0	0

NAME:	Julian Watts
CLUB:	Sheffield Wed
BORN:	Sheffield, 17/3/71
DEBUT v:	Huddersfield, 13/10/90
SUBSTITUTED:	0
BOOKINGS:	3
SENDINGS OFF:	0
OWN GOALS:	0
DOMESTIC PENS:	0
HAT-TRICKS:	0
STRIKE RATE (%):	–
EVER PRESENT:	–

LEAGUE CLUBS	YEARS	APPS	GOALS	FEE
Sheffield Wed	92-95	5	0	£80,000
Shrewsbury	92	9	0	Loan
Rotherham	90-92	20	1	Appr

OVERALL RECORD

COMPETITION	APPS	GOALS	(PENS)	SUBS
League	29	1	0	5
FA Cup	4	0	0	0
League Cup	1	0	0	0
Europe	1	0	–	–
Scotland	0	0	–	–
Other	2	0	–	–

HONOURS

None

INTERNATIONAL APPEARANCES

COUNTRY	LEVEL	GAMES	GOALS
	Full	0	0
	B	0	0
	U-21	0	0
	Youth	0	0

NAME:	Simon Webster
CLUB:	West Ham
BORN:	Earl Shilton, 20/1/64
DEBUT v:	Everton, 3/1/83
SUBSTITUTED:	11
BOOKINGS:	10
SENDINGS OFF:	2
OWN GOALS:	1
DOMESTIC PENS:	0
HAT-TRICKS:	0
STRIKE RATE (%):	3.88
EVER PRESENT:	–

LEAGUE CLUBS	YEARS	APPS	GOALS	FEE
West Ham	93-95	5	0	£525,000
Oldham	95	7	0	Loan
Charlton	90-93	127	7	£50,000
Sheffield Utd	88-90	37	3	£35,000
Huddersfield	85-88	118	4	£15,000
Exeter	83-84	26	0	Loan
Tottenham	81-85	3	0	Appr

OVERALL RECORD

COMPETITION	APPS	GOALS	(PENS)	SUBS
League	306	14	0	17
FA Cup	18	0	0	1
League Cup	19	0	0	0
Europe	0	0	–	–
Scotland	0	0	–	–
Other	12	0	–	–

HONOURS

None

INTERNATIONAL APPEARANCES

COUNTRY	LEVEL	GAMES	GOALS
	Full	0	0
	B	0	0
	U-21	0	0
	Youth	0	0

NAME:	David Wetherall
CLUB:	Leeds
BORN:	Sheffield, 14/3/71
DEBUT v:	Arsenal, 3/9/91
SUBSTITUTED:	7
BOOKINGS:	12
SENDINGS OFF:	0
OWN GOALS:	0
DOMESTIC PENS:	0
HAT-TRICKS:	0
STRIKE RATE (%):	8.25
EVER PRESENT:	–

LEAGUE CLUBS	YEARS	APPS	GOALS	FEE
Leeds	91-95	83	5	£125,000
Sheffield Wed	89-91	0	0	School

OVERALL RECORD

COMPETITION	APPS	GOALS	(PENS)	SUBS
League	81	5	0	2
FA Cup	8	3	0	1
League Cup	5	0	0	0
Europe	0	0	–	–
Scotland	0	0	–	–

HONOURS

None

INTERNATIONAL APPEARANCES

COUNTRY	LEVEL	GAMES	GOALS
	Full	0	0
	B	0	0
	U-21	0	0
	Youth	0	0

NAME:	Phil Whelan
CLUB:	Middlesbrough
BORN:	Stockport, 7/3/72
DEBUT v:	Southend, 4/4/92
SUBSTITUTED:	12
BOOKINGS:	16
SENDINGS OFF:	1
OWN GOALS:	2
DOMESTIC PENS:	0
HAT-TRICKS:	0
STRIKE RATE (%):	2.17
EVER PRESENT:	–

LEAGUE CLUBS	YEARS	APPS	GOALS	FEE
Middlesbrough	95	0	0	£300,000
Ipswich	90-95	81	2	Appr

OVERALL RECORD

COMPETITION	APPS	GOALS	(PENS)	SUBS
League	75	2	0	6
FA Cup	3	0	0	1
League Cup	6	0	0	1
Europe	0	0	–	–
Scotland	0	0	–	–
Other	1	0	–	–

HONOURS

None

INTERNATIONAL APPEARANCES

COUNTRY	LEVEL	GAMES	GOALS
England	Full	0	0
	B	0	0
	U-21	3	1
	Youth	0	0

NAME: Adrian Whitbread
CLUB: West Ham
BORN: Epping, 22/10/71
DEBUT v: Brentford, 3/12/89
SUBSTITUTED: 11
BOOKINGS: 7
SENDINGS OFF: 0
OWN GOALS: 2
DOMESTIC PENS: 0
HAT-TRICKS: 0
STRIKE RATE (%): 2.08
EVER PRESENT: –

LEAGUE CLUBS	YEARS	APPS	GOALS	FEE
West Ham	94-95	6	0	£500,000
Swindon	93-94	35	1	£500,000
Leyton Orient	89-93	125	2	Trainee

OVERALL RECORD

COMPETITION	APPS	GOALS	(PENS)	SUBS
League	162	3	0	4
FA Cup	13	1	0	0
League Cup	11	0	0	2
Europe	0	0	–	–
Scotland	0	0	–	–
Other	9	0	–	–

HONOURS

None

INTERNATIONAL APPEARANCES

COUNTRY	LEVEL	GAMES	GOALS
	Full	0	0
	B	0	0
	U-21	0	0
	Youth	0	0

NAME: Derek Whyte
CLUB: Middlesbrough
BORN: Glasgow, 31/8/68
DEBUT v: Hearts, 22/2/86
SUBSTITUTED: 5
BOOKINGS: 16
SENDINGS OFF: 1
OWN GOALS: 1
DOMESTIC PENS: 0
HAT-TRICKS: 0
STRIKE RATE (%): 2.38
EVER PRESENT: –

LEAGUE CLUBS	YEARS	APPS	GOALS	FEE
Middlesbrough	92-95	113	2	£700,000
Celtic	85-92	216	7	Appr

OVERALL RECORD

COMPETITION	APPS	GOALS	(PENS)	SUBS
League	112	2	0	1
FA Cup	5	1	0	0
League Cup	8	0	0	0
Europe	15	1	–	–
Scotland	261	7	–	–
Other	7	0	–	–

HONOURS

First Division Championship 94-95, Scottish Premier
League 85-86, 87-88, Scottish Cup 86-87, 88-89, Scottish
Cup r/u 89-90, Scottish League Cup r/u 86-87

INTERNATIONAL APPEARANCES

COUNTRY	LEVEL	GAMES	GOALS
Scotland	Full	7	0
	B	2	0
	U-21	9	1
	Youth	0	0

NAME: Tom Widdrington
CLUB: Southampton
BORN: Newcastle, 1/10/71
DEBUT v: Hull, 14/9/91
SUBSTITUTED: 14
BOOKINGS: 14
SENDINGS OFF: 1
OWN GOALS: 0
DOMESTIC PENS: 0
HAT-TRICKS: 0
STRIKE RATE (%): 1.41
EVER PRESENT: –

LEAGUE CLUBS	YEARS	APPS	GOALS	FEE
Southampton	90-95	54	1	Trainee
Wigan	91	6	0	Loan

OVERALL RECORD

COMPETITION	APPS	GOALS	(PENS)	SUBS
League	52	1	0	8
FA Cup	7	0	0	0
League Cup	3	0	0	1
Europe	0	0	–	–
Scotland	0	0	–	–

HONOURS

None

INTERNATIONAL APPEARANCES

COUNTRY	LEVEL	GAMES	GOALS
	Full	0	0
	B	0	0
	U-21	0	0
	Youth	0	0

NAME:	Mark Wright
CLUB:	Liverpool
BORN:	Dorchester, 1/8/63
DEBUT v:	Bristol City, 17/10/81
SUBSTITUTED:	12
BOOKINGS:	17
SENDINGS OFF:	0
OWN GOALS:	5
DOMESTIC PENS:	0
HAT-TRICKS:	0
STRIKE RATE (%):	4.85
EVER PRESENT:	–

LEAGUE CLUBS	YEARS	APPS	GOALS	FEE
Liverpool	91-95	91	3	£2.2m
Derby	87-91	144	10	£760,000
Southampton	82-87	170	7	£80,000
Oxford	80-82	10	0	Amateur

OVERALL RECORD

COMPETITION	APPS	GOALS	(PENS)	SUBS
League	411	20	0	4
FA Cup	32	1	0	0
League Cup	48	3	0	0
Europe	11	1	–	–
Scotland	0	0	–	–
Other	14	1	–	–

HONOURS

FA Cup 91-92, Charity Shield medal 92, PFA Team Award Div 1. 91

INTERNATIONAL APPEARANCES

COUNTRY	LEVEL	GAMES	GOALS
England	Full	43	1
	B	1	0
	U-21	4	0
	Youth	0	0

NAME:	Steve Yates
CLUB:	Q.P.R.
BORN:	Bristol, 29/1/70
DEBUT v:	Darlington, 3/3/87
SUBSTITUTED:	7
BOOKINGS:	3
SENDINGS OFF:	0
OWN GOALS:	2
DOMESTIC PENS:	0
HAT-TRICKS:	0
STRIKE RATE (%):	0.37
EVER PRESENT:	–

LEAGUE CLUBS	YEARS	APPS	GOALS	FEE
Q.P.R.	93-95	52	1	£650,000
Bristol Rovers	87-93	197	0	Trainee

OVERALL RECORD

COMPETITION	APPS	GOALS	(PENS)	SUBS
League	245	1	0	4
FA Cup	12	0	0	0
League Cup	12	0	0	0
Europe	0	0	–	–
Scotland	0	0	–	–
Other	21	0	–	–

HONOURS

Division Three Championship 89-90

INTERNATIONAL APPEARANCES

COUNTRY	LEVEL	GAMES	GOALS
	Full	0	0
	B	0	0
	U-21	0	0
	Youth	0	0

INTRODUCTION – MIDFIELDERS

Where do you start when trying to assess the glittering array of midfield talent currently on display in the Premiership? The list of quality midfielders is mind-blowing . . . Le Tissier, Redknapp, Platt, McAllister, Barmby; just a few of the names which spring instantly to mind. Arguably the cream of the crop is Jamie Redknapp who has developed into one of the most complete midfielders in the country since leaving Bournemouth after just 13 first team games. It took him a while to become established at Anfield but he has slotted perfectly into Roy Evans' new formation and his performances for the Reds took him to the verge of Venables' England squad in 1995. And at 22 the future looks bright for the son of West Ham manager Harry.

But Rednapp is not the only midfielder to make his mark on the south coast. While young Jamie was learning his trade from his Dad, Matt Le Tissier was already dazzling the crowd down at the Dell. The Guernsey-born maestro is one of the most naturally gifted players this country has seen in recent years and it remains a mystery why he is not an England regular. For a midfield player his goalscoring prowess is incredible and there are a few strikers around who would envy a record of something like 100 league goals in the last six seasons. He's a master craftsmen and few people on the South Coast would argue with the fact that Le Tissier kept the Saints in the Premiership virtually single-handed last season. He's been a one-club man since joining Southampton from Vale Recreation in 1986 and, even with top clubs waiting with cheque books open, he's likely to remain a Dell boy for some time.

Leeds United's equivalent of the super Saint is Gary McAllister, probably the most elegant midfielder in the country. His touch, vision and passing ability is second to none and, like Le Tissier, he's capable of chipping in with a few spectacular goals from long range. McAllister, now captain of Scotland and Leeds, arrived in England as a raw recruit from Motherwell in 1985 when he signed for Leicester and developed into an accomplished midfield playmaker. Clubs were queuing up for his signature when he made it clear he wanted to leave Leicester in the summer of 1990, but it was Leeds who won the race. And what a signing McAllister has proved to be, helping Leeds to the League Championship in 1992 just a year after rising from the ashes of the First Division.

But while Rednapp, Le Tissier and McAllister are now established Premiership stars with a wealth of experience behind them, there is an abundance of talent ready to knock them off their perch. Manchester United's Roy Keane has come on in leaps and bounds since he joined the club from Nottingham Forest, while City rival Gary Flitcroft is also making a name for himself in Manchester.

But the versatile Nicky Barmby is one to watch this season after stepping up from the successful England Under-21 side to stake his claim for a place in the full international XI. Barmby came to the fore last season as an attacking midfield player in Gerry Francis' rejuvenated Spurs side. And, with Jurgen Klinsmann a thing of the past, his goals are going to be all the more important for the North London club. But it will be a tough battle for him to establish himself in the England midfield where David Platt, Paul Gascoigne and Paul Ince are dominant figures and the likes of Matt le Tissier and Steve McManaman are often on bench-warming duty.

NAME: Martin Allen
CLUB: West Ham
BORN: Reading, 14/8/65
DEBUT v: Luton, 23/3/85
SUBSTITUTED: 30
BOOKINGS: 33
SENDINGS OFF: 2
OWN GOALS: 0
DOMESTIC PENS: 0
HAT-TRICKS: 0
STRIKE RATE (%): 13.58
EVER PRESENT: –

LEAGUE CLUBS	YEARS	APPS	GOALS	FEE
West Ham	89-95	187	25	£675,000
Q.P.R.	83-89	136	16	Appr

OVERALL RECORD

COMPETITION	APPS	GOALS	(PENS)	SUBS
League	288	41	0	35
FA Cup	23	5	0	0
League Cup	31	6	0	6
Europe	1	0	–	–
Scottish	0	0	–	–
Other	14	1	–	–

HONOURS

League Cup r/u 85-86, PFA Team Award Div 1. 93

INTERNATIONAL APPEARANCES

COUNTRY	LEVEL	GAMES	GOALS
England	Full	0	0
	B	1	1
	U-21	2	0
	Youth	3	0

NAME: Paul Allen
CLUB: Southampton
BORN: Aveley, 28/8/62
DEBUT v: Burnley, 29/9/79
SUBSTITUTED: 36
BOOKINGS: 19
SENDINGS OFF: 0
OWN GOALS: 0
DOMESTIC PENS: 0
HAT-TRICKS: 0
STRIKE RATE (%): 6.54
EVER PRESENT: –

LEAGUE CLUBS	YEARS	APPS	GOALS	FEE
Southampton	93-95	43	1	£400,000
Stoke	95	17	1	Loan
Luton	94	4	0	Loan
Tottenham	85-93	292	23	£400,000
West Ham	79-85	152	6	Appr

OVERALL RECORD

COMPETITION	APPS	GOALS	(PENS)	SUBS
League	486	31	0	22
FA Cup	43	4	0	4
League Cup	66	6	0	6
Europe	8	0	–	–
Scottish	0	0	–	–
Other	12	0	–	–

HONOURS

FA Cup 79-80, 90-91, FA Cup r/u 86-87, Charity Shield medal, 80, 91

INTERNATIONAL APPEARANCES

COUNTRY	LEVEL	GAMES	GOALS
England	Full	0	0
	B	1	0
	U-21	3	0
	Youth	27	2

NAME: Darren Anderton
CLUB: Tottenham
BORN: Southampton, 3/3/72
DEBUT v: Wolves, 3/11/90
SUBSTITUTED: 28
BOOKINGS: 4
SENDINGS OFF: 0
OWN GOALS: 0
DOMESTIC PENS: 0
HAT-TRICKS: 0
STRIKE RATE (%): 16.50
EVER PRESENT: –

LEAGUE CLUBS	YEARS	APPS	GOALS	FEE
Tottenham	92-95	108	17	£1.75m
Portsmouth	90-92	62	7	Trainee

OVERALL RECORD

COMPETITION	APPS	GOALS	(PENS)	SUBS
League	157	24	0	13
FA Cup	20	7	0	2
League Cup	12	3	0	2
Europe	0	0	–	–
Scottish	0	0	–	–
Other	4	1	–	–

HONOURS

None

INTERNATIONAL APPEARANCES

COUNTRY	LEVEL	GAMES	GOALS
England	Full	9	3
	B	0	0
	U-21	11	4
	Youth	1	0

NAME:	Steve Anthrobus
CLUB:	Wimbledon
BORN:	Lewisham, 10/11/68
DEBUT v:	Plymouth, 20/10/87
SUBSTITUTED:	19
BOOKINGS:	8
SENDINGS OFF:	0
OWN GOALS:	0
DOMESTIC PENS:	0
HAT-TRICKS:	0
STRIKE RATE (%):	6.25
EVER PRESENT:	–

LEAGUE CLUBS	**YEARS**	**APPS**	**GOALS**	**FEE**
Wimbledon	90-95	28	0	£150,000
Chester	94	7	0	Loan
Peterborough	93	2	0	Loan
Millwall	86-90	21	4	Trainee

OVERALL RECORD

COMPETITION	**APPS**	**GOALS**	**(PENS)**	**SUBS**
League	55	4	0	3
FA Cup	2	0	0	0
League Cup	4	0	0	0
Europe	0	0	–	–
Scottish	0	0	–	–
Other	1	0	–	–

HONOURS

None

INTERNATIONAL APPEARANCES

COUNTRY	**LEVEL**	**GAMES**	**GOALS**
	Full	0	0
	B	0	0
	U-21	0	0
	Youth	0	0

NAME:	Neil Ardley
CLUB:	Wimbledon
BORN:	Epsom, 1/9/72
DEBUT v:	Aston Villa, 20/4/91
SUBSTITUTED:	13
BOOKINGS:	5
SENDINGS OFF:	0
OWN GOALS:	0
DOMESTIC PENS:	0
HAT-TRICKS:	0
STRIKE RATE (%):	9.64
EVER PRESENT:	–

LEAGUE CLUBS	**YEARS**	**APPS**	**GOALS**	**FEE**
Wimbledon	91-95	65	6	Trainee

OVERALL RECORD

COMPETITION	**APPS**	**GOALS**	**(PENS)**	**SUBS**
League	55	6	0	10
FA Cup	8	0	0	0
League Cup	8	2	0	2
Europe	0	0	–	–
Scottish	0	0	–	–

HONOURS

None

INTERNATIONAL APPEARANCES

COUNTRY	**LEVEL**	**GAMES**	**GOALS**
England	Full	0	0
	B	0	0
	U-21	9	0
	Youth	0	0

NAME:	Mark Atkins
CLUB:	Blackburn
BORN:	Doncaster, 14/8/68
DEBUT v:	Wrexham, 27/4/85
SUBSTITUTED:	24
BOOKINGS:	10
SENDINGS OFF:	0
OWN GOALS:	2
DOMESTIC PENS:	1
HAT-TRICKS:	0
STRIKE RATE (%):	11.14
EVER PRESENT:	88-89

LEAGUE CLUBS	**YEARS**	**APPS**	**GOALS**	**FEE**
Blackburn	88-95	253	33	£45,000
Scunthorpe	85-88	50	2	Appr

OVERALL RECORD

COMPETITION	**APPS**	**GOALS**	**(PENS)**	**SUBS**
League	269	35	1	34
FA Cup	16	0	0	3
League Cup	23	4	0	5
Europe	2	0	–	–
Scottish	0	0	–	–
Other	22	1	–	–

HONOURS

League Championship 94-95, Charity Shield medal 94

INTERNATIONAL APPEARANCES

COUNTRY	**LEVEL**	**GAMES**	**GOALS**
	Full	0	0
	B	0	0
	U-21	0	0
	Youth	0	0

NAME:	Dennis Bailey
CLUB:	Q.P.R.
BORN:	Lambeth, 13/11/65
DEBUT v:	Hull, 19/12/87
SUBSTITUTED:	22
BOOKINGS:	2
SENDINGS OFF:	0
OWN GOALS:	0
DOMESTIC PENS:	5
HAT-TRICKS:	1
STRIKE RATE (%):	31.28
EVER PRESENT:	–

LEAGUE CLUBS	YEARS	APPS	GOALS	FEE
Q.P.R.	91-95	39	10	£175,000
Brentford	95	6	3	Loan
Watford	94	7	3	Loan
Charlton	93	4	0	Loan
Bristol Rovers	91	6	1	Loan
Birmingham	89-91	75	23	£80,000
Bristol Rovers	89	17	9	Loan
Crystal Palace	87-89	5	1	£10,000
From: Farnborough Town				

OVERALL RECORD

COMPETITION	APPS	GOALS	(PENS)	SUBS
League	127	50	5	32
FA Cup	8	1	0	1
League Cup	11	5	0	0
Europe	0	0	–	–
Scottish	0	0	–	–
Other	10	2	–	–

HONOURS

None

INTERNATIONAL APPEARANCES

COUNTRY	LEVEL	GAMES	GOALS
	Full	0	0
	B	0	0
	U-21	0	0
	Youth	0	0

NAME:	Simon Barker
CLUB:	Q.P.R.
BORN:	Farnworth, 4/11/64
DEBUT v:	Swansea, 29/10/83
SUBSTITUTED:	24
BOOKINGS:	23
SENDINGS OFF:	1
OWN GOALS:	1
DOMESTIC PENS:	12
HAT-TRICKS:	0
STRIKE RATE (%):	14.41
EVER PRESENT:	86-87

LEAGUE CLUBS	YEARS	APPS	GOALS	FEE
Q.P.R.	88-95	223	21	£400,000
Blackburn	82-88	182	35	Appr

OVERALL RECORD

COMPETITION	APPS	GOALS	(PENS)	SUBS
League	380	56	11	25
FA Cup	32	3	1	1
League Cup	32	9	0	2
Europe	0	0	–	–
Scottish	0	0	–	–
Other	14	2	–	–

HONOURS

None

INTERNATIONAL APPEARANCES

COUNTRY	LEVEL	GAMES	GOALS
England	Full	0	0
	B	0	0
	U-21	4	0
	Youth	0	0

NAME:	Darren Barnard
CLUB:	Chelsea
BORN:	Germany, 30/11/71
DEBUT v:	West Ham, 4/4/92
SUBSTITUTED:	9
BOOKINGS:	1
SENDINGS OFF:	0
OWN GOALS:	0
DOMESTIC PENS:	0
HAT-TRICKS:	0
STRIKE RATE (%):	5.26
EVER PRESENT:	–

LEAGUE CLUBS	YEARS	APPS	GOALS	FEE
Chelsea	90-95	30	2	£50,000
Reading	94	4	0	Loan
From: Wokingham				

OVERALL RECORD

COMPETITION	APPS	GOALS	(PENS)	SUBS
League	22	2	0	12
FA Cup	1	0	0	1
League Cup	1	0	0	1
Europe	0	0	–	–
Scottish	0	0	–	–
Other	1	0	–	–

HONOURS

None

INTERNATIONAL APPEARANCES

COUNTRY	LEVEL	GAMES	GOALS
	Full	0	0
	B	0	0
	U-21	0	0
	Youth	0	0

NAME:	John Barnes
CLUB:	Liverpool
BORN:	Jamaica, 7/11/63
DEBUT v:	Oldham, 5/9/81
SUBSTITUTED:	35
BOOKINGS:	0
SENDINGS OFF:	0
OWN GOALS:	0
DOMESTIC PENS:	9
HAT-TRICKS:	3
STRIKE RATE (%):	30.34
EVER PRESENT:	82-83

LEAGUE CLUBS	YEARS	APPS	GOALS	FEE
Liverpool	87-95	243	77	£900,000
Watford	81-87	233	65	Appr

OVERALL RECORD

COMPETITION	APPS	GOALS	(PENS)	SUBS
League	472	142	7	4
FA Cup	73	27	2	0
League Cup	41	10	0	0
Europe	7	0	–	–
Scottish	0	0	–	–
Other	9	3	–	–

HONOURS

League Championship 87-88, 89-90, FA Cup 88-89, FA Cup r/u 83-84, 87-88, FA Youth Cup 81-82, League Cup 94-95, Charity Shield medal 88, 89, 90, 92, Footballer of the Year 87-88, 89-90, PFA Player of the Year 87-88, PFA Team Award Div 1. 88, 90, 91

INTERNATIONAL APPEARANCES

COUNTRY	LEVEL	GAMES	GOALS
England	Full	79	11
	B	1	0
	U-21	2	1
	Youth	0	0

NAME:	Chris Bart-Williams
CLUB:	Nottingham Forest
BORN:	Sierre Leone, 16/6/74
DEBUT v:	Grimsby, 23/10/90
SUBSTITUTED:	38
BOOKINGS:	10
SENDINGS OFF:	0
OWN GOALS:	0
DOMESTIC PENS:	0
HAT-TRICKS:	1
STRIKE RATE (%):	12.44
EVER PRESENT:	–

LEAGUE CLUBS	YEARS	APPS	GOALS	FEE
Nottingham Forest	95	0	0	Undisclosed
Sheffield Wed	91-95	125	16	£275,000
Leyton Orient	90-91	36	2	Trainee

OVERALL RECORD

COMPETITION	APPS	GOALS	(PENS)	SUBS
League	130	18	0	31
FA Cup	9	2	0	3
League Cup	14	4	0	6
Europe	4	2	–	–
Scottish	0	0	–	–
Other	2	0	–	–

HONOURS

FA Cup r/u 92-93

INTERNATIONAL APPEARANCES

COUNTRY	LEVEL	GAMES	GOALS
England	Full	0	0
	B	1	0
	U-21	14	1
	Youth	12	2

NAME:	David Batty
CLUB:	Blackburn
BORN:	Leeds, 2/12/68
DEBUT v:	Swindon, 21/11/87
SUBSTITUTED:	13
BOOKINGS:	25
SENDINGS OFF:	0
OWN GOALS:	0
DOMESTIC PENS:	0
HAT-TRICKS:	0
STRIKE RATE (%):	1.44
EVER PRESENT:	–

LEAGUE CLUBS	YEARS	APPS	GOALS	FEE
Blackburn	93-95	31	0	£2.75m
Leeds	87-93	211	4	Appr

OVERALL RECORD

COMPETITION	APPS	GOALS	(PENS)	SUBS
League	231	4	0	11
FA Cup	16	0	0	0
League Cup	19	0	0	0
Europe	4	0	–	–
Scottish	0	0	–	–
Other	15	0	–	–

HONOURS

League Championship 91-92, Division Two Championship 89-90, Charity Shield medal 92, PFA Team Award Premier League 94

INTERNATIONAL APPEARANCES

COUNTRY	LEVEL	GAMES	GOALS
England	Full	17	0
	B	4	0
	U-21	6	0
	Youth	0	0

NAME:	Peter Beagrie
CLUB:	Manchester City
BORN:	Middlesbrough, 29/11/65
DEBUT v:	Oldham, 2/10/84
SUBSTITUTED:	33
BOOKINGS:	15
SENDINGS OFF:	0
OWN GOALS:	0
DOMESTIC PENS:	1
HAT-TRICKS:	0
STRIKE RATE (%):	11.05
EVER PRESENT:	–

LEAGUE CLUBS	YEARS	APPS	GOALS	FEE
Manchester City	94-95	46	3	£1.1m
Sunderland	91	5	1	Loan
Everton	89-94	114	12	£750,000
Stoke	88-89	54	7	£210,000
Sheffield Utd	86-88	84	12	£35,000
Middlesbrough	83-86	32	2	Appr

OVERALL RECORD

COMPETITION	APPS	GOALS	(PENS)	SUBS
League	294	36	1	41
FA Cup	19	2	0	2
League Cup	22	4	0	2
Europe	0	0	–	–
Scottish	0	0	–	–
Other	12	1	–	–

INTERNATIONAL APPEARANCES

COUNTRY	LEVEL	GAMES	GOALS
England	Full	0	0
	B	2	0
	U-21	2	0
	Youth	0	0

HONOURS

None

NAME:	David Beckham
CLUB:	Manchester Utd
BORN:	Leytonstone, 2/5/75
DEBUT v:	Doncaster, 4/3/95
SUBSTITUTED:	1
BOOKINGS:	1
SENDINGS OFF:	0
OWN GOALS:	0
DOMESTIC PENS:	0
HAT-TRICKS:	0
STRIKE RATE (%):	–
EVER PRESENT:	–

LEAGUE CLUBS	YEARS	APPS	GOALS	FEE
Manchester Utd	92-95	4	0	Trainee
Preston	95	5	1	Loan

OVERALL RECORD

COMPETITION	APPS	GOALS	(PENS)	SUBS
League	6	1	0	3
FA Cup	1	0	0	1
League Cup	3	0	0	0
Europe	2	1	–	–
Scottish	0	0	–	–

HONOURS

FA Youth Cup 91-92, 92-93

INTERNATIONAL APPEARANCES

COUNTRY	LEVEL	GAMES	GOALS
England	Full	0	0
	B	0	0
	U-21	0	0
	Youth	4	0

NAME:	Ian Bishop
CLUB:	West Ham
BORN:	Liverpool, 29/5/65
DEBUT v:	Darlington, 27/3/84
SUBSTITUTED:	15
BOOKINGS:	10
SENDINGS OFF:	0
OWN GOALS:	0
DOMESTIC PENS:	1
HAT-TRICKS:	0
STRIKE RATE (%):	7.66
EVER PRESENT:	–

LEAGUE CLUBS	YEARS	APPS	GOALS	FEE
West Ham	89-95	187	10	£500,000
Manchester City	89	19	2	£465,000
Bournemouth	88-89	44	2	£35,000
Carlisle	84-88	132	14	£15,000
Crewe	84	4	0	Loan
Everton	83-84	1	0	Appr

OVERALL RECORD

COMPETITION	APPS	GOALS	(PENS)	SUBS
League	373	28	1	14
FA Cup	27	4	0	1
League Cup	29	2	0	0
Europe	0	0	–	–
Scottish	0	0	–	–
Other	13	1	–	–

HONOURS

PFA Team Award Div 2. 1991

INTERNATIONAL APPEARANCES

COUNTRY	LEVEL	GAMES	GOALS
England	Full	0	0
	B	1	0
	U-21	0	0
	Youth	0	0

NAME:	Kingsley Black
CLUB:	Nottm Forest
BORN:	Luton, 22/6/68
DEBUT v:	Q.P.R., 26/9/87
SUBSTITUTED:	31
BOOKINGS:	2
SENDINGS OFF:	0
OWN GOALS:	0
DOMESTIC PENS:	0
HAT-TRICKS:	0
STRIKE RATE (%):	17.50
EVER PRESENT:	–

LEAGUE CLUBS	YEARS	APPS	GOALS	FEE
Nottm Forest	91-95	94	14	£1.5m
Sheffield Utd	95	11	2	Loan
Luton	86-91	127	25	Appr

OVERALL RECORD

COMPETITION	APPS	GOALS	(PENS)	SUBS
League	210	41	0	22
FA Cup	9	2	0	1
League Cup	35	6	0	3
Europe	0	0	–	–
Scottish	0	0	–	–
Other	11	2	–	–

HONOURS

League Cup 87-88, League Cup r/u 88-89

INTERNATIONAL APPEARANCES

COUNTRY	LEVEL	GAMES	GOALS
N. Ireland	Full	30	1
	B	1	0
	U-21	1	0
	Youth	0	0

NAME:	Lars Bohinen
CLUB:	Nottm Forest
BORN:	Norway, 8/9/69
DEBUT v:	Birmingham, 6/11/93
SUBSTITUTED:	13
BOOKINGS:	9
SENDINGS OFF:	0
OWN GOALS:	0
DOMESTIC PENS:	0
HAT-TRICKS:	0
STRIKE RATE (%):	13.85
EVER PRESENT:	–

LEAGUE CLUBS	YEARS	APPS	GOALS	FEE
Nottm Forest	93-95	56	8	£450,000
From: Lillestrom				

OVERALL RECORD

COMPETITION	APPS	GOALS	(PENS)	SUBS
League	51	8	0	5
FA Cup	3	1	0	0
League Cup	6	0	0	1
Europe	0	0	–	–
Scottish	0	0	–	–

HONOURS

None

INTERNATIONAL APPEARANCES

COUNTRY	LEVEL	GAMES	GOALS
Norway	Full	38	8
	B	0	0
	U-21	0	0
	Youth	0	0

NAME:	Willie Boland
CLUB:	Coventry
BORN:	Ennis, 6/8/75
DEBUT v:	Chelsea, 1/5/93
SUBSTITUTED:	6
BOOKINGS:	2
SENDINGS OFF:	0
OWN GOALS:	0
DOMESTIC PENS:	0
HAT-TRICKS:	0
STRIKE RATE (%):	–
EVER PRESENT:	–

LEAGUE CLUBS	YEARS	APPS	GOALS	FEE
Coventry	92-95	40	0	Trainee

OVERALL RECORD

COMPETITION	APPS	GOALS	(PENS)	SUBS
League	33	0	0	7
FA Cup	0	0	0	0
League Cup	4	0	0	0
Europe	0	0	–	–
Scottish	0	0	–	–

HONOURS

None

INTERNATIONAL APPEARANCES

COUNTRY	LEVEL	GAMES	GOALS
Eire	Full	0	0
	B	0	0
	U-21	5	0
	Youth	0	0

NAME:	Robert Bowman
CLUB:	Leeds
BORN:	Durham, 21/11/75
DEBUT v:	Wimbledon, 6/2/93
SUBSTITUTED:	0
BOOKINGS:	0
SENDINGS OFF:	0
OWN GOALS:	0
DOMESTIC PENS:	0
HAT-TRICKS:	0
STRIKE RATE (%):	–
EVER PRESENT:	–

LEAGUE CLUBS	YEARS	APPS	GOALS	FEE
Leeds	92-95	4	0	Trainee

OVERALL RECORD

COMPETITION	APPS	GOALS	(PENS)	SUBS
League	3	0	0	1
FA Cup	0	0	0	0
League Cup	0	0	0	0
Europe	0	0	–	–
Scottish	0	0	–	–

HONOURS

FA Youth Cup 92-93

INTERNATIONAL APPEARANCES

COUNTRY	LEVEL	GAMES	GOALS
England	Full	0	0
	B	0	0
	U-21	0	0
	Youth	7	0

NAME:	David Brightwell
CLUB:	Manchester City
BORN:	Lutterworth, 7/1/71
DEBUT v:	Cambridge, 25/3/91
SUBSTITUTED:	6
BOOKINGS:	3
SENDINGS OFF:	0
OWN GOALS:	0
DOMESTIC PENS:	0
HAT-TRICKS:	0
STRIKE RATE (%):	3.28
EVER PRESENT:	–

LEAGUE CLUBS	YEARS	APPS	GOALS	FEE
Manchester City	88-95	45	1	Trainee
Chester	91	6	0	Loan

OVERALL RECORD

COMPETITION	APPS	GOALS	(PENS)	SUBS
League	42	1	0	9
FA Cup	5	1	0	2
League Cup	2	0	0	1
Europe	0	0	–	–
Scottish	0	0	–	–

HONOURS

None

INTERNATIONAL APPEARANCES

COUNTRY	LEVEL	GAMES	GOALS
	Full	0	0
	B	0	0
	U-21	0	0
	Youth	0	0

NAME:	Ian Brightwell
CLUB:	Manchester City
BORN:	Lutterworth, 9/4/68
DEBUT v:	Wimbledon, 23/8/86
SUBSTITUTED:	18
BOOKINGS:	13
SENDINGS OFF:	0
OWN GOALS:	2
DOMESTIC PENS:	0
HAT-TRICKS:	0
STRIKE RATE (%):	6.18
EVER PRESENT:	–

LEAGUE CLUBS	YEARS	APPS	GOALS	FEE
Manchester City	86-95	232	16	Trainee

OVERALL RECORD

COMPETITION	APPS	GOALS	(PENS)	SUBS
League	203	16	0	29
FA Cup	13	1	0	4
League Cup	24	0	0	2
Europe	0	0	–	–
Scottish	0	0	–	–
Other	7	0	–	–

HONOURS

None

INTERNATIONAL APPEARANCES

COUNTRY	LEVEL	GAMES	GOALS
England	Full	0	0
	B	0	0
	U-21	4	2
	Youth	3	0

NAME:	Lee Briscoe
CLUB:	Sheffield Wed
BORN:	Pontefract, 30/9/75
DEBUT v:	Tottenham, 5/2/94
SUBSTITUTED:	3
BOOKINGS:	0
SENDINGS OFF:	0
OWN GOALS:	0
DOMESTIC PENS:	0
HAT-TRICKS:	0
STRIKE RATE (%):	–
EVER PRESENT:	–

LEAGUE CLUBS	YEARS	APPS	GOALS	FEE
Sheffield Wed	92-95	7	0	Trainee

OVERALL RECORD

COMPETITION	APPS	GOALS	(PENS)	SUBS
League	6	0	0	1
FA Cup	0	0	0	0
League Cup	0	0	0	0
Europe	0	0	–	–
Scottish	0	0	–	–

HONOURS

None

INTERNATIONAL APPEARANCES

COUNTRY	LEVEL	GAMES	GOALS
	Full	0	0
	B	0	0
	U-21	0	0
	Youth	0	0

NAME:	Craig Burley
CLUB:	Chelsea
BORN:	Irvine, 24/9/71
DEBUT v:	Nottm Forest, 20/4/91
SUBSTITUTED:	12
BOOKINGS:	5
SENDINGS OFF:	0
OWN GOALS:	2
DOMESTIC PENS:	0
HAT-TRICKS:	0
STRIKE RATE (%):	11.27
EVER PRESENT:	–

LEAGUE CLUBS	YEARS	APPS	GOALS	FEE
Chelsea	89-95	60	5	Trainee

OVERALL RECORD

COMPETITION	APPS	GOALS	(PENS)	SUBS
League	43	5	0	17
FA Cup	9	3	0	2
League Cup	0	0	0	0
Europe	1	0	–	–
Scottish	0	0	–	–
Other	3	0	–	–

HONOURS

FA Cup r/u 93-94

INTERNATIONAL APPEARANCES

COUNTRY	LEVEL	GAMES	GOALS
Scotland	Full	3	0
	B	0	0
	U-21	8	0
	Youth	0	0

NAME:	Nicky Butt
CLUB:	Manchester Utd
BORN:	Manchester, 21/1/75
DEBUT v:	Oldham, 21/11/92
SUBSTITUTED:	4
BOOKINGS:	6
SENDINGS OFF:	0
OWN GOALS:	0
DOMESTIC PENS:	0
HAT-TRICKS:	0
STRIKE RATE (%):	–
EVER PRESENT:	–

LEAGUE CLUBS	YEARS	APPS	GOALS	FEE
Manchester Utd	92-95	24	1	Appr

OVERALL RECORD

COMPETITION	APPS	GOALS	(PENS)	SUBS
League	11	1	0	13
FA Cup	3	0	0	2
League Cup	2	0	0	0
Europe	6	0	–	–
Scottish	0	0	–	–

HONOURS

FA Cup r/u 94-95, FA Youth Cup 91-92, Charity Shield medal 94, FA Youth Cup r/u 92-93

INTERNATIONAL APPEARANCES

COUNTRY	LEVEL	GAMES	GOALS
England	Full	0	0
	B	0	0
	U-21	3	0
	Youth	7	0

NAME:	Franz Carr
CLUB:	Aston Villa
BORN:	Preston, 24/9/66
DEBUT v:	Aston Villa, 12/10/85
SUBSTITUTED:	31
BOOKINGS:	0
SENDINGS OFF:	0
OWN GOALS:	0
DOMESTIC PENS:	0
HAT-TRICKS:	0
STRIKE RATE (%):	12.66
EVER PRESENT:	–

LEAGUE CLUBS	YEARS	APPS	GOALS	FEE
Aston Villa	95	2	0	£150,000
Leicester	94-95	13	1	£100,000
Sheffield Utd	93-94	18	4	£120,000
Newcastle	91-93	25	3	£250,000
West Ham	91	3	0	Loan
Sheffield Wed	89-90	12	0	Loan
Nottm Forest	84-91	131	17	£100,000
Blackburn	84	0	0	Appr

OVERALL RECORD

COMPETITION	APPS	GOALS	(PENS)	SUBS
League	184	25	0	20
FA Cup	10	0	0	0
League Cup	19	5	0	4
Europe	0	0	–	–
Scottish	0	0	–	–
Other	12	2	–	–

HONOURS

League Cup 89-90

INTERNATIONAL APPEARANCES

COUNTRY	LEVEL	GAMES	GOALS
England	Full	0	0
	B	0	0
	U-21	9	1
	Youth	14	4

NAME:	Darren Caskey
CLUB:	Tottenham
BORN:	Basildon, 21/8/74
DEBUT v:	Arsenal, 16/8/93
SUBSTITUTED:	3
BOOKINGS:	3
SENDINGS OFF:	1
OWN GOALS:	0
DOMESTIC PENS:	0
HAT-TRICKS:	0
STRIKE RATE (%):	–
EVER PRESENT:	–

LEAGUE CLUBS	YEARS	APPS	GOALS	FEE
Tottenham	92-95	29	4	Trainee

OVERALL RECORD

COMPETITION	APPS	GOALS	(PENS)	SUBS
League	17	4	0	12
FA Cup	3	0	0	0
League Cup	3	1	0	1
Europe	0	0	–	–
Scottish	0	0	–	–
Other	2	0	–	–

HONOURS

None

INTERNATIONAL APPEARANCES

COUNTRY	LEVEL	GAMES	GOALS
England	Full	0	0
	B	0	0
	U-21	0	0
	Youth	19	2

NAME:	Stuart Castledine
CLUB:	Wimbledon
BORN:	Wandsworth, 23/1/73
DEBUT v:	Norwich, 25/4/92
SUBSTITUTED:	2
BOOKINGS:	0
SENDINGS OFF:	0
OWN GOALS:	0
DOMESTIC PENS:	0
HAT-TRICKS:	0
STRIKE RATE (%):	–
EVER PRESENT:	–

LEAGUE CLUBS	YEARS	APPS	GOALS	FEE
Wimbledon	91-95	12	2	Trainee

OVERALL RECORD

COMPETITION	APPS	GOALS	(PENS)	SUBS
League	9	2	0	3
FA Cup	0	0	0	0
League Cup	0	0	0	0
Europe	0	0	–	–
Scottish	0	0	–	–

HONOURS

None

INTERNATIONAL APPEARANCES

COUNTRY	LEVEL	GAMES	GOALS
	Full	0	0
	B	0	0
	U-21	0	0
	Youth	0	0

NAME: Philip Charnock
CLUB: Liverpool
BORN: Southport, 14/2/75
DEBUT v: –
SUBSTITUTED: 0
BOOKINGS: 0
SENDINGS OFF: 0
OWN GOALS: 0
DOMESTIC PENS: 0
HAT-TRICKS: 0
STRIKE RATE (%): –
EVER PRESENT: –

LEAGUE CLUBS	YEARS	APPS	GOALS	FEE
Liverpool	92-95	0	0	Trainee

OVERALL RECORD

COMPETITION	APPS	GOALS	(PENS)	SUBS
League	0	0	0	0
FA Cup	0	0	0	0
League Cup	1	0	0	0
Europe	1	0	–	–
Scottish	0	0	–	–

HONOURS

None

INTERNATIONAL APPEARANCES

COUNTRY	LEVEL	GAMES	GOALS
	Full	0	0
	B	0	0
	U-21	0	0
	Youth	0	0

NAME: Lee Clark
CLUB: Newcastle
BORN: Wallsend, 27/10/72
DEBUT v: Bristol City, 29/9/90
SUBSTITUTED: 11
BOOKINGS: 7
SENDINGS OFF: 0
OWN GOALS: 0
DOMESTIC PENS: 0
HAT-TRICKS: 0
STRIKE RATE (%): 12.65
EVER PRESENT: 92-93

LEAGUE CLUBS	YEARS	APPS	GOALS	FEE
Newcastle	89-95	142	19	Trainee

OVERALL RECORD

COMPETITION	APPS	GOALS	(PENS)	SUBS
League	122	19	0	20
FA Cup	11	2	0	0
League Cup	13	0	0	0
Europe	3	0	–	–
Scottish	0	0	–	–
Other	4	1	–	–

HONOURS

First Division Championship 92-93, PFA Team Award
Div 1. 93

INTERNATIONAL APPEARANCES

COUNTRY	LEVEL	GAMES	GOALS
England	Full	0	0
	B	0	0
	U-21	11	0
	Youth	8	0

NAME: Adrian Clarke
CLUB: Arsenal
BORN: Cambridge, 28/9/74
DEBUT v: Q.P.R., 31/12/94
SUBSTITUTED: 0
BOOKINGS: 0
SENDINGS OFF: 0
OWN GOALS: 0
DOMESTIC PENS: 0
HAT-TRICKS: 0
STRIKE RATE (%): –
EVER PRESENT: –

LEAGUE CLUBS	YEARS	APPS	GOALS	FEE
Arsenal	93-95	1	0	Trainee

OVERALL RECORD

COMPETITION	APPS	GOALS	(PENS)	SUBS
League	0	0	0	1
FA Cup	0	0	0	0
League Cup	0	0	0	0
Europe	0	0	–	–
Scottish	0	0	–	–

HONOURS

FA Youth Cup 93-94

INTERNATIONAL APPEARANCES

COUNTRY	LEVEL	GAMES	GOALS
England	Full	0	0
	B	0	0
	U-21	1	0
	Youth	0	0

NAME:	Nigel Clough
CLUB:	Liverpool
BORN:	Sunderland, 19/3/66
DEBUT v:	Ipswich, 26/12/84
SUBSTITUTED:	14
BOOKINGS:	4
SENDINGS OFF:	1
OWN GOALS:	0
DOMESTIC PENS:	20
HAT-TRICKS:	2
STRIKE RATE (%):	31.86
EVER PRESENT:	86-87, 89-90, 92-93

LEAGUE CLUBS	YEARS	APPS	GOALS	FEE
Liverpool	93-95	37	6	£2.275m
Nottm Forest	84-93	311	101	–
From: ACT Hunters				

OVERALL RECORD

COMPETITION	APPS	GOALS	(PENS)	SUBS
League	335	107	17	13
FA Cup	30	6	0	0
League Cup	52	24	3	0
Europe	0	0	–	–
Scottish	0	0	–	–
Other	15	1	–	–

HONOURS

FA Cup r/u 90-91, League Cup 88-89, 89-90, League Cup r/u 91-92

INTERNATIONAL APPEARANCES

COUNTRY	LEVEL	GAMES	GOALS
England	Full	14	0
	B	4	1
	U-21	15	4
	Youth	0	0

NAME:	Paul Cook
CLUB:	Coventry
BORN:	Liverpool, 22/2/67
DEBUT v:	Reading, 13/5/85
SUBSTITUTED:	41
BOOKINGS:	19
SENDINGS OFF:	3
OWN GOALS:	0
DOMESTIC PENS:	7
HAT-TRICKS:	0
STRIKE RATE (%):	10.89
EVER PRESENT:	–

LEAGUE CLUBS	YEARS	APPS	GOALS	FEE
Coventry	94-95	34	3	£600,000
Wolverhampton	89-94	193	19	£250,000
Norwich	88-89	6	0	£73,000
Wigan	84-88	83	14	–

OVERALL RECORD

COMPETITION	APPS	GOALS	(PENS)	SUBS
League	304	36	7	12
FA Cup	15	0	0	3
League Cup	15	2	0	0
Europe	0	0	–	–
Scottish	0	0	–	–
Other	15	2	–	–

HONOURS

None

INTERNATIONAL APPEARANCES

COUNTRY	LEVEL	GAMES	GOALS
England	Full	0	0
	B	1	0
	U-21	0	0
	Youth	0	0

NAME:	Julian Darby
CLUB:	Coventry
BORN:	Bolton, 3/10/67
DEBUT v:	Blackpool, 31/3/86
SUBSTITUTED:	13
BOOKINGS:	13
SENDINGS OFF:	1
OWN GOALS:	1
DOMESTIC PENS:	0
HAT-TRICKS:	0
STRIKE RATE (%):	14.10
EVER PRESENT:	89-90

LEAGUE CLUBS	YEARS	APPS	GOALS	FEE
Coventry	93-95	55	5	£500,000
Bolton	86-93	270	36	Appr

OVERALL RECORD

COMPETITION	APPS	GOALS	(PENS)	SUBS
League	310	41	0	15
FA Cup	21	3	0	2
League Cup	28	9	0	0
Europe	0	0	–	–
Scottish	0	0	–	–
Other	32	5	–	–

HONOURS

None

INTERNATIONAL APPEARANCES

COUNTRY	LEVEL	GAMES	GOALS
	Full	0	0
	B	0	0
	U-21	0	0
	Youth	0	0

NAME:	Simon Davies
CLUB:	Manchester Utd
BORN:	Winsford, 23/4/74
DEBUT v:	Brentford, 18/12/93
SUBSTITUTED:	4
BOOKINGS:	1
SENDINGS OFF:	0
OWN GOALS:	0
DOMESTIC PENS:	0
HAT-TRICKS:	0
STRIKE RATE (%):	–
EVER PRESENT:	–

LEAGUE CLUBS	YEARS	APPS	GOALS	FEE
Manchester Utd	92-95	5	0	Trainee
Exeter	93-94	6	1	Loan

OVERALL RECORD

COMPETITION	APPS	GOALS	(PENS)	SUBS
League	8	1	0	3
FA Cup	1	0	0	0
League Cup	3	0	0	0
Europe	2	1	–	–
Scottish	0	0	–	–

HONOURS

FA Youth Cup 91-92

INTERNATIONAL APPEARANCES

COUNTRY	LEVEL	GAMES	GOALS
	Full	0	0
	B	0	0
	U-21	0	0
	Youth	0	0

NAME:	Paul Davis
CLUB:	Arsenal
BORN:	Dulwich, 9/12/61
DEBUT v:	Tottenham, 7/4/80
SUBSTITUTED:	25
BOOKINGS:	7
SENDINGS OFF:	0
OWN GOALS:	0
DOMESTIC PENS:	1
HAT-TRICKS:	0
STRIKE RATE (%):	8.60
EVER PRESENT:	–

LEAGUE CLUBS	YEARS	APPS	GOALS	FEE
Arsenal	79-95	351	30	Appr

OVERALL RECORD

COMPETITION	APPS	GOALS	(PENS)	SUBS
League	331	30	1	20
FA Cup	22	3	0	5
League Cup	46	4	0	6
Europe	16	0	–	–
Scottish	0	0	–	–
Other	12	2	–	–

HONOURS

League Championship 88-89, 90-91, FA Cup 92-93, League Cup 86-87, 92-93, League Cup r/u 87-88, Charity Shield medal 91, 93, European Cup Winners' Cup 93-94

INTERNATIONAL APPEARANCES

COUNTRY	LEVEL	GAMES	GOALS
England	Full	0	0
	B	2	1
	U-21	11	2
	Youth	0	0

NAME:	Fabian De Freitas
CLUB:	Bolton
BORN:	Surinam, 28/7/72
DEBUT v:	Middlesbrough, 27/8/94
SUBSTITUTED:	6
BOOKINGS:	0
SENDINGS OFF:	0
OWN GOALS:	0
DOMESTIC PENS:	0
HAT-TRICKS:	0
STRIKE RATE (%):	–
EVER PRESENT:	–

LEAGUE CLUBS	YEARS	APPS	GOALS	FEE
Bolton	94-95	12	2	£400,000
From: FC Volendem				

OVERALL RECORD

COMPETITION	APPS	GOALS	(PENS)	SUBS
League	7	2	0	5
FA Cup	0	0	0	0
League Cup	0	0	0	2
Europe	0	0	–	–
Scottish	0	0	–	–
Other	2	2	–	–

HONOURS

None

INTERNATIONAL APPEARANCES

COUNTRY	LEVEL	GAMES	GOALS
Holland	Full	0	0
	B	0	0
	U-21	3	0
	Youth	0	0

NAME:	Gerald Dobbs
CLUB:	Wimbledon
BORN:	Lambeth, 24/1/71
DEBUT v:	Nottm Forest, 2/4/92
SUBSTITUTED:	5
BOOKINGS:	4
SENDINGS OFF:	1
OWN GOALS:	0
DOMESTIC PENS:	0
HAT-TRICKS:	0
STRIKE RATE (%):	–
EVER PRESENT:	–

LEAGUE CLUBS	YEARS	APPS	GOALS	FEE
Wimbledon	89-95	33	1	Trainee

OVERALL RECORD

COMPETITION	APPS	GOALS	(PENS)	SUBS
League	21	1	0	12
FA Cup	1	1	0	1
League Cup	2	0	0	0
Europe	0	0	–	–
Scottish	0	0	–	–

HONOURS

None

INTERNATIONAL APPEARANCES

COUNTRY	LEVEL	GAMES	GOALS
	Full	0	0
	B	0	0
	U-21	0	0
	Youth	0	0

NAME:	Jason Dozzell
CLUB:	Tottenham
BORN:	Ipswich, 9/12/67
DEBUT v:	Coventry, 4/2/84
SUBSTITUTED:	16
BOOKINGS:	9
SENDINGS OFF:	0
OWN GOALS:	0
DOMESTIC PENS:	0
HAT-TRICKS:	0
STRIKE RATE (%):	17.80
EVER PRESENT:	86-87, 89-90

LEAGUE CLUBS	YEARS	APPS	GOALS	FEE
Tottenham	93-95	39	8	£1.7m
Ipswich	84-93	332	52	Appr

OVERALL RECORD

COMPETITION	APPS	GOALS	(PENS)	SUBS
League	346	60	0	25
FA Cup	24	13	0	0
League Cup	31	3	0	1
Europe	0	0	–	–
Scottish	0	0	–	–
Other	22	4	–	–

HONOURS

Division Two Championship 91-92

INTERNATIONAL APPEARANCES

COUNTRY	LEVEL	GAMES	GOALS
England	Full	0	0
	B	0	0
	U-21	8	0
	Youth	5	2

NAME:	Ilie Dumitrescu
CLUB:	Tottenham
BORN:	Bucharest, 6/1/69
DEBUT v:	Sheffield Wed, 20/8/94
SUBSTITUTED:	3
BOOKINGS:	2
SENDINGS OFF:	1
OWN GOALS:	0
DOMESTIC PENS:	1
HAT-TRICKS:	0
STRIKE RATE (%):	–
EVER PRESENT:	–

LEAGUE CLUBS	YEARS	APPS	GOALS	FEE
Tottenham	94-95	12	4	£2.6m
From: Steau Bucharest				

OVERALL RECORD

COMPETITION	APPS	GOALS	(PENS)	SUBS
League	10	4	1	2
FA Cup	0	0	0	0
League Cup	2	1	0	0
Europe	0	0	–	–
Scottish	0	0	–	–

HONOURS

None

INTERNATIONAL APPEARANCES

COUNTRY	LEVEL	GAMES	GOALS
Romania	Full	47	18
	B	0	0
	U-21	0	0
	Youth	0	0

NAME:	Robbie Earle
CLUB:	Wimbledon
BORN:	Staffs, 27/1/65
DEBUT v:	Swindon, 28/8/82
SUBSTITUTED:	16
BOOKINGS:	12
SENDINGS OFF:	0
OWN GOALS:	0
DOMESTIC PENS:	1
HAT-TRICKS:	1
STRIKE RATE (%):	23.94
EVER PRESENT:	84-85, 85-86, 92-93 93-94

LEAGUE CLUBS	YEARS	APPS	GOALS	FEE
Wimbledon	91-95	133	30	£775,000
Port Vale	82-91	294	77	Appr

OVERALL RECORD

COMPETITION	APPS	GOALS	(PENS)	SUBS
League	417	107	1	10
FA Cup	34	5	0	1
League Cup	33	7	0	2
Europe	0	0	–	–
Scottish	0	0	–	–
Other	20	6	–	–

HONOURS

None

INTERNATIONAL APPEARANCES

COUNTRY	LEVEL	GAMES	GOALS
	Full	0	0
	B	0	0
	U-21	0	0
	Youth	0	0

NAME:	John Ebbrell
CLUB:	Everton
BORN:	Bromborough, 1/10/69
DEBUT v:	Wimbledon, 4/2/89
SUBSTITUTED:	10
BOOKINGS:	26
SENDINGS OFF:	0
OWN GOALS:	0
DOMESTIC PENS:	0
HAT-TRICKS:	0
STRIKE RATE (%):	5.53
EVER PRESENT:	–

LEAGUE CLUBS	YEARS	APPS	GOALS	FEE
Everton	86-95	185	9	Appr

OVERALL RECORD

COMPETITION	APPS	GOALS	(PENS)	SUBS
League	176	9	0	9
FA Cup	16	2	0	0
League Cup	16	1	0	0
Europe	0	0	–	–
Scottish	0	0	–	–
Other	8	1	–	–

HONOURS

None

INTERNATIONAL APPEARANCES

COUNTRY	LEVEL	GAMES	GOALS
England	Full	0	0
	B	1	0
	U-21	14	1
	Youth	2	1

NAME:	Rob Elliott
CLUB:	Newcastle
BORN:	Newcastle, 25/12/73
DEBUT v:	Middlesbrough, 12/3/91
SUBSTITUTED:	6
BOOKINGS:	5
SENDINGS OFF:	1
OWN GOALS:	0
DOMESTIC PENS:	0
HAT-TRICKS:	0
STRIKE RATE (%):	4.00
EVER PRESENT:	–

LEAGUE CLUBS	YEARS	APPS	GOALS	FEE
Newcastle	91-95	43	2	Trainee

OVERALL RECORD

COMPETITION	APPS	GOALS	(PENS)	SUBS
League	37	2	0	6
FA Cup	5	0	0	1
League Cup	1	0	0	0
Europe	0	0	–	–
Scottish	0	0	–	–
Other	1	0	–	–

HONOURS

None

INTERNATIONAL APPEARANCES

COUNTRY	LEVEL	GAMES	GOALS
England	Full	0	0
	B	0	0
	U-21	0	0
	Youth	1	0

NAME:	Gareth Farrelly
CLUB:	Aston Villa
BORN:	Dublin, 28/8/75
DEBUT v:	Bristol Rovers, 22/3/95
SUBSTITUTED:	0
BOOKINGS:	2
SENDINGS OFF:	0
OWN GOALS:	0
DOMESTIC PENS:	0
HAT-TRICKS:	0
STRIKE RATE (%):	–
EVER PRESENT:	–

LEAGUE CLUBS	YEARS	APPS	GOALS	FEE
Aston Villa	92-95	0	0	£40,000
Rotherham	95	10	1	Loan
From: Home Farm				

OVERALL RECORD

COMPETITION	APPS	GOALS	(PENS)	SUBS
League	9	1	0	1
FA Cup	0	0	0	0
League Cup	0	0	0	0
Europe	0	0	–	–
Scottish	0	0	–	–

HONOURS

None

INTERNATIONAL APPEARANCES

COUNTRY	LEVEL	GAMES	GOALS
Eire	Full	0	0
	B	0	0
	U-21	4	0
	Youth	0	0

NAME:	Peter Fear
CLUB:	Wimbledon
BORN:	Sutton, 10/9/73
DEBUT v:	Arsenal, 10/2/93
SUBSTITUTED:	7
BOOKINGS:	6
SENDINGS OFF:	0
OWN GOALS:	0
DOMESTIC PENS:	0
HAT-TRICKS:	0
STRIKE RATE (%):	4.17
EVER PRESENT:	–

LEAGUE CLUBS	YEARS	APPS	GOALS	FEE
Wimbledon	92-95	41	2	Trainee

OVERALL RECORD

COMPETITION	APPS	GOALS	(PENS)	SUBS
League	33	2	0	8
FA Cup	2	0	0	0
League Cup	3	0	0	2
Europe	0	0	–	–
Scottish	0	0	–	–

HONOURS

None

INTERNATIONAL APPEARANCES

COUNTRY	LEVEL	GAMES	GOALS
	Full	0	0
	B	0	0
	U-21	0	0
	Youth	0	0

NAME:	Mark Flatts
CLUB:	Arsenal
BORN:	Islington, 14/10/72
DEBUT v:	Sheffield Utd, 19/9/92
SUBSTITUTED:	3
BOOKINGS:	0
SENDINGS OFF:	0
OWN GOALS:	0
DOMESTIC PENS:	0
HAT-TRICKS:	0
STRIKE RATE (%):	5.00
EVER PRESENT:	–

LEAGUE CLUBS	YEARS	APPS	GOALS	FEE
Arsenal	90-95	16	0	Trainee
Bristol City	95	6	0	Loan
Brighton	94	11	1	Loan
Cambridge	93	5	1	Loan

OVERALL RECORD

COMPETITION	APPS	GOALS	(PENS)	SUBS
League	28	2	0	10
FA Cup	0	0	0	1
League Cup	1	0	0	0
Europe	0	0	–	–
Scottish	0	0	–	–
Other	1	0	–	–

HONOURS

None

INTERNATIONAL APPEARANCES

COUNTRY	LEVEL	GAMES	GOALS
England	Full	0	0
	B	0	0
	U-21	0	0
	Youth	1	0

NAME:	Garry Flitcroft
CLUB:	Manchester City
BORN:	Bolton, 6/11/72
DEBUT v:	Chester, 7/3/92
SUBSTITUTED:	4
BOOKINGS:	14
SENDINGS OFF:	1
OWN GOALS:	1
DOMESTIC PENS:	0
HAT-TRICKS:	0
STRIKE RATE (%):	11.38
EVER PRESENT:	–

LEAGUE CLUBS	YEARS	APPS	GOALS	FEE
Manchester City	91-95	90	13	Trainee
Bury	92	12	0	Loan

OVERALL RECORD

COMPETITION	APPS	GOALS	(PENS)	SUBS
League	96	13	0	6
FA Cup	10	1	0	0
League Cup	10	0	0	1
Europe	0	0	–	–
Scottish	0	0	–	–

HONOURS

None

INTERNATIONAL APPEARANCES

COUNTRY	LEVEL	GAMES	GOALS
England	Full	0	0
	B	0	0
	U-21	11	3
	Youth	1	0

NAME:	Mark Ford
CLUB:	Leeds
BORN:	Pontefract, 10/10/75
DEBUT v:	Swindon, 7/5/94
SUBSTITUTED:	0
BOOKINGS:	0
SENDINGS OFF:	0
OWN GOALS:	0
DOMESTIC PENS:	0
HAT-TRICKS:	0
STRIKE RATE (%):	–
EVER PRESENT:	–

LEAGUE CLUBS	YEARS	APPS	GOALS	FEE
Leeds	93-95	1	0	Trainee

OVERALL RECORD

COMPETITION	APPS	GOALS	(PENS)	SUBS
League	0	0	0	1
FA Cup	0	0	0	0
League Cup	0	0	0	0
Europe	0	0	–	–
Scottish	0	0	–	–

HONOURS

FA Youth Cup 92-93

INTERNATIONAL APPEARANCES

COUNTRY	LEVEL	GAMES	GOALS
England	Full	0	0
	B	0	0
	U-21	0	0
	Youth	5	0

NAME:	Sean Flynn
CLUB:	Coventry
BORN:	Birmingham, 13/3/68
DEBUT v:	Sheffield Utd, 26/12/91
SUBSTITUTED:	13
BOOKINGS:	5
SENDINGS OFF:	0
OWN GOALS:	0
DOMESTIC PENS:	0
HAT-TRICKS:	0
STRIKE RATE (%):	9.52
EVER PRESENT:	–

LEAGUE CLUBS	YEARS	APPS	GOALS	FEE
Coventry	91-95	97	9	£30,000
From: Halesowen Town				

OVERALL RECORD

COMPETITION	APPS	GOALS	(PENS)	SUBS
League	90	9	0	7
FA Cup	3	0	0	0
League Cup	5	1	0	0
Europe	0	0	–	–
Scottish	0	0	–	–

HONOURS

None

INTERNATIONAL APPEARANCES

COUNTRY	LEVEL	GAMES	GOALS
	Full	0	0
	B	0	0
	U-21	0	0
	Youth	0	0

NAME:	Ruel Fox
CLUB:	Newcastle
BORN:	Ipswich, 14/1/68
DEBUT v:	Oxford, 29/11/86
SUBSTITUTED:	23
BOOKINGS:	0
SENDINGS OFF:	0
OWN GOALS:	0
DOMESTIC PENS:	2
HAT-TRICKS:	0
STRIKE RATE (%):	14.34
EVER PRESENT:	–

LEAGUE CLUBS	YEARS	APPS	GOALS	FEE
Newcastle	94-95	55	12	£2.1m
Norwich	86-94	172	22	Appr

OVERALL RECORD

COMPETITION	APPS	GOALS	(PENS)	SUBS
League	203	34	2	24
FA Cup	16	0	0	4
League Cup	15	4	0	3
Europe	10	1	–	–
Scottish	0	0	–	–
Other	9	0	–	–

HONOURS

None

INTERNATIONAL APPEARANCES

COUNTRY	LEVEL	GAMES	GOALS
England	Full	0	0
	B	2	0
	U-21	0	0
	Youth	0	0

NAME:	Scot Gemmill
CLUB:	Nottm Forest
BORN:	Paisley, 2/1/71
DEBUT v:	Wimbledon, 30/3/91
SUBSTITUTED:	9
BOOKINGS:	6
SENDINGS OFF:	0
OWN GOALS:	0
DOMESTIC PENS:	0
HAT-TRICKS:	0
STRIKE RATE (%):	13.84
EVER PRESENT:	–

LEAGUE CLUBS	YEARS	APPS	GOALS	FEE
Nottm Forest	90-95	126	18	Appr

OVERALL RECORD

COMPETITION	APPS	GOALS	(PENS)	SUBS
League	123	18	0	3
FA Cup	11	1	0	0
League Cup	21	3	0	1
Europe	0	0	–	–
Scottish	0	0	–	–
Other	9	3	–	–

HONOURS

League Cup r/u 91-92, PFA Team Award Div 1. 94

INTERNATIONAL APPEARANCES

COUNTRY	LEVEL	GAMES	GOALS
Scotland	Full	2	0
	B	1	0
	U-21	4	0
	Youth	0	0

NAME:	Ryan Giggs
CLUB:	Manchester Utd
BORN:	Cardiff, 29/11/73
DEBUT v:	Everton, 2/3/91
SUBSTITUTED:	24
BOOKINGS:	6
SENDINGS OFF:	0
OWN GOALS:	0
DOMESTIC PENS:	0
HAT-TRICKS:	0
STRIKE RATE (%):	20.00
EVER PRESENT:	–

LEAGUE CLUBS	YEARS	APPS	GOALS	FEE
Manchester Utd	90-95	148	27	Appr

OVERALL RECORD

COMPETITION	APPS	GOALS	(PENS)	SUBS
League	134	27	0	14
FA Cup	17	4	0	2
League Cup	14	6	0	4
Europe	9	2	–	–
Scottish	0	0	–	–
Other	3	0	–	–

HONOURS

League Championship 92-93, 93-94, FA Cup 93-94, FA Cup r/u 94-95, League Cup 91-92, League Cup r/u 93-94, Charity Shield medal 93, 94, PFA Young Player of the Year 91-92, 92-93, PFA Team Award Premier League 93

INTERNATIONAL APPEARANCES

COUNTRY	LEVEL	GAMES	GOALS
Wales	Full	13	3
	B	0	0
	U-21	1	0
	Youth	0	0

NAME:	Keith Gillespie
CLUB:	Newcastle
BORN:	Bangor, 18/2/75
DEBUT v:	Doncaster, 4/9/93
SUBSTITUTED:	5
BOOKINGS:	8
SENDINGS OFF:	0
OWN GOALS:	0
DOMESTIC PENS:	0
HAT-TRICKS:	0
STRIKE RATE (%):	24.39
EVER PRESENT:	–

LEAGUE CLUBS	YEARS	APPS	GOALS	FEE
Newcastle	95	17	2	£1m
Wigan	93-94	8	4	Loan
Manchester Utd	93-95	9	1	Trainee

OVERALL RECORD

COMPETITION	APPS	GOALS	(PENS)	SUBS
League	26	7	0	8
FA Cup	4	3	0	0
League Cup	3	0	0	0
Europe	0	0	–	–
Scottish	0	0	–	–
Other	2	0	–	–

HONOURS

Charity Shield medal 94, FA Youth Cup r/u 92-93

INTERNATIONAL APPEARANCES

COUNTRY	LEVEL	GAMES	GOALS
N. Ireland	Full	6	1
	B	0	0
	U-21	1	0
	Youth	0	0

NAME:	Dale Gordon
CLUB:	West Ham
BORN:	Great Yarmouth, 9/1/67
DEBUT v:	Liverpool, 25/8/84
SUBSTITUTED:	23
BOOKINGS:	11
SENDINGS OFF:	0
OWN GOALS:	0
DOMESTIC PENS:	0
HAT-TRICKS:	0
STRIKE RATE (%):	15.91
EVER PRESENT:	88-89

LEAGUE CLUBS	YEARS	APPS	GOALS	FEE
West Ham	93-95	8	1	£750,000
Peterborough	95	6	1	Loan
Rangers	91-93	44	6	£1.2m
Norwich	84-91	206	31	Appr

OVERALL RECORD

COMPETITION	APPS	GOALS	(PENS)	SUBS
League	208	33	0	12
FA Cup	19	6	0	0
League Cup	25	3	0	0
Europe	1	0	–	–
Scottish	53	7	–	–
Other	16	3	–	–

HONOURS

Scottish Premier League 91-92, 92-93, Scottish Cup 91-92, Scottish League Cup 92-93

INTERNATIONAL APPEARANCES

COUNTRY	LEVEL	GAMES	GOALS
England	Full	0	0
	B	2	0
	U-21	4	0
	Youth	1	0

NAME:	Tony Grant
CLUB:	Everton
BORN:	Liverpool, 14/11/74
DEBUT v:	Newcastle, 1/2/95
SUBSTITUTED:	1
BOOKINGS:	0
SENDINGS OFF:	0
OWN GOALS:	0
DOMESTIC PENS:	0
HAT-TRICKS:	0
STRIKE RATE (%):	–
EVER PRESENT:	–

LEAGUE CLUBS	YEARS	APPS	GOALS	FEE
Everton	92-95	5	0	Trainee

OVERALL RECORD

COMPETITION	APPS	GOALS	(PENS)	SUBS
League	1	0	0	4
FA Cup	0	0	0	0
League Cup	0	0	0	0
Europe	0	0	–	–
Scottish	0	0	–	–
Other	0	0	–	–

HONOURS

None

INTERNATIONAL APPEARANCES

COUNTRY	LEVEL	GAMES	GOALS
	Full	0	0
	B	0	0
	U-21	0	0
	Youth	0	0

NAME:	Ruud Gullit
CLUB:	Chelsea
BORN:	Amsterdam, 1/9/62
DEBUT v:	–
SUBSTITUTED:	0
BOOKINGS:	0
SENDINGS OFF:	0
OWN GOALS:	0
DOMESTIC PENS:	0
HAT-TRICKS:	0
STRIKE RATE (%):	–
EVER PRESENT:	–

LEAGUE CLUBS	YEARS	APPS	GOALS	FEE
Chelsea	95	0	0	Free
From: Sampdoria				

OVERALL RECORD

COMPETITION	APPS	GOALS	(PENS)	SUBS
League	0	0	0	0
FA Cup	0	0	0	0
League Cup	0	0	0	0
Europe	30	7	–	–
Scottish	0	0	–	–

HONOURS

European Nations Cup 88, Dutch Championship 83-84, 85-86, 86-87, Dutch Cup 83-84, Italian Championship 87-88, 91-92, 92-93, Italian Cup 93-94, Italian Cup r/u 89-90, European Cup 88-89, 89-90, European and World Footballer of the Year 87

INTERNATIONAL APPEARANCES

COUNTRY	LEVEL	GAMES	GOALS
Holland	Full	66	16
	B	0	0
	U-21	0	0
	Youth	0	0

NAME:	Alf Inge Haaland
CLUB:	Nottingham Forest
BORN:	Norway, 23/11/72
DEBUT v:	Leicester, 6/2/94
SUBSTITUTED:	1
BOOKINGS:	3
SENDINGS OFF:	0
OWN GOALS:	0
DOMESTIC PENS:	0
HAT-TRICKS:	–
STRIKE RATE (%):	–
EVER PRESENT:	

LEAGUE CLUBS	YEARS	APPS	GOALS	FEE
Nottingham Forest	94-95	23	1	£250,000
From: Byrne SK				

OVERALL RECORD

COMPETITION	APPS	GOALS	(PENS)	SUBS
League	21	1	0	2
FA Cup	1	0	0	0
League Cup	0	0	0	1
Europe	0	0	–	–
Scottish	0	0	–	–

HONOURS

None

INTERNATIONAL APPEARANCES

COUNTRY	LEVEL	GAMES	GOALS
Norway	Full	6	0
	B	0	0
	U-21	0	0
	Youth	0	0

NAME:	Marcus Hall
CLUB:	Coventry
BORN:	Coventry, 24/4/76
DEBUT v:	Tottenham, 31/12/94
SUBSTITUTED:	0
BOOKINGS:	1
SENDINGS OFF:	0
OWN GOALS:	0
DOMESTIC PENS:	0
HAT-TRICKS:	0
STRIKE RATE (%):	–
EVER PRESENT:	–

LEAGUE CLUBS	YEARS	APPS	GOALS	FEE
Coventry	94-95	5	0	Trainee

OVERALL RECORD

COMPETITION	APPS	GOALS	(PENS)	SUBS
League	2	0	0	3
FA Cup	0	0	0	0
League Cup	0	0	0	0
Europe	0	0	–	–
Scottish	0	0	–	–

HONOURS

None

INTERNATIONAL APPEARANCES

COUNTRY	LEVEL	GAMES	GOALS
	Full	0	0
	B	0	0
	U-21	0	0
	Youth	0	0

NAME:	Mickey Hazard
CLUB:	Tottenham
BORN:	Sunderland, 5/2/60
DEBUT v:	Everton, 19/4/80
SUBSTITUTED:	56
BOOKINGS:	11
SENDINGS OFF:	0
OWN GOALS:	0
DOMESTIC PENS:	11
HAT-TRICKS:	0
STRIKE RATE (%):	13.33
EVER PRESENT:	–

LEAGUE CLUBS	YEARS	APPS	GOALS	FEE
Tottenham	93-95	28	2	£50,000
Swindon	90-93	119	17	£130,000
Portsmouth	90	8	1	£100,000
Chelsea	85-90	81	9	£310,000
Tottenham	78-85	91	13	Appr

OVERALL RECORD

COMPETITION	APPS	GOALS	(PENS)	SUBS
League	286	42	11	41
FA Cup	20	3	0	5
League Cup	31	7	0	7
Europe	22	2	–	–
Scottish	0	0	–	–
Other	13	3	–	–

HONOURS

FA Cup 81-82, League Cup r/u 81-82, Charity Shield medal 82, UEFA Cup 83-84, PFA Team Awards: Div 2. 92; Div 1. 93

INTERNATIONAL APPEARANCES

COUNTRY	LEVEL	GAMES	GOALS
England	Full	0	0
	B	1	0
	U-21	0	0
	Youth	0	0

NAME:	Neil Heaney
CLUB:	Southampton
BORN:	Middlesbrough, 3/11/71
DEBUT v:	Chesterfield, 19/1/91
SUBSTITUTED:	11
BOOKINGS:	4
SENDINGS OFF:	0
OWN GOALS:	1
DOMESTIC PENS:	0
HAT-TRICKS:	0
STRIKE RATE (%):	8.70
EVER PRESENT:	–

LEAGUE CLUBS	YEARS	APPS	GOALS	FEE
Southampton	94-95	36	2	£300,000
Cambridge	92	13	2	Loan
Hartlepool	91	3	0	Loan
Arsenal	89-94	7	0	Trainee

OVERALL RECORD

COMPETITION	APPS	GOALS	(PENS)	SUBS
League	38	4	0	21
FA Cup	6	2	0	0
League Cup	2	0	0	2
Europe	0	0	–	–
Scottish	0	0	–	–

HONOURS

FA Youth Cup 87-88

INTERNATIONAL APPEARANCES

COUNTRY	LEVEL	GAMES	GOALS
England	Full	0	0
	B	0	0
	U-21	6	0
	Youth	2	1

NAME:	Glenn Helder
CLUB:	Arsenal
BORN:	Holland, 28/10/68
DEBUT v:	Nottm Forest, 21/2/95
SUBSTITUTED:	5
BOOKINGS:	0
SENDINGS OFF:	0
OWN GOALS:	0
DOMESTIC PENS:	0
HAT-TRICKS:	0
STRIKE RATE (%):	–
EVER PRESENT:	–

LEAGUE CLUBS	YEARS	APPS	GOALS	FEE
Arsenal	95	13	0	£2m
From: Vitesse Arnhem				

OVERALL RECORD

COMPETITION	APPS	GOALS	(PENS)	SUBS
League	12	0	0	1
FA Cup	0	0	0	0
League Cup	0	0	0	0
Europe	4	0	–	–
Scottish	0	0	–	–

HONOURS

None

INTERNATIONAL APPEARANCES

COUNTRY	LEVEL	GAMES	GOALS
Holland	Full	1	0
	B	0	0
	U-21	0	0
	Youth	0	0

NAME:	Danny Hill
CLUB:	Tottenham
BORN:	Enfield, 1/10/74
DEBUT v:	Chelsea, 20/3/93
SUBSTITUTED:	1
BOOKINGS:	0
SENDINGS OFF:	0
OWN GOALS:	0
DOMESTIC PENS:	0
HAT-TRICKS:	0
STRIKE RATE (%):	–
EVER PRESENT:	–

LEAGUE CLUBS	YEARS	APPS	GOALS	FEE
Tottenham	92-95	10	0	Trainee

OVERALL RECORD

COMPETITION	APPS	GOALS	(PENS)	SUBS
League	5	0	0	5
FA Cup	0	0	0	0
League Cup	0	0	0	2
Europe	0	0		
Scottish	0	0		
Other	1	0		

CLUB HONOURS

None

INTERNATIONAL APPEARANCES

COUNTRY	LEVEL	GAMES	GOALS
England	Full	0	0
	B	0	0
	U-21	4	0
	Youth	1	0

NAME:	David Hillier
CLUB:	Arsenal
BORN:	Blackheath, 19/12/69
DEBUT v:	Leeds, 29/9/90
SUBSTITUTED:	20
BOOKINGS:	8
SENDINGS OFF:	0
OWN GOALS:	0
DOMESTIC PENS:	0
HAT-TRICKS:	0
STRIKE RATE (%):	1.60
EVER PRESENT:	–

LEAGUE CLUBS	YEARS	APPS	GOALS	FEE
Arsenal	88-95	97	2	Trainee

OVERALL RECORD

COMPETITION	APPS	GOALS	(PENS)	SUBS
League	79	2	0	18
FA Cup	13	0	0	2
League Cup	11	0	0	2
Europe	7	0	–	–
Scottish	0	0	–	–
Other	4	0	–	–

HONOURS

League Championship 90-91, FA Youth Cup 87-88, Charity Shield medal 91, European Cup Winners' Cup r/u 94-95

INTERNATIONAL APPEARANCES

COUNTRY	LEVEL	GAMES	GOALS
England	Full	0	0
	B	0	0
	U-21	1	0
	Youth	0	0

NAME:	Glenn Hoddle
CLUB:	Chelsea
BORN:	Hayes, 27/10/57
DEBUT v:	Norwich, 30/8/75
SUBSTITUTED:	22
BOOKINGS:	3
SENDINGS OFF:	0
OWN GOALS:	0
DOMESTIC PENS:	28
HAT-TRICKS:	1
STRIKE RATE (%):	19.41
EVER PRESENT:	–

LEAGUE CLUBS	YEARS	APPS	GOALS	FEE
Chelsea	93-95	31	1	£175,000
Swindon	91-93	64	1	Free
From: Monaco				
Tottenham	75-87	378	88	Appr

OVERALL RECORD

COMPETITION	APPS	GOALS	(PENS)	SUBS
League	453	90	25	20
FA Cup	48	11	2	3
League Cup	53	11	1	0
Europe	28	1	–	–
Scottish	0	0	–	–
Other	10	0	–	–

HONOURS

FA Cup 80-81, 81-82, FA Cup r/u 86-87, 93-94, League Cup r/u 81-82, French Championship 87-88, French Cup 90-91, French Cup r/u 88-89, Charity Shield medal 81, 82, PFA Young Player of the Year 79-80, PFA Team Awards: Div 2. 78; Div 1. 80, 82, 84, 86, 87

INTERNATIONAL APPEARANCES

COUNTRY	LEVEL	GAMES	GOALS
England	Full	53	8
	B	4	1
	U-21	12	2
	Youth	2	0

NAME:	Steve Hodge
CLUB:	Q.P.R.
BORN:	Nottingham, 25/10/62
DEBUT v:	Ipswich, 15/5/82
SUBSTITUTED:	29
BOOKINGS:	16
SENDINGS OFF:	0
OWN GOALS:	1
DOMESTIC PENS:	0
HAT-TRICKS:	0
STRIKE RATE (%):	21.03
EVER PRESENT:	84-85

LEAGUE CLUBS	YEARS	APPS	GOALS	FEE
Q.P.R.	94-95	15	0	£250,000
Derby	94	9	2	Loan
Leeds	91-94	54	10	£900,000
Nottm Forest	88-91	82	20	£550,000
Tottenham	86-88	45	7	£650,000
Aston Villa	85-86	53	12	£450,000
Nottm Forest	80-85	123	30	Appr

OVERALL RECORD

COMPETITION	APPS	GOALS	(PENS)	SUBS
League	349	81	0	32
FA Cup	31	6	0	2
League Cup	48	11	0	4
Europe	13	5	–	–
Scottish	0	0	–	–
Other	13	4	–	–

HONOURS

League Championship 91-92, FA Cup r/u 86-87, 90-91, League Cup 88-89, 89-90, Charity Shield medal 92

INTERNATIONAL APPEARANCES

COUNTRY	LEVEL	GAMES	GOALS
England	Full	24	0
	B	2	1
	U-21	6	3
	Youth	0	0

NAME:	Chris Holland
CLUB:	Newcastle
BORN:	Whalley, 11/9/75
DEBUT v:	Wigan, 16/10/93
SUBSTITUTED:	1
BOOKINGS:	0
SENDINGS OFF:	0
OWN GOALS:	0
DOMESTIC PENS:	0
HAT-TRICKS:	0
STRIKE RATE (%):	–
EVER PRESENT:	–

LEAGUE CLUBS	YEARS	APPS	GOALS	FEE
Newcastle	93-95	3	0	£60,000
Preston	93	1	0	Trainee

OVERALL RECORD

COMPETITION	APPS	GOALS	(PENS)	SUBS
League	2	0	0	2
FA Cup	0	0	0	0
League Cup	0	0	0	0
Europe	0	0	–	–
Scottish	0	0	–	–
Other	1	0	–	–

HONOURS

None

INTERNATIONAL APPEARANCES

COUNTRY	LEVEL	GAMES	GOALS
England	Full	0	0
	B	0	0
	U-21	0	0
	Youth	9	0

NAME:	Ian Holloway
CLUB:	Q.P.R.
BORN:	Kingswood, 12/3/63
DEBUT v:	Wrexham, 25/4/81
SUBSTITUTED:	26
BOOKINGS:	23
SENDINGS OFF:	1
OWN GOALS:	1
DOMESTIC PENS:	12
HAT-TRICKS:	0
STRIKE RATE (%):	10.06
EVER PRESENT:	89-90, 90-91

LEAGUE CLUBS	YEARS	APPS	GOALS	FEE
Q.P.R.	91-95	114	3	£230,000
Bristol Rovers	87-91	179	26	£10,000
Torquay	87	5	0	Loan
Brentford	86-87	29	2	£25,000
Wimbledon	85-86	19	2	£35,000
Bristol Rovers	81-85	111	14	Appr

OVERALL RECORD

COMPETITION	APPS	GOALS	(PENS)	SUBS
League	432	47	11	26
FA Cup	28	4	1	1
League Cup	30	1	0	1
Europe	0	0	–	–
Scottish	0	0	–	–
Other	28	3	–	–

HONOURS

Division Three Championship 89-90

INTERNATIONAL APPEARANCES

COUNTRY	LEVEL	GAMES	GOALS
	Full	0	0
	B	0	0
	U-21	0	0
	Youth	0	0

NAME:	Matt Holmes
CLUB:	West Ham
BORN:	Luton, 1/8/69
DEBUT v:	Aldershot, 25/3/89
SUBSTITUTED:	49
BOOKINGS:	7
SENDINGS OFF:	0
OWN GOALS:	0
DOMESTIC PENS:	0
HAT-TRICKS:	0
STRIKE RATE (%):	5.96
EVER PRESENT:	91-92

LEAGUE CLUBS	YEARS	APPS	GOALS	FEE
West Ham	92-95	76	5	£40,000
Cardiff	89	1	0	Loan
Bournemouth	88-92	114	8	Appr

OVERALL RECORD

COMPETITION	APPS	GOALS	(PENS)	SUBS
League	168	13	0	23
FA Cup	14	0	0	2
League Cup	11	0	0	0
Europe	0	0	–	–
Scottish	0	0	–	–
Other	8	1	–	–

HONOURS

None

INTERNATIONAL APPEARANCES

COUNTRY	LEVEL	GAMES	GOALS
	Full	0	0
	B	0	0
	U-21	0	0
	Youth	0	0

NAME:	Paul Holmes
CLUB:	Everton
BORN:	Stocksbridge, 18/2/68
DEBUT v:	Wigan, 5/11/85
SUBSTITUTED:	16
BOOKINGS:	5
SENDINGS OFF:	0
OWN GOALS:	1
DOMESTIC PENS:	0
HAT-TRICKS:	0
STRIKE RATE (%):	2.43
EVER PRESENT:	–

LEAGUE CLUBS	YEARS	APPS	GOALS	FEE
Everton	93-95	20	0	£100,000
Birmingham	92-93	12	0	£40,000
Torquay	88-92	138	4	£6,000
Doncaster	85-88	47	1	Appr

OVERALL RECORD

COMPETITION	APPS	GOALS	(PENS)	SUBS
League	201	5	0	16
FA Cup	13	1	0	4
League Cup	13	0	0	0
Europe	0	0	–	–
Scottish	0	0	–	–
Other	17	0	–	–

HONOURS

None

INTERNATIONAL APPEARANCES

COUNTRY	LEVEL	GAMES	GOALS
	Full	0	0
	B	0	0
	U-21	0	0
	Youth	0	0

NAME:	David Hopkin
CLUB:	Chelsea
BORN:	Greenock, 21/8/70
DEBUT v:	Albion, 17/3/91
SUBSTITUTED:	10
BOOKINGS:	2
SENDINGS OFF:	0
OWN GOALS:	0
DOMESTIC PENS:	0
HAT-TRICKS:	0
STRIKE RATE (%):	4.35
EVER PRESENT:	–

LEAGUE CLUBS	YEARS	APPS	GOALS	FEE
Chelsea	92-95	40	2	£300,000
Morton	89-92	48	4	Appr

OVERALL RECORD

COMPETITION	APPS	GOALS	(PENS)	SUBS
League	21	2	0	19
FA Cup	3	0	0	2
League Cup	0	0	0	1
Europe	0	0	–	–
Scottish	52	7	–	–

HONOURS

None

INTERNATIONAL APPEARANCES

COUNTRY	LEVEL	GAMES	GOALS
	Full	0	0
	B	0	0
	U-21	0	0
	Youth	0	0

NAME:	Barry Horne
CLUB:	Everton
BORN:	St. Asaph, 18/5/62
DEBUT v:	Swindon, 24/8/84
SUBSTITUTED:	18
BOOKINGS:	26
SENDINGS OFF:	3
OWN GOALS:	0
DOMESTIC PENS:	0
HAT-TRICKS:	0
STRIKE RATE (%):	8.33
EVER PRESENT:	85-86, 86-87, 90-91

LEAGUE CLUBS	YEARS	APPS	GOALS	FEE
Everton	92-95	97	2	£675,000
Southampton	89-92	112	6	£700,000
Portsmouth	87-89	70	7	£60,000
Wrexham	84-87	136	17	–
From: Rwyl				

OVERALL RECORD

COMPETITION	APPS	GOALS	(PENS)	SUBS
League	406	32	0	9
FA Cup	35	5	0	1
League Cup	38	4	0	3
Europe	6	1	–	–
Scottish	0	0	–	–
Other	16	3	–	–

HONOURS

FA Cup 94-95

INTERNATIONAL APPEARANCES

COUNTRY	LEVEL	GAMES	GOALS
Wales	Full	49	2
	B	0	0
	U-21	0	0
	Youth	0	0

NAME:	Steve Howe
CLUB:	Nottm Forest
BORN:	Annitsford, 6/11/73
DEBUT v:	Bolton, 6/9/93
SUBSTITUTED:	1
BOOKINGS:	0
SENDINGS OFF:	0
OWN GOALS:	0
DOMESTIC PENS:	0
HAT-TRICKS:	0
STRIKE RATE (%):	–
EVER PRESENT:	–

LEAGUE CLUBS	YEARS	APPS	GOALS	FEE
Nottm Forest	91-95	4	0	Trainee

OVERALL RECORD

COMPETITION	APPS	GOALS	(PENS)	SUBS
League	2	0	0	2
FA Cup	0	0	0	0
League Cup	1	0	0	0
Europe	0	0	–	–
Scottish	0	0	–	–

HONOURS

None

INTERNATIONAL APPEARANCES

COUNTRY	LEVEL	GAMES	GOALS
England	Full	0	0
	B	0	0
	U-21	0	0
	Youth	5	0

NAME:	David Howells
CLUB:	Tottenham
BORN:	Guildford, 15/12/67
DEBUT v:	Sheffield Wed, 22/2/86
SUBSTITUTED:	42
BOOKINGS:	8
SENDINGS OFF:	0
OWN GOALS:	0
DOMESTIC PENS:	0
HAT-TRICKS:	0
STRIKE RATE (%):	8.86
EVER PRESENT:	–

LEAGUE CLUBS	YEARS	APPS	GOALS	FEE
Tottenham	85-95	196	17	Trainee

OVERALL RECORD

COMPETITION	APPS	GOALS	(PENS)	SUBS
League	163	17	0	33
FA Cup	14	1	0	3
League Cup	19	3	0	5
Europe	6	0	–	–
Scottish	0	0	–	–
Other	1	0	–	–

HONOURS

FA Cup 90-91, Charity Shield medal 91

INTERNATIONAL APPEARANCES

COUNTRY	LEVEL	GAMES	GOALS
England	Full	0	0
	B	1	0
	U-21	0	0
	Youth	7	1

NAME:	David Hughes
CLUB:	Southampton
BORN:	St Albans, 30/12/72
DEBUT v:	Oldham, 3/1/94
SUBSTITUTED:	1
BOOKINGS:	2
SENDINGS OFF:	0
OWN GOALS:	0
DOMESTIC PENS:	0
HAT-TRICKS:	0
STRIKE RATE (%):	–
EVER PRESENT:	–

LEAGUE CLUBS	YEARS	APPS	GOALS	FEE
Southampton	91-95	14	2	Trainee

OVERALL RECORD

COMPETITION	APPS	GOALS	(PENS)	SUBS
League	2	2	0	12
FA Cup	0	1	0	4
League Cup	0	0	0	0
Europe	0	0	–	–
Scottish	0	0	–	–

HONOURS

None

INTERNATIONAL APPEARANCES

COUNTRY	LEVEL	GAMES	GOALS
Wales	Full	0	0
	B	0	0
	U-21	1	0
	Youth	0	0

NAME:	Michael Hughes
CLUB:	West Ham
BORN:	Larne 2/8/71
DEBUT v:	Plymouth 15/10/98
SUBSTITUTED:	12
BOOKINGS:	0
SENDINGS OFF:	0
OWN GOALS:	0
DOMESTIC PENS:	0
HAT-TRICKS:	0
STRIKE RATE (%):	5.88
EVER PRESENT:	–

LEAGUE CLUBS	YEARS	APPS	GOALS	FEE
West Ham	94-95	17	2	Loan
Strasbourg	92-94	57	11	£700,000
Manchester City	88-92	26	1	£10,000

OVERALL RECORD

COMPETITION	APPS	GOALS	(PENS)	SUBS
League	40	3	0	3
FA Cup	3	0	0	0
League Cup	5	0	0	0
Europe	0	0	–	–
Scottish	0	0	–	–
Other	62	11		

HONOURS

FA Youth Cup r/u 88-89

INTERNATIONAL APPEARANCES

COUNTRY	LEVEL	GAMES	GOALS
N. Ireland	Full	24	1
	B	0	0
	U-21	2	0
	Youth	0	0

NAME:	Stephen Hughes
CLUB:	Arsenal
BORN:	Wokingham, 18/9/76
DEBUT v:	Aston Villa, 26/12/94
SUBSTITUTED:	1
BOOKINGS:	0
SENDINGS OFF:	0
OWN GOALS:	0
DOMESTIC PENS:	0
HAT-TRICKS:	0
STRIKE RATE (%):	–
EVER PRESENT:	–

LEAGUE CLUBS	YEARS	APPS	GOALS	FEE
Arsenal	94-95	1	0	Appr

OVERALL RECORD

COMPETITION	APPS	GOALS	(PENS)	SUBS
League	1	0	0	0
FA Cup	0	0	0	0
League Cup	0	0	0	0
Europe	0	0	–	–
Scottish	0	0	–	–

HONOURS

FA Youth Cup 93-94

INTERNATIONAL APPEARANCES

COUNTRY	LEVEL	GAMES	GOALS
	Full	0	0
	B	0	0
	U-21	0	0
	Youth	0	0

NAME:	Don Hutchison
CLUB:	West Ham
BORN:	Gateshead, 9/5/71
DEBUT v:	Scunthorpe, 7/10/89
SUBSTITUTED:	18
BOOKINGS:	12
SENDINGS OFF:	2
OWN GOALS:	0
DOMESTIC PENS:	1
HAT-TRICKS:	0
STRIKE RATE (%):	20.91
EVER PRESENT:	–

LEAGUE CLUBS	YEARS	APPS	GOALS	FEE
West Ham	94-95	23	9	£1.5m
Liverpool	90-94	45	7	£175,000
Hartlepool	89-90	24	3	Trainee

OVERALL RECORD

COMPETITION	APPS	GOALS	(PENS)	SUBS
League	74	19	1	18
FA Cup	3	0	0	3
League Cup	11	4	0	1
Europe	3	1	–	–
Scottish	0	0	–	–
Other	2	0	–	–

HONOURS

Charity Shield medal 92

INTERNATIONAL APPEARANCES

COUNTRY	LEVEL	GAMES	GOALS
Scotland	Full	0	0
	B	1	0
	U-21	0	0
	Youth	0	0

NAME:	Graham Hyde
CLUB:	Sheffield Wed
BORN:	Doncaster, 10/11/70
DEBUT v:	Man City, 14/9/91
SUBSTITUTED:	15
BOOKINGS:	14
SENDINGS OFF:	0
OWN GOALS:	0
DOMESTIC PENS:	0
HAT-TRICKS:	0
STRIKE RATE (%):	7.52
EVER PRESENT:	–

LEAGUE CLUBS	YEARS	APPS	GOALS	FEE
Sheffield Wed	88-95	104	7	Trainee

OVERALL RECORD

COMPETITION	APPS	GOALS	(PENS)	SUBS
League	84	7	0	20
FA Cup	7	1	0	6
League Cup	14	2	0	2
Europe	3	0	–	–
Scottish	0	0	–	–
Other	1	1	–	–

HONOURS

FA Cup r/u 92-93, League Cup r/u 92-93

INTERNATIONAL APPEARANCES

COUNTRY	LEVEL	GAMES	GOALS
	Full	0	0
	B	0	0
	U-21	0	0
	Youth	0	0

NAME:	Andy Impey
CLUB:	Q.P.R.
BORN:	Hammersmith, 30/9/71
DEBUT v:	Coventry, 11/1/92
SUBSTITUTED:	10
BOOKINGS:	9
SENDINGS OFF:	0
OWN GOALS:	0
DOMESTIC PENS:	0
HAT-TRICKS:	0
STRIKE RATE (%):	7.09
EVER PRESENT:	–

LEAGUE CLUBS	YEARS	APPS	GOALS	FEE
Q.P.R.	90-95	125	8	£35,000
From: Yeading				

OVERALL RECORD

COMPETITION	APPS	GOALS	(PENS)	SUBS
League	122	8	0	3
FA Cup	4	1	0	2
League Cup	9	1	0	1
Europe	0	0	–	–
Scottish	0	0	–	–
Other	2	1	–	–

HONOURS

None

INTERNATIONAL APPEARANCES

COUNTRY	LEVEL	GAMES	GOALS
England	Full	0	0
	B	0	0
	U-21	1	0
	Youth	0	0

NAME:	Klas Ingesson
CLUB:	Sheffield Wed
BORN:	Sweden, 20/8/68
DEBUT v:	Nottm Forest, 10/9/94
SUBSTITUTED:	3
BOOKINGS:	2
SENDINGS OFF:	0
OWN GOALS:	0
DOMESTIC PENS:	0
HAT-TRICKS:	0
STRIKE RATE (%):	–
EVER PRESENT:	–

LEAGUE CLUBS	YEARS	APPS	GOALS	FEE
Sheffield Wed	94-95	13	2	£2m
From: PSV Eindhoven				

OVERALL RECORD

COMPETITION	APPS	GOALS	(PENS)	SUBS
League	9	2	0	4
FA Cup	1	0	0	0
League Cup	1	0	0	0
Europe	0	0	–	–
Scottish	0	0	–	–

HONOURS

Belgian Cup r/u 91-92

INTERNATIONAL APPEARANCES

COUNTRY	LEVEL	GAMES	GOALS
Sweden	Full	50	11
	B	0	0
	U-21	0	0
	Youth	0	0

NAME:	Leigh Jenkinson
CLUB:	Coventry
BORN:	Thorne, 9/7/69
DEBUT v:	Sheffield Utd, 27/2/88
SUBSTITUTED:	20
BOOKINGS:	6
SENDINGS OFF:	1
OWN GOALS:	0
DOMESTIC PENS:	1
HAT-TRICKS:	0
STRIKE RATE (%):	7.85
EVER PRESENT:	–

LEAGUE CLUBS	YEARS	APPS	GOALS	FEE
Coventry	93-95	32	1	£300,000
Birmingham	94	3	0	Loan
Rotherham	90	7	0	Loan
Hull	87-93	130	13	Trainee

OVERALL RECORD

COMPETITION	APPS	GOALS	(PENS)	SUBS
League	124	14	1	48
FA Cup	9	0	0	0
League Cup	7	1	0	3
Europe	0	0	–	–
Scottish	0	0	–	–
Other	11	1	–	–

HONOURS

None

INTERNATIONAL APPEARANCES

COUNTRY	LEVEL	GAMES	GOALS
	Full	0	0
	B	0	0
	U-21	0	0
	Youth	0	0

NAME:	John Jensen
CLUB:	Arsenal
BORN:	Copenhagen, 3/5/65
DEBUT v:	Norwich, 15/8/92
SUBSTITUTED:	25
BOOKINGS:	10
SENDINGS OFF:	0
OWN GOALS:	0
DOMESTIC PENS:	0
HAT-TRICKS:	0
STRIKE RATE (%):	1.01
EVER PRESENT:	–

LEAGUE CLUBS	YEARS	APPS	GOALS	FEE
Arsenal	92-95	83	1	£1.1m
From: Brondby				

OVERALL RECORD

COMPETITION	APPS	GOALS	(PENS)	SUBS
League	80	1	0	3
FA Cup	6	0	0	0
League Cup	9	0	0	1
Europe	13	0	–	–
Scottish	0	0	–	–
Other	3	0	–	–

HONOURS

European Nations Cup 92, FA Cup 92-93, Charity Shield medal 93, European Cup Winners' Cup 93-94, Danish Championship 86-87, Danish Cup r/u 87

INTERNATIONAL APPEARANCES

COUNTRY	LEVEL	GAMES	GOALS
Denmark	Full	72	3
	B	0	0
	U-21	0	0
	Youth	0	0

Flower-power:
Tim looks forward to the European Cup
and tries to forget the Umbro Cup

Bardsley: England seem to have slammed the door in his face

More goals than sendings-off in 94-95.
Is West Ham's 'terminator' reformed ?

Liverpool's attacking central defender Dr Ruddock recommends opthalmic treatment for his friend the ref

*Anderton… in search of
that elusive 25th League goal*

Fox: was he Chased or did this canary fly into Keegan's nest of his own accord

Haircuts and goals: Stan's always good for the 'odd' one or two

Sharp-shooter Cole looks forward to French lessons from the master

NAME:	Ryan Jones
CLUB:	Sheffield Wed
BORN:	Sheffield, 23/7/73
DEBUT v:	Coventry, 3/3/93
SUBSTITUTED:	4
BOOKINGS:	2
SENDINGS OFF:	0
OWN GOALS:	0
DOMESTIC PENS:	0
HAT-TRICKS:	0
STRIKE RATE (%):	14.29
EVER PRESENT:	–

LEAGUE CLUBS	YEARS	APPS	GOALS	FEE
Sheffield Wed	91-95	41	6	Trainee

OVERALL RECORD

COMPETITION	APPS	GOALS	(PENS)	SUBS
League	36	6	0	5
FA Cup	3	0	0	0
League Cup	4	1	0	1
Europe	0	0	–	–
Scottish	0	0	–	–

HONOURS

FA Youth Cup r/u 90-91

INTERNATIONAL APPEARANCES

COUNTRY	LEVEL	GAMES	GOALS
Wales	Full	1	0
	B	1	0
	U-21	3	0
	Youth	0	0

NAME:	Vinnie Jones
CLUB:	Wimbledon
BORN:	Watford, 5/1/65
DEBUT v:	Nottm Forest, 22/11/86
SUBSTITUTED:	22
BOOKINGS:	53
SENDINGS OFF:	5
OWN GOALS:	1
DOMESTIC PENS:	1
HAT-TRICKS:	0
STRIKE RATE (%):	8.70
EVER PRESENT:	–

LEAGUE CLUBS	YEARS	APPS	GOALS	FEE
Wimbledon	92-95	92	6	£700,000
Chelsea	91-92	42	4	£575,000
Sheffield Utd	90-91	35	2	£700,000
Leeds	89-90	46	5	£650,000
Wimbledon	86-89	77	9	£10,000
From: Wealdstone				

OVERALL RECORD

COMPETITION	APPS	GOALS	(PENS)	SUBS
League	290	26	1	2
FA Cup	25	2	0	2
League Cup	24	2	0	2
Europe	0	0	–	–
Scottish	0	0	–	–
Other	13	2	–	–

HONOURS

Division Two Championship 89-90, FA Cup 87-88

INTERNATIONAL APPEARANCES

COUNTRY	LEVEL	GAMES	GOALS
Wales	Full	4	0
	B	0	0
	U-21	0	0
	Youth	0	0

NAME:	Andrei Kanchelskis
CLUB:	Manchester Utd
BORN:	Kirovograd, USSR 23/1/69
DEBUT v:	Crystal Palace, 11/5/91
SUBSTITUTED:	30
BOOKINGS:	3
SENDINGS OFF:	1
OWN GOALS:	0
DOMESTIC PENS:	0
HAT-TRICKS:	1
STRIKE RATE (%):	22.52
EVER PRESENT:	–

LEAGUE CLUBS	YEARS	APPS	GOALS	FEE
Manchester Utd	91-95	123	27	£650,000
From: Donezts				

OVERALL RECORD

COMPETITION	APPS	GOALS	(PENS)	SUBS
League	96	27	0	27
FA Cup	11	4	0	1
League Cup	15	3	0	1
Europe	8	1	–	–
Scottish	0	0	–	–
Other	3	0	–	–

HONOURS

League Championship 92-93, 93-94, FA Cup 93-94, League Cup 91-92, League Cup r/u 93-94, Charity Shield medal 93, 94

INTERNATIONAL APPEARANCES

COUNTRY	LEVEL	GAMES	GOALS
Russia	Full	34	6
	B	0	0
	U-21	0	0
	Youth	0	0

NAME:	Graham Kavanagh
CLUB:	Middlesbrough
BORN:	Dublin, 2/12/73
DEBUT v:	Nottm Forest, 21/10/92
SUBSTITUTED:	6
BOOKINGS:	4
SENDINGS OFF:	0
OWN GOALS:	0
DOMESTIC PENS:	0
HAT-TRICKS:	0
STRIKE RATE (%):	–
EVER PRESENT:	–

LEAGUE CLUBS	**YEARS**	**APPS**	**GOALS**	**FEE**
Middlesbrough	91-95	28	2	
Darlington	94	5	0	Loan
From: Home Farm				

OVERALL RECORD

COMPETITION	**APPS**	**GOALS**	**(PENS)**	**SUBS**
League	21	2	0	12
FA Cup	2	1	0	2
League Cup	1	0	0	0
Europe	0	0	–	–
Scottish	0	0	–	–
Other	7	0	–	–

HONOURS

None

INTERNATIONAL APPEARANCES

COUNTRY	**LEVEL**	**GAMES**	**GOALS**
Eire	Full	0	0
	B	0	0
	U-21	9	0
	Youth	0	0

NAME:	Roy Keane
CLUB:	Manchester Utd
BORN:	Cork, 10/8/71
DEBUT v:	Liverpool, 28/8/90
SUBSTITUTED:	15
BOOKINGS:	35
SENDINGS OFF:	1
OWN GOALS:	0
DOMESTIC PENS:	0
HAT-TRICKS:	0
STRIKE RATE (%):	16.74
EVER PRESENT:	–

LEAGUE CLUBS	**YEARS**	**APPS**	**GOALS**	**FEE**
Manchester Utd	93-95	63	7	£3.75m
Nottm Forest	90-93	114	22	£10,000
From: Cobh Ramblers				

OVERALL RECORD

COMPETITION	**APPS**	**GOALS**	**(PENS)**	**SUBS**
League	172	29	0	5
FA Cup	30	4	0	1
League Cup	24	6	0	1
Europe	7	3	–	–
Scottish	0	0	–	–
Other	7	2	–	–

HONOURS

League Championship 93-94, FA Cup 93-94, FA Cup r/u 90-91, 94-95, League Cup r/u 93-94, Charity Shield medal 93, PFA Team Award Premier League 93

INTERNATIONAL APPEARANCES

COUNTRY	**LEVEL**	**GAMES**	**GOALS**
Eire	Full	28	1
	B	1	0
	U-21	4	0
	Youth	0	0

NAME:	Mark Kennedy
CLUB:	Liverpool
BORN:	Dublin, 15/5/76
DEBUT v:	Charlton, 24/4/93
SUBSTITUTED:	14
BOOKINGS:	3
SENDINGS OFF:	0
OWN GOALS:	0
DOMESTIC PENS:	1
HAT-TRICKS:	0
STRIKE RATE (%):	20.00
EVER PRESENT:	–

LEAGUE CLUBS	**YEARS**	**APPS**	**GOALS**	**FEE**
Liverpool	95	5	0	£1.5m
Millwall	93-95	43	9	Trainee

OVERALL RECORD

COMPETITION	**APPS**	**GOALS**	**(PENS)**	**SUBS**
League	41	9	1	7
FA Cup	3	1	0	1
League Cup	7	2	0	1
Europe	0	0	–	–
Scottish	0	0	–	–

HONOURS

FA Youth Cup r/u 93-94

INTERNATIONAL APPEARANCES

COUNTRY	**LEVEL**	**GAMES**	**GOALS**
Eire	Full	0	0
	B	0	0
	U-21	6	0
	Youth	0	0

NAME:	David Kerr
CLUB:	Manchester City
BORN:	Dumfries, 6/9/74
DEBUT v:	Crystal Palace, 5/5/93
SUBSTITUTED:	3
BOOKINGS:	0
SENDINGS OFF:	0
OWN GOALS:	0
DOMESTIC PENS:	0
HAT-TRICKS:	0
STRIKE RATE (%):	–
EVER PRESENT:	–

LEAGUE CLUBS	YEARS	APPS	GOALS	FEE
Manchester City	91-95	6	0	Trainee

OVERALL RECORD

COMPETITION	APPS	GOALS	(PENS)	SUBS
League	5	0	0	1
FA Cup	0	0	0	0
League Cup	0	0	0	0
Europe	0	0	–	–
Scottish	0	0	–	–

HONOURS

None

INTERNATIONAL APPEARANCES

COUNTRY	LEVEL	GAMES	GOALS
	Full	0	0
	B	0	0
	U-21	0	0
	Youth	0	0

NAME:	Paul Lake
CLUB:	Manchester City
BORN:	Denton, 28/10/68
DEBUT v:	Wimbledon, 24/1/87
SUBSTITUTED:	21
BOOKINGS:	0
SENDINGS OFF:	0
OWN GOALS:	0
DOMESTIC PENS:	1
HAT-TRICKS:	0
STRIKE RATE (%):	7.75
EVER PRESENT:	–

LEAGUE CLUBS	YEARS	APPS	GOALS	FEE
Manchester City	87-95	110	7	Trainee

OVERALL RECORD

COMPETITION	APPS	GOALS	(PENS)	SUBS
League	106	7	1	4
FA Cup	9	2	0	0
League Cup	10	1	0	0
Europe	0	0	–	–
Scottish	0	0	–	–
Other	5	1	–	–

HONOURS

None

INTERNATIONAL APPEARANCES

COUNTRY	LEVEL	GAMES	GOALS
England	Full	0	0
	B	1	0
	U-21	5	0
	Youth	0	0

NAME:	David Lee
CLUB:	Bolton
BORN:	Manchester, 5/11/67
DEBUT v:	Chesterfield, 17/8/85
SUBSTITUTED:	38
BOOKINGS:	3
SENDINGS OFF:	0
OWN GOALS:	0
DOMESTIC PENS:	3
HAT-TRICKS:	1
STRIKE RATE (%):	13.47
EVER PRESENT:	–

LEAGUE CLUBS	YEARS	APPS	GOALS	FEE
Bolton	92-95	112	14	£300,000
Southampton	91-92	20	0	£350,000
Bury	86-91	208	35	Appr

OVERALL RECORD

COMPETITION	APPS	GOALS	(PENS)	SUBS
League	316	49	3	24
FA Cup	17	0	0	2
League Cup	27	3	0	0
Europe	0	0	–	–
Scottish	0	0	–	–
Other	31	5	–	–

HONOURS

League Cup r/u 94-95

INTERNATIONAL APPEARANCES

COUNTRY	LEVEL	GAMES	GOALS
	Full	0	0
	B	0	0
	U-21	0	0
	Youth	0	0

NAME:	Robert Lee
CLUB:	Newcastle
BORN:	West Ham, 1/2/66
DEBUT v:	Grimsby, 10/3/84
SUBSTITUTED:	26
BOOKINGS:	19
SENDINGS OFF:	1
OWN GOALS:	0
DOMESTIC PENS:	0
HAT-TRICKS:	1
STRIKE RATE (%):	20.09
EVER PRESENT:	93-94

LEAGUE CLUBS	YEARS	APPS	GOALS	FEE
Newcastle	92-95	113	26	£700,000
Charlton	83-92	298	59	
From: Hornchurch				

OVERALL RECORD

COMPETITION	APPS	GOALS	(PENS)	SUBS
League	387	85	0	24
FA Cup	25	5	0	0
League Cup	24	3	0	3
Europe	3	4	–	–
Scottish	0	0	–	–
Other	13	3	–	–

HONOURS

First Division Championship 92-93

INTERNATIONAL APPEARANCES

COUNTRY	LEVEL	GAMES	GOALS
England	Full	2	1
	B	1	0
	U-21	2	0
	Youth	0	0

NAME:	Oyvind Leonhardsen
CLUB:	Wimbledon
BORN:	Norway, 17/8/70
DEBUT v:	Aston Villa, 2/11/94
SUBSTITUTED:	4
BOOKINGS:	3
SENDINGS OFF:	0
OWN GOALS:	0
DOMESTIC PENS:	0
HAT-TRICKS:	0
STRIKE RATE (%):	–
EVER PRESENT:	–

LEAGUE CLUBS	YEARS	APPS	GOALS	FEE
Wimbledon	94-95	20	3	£650,000
From: Rosenborg B.K.				

OVERALL RECORD

COMPETITION	APPS	GOALS	(PENS)	SUBS
League	18	3	0	2
FA Cup	3	0	0	0
League Cup	0	0	0	0
Europe	6	1	–	–
Scottish	0	0	–	–

HONOURS

Norwegian Championship 92-93, 93-94, Norwegian Cup 92-93

INTERNATIONAL APPEARANCES

COUNTRY	LEVEL	GAMES	GOALS
Norway	Full	35	5
	B	0	0
	U-21	0	0
	Youth	0	0

NAME:	Matthew Le Tissier
CLUB:	Southampton
BORN:	Guernsey, 14/10/68
DEBUT v:	Norwich, 30/8/86
SUBSTITUTED:	40
BOOKINGS:	32
SENDINGS OFF:	1
OWN GOALS:	0
DOMESTIC PENS:	31
HAT-TRICKS:	7
STRIKE RATE (%):	42.24
EVER PRESENT:	–

LEAGUE CLUBS	YEARS	APPS	GOALS	FEE
Southampton	86-95	292	118	Trainee

OVERALL RECORD

COMPETITION	APPS	GOALS	(PENS)	SUBS
League	262	118	25	30
FA Cup	23	11	3	1
League Cup	26	18	3	6
Europe	0	0	–	–
Scottish	0	0	–	–
Other	12	9	–	–

HONOURS

PFA Young Player of the Year 89-90, PFA Team Award Premier League 95

INTERNATIONAL APPEARANCES

COUNTRY	LEVEL	GAMES	GOALS
England	Full	6	0
	B	6	0
	U-21	0	0
	Youth	1	0

NAME:	Craig Liddle
CLUB:	Middlesbrough
BORN:	Chester-Le-Street, 21/10/71
DEBUT v:	Tranmere, 7/5/95
SUBSTITUTED:	0
BOOKINGS:	0
SENDINGS OFF:	0
OWN GOALS:	0
DOMESTIC PENS:	0
HAT-TRICKS:	0
STRIKE RATE (%):	–
EVER PRESENT:	–

LEAGUE CLUBS	YEARS	APPS	GOALS	FEE
Middlesbrough	94-95	1	0	Trainee

OVERALL RECORD

COMPETITION	APPS	GOALS	(PENS)	SUBS
League	1	0	0	0
FA Cup	0	0	0	0
League Cup	0	0	0	0
Europe	0	0	–	–
Scottish	0	0	–	–

HONOURS

None

INTERNATIONAL APPEARANCES

COUNTRY	LEVEL	GAMES	GOALS
	Full	0	0
	B	0	0
	U-21	0	0
	Youth	0	0

NAME:	Anders Limpar
CLUB:	Everton
BORN:	Solna, Sweden, 24/9/65
DEBUT v:	Wimbledon, 25/8/90
SUBSTITUTED:	47
BOOKINGS:	16
SENDINGS OFF:	0
OWN GOALS:	0
DOMESTIC PENS:	0
HAT-TRICKS:	1
STRIKE RATE (%):	15.03
EVER PRESENT:	–

LEAGUE CLUBS	YEARS	APPS	GOALS	FEE
Everton	94-95	36	2	£1.6m
Arsenal	90-94	95	18	£1m
From: Cremonese				

OVERALL RECORD

COMPETITION	APPS	GOALS	(PENS)	SUBS
League	103	20	0	28
FA Cup	12	3	0	1
League Cup	9	0	0	0
Europe	3	1	–	–
Scottish	0	0	–	–
Other	149	31	–	–

HONOURS

League Championship 90-91, FA Cup 94-95

INTERNATIONAL APPEARANCES

COUNTRY	LEVEL	GAMES	GOALS
Sweden	Full	52	5
	B	1	0
	U-21	0	0
	Youth	0	0

NAME:	Gary McAllister
CLUB:	Leeds
BORN:	Motherwell, 25/12/64
DEBUT v:	Queen of the South, 1/5/82
SUBSTITUTED:	22
BOOKINGS:	8
SENDINGS OFF:	0
OWN GOALS:	1
DOMESTIC PENS:	20
HAT-TRICKS:	0
STRIKE RATE (%):	18.40
EVER PRESENT:	88-89, 90-91, 91-92 93-94

LEAGUE CLUBS	YEARS	APPS	GOALS	FEE
Leeds	90-95	195	27	£1m
Leicester	85-90	201	46	£125,000
Motherwell	82-85	70	8	Appr

OVERALL RECORD

COMPETITION	APPS	GOALS	(PENS)	SUBS
League	393	73	19	3
FA Cup	22	4	1	0
League Cup	32	6	0	1
Europe	5	2	–	–
Scottish	70	8	–	–
Other	10	0	–	–

HONOURS

League Championship 91-92, Scottish First Division Championship 84-85, Charity Shield medal 92, PFA Team Awards: Div 2. 89, 90; Div 1. 92; Premier League 94

INTERNATIONAL APPEARANCES

COUNTRY	LEVEL	GAMES	GOALS
Scotland	Full	33	4
	B	3	1
	U-21	1	0
	Youth	0	0

NAME:	Jason McAteer
CLUB:	Bolton
BORN:	Liverpool, 18/6/71
DEBUT v:	Burnley, 28/11/92
SUBSTITUTED:	2
BOOKINGS:	11
SENDINGS OFF:	0
OWN GOALS:	0
DOMESTIC PENS:	0
HAT-TRICKS:	0
STRIKE RATE (%):	8.33
EVER PRESENT:	93-94

LEAGUE CLUBS	YEARS	APPS	GOALS	FEE
Bolton	92-95	110	9	Free
From: Marine				

OVERALL RECORD

COMPETITION	APPS	GOALS	(PENS)	SUBS
League	105	9	0	5
FA Cup	11	0	0	0
League Cup	11	2	0	0
Europe	0	0	–	–
Scottish	0	0	–	–
Other	9	2	–	–

HONOURS

League Cup r/u 94-95, PFA Team Award Div 1. 94, 95

INTERNATIONAL APPEARANCES

COUNTRY	LEVEL	GAMES	GOALS
Eire	Full	14	0
	B	1	0
	U-21	0	0
	Youth	0	0

NAME:	Brian McClair
CLUB:	Manchester Utd
BORN:	Bellshill, 8/12/63
DEBUT v:	Kilmarnock, 21/8/81
SUBSTITUTED:	11
BOOKINGS:	8
SENDINGS OFF:	0
OWN GOALS:	0
DOMESTIC PENS:	7
HAT-TRICKS:	2
STRIKE RATE (%):	30.97
EVER PRESENT:	87-88, 88-89, 91-92
	92-93

LEAGUE CLUBS	YEARS	APPS	GOALS	FEE
Manchester Utd	87-95	301	85	£850,000
Celtic	83-87	145	99	£100,000
Motherwell	81-83	40	15	Free
Aston Villa	81	0	0	Appr

OVERALL RECORD

COMPETITION	APPS	GOALS	(PENS)	SUBS
League	278	85	5	23
FA Cup	34	14	1	5
League Cup	40	19	1	1
Europe	30	9	–	–
Scottish	235	139	–	–
Other	6	2	–	–

HONOURS

League Championship 92-93, 93-94, FA Cup 89-90, 93-94, FA Cup r/u 94-95, League Cup 91-92, League Cup r/u 90-91, 93-94, Charity Shield medal 90, 94, Scottish Premier League 85-86, Scottish FA Cup 84-85, Scottish FA Cup r/u 83-84, Scottish League Cup r/u 83-84, 86-87, European Cup Winners' Cup 90-91, Scottish PFA Player of the Year 86-87

INTERNATIONAL APPEARANCES

COUNTRY	LEVEL	GAMES	GOALS
Scotland	Full	30	2
	B	1	0
	U-21	8	2
	Youth	0	0

NAME:	Neil McDonald
CLUB:	Bolton
BORN:	Wallsend, 2/11/65
DEBUT v:	Barnsley, 25/9/82
SUBSTITUTED:	26
BOOKINGS:	5
SENDINGS OFF:	1
OWN GOALS:	0
DOMESTIC PENS:	9
HAT-TRICKS:	0
STRIKE RATE (%):	10.29
EVER PRESENT:	87-88

LEAGUE CLUBS	YEARS	APPS	GOALS	FEE
Bolton	94-95	4	0	Free
Oldham	91-94	24	1	£500,000
Everton	88-91	90	4	£525,000
Newcastle	82-88	180	24	Appr

OVERALL RECORD

COMPETITION	APPS	GOALS	(PENS)	SUBS
League	262	29	8	36
FA Cup	29	1	0	1
League Cup	22	6	1	0
Europe	0	0	–	–
Scottish	0	0	–	–
Other	16	0	–	–

HONOURS

FA Cup r/u 88-89

INTERNATIONAL APPEARANCES

COUNTRY	LEVEL	GAMES	GOALS
England	Full	0	0
	B	0	0
	U-21	5	0
	Youth	7	1

NAME:	Paul McDonald
CLUB:	Southampton
BORN:	Motherwell, 20/4/68
DEBUT v:	Hibernian, 4/10/86
SUBSTITUTED:	0
BOOKINGS:	0
SENDINGS OFF:	0
OWN GOALS:	0
DOMESTIC PENS:	0
HAT-TRICKS:	0
STRIKE RATE (%):	–
EVER PRESENT:	–

LEAGUE CLUBS	YEARS	APPS	GOALS	FEE
Southampton	93-95	2	0	£75,000
Hamilton	86-93	215	26	Appr

OVERALL RECORD

COMPETITION	APPS	GOALS	(PENS)	SUBS
League	0	0	0	2
FA Cup	0	0	0	0
League Cup	0	0	0	0
Europe	0	0	–	–
Scottish	240	30	–	–

HONOURS

Scottish Division One Championship 87-88, B & Q Cup 91-92, 92-93

INTERNATIONAL APPEARANCES

COUNTRY	LEVEL	GAMES	GOALS
	Full	0	0
	B	0	0
	U-21	0	0
	Youth	0	0

NAME:	Eddie McGoldrick
CLUB:	Arsenal
BORN:	Islington, 30/4/65
DEBUT v:	Scunthorpe, 23/8/86
SUBSTITUTED:	27
BOOKINGS:	15
SENDINGS OFF:	0
OWN GOALS:	1
DOMESTIC PENS:	0
HAT-TRICKS:	0
STRIKE RATE (%):	6.61
EVER PRESENT:	87-88, 92-93

LEAGUE CLUBS	YEARS	APPS	GOALS	FEE
Arsenal	93-95	37	0	£1m
Crystal Palace	89-93	147	11	£200,000
Northampton	86-89	107	9	£10,000
From: Kettering Town				

OVERALL RECORD

COMPETITION	APPS	GOALS	(PENS)	SUBS
League	268	20	0	23
FA Cup	15	1	0	2
League Cup	37	2	0	3
Europe	7	1	–	–
Scottish	0	0	–	–
Other	24	3	–	–

HONOURS

Division Four Championship 86-87, FA Cup r/u 89-90, Charity Shield medal 93, European Cup Winners' Cup 93-94, European Cup Winners' Cup r/u 94-95

INTERNATIONAL APPEARANCES

COUNTRY	LEVEL	GAMES	GOALS
Eire	Full	14	0
	B	1	0
	U-21	0	0
	Youth	0	0

NAME:	Paul McGregor
CLUB:	Nottm Forest
BORN:	Liverpool, 17/12/74
DEBUT v:	Ipswich, 10/12/94
SUBSTITUTED:	0
BOOKINGS:	1
SENDINGS OFF:	0
OWN GOALS:	0
DOMESTIC PENS:	0
HAT-TRICKS:	0
STRIKE RATE (%):	–
EVER PRESENT:	–

LEAGUE CLUBS	YEARS	APPS	GOALS	FEE
Nottm Forest	94-95	10	1	Trainee

OVERALL RECORD

COMPETITION	APPS	GOALS	(PENS)	SUBS
League	0	1	0	10
FA Cup	0	0	0	0
League Cup	0	0	0	0
Europe	0	0	–	–
Scottish	0	0	–	–

HONOURS

None

INTERNATIONAL APPEARANCES

COUNTRY	LEVEL	GAMES	GOALS
	Full	0	0
	B	0	0
	U-21	0	0
	Youth	0	0

NAME: Gerry McMahon
CLUB: Tottenham
BORN: Belfast, 29/12/73
DEBUT v: Carlisle, 22/10/94
SUBSTITUTED: 2
BOOKINGS: 1
SENDINGS OFF: 0
OWN GOALS: 0
DOMESTIC PENS: 0
HAT-TRICKS: 0
STRIKE RATE (%): –
EVER PRESENT: –

LEAGUE CLUBS	YEARS	APPS	GOALS	FEE
Tottenham	92-95	2	0	£100,000
Barnet	94-95	10	2	Loan
Glenavon	90-92	0	0	Appr

OVERALL RECORD

COMPETITION	APPS	GOALS	(PENS)	SUBS
League	12	2	0	0
FA Cup	2	1	0	0
League Cup	0	0	0	0
Europe	0	0	–	–
Scottish	0	0	–	–

HONOURS

None

INTERNATIONAL APPEARANCES

COUNTRY	LEVEL	GAMES	GOALS
N. Ireland	Full	3	0
	B	1	0
	U-21	1	0
	Youth	0	0

NAME: Steve McManaman
CLUB: Liverpool
BORN: Bootle, 11/2/72
DEBUT v: Sheffield Utd, 15/12/90
SUBSTITUTED: 12
BOOKINGS: 7
SENDINGS OFF: 0
OWN GOALS: 0
DOMESTIC PENS: 0
HAT-TRICKS: 0
STRIKE RATE (%): 16.28
EVER PRESENT: –

LEAGUE CLUBS	YEARS	APPS	GOALS	FEE
Liverpool	90-95	133	18	Appr

OVERALL RECORD

COMPETITION	APPS	GOALS	(PENS)	SUBS
League	122	18	0	11
FA Cup	18	3	0	1
League Cup	19	7	0	1
Europe	11	1	–	–
Scottish	0	0	–	–

HONOURS

FA Cup 91-92, League Cup 94-95

INTERNATIONAL APPEARANCES

COUNTRY	LEVEL	GAMES	GOALS
England	Full	3	0
	B	0	0
	U-21	7	1
	Youth	2	0

NAME: Jim Magilton
CLUB: Southampton
BORN: Belfast, 6/5/69
DEBUT v: West Ham, 3/10/90
SUBSTITUTED: 3
BOOKINGS: 16
SENDINGS OFF: 2
OWN GOALS: 0
DOMESTIC PENS: 14
HAT-TRICKS: 0
STRIKE RATE (%): 19.57
EVER PRESENT: 94-95

LEAGUE CLUBS	YEARS	APPS	GOALS	FEE
Southampton	94-95	57	6	£750,000
Oxford	90-94	152	34	£100,000
Liverpool	86-90	0	0	Appr

OVERALL RECORD

COMPETITION	APPS	GOALS	(PENS)	SUBS
League	209	40	12	0
FA Cup	13	5	2	0
League Cup	13	1	0	0
Europe	0	0	–	–
Scottish	0	0	–	–
Other	6	3	–	–

HONOURS

None

INTERNATIONAL APPEARANCES

COUNTRY	LEVEL	GAMES	GOALS
N. Ireland	Full	29	4
	B	1	0
	U-21	2	0
	Youth	0	0

NAME:	Dominic Matteo
CLUB:	Liverpool
BORN:	Dumfries, 28/4/74
DEBUT v:	Man City, 23/10/93
SUBSTITUTED:	6
BOOKINGS:	0
SENDINGS OFF:	0
OWN GOALS:	0
DOMESTIC PENS:	0
HAT-TRICKS:	0
STRIKE RATE (%):	–
EVER PRESENT:	–

LEAGUE CLUBS	YEARS	APPS	GOALS	FEE
Liverpool	92-95	18	1	Trainee
Sunderland	95	1	0	Loan

OVERALL RECORD

COMPETITION	APPS	GOALS	(PENS)	SUBS
League	14	1	0	5
FA Cup	1	0	0	0
League Cup	2	0	0	0
Europe	0	0	–	–
Scottish	0	0	–	–

HONOURS

None

INTERNATIONAL APPEARANCES

COUNTRY	LEVEL	GAMES	GOALS
England	Full	0	0
	B	0	0
	U-21	3	0
	Youth	1	0

NAME:	Michael Meaker
CLUB:	Q.P.R.
BORN:	Greenford, 18/8/71
DEBUT v:	Man City, 1/12/90
SUBSTITUTED:	6
BOOKINGS:	3
SENDINGS OFF:	0
OWN GOALS:	0
DOMESTIC PENS:	0
HAT-TRICKS:	0
STRIKE RATE (%):	7.14
EVER PRESENT:	–

LEAGUE CLUBS	YEARS	APPS	GOALS	FEE
Q.P.R.	90-95	33	1	Trainee
Plymouth	91-92	4	0	Loan

OVERALL RECORD

COMPETITION	APPS	GOALS	(PENS)	SUBS
League	25	1	0	12
FA Cup	3	1	0	0
League Cup	2	1	0	0
Europe	0	0	–	–
Scottish	0	0	–	–
Other	2	0	–	–

HONOURS

None

INTERNATIONAL APPEARANCES

COUNTRY	LEVEL	GAMES	GOALS
Wales	Full	0	0
	B	1	0
	U-21	2	0
	Youth	0	0

NAME:	Paul Merson
CLUB:	Arsenal
BORN:	Harlesden, 20/3/68
DEBUT v:	Man City, 22/11/86
SUBSTITUTED:	69
BOOKINGS:	13
SENDINGS OFF:	0
OWN GOALS:	0
DOMESTIC PENS:	0
HAT-TRICKS:	1
STRIKE RATE (%):	25.00
EVER PRESENT:	91-92

LEAGUE CLUBS	YEARS	APPS	GOALS	FEE
Arsenal	85-95	257	67	Appr
Brentford	87	7	0	Loan

OVERALL RECORD

COMPETITION	APPS	GOALS	(PENS)	SUBS
League	225	67	0	39
FA Cup	23	4	0	3
League Cup	28	9	0	2
Europe	19	5	–	–
Scottish	0	0	–	–
Other	20	2	–	–

HONOURS

League Championship 88-89, 90-91, FA Cup 92-93, League
Cup 92-93, Charity Shield medal 89, 91, 93, European Cup
Winners' Cup 93-94, European Cup Winners' Cup r/u 94-95,
PFA Young Player of the Year 88-89

INTERNATIONAL APPEARANCES

COUNTRY	LEVEL	GAMES	GOALS
England	Full	14	1
	B	3	2
	U-21	4	0
	Youth	3	0

NAME: Adrian Mike
CLUB: Manchester City
BORN: Manchester, 16/11/73
DEBUT v: Notts County, 25/4/92
SUBSTITUTED: 3
BOOKINGS: 0
SENDINGS OFF: 0
OWN GOALS: 0
DOMESTIC PENS: 0
HAT-TRICKS: 0
STRIKE RATE (%): –
EVER PRESENT: –

LEAGUE CLUBS	YEARS	APPS	GOALS	FEE
Manchester City	92-95	14	2	Trainee
Bury	93	7	1	Loan

OVERALL RECORD

COMPETITION	APPS	GOALS	(PENS)	SUBS
League	10	3	0	11
FA Cup	0	0	0	1
League Cup	1	0	0	1
Europe	0	0	–	–
Scottish	0	0	–	–

HONOURS

None

INTERNATIONAL APPEARANCES

COUNTRY	LEVEL	GAMES	GOALS
England	Full	0	0
	B	0	0
	U-21	0	0
	Youth	5	0

NAME: Jan Molby
CLUB: Liverpool
BORN: Kolding, Denmark, 4/7/63
DEBUT v: Norwich, 25/8/84
SUBSTITUTED: 27
BOOKINGS: 7
SENDINGS OFF: 0
OWN GOALS: 0
DOMESTIC PENS: 39
HAT-TRICKS: 1
STRIKE RATE (%): 20.8
EVER PRESENT: –

LEAGUE CLUBS	YEARS	APPS	GOALS	FEE
Liverpool	84-95	218	44	£575,000
From: Ajax				

OVERALL RECORD

COMPETITION	APPS	GOALS	(PENS)	SUBS
League	195	44	30	23
FA Cup	24	4	2	4
League Cup	25	9	7	3
Europe	11	1	–	–
Scottish	0	0	–	–
Other	85	24	–	–

HONOURS

League Championship 85-86, 89-90, FA Cup 85-86, 91-92, FA Cup r/u 87-88, League Cup r/u 86-87, Charity Shield medal 86

INTERNATIONAL APPEARANCES

COUNTRY	LEVEL	GAMES	GOALS
Denmark	Full	26	1
	B	0	0
	U-21	0	0
	Youth	0	0

NAME: John Moncur
CLUB: West Ham
BORN: Stepney, 22/9/66
DEBUT v: York City, 27/9/86
SUBSTITUTED: 13
BOOKINGS: 18
SENDINGS OFF: 0
OWN GOALS: 0
DOMESTIC PENS: 0
HAT-TRICKS: 0
STRIKE RATE (%): 6.33
EVER PRESENT: –

LEAGUE CLUBS	YEARS	APPS	GOALS	FEE
West Ham	94-95	30	2	£1m
Swindon	92-94	68	5	£80,000
Ipswich	91	6	0	Loan
Brentford	89	5	1	Loan
Portsmouth	89	7	0	Loan
Cambridge	87	4	0	Loan
Doncaster	86	4	0	Loan
Tottenham	84-92	21	1	Appr

OVERALL RECORD

COMPETITION	APPS	GOALS	(PENS)	SUBS
League	127	9	0	18
FA Cup	3	0	0	0
League Cup	8	1	0	2
Europe	0	0	–	–
Scottish	0	0	–	–
Other	5	1	–	–

HONOURS

None

INTERNATIONAL APPEARANCES

COUNTRY	LEVEL	GAMES	GOALS
England	Full	0	0
	B	0	0
	U-21	0	0
	Youth	1	0

NAME:	Alan Moore
CLUB:	Middlesbrough
BORN:	Dublin, 25/11/74
DEBUT v:	Everton, 10/4/93
SUBSTITUTED:	10
BOOKINGS:	8
SENDINGS OFF:	0
OWN GOALS:	0
DOMESTIC PENS:	0
HAT-TRICKS:	0
STRIKE RATE (%):	19.78
EVER PRESENT:	–

LEAGUE CLUBS	YEARS	APPS	GOALS	FEE
Middlesbrough	91-95	82	15	–
From: Rivermount				

OVERALL RECORD

COMPETITION	APPS	GOALS	(PENS)	SUBS
League	78	15	0	4
FA Cup	2	2	0	1
League Cup	6	1	0	0
Europe	0	0	–	–
Scottish	0	0	–	–
Other	4	0	–	–

HONOURS

First Division Championship 94-95

INTERNATIONAL APPEARANCES

COUNTRY	LEVEL	GAMES	GOALS
Eire	Full	0	0
	B	0	0
	U-21	6	1
	Youth	0	0

NAME:	Moreno-Jamie Morales
CLUB:	Middlesbrough
BORN:	Cindad, Bolivia, 19/1/74
DEBUT v:	Millwall, 1/10/94
SUBSTITUTED:	2
BOOKINGS:	0
SENDINGS OFF:	0
OWN GOALS:	0
DOMESTIC PENS:	0
HAT-TRICKS:	0
STRIKE RATE (%):	–
EVER PRESENT:	–

LEAGUE CLUBS	YEARS	APPS	GOALS	FEE
Middlesbrough	94-95	13	1	£250,000
From: Ciudad				

OVERALL RECORD

COMPETITION	APPS	GOALS	(PENS)	SUBS
League	5	1	0	8
FA Cup	0	0	0	0
League Cup	1	0	0	0
Europe	0	0	–	–
Scottish	0	0	–	–
Other	3	1	–	–

HONOURS

None

INTERNATIONAL APPEARANCES

COUNTRY	LEVEL	GAMES	GOALS
Bolivia	Full	0	0
	B	0	0
	U-21	0	0
	Youth	0	0

NAME:	Robbie Mustoe
CLUB:	Middlesbrough
BORN:	Witney, 28/8/68
DEBUT v:	Norwich, 29/11/86
SUBSTITUTED:	42
BOOKINGS:	12
SENDINGS OFF:	1
OWN GOALS:	0
DOMESTIC PENS:	0
HAT-TRICKS:	0
STRIKE RATE (%):	10.14
EVER PRESENT:	–

LEAGUE CLUBS	YEARS	APPS	GOALS	FEE
Middlesbrough	90-95	159	12	£375,000
Oxford	86-90	91	10	Appr

OVERALL RECORD

COMPETITION	APPS	GOALS	(PENS)	SUBS
League	228	22	0	22
FA Cup	12	1	0	0
League Cup	23	6	0	1
Europe	0	0	–	–
Scottish	0	0	–	–
Other	16	1	–	–

HONOURS

First Division Championship 94-95

INTERNATIONAL APPEARANCES

COUNTRY	LEVEL	GAMES	GOALS
	Full	0	0
	B	0	0
	U-21	0	0
	Youth	0	0

NAME:	Aidan Newhouse
CLUB:	Wimbledon
BORN:	Wallasey, 23/5/72
DEBUT v:	Bury, 7/5/88
SUBSTITUTED:	17
BOOKINGS:	3
SENDINGS OFF:	0
OWN GOALS:	0
DOMESTIC PENS:	1
HAT-TRICKS:	0
STRIKE RATE (%):	11.49
EVER PRESENT:	–

LEAGUE CLUBS	YEARS	APPS	GOALS	FEE
Wimbledon	90-95	23	3	£100,000
Portsmouth	94	6	1	Loan
Port Vale	94	2	0	Loan
Chester	88-90	44	6	Trainee

OVERALL RECORD

COMPETITION	APPS	GOALS	(PENS)	SUBS
League	42	10	1	33
FA Cup	2	0	0	2
League Cup	6	0	0	2
Europe	0	0	–	–
Scottish	0	0	–	–
Other	6	1	–	–

HONOURS

None

INTERNATIONAL APPEARANCES

COUNTRY	LEVEL	GAMES	GOALS
England	Full	0	0
	B	0	0
	U-21	0	0
	Youth	13	4

NAME:	Eddie Newton
CLUB:	Chelsea
BORN:	Hammersmith, 13/12/71
DEBUT v:	Chesterfield, 25/1/92
SUBSTITUTED:	5
BOOKINGS:	2
SENDINGS OFF:	0
OWN GOALS:	0
DOMESTIC PENS:	0
HAT-TRICKS:	0
STRIKE RATE (%):	7.86
EVER PRESENT:	–

LEAGUE CLUBS	YEARS	APPS	GOALS	FEE
Chelsea`	90-95	101	7	Trainee
Cardiff	92	18	4	Loan

OVERALL RECORD

COMPETITION	APPS	GOALS	(PENS)	SUBS
League	105	11	0	14
FA Cup	7	0	0	2
League Cup	11	0	0	1
Europe	5	0	–	–
Scottish	0	0	–	–
Other	2	0	–	–

HONOURS

FA Cup r/u 93-94

INTERNATIONAL APPEARANCES

COUNTRY	LEVEL	GAMES	GOALS
England	Full	0	0
	B	0	0
	U-21	1	0
	Youth	0	0

NAME:	Matt Oakley
CLUB:	Southampton
BORN:	Peterborough, 17/8/77
DEBUT v:	Everton, 6/5/95
SUBSTITUTED:	0
BOOKINGS:	0
SENDINGS OFF:	0
OWN GOALS:	0
DOMESTIC PENS:	0
HAT-TRICKS:	0
STRIKE RATE (%):	–
EVER PRESENT:	–

LEAGUE CLUBS	YEARS	APPS	GOALS	FEE
Southampton	95	1	0	Trainee

OVERALL RECORD

COMPETITION	APPS	GOALS	(PENS)	SUBS
League	0	0	0	1
FA Cup	0	0	0	0
League Cup	0	0	0	0
Europe	0	0	–	–
Scottish	0	0	–	–

HONOURS

None

INTERNATIONAL APPEARANCES

COUNTRY	LEVEL	GAMES	GOALS
	Full	0	0
	B	0	0
	U-21	0	0
	Youth	0	0

NAME:	Ray Parlour
CLUB:	Arsenal
BORN:	Romford, 7/3/73
DEBUT v:	Liverpool, 29/1/92
SUBSTITUTED:	12
BOOKINGS:	6
SENDINGS OFF:	0
OWN GOALS:	0
DOMESTIC PENS:	0
HAT-TRICKS:	0
STRIKE RATE (%):	4.85
EVER PRESENT:	–

LEAGUE CLUBS	YEARS	APPS	GOALS	FEE
Arsenal	91-95	83	4	Trainee

OVERALL RECORD

COMPETITION	APPS	GOALS	(PENS)	SUBS
League	64	4	0	19
FA Cup	9	1	0	0
League Cup	10	0	0	1
Europe	8	0	–	–
Scottish	0	0	–	–
Other	1	0	–	–

HONOURS

FA Cup 92-93, League Cup 92-93, European Cup Winners' Cup 93-94, European Cup Winners' Cup r/u 94-95

INTERNATIONAL APPEARANCES

COUNTRY	LEVEL	GAMES	GOALS
England	Full	0	0
	B	0	0
	U-21	12	0
	Youth	0	0

NAME:	Mark Patterson
CLUB:	Bolton
BORN:	Darwen, 24/5/65
DEBUT v:	Man City, 17/9/83
SUBSTITUTED:	31
BOOKINGS:	21
SENDINGS OFF:	0
OWN GOALS:	0
DOMESTIC PENS:	7
HAT-TRICKS:	1
STRIKE RATE (%):	15.71
EVER PRESENT:	–

LEAGUE CLUBS	YEARS	APPS	GOALS	FEE
Bolton	91-95	153	10	£65,000
Bury	90-91	42	10	£40,000
Preston	88-90	55	19	£20,000
Blackburn	83-88	101	20	Appr

OVERALL RECORD

COMPETITION	APPS	GOALS	(PENS)	SUBS
League	331	59	7	20
FA Cup	25	1	0	1
League Cup	20	3	0	4
Europe	0	0	–	–
Scottish	0	0	–	–
Other	26	3	–	–

HONOURS

League Cup r/u 94-95

INTERNATIONAL APPEARANCES

COUNTRY	LEVEL	GAMES	GOALS
	Full	0	0
	B	0	0
	U-21	0	0
	Youth	0	0

NAME:	Gavin Peacock
CLUB:	Chelsea
BORN:	Eltham, 18/11/67
DEBUT v:	Sheffield Wed, 29/11/86
SUBSTITUTED:	26
BOOKINGS:	10
SENDINGS OFF:	0
OWN GOALS:	0
DOMESTIC PENS:	6
HAT-TRICKS:	2
STRIKE RATE (%):	22.68
EVER PRESENT:	91-92

LEAGUE CLUBS	YEARS	APPS	GOALS	FEE
Chelsea	93-95	75	12	£1.25m
Newcastle	90-93	105	35	£275,000
Bournemouth	89-90	56	8	£250,000
Gillingham	87-89	70	11	£40,000
Q.P.R.	84-87	17	1	Appr

OVERALL RECORD

COMPETITION	APPS	GOALS	(PENS)	SUBS
League	309	67	6	14
FA Cup	21	10	0	1
League Cup	21	6	0	0
Europe	7	0	–	–
Scottish	0	0	–	–
Other	14	6	–	–

HONOURS

First Division Championship 92-93, FA Cup r/u 93-94, PFA Team Award Div 1. 93

INTERNATIONAL APPEARANCES

COUNTRY	LEVEL	GAMES	GOALS
England	Full	0	0
	B	1	0
	U-21	0	0
	Youth	6	0

NAME:	Dan Petrescu
CLUB:	Sheffield Wed
BORN:	Romania, 22/12/67
DEBUT v:	Tottenham, 20/8/94
SUBSTITUTED:	8
BOOKINGS:	3
SENDINGS OFF:	0
OWN GOALS:	0
DOMESTIC PENS:	0
HAT-TRICKS:	0
STRIKE RATE (%):	–
EVER PRESENT:	–

LEAGUE CLUBS	YEARS	APPS	GOALS	FEE
Sheffield Wed	94-95	29	3	£1.3m
From: Genoa				

OVERALL RECORD

COMPETITION	APPS	GOALS	(PENS)	SUBS
League	20	3	0	9
FA Cup	0	0	0	2
League Cup	2	0	0	0
Europe	0	0	–	–
Scottish	0	0	–	–

HONOURS

European Cup r/u 88-89, Romanian League Championship 87-88, 88-89, Romanian Cup 87-88, 88-89, Romanian Cup r/u 89-90

INTERNATIONAL APPEARANCES

COUNTRY	LEVEL	GAMES	GOALS
Romania	Full	41	5
	B	0	0
	U-21	0	0
	Youth	0	0

NAME:	Dave Phillips
CLUB:	Nottm Forest
BORN:	Germany, 29/7/63
DEBUT v:	Oxford, 29/8/81
SUBSTITUTED:	20
BOOKINGS:	2
SENDINGS OFF:	0
OWN GOALS:	0
DOMESTIC PENS:	2
HAT-TRICKS:	0
STRIKE RATE (%):	10.42
EVER PRESENT:	84-85, 89-90, 90-91 92-93

LEAGUE CLUBS	YEARS	APPS	GOALS	FEE
Nottm Forest	93-95	82	5	£500,000
Norwich	89-93	152	17	£525,000
Coventry	86-89	100	8	£150,000
Manchester City	84-86	81	13	£65,000
Plymouth	81-84	73	15	Appr

OVERALL RECORD

COMPETITION	APPS	GOALS	(PENS)	SUBS
League	470	58	2	18
FA Cup	45	2	0	1
League Cup	41	0	0	1
Europe	0	0	–	–
Scottish	0	0	–	–
Other	27	7	–	–

HONOURS

FA Cup 86-87, Charity Shield medal 87

INTERNATIONAL APPEARANCES

COUNTRY	LEVEL	GAMES	GOALS
Wales	Full	60	2
	B	0	0
	U-21	3	0
	Youth	0	0

NAME:	Jamie Pollock
CLUB:	Middlesbrough
BORN:	Stockton, 16/2/74
DEBUT v:	Wolves, 27/4/91
SUBSTITUTED:	23
BOOKINGS:	27
SENDINGS OFF:	1
OWN GOALS:	0
DOMESTIC PENS:	0
HAT-TRICKS:	0
STRIKE RATE (%):	12.16
EVER PRESENT:	–

LEAGUE CLUBS	YEARS	APPS	GOALS	FEE
Middlesbrough	91-95	124	16	Trainee

OVERALL RECORD

COMPETITION	APPS	GOALS	(PENS)	SUBS
League	113	16	0	11
FA Cup	10	1	0	1
League Cup	11	1	0	2
Europe	0	0	–	–
Scottish	0	0	–	–
Other	5	0	–	–

HONOURS

First Division Championship 94-95, PFA Team Award Div 1. 95

INTERNATIONAL APPEARANCES

COUNTRY	LEVEL	GAMES	GOALS
England	Full	0	0
	B	0	0
	U-21	1	0
	Youth	8	2

NAME:	Adam Poric
CLUB:	Sheffield Wed
BORN:	London, 22/4/73
DEBUT v:	Wimbledon, 16/10/93
SUBSTITUTED:	1
BOOKINGS:	1
SENDINGS OFF:	0
OWN GOALS:	0
DOMESTIC PENS:	0
HAT-TRICKS:	0
STRIKE RATE (%):	–
EVER PRESENT:	–

LEAGUE CLUBS	YEARS	APPS	GOALS	FEE
Sheffield Wed	93-95	10	0	£60,000
From: St Georges				

OVERALL RECORD

COMPETITION	APPS	GOALS	(PENS)	SUBS
League	3	0	0	7
FA Cup	0	0	0	0
League Cup	0	0	0	2
Europe	0	0	–	–
Scottish	0	0	–	–

HONOURS

None

INTERNATIONAL APPEARANCES

COUNTRY	LEVEL	GAMES	GOALS
	Full	0	0
	B	0	0
	U-21	0	0
	Youth	0	0

NAME:	Lucas Radebe
CLUB:	Leeds
BORN:	Johanesburg, 12/4/69
DEBUT v:	Sheffield Wed, 26/9/94
SUBSTITUTED:	5
BOOKINGS:	2
SENDINGS OFF:	0
OWN GOALS:	0
DOMESTIC PENS:	0
HAT-TRICKS:	0
STRIKE RATE (%):	–
EVER PRESENT:	–

LEAGUE CLUBS	YEARS	APPS	GOALS	FEE
Leeds	94-95	12	0	£250,000
From: Kaiser Chiefs				

OVERALL RECORD

COMPETITION	APPS	GOALS	(PENS)	SUBS
League	9	0	0	3
FA Cup	1	0	0	1
League Cup	0	0	0	1
Europe	0	0	–	–
Scottish	0	0	–	–

HONOURS

None

INTERNATIONAL APPEARANCES

COUNTRY	LEVEL	GAMES	GOALS
South Africa	Full	15	0
	B	0	0
	U-21	0	0
	Youth	0	0

NAME:	Jamie Redknapp
CLUB:	Liverpool
BORN:	Barton-On-Sea, 25/6/73
DEBUT v:	Hull, 13/1/90
SUBSTITUTED:	8
BOOKINGS:	12
SENDINGS OFF:	1
OWN GOALS:	0
DOMESTIC PENS:	0
HAT-TRICKS:	0
STRIKE RATE (%):	8.81
EVER PRESENT:	–

LEAGUE CLUBS	YEARS	APPS	GOALS	FEE
Liverpool	91-95	111	10	£350,000
Bournemouth	90-91	13	0	Trainee

OVERALL RECORD

COMPETITION	APPS	GOALS	(PENS)	SUBS
League	103	10	0	21
FA Cup	14	1	0	0
League Cup	21	3	0	0
Europe	6	0	–	–
Scottish	0	0	–	–
Other	2	0	–	–

HONOURS

League Cup 94-95

INTERNATIONAL APPEARANCES

COUNTRY	LEVEL	GAMES	GOALS
England	Full	0	0
	B	1	0
	U-21	18	5
	Youth	2	0

NAME:	Kevin Richardson
CLUB:	Coventry
BORN:	Newcastle, 4/12/62
DEBUT v:	Sunderland, 21/11/81
SUBSTITUTED:	29
BOOKINGS:	18
SENDINGS OFF:	0
OWN GOALS:	0
DOMESTIC PENS:	0
HAT-TRICKS:	0
STRIKE RATE (%):	9.37
EVER PRESENT:	91-92, 92-93

LEAGUE CLUBS	YEARS	APPS	GOALS	FEE
Coventry	95	14	0	£300,000
Aston Villa	91-95	143	13	£450,000
Real Sociedad	90-91	31	1	£750,000
Arsenal	87-90	96	5	£200,000
Watford	86-87	39	2	£225,000
Everton	80-86	109	16	Appr

OVERALL RECORD

COMPETITION	APPS	GOALS	(PENS)	SUBS
League	378	36	0	23
FA Cup	41	2	0	0
League Cup	42	8	0	6
Europe	15	0	–	–
Scottish	0	0	–	–
Other	17	0	–	–

INTERNATIONAL APPEARANCES

COUNTRY	LEVEL	GAMES	GOALS
England	Full	2	0
	B	0	0
	U-21	0	0
	Youth	0	0

HONOURS

League Championship 84-85, 88-89, FA Cup 83-84, League Cup 93-94, League Cup r/u 83-84, 87-88, Charity Shield medal 84, 86, 90

NAME:	Stuart Ripley
CLUB:	Blackburn
BORN:	Middlesbrough, 20/11/67
DEBUT v:	Oldham, 5/2/85
SUBSTITUTED:	65
BOOKINGS:	7
SENDINGS OFF:	1
OWN GOALS:	0
DOMESTIC PENS:	0
HAT-TRICKS:	1
STRIKE RATE (%):	10.11
EVER PRESENT:	–

LEAGUE CLUBS	YEARS	APPS	GOALS	FEE
Blackburn	92-95	117	11	£1.3m
Bolton	86	5	1	Loan
Middlesbrough	85-92	249	26	Appr

OVERALL RECORD

COMPETITION	APPS	GOALS	(PENS)	SUBS
League	329	38	0	42
FA Cup	26	3	0	1
League Cup	35	3	0	2
Europe	2	0	–	–
Scottish	0	0	–	–
Other	21	1	–	–

HONOURS

League Championship 94-95, Charity Shield medal 94

INTERNATIONAL APPEARANCES

COUNTRY	LEVEL	GAMES	GOALS
England	Full	1	0
	B	0	0
	U-21	8	1
	Youth	2	0

NAME:	Graham Rix
CLUB:	Chelsea
BORN:	Doncaster, 23/10/57
DEBUT v:	Leicester, 2/4/77
SUBSTITUTED:	15
BOOKINGS:	0
SENDINGS OFF:	0
OWN GOALS:	0
DOMESTIC PENS:	0
HAT-TRICKS:	0
STRIKE RATE (%):	11.36
EVER PRESENT:	–

LEAGUE CLUBS	YEARS	APPS	GOALS	FEE
Chelsea	93-95	1	0	Free
Dundee	92-93	14	2	Free
From: Le Havre				
Brentford	87-88	6	0	Loan
Arsenal	74-88	351	41	Appr

OVERALL RECORD

COMPETITION	APPS	GOALS	(PENS)	SUBS
League	344	41	0	14
FA Cup	42	7	0	2
League Cup	45	2	0	0
Europe	24	1	–	–
Scottish	16	2	–	–
Other	1	0	–	–

HONOURS

FA Cup 78-79, FA Cup r/u 77-78, 79-80, Charity Shield medal 79, European Cup Winners' Cup r/u 79-80

INTERNATIONAL APPEARANCES

COUNTRY	LEVEL	GAMES	GOALS
England	Full	17	0
	B	3	0
	U-21	7	0
	Youth	0	0

NAME:	Matt Robinson
CLUB:	Southampton
BORN:	Exeter, 23/12/74
DEBUT v:	Sheffield Wed, 30/4/95
SUBSTITUTED:	0
BOOKINGS:	0
SENDINGS OFF:	0
OWN GOALS:	0
DOMESTIC PENS:	0
HAT-TRICKS:	0
STRIKE RATE (%):	–
EVER PRESENT:	–

LEAGUE CLUBS	YEARS	APPS	GOALS	FEE
Southampton	93-95	1	0	Trainee

OVERALL RECORD

COMPETITION	APPS	GOALS	(PENS)	SUBS
League	0	0	0	1
FA Cup	0	0	0	0
League Cup	0	0	0	0
Europe	0	0	–	–
Scottish	0	0	–	–

HONOURS

None

INTERNATIONAL APPEARANCES

COUNTRY	LEVEL	GAMES	GOALS
	Full	0	0
	B	0	0
	U-21	0	0
	Youth	0	0

NAME:	Bryan Robson
CLUB:	Middlesbrough
BORN:	Witton Gilbert, 11/1/57
DEBUT v:	York, 12/4/75
SUBSTITUTED:	37
BOOKINGS:	8
SENDINGS OFF:	0
OWN GOALS:	1
DOMESTIC PENS:	2
HAT-TRICKS:	1
STRIKE RATE (%):	19.53
EVER PRESENT:	–

LEAGUE CLUBS	YEARS	APPS	GOALS	FEE
Middlesbrough	94-95	22	1	Free
Manchester Utd	81-94	345	74	£1.5m
West Brom	74-81	198	39	Appr

OVERALL RECORD

COMPETITION	APPS	GOALS	(PENS)	SUBS
League	541	114	2	24
FA Cup	43	12	0	4
League Cup	67	7	0	2
Europe	38	10	–	–
Scottish	0	0	–	–
Other	8	4	–	–

HONOURS

League Championship 92-93, 93-94, First Division
Championship 94-95, FA Cup 82-83, 84-85, 89-90, League
Cup r/u 90-91, Charity Shield medal 83, 85, 93, European
Cup Winners' Cup 90-91, PFA Team Awards: Div 1. 82, 83,
84, 85, 86, 89

INTERNATIONAL APPEARANCES

COUNTRY	LEVEL	GAMES	GOALS
England	Full	90	26
	B	6	2
	U-21	7	2
	Youth	7	0

NAME:	David Rocastle
CLUB:	Chelsea
BORN:	Lewisham, 2/5/67
DEBUT v:	Newcastle, 28/9/85
SUBSTITUTED:	75
BOOKINGS:	12
SENDINGS OFF:	0
OWN GOALS:	0
DOMESTIC PENS:	0
HAT-TRICKS:	0
STRIKE RATE (%):	10.96
EVER PRESENT:	87-88, 88-89

LEAGUE CLUBS	YEARS	APPS	GOALS	FEE
Chelsea	94-95	28	0	£1.25
Manchester City	93-94	21	2	£2m
Leeds	92-93	25	2	£2m
Arsenal	84-92	218	24	Appr

OVERALL RECORD

COMPETITION	APPS	GOALS	(PENS)	SUBS
League	268	28	0	24
FA Cup	20	4	0	5
League Cup	35	7	0	4
Europe	15	1	–	–
Scottish	0	0	–	–
Other	17	4	–	–

HONOURS

League Championship 88-89, 90-91, League Cup 86-87,
League Cup r/u 87-88, Charity Shield medal 89, 91, PFA
Team Awards Div 1. 87, 89

INTERNATIONAL APPEARANCES

COUNTRY	LEVEL	GAMES	GOALS
England	Full	14	0
	B	2	0
	U-21	14	2
	Youth	0	0

NAME:	Gary Rowett
CLUB:	Everton
BORN:	Bromsgrove, 6/3/74
DEBUT v:	Millwall, 7/9/91
SUBSTITUTED:	20
BOOKINGS:	5
SENDINGS OFF:	0
OWN GOALS:	0
DOMESTIC PENS:	0
HAT-TRICKS:	0
STRIKE RATE (%):	10.31
EVER PRESENT:	–

LEAGUE CLUBS	YEARS	APPS	GOALS	FEE
Everton	94-95	4	0	£200,000
Blackpool	95	17	0	Loan
Cambridge	91-94	62	9	Trainee

OVERALL RECORD

COMPETITION	APPS	GOALS	(PENS)	SUBS
League	70	9	0	13
FA Cup	5	0	0	2
League Cup	7	1	0	0
Europe	0	0	–	–
Scottish	0	0	–	–
Other	5	3	–	–

HONOURS

None

INTERNATIONAL APPEARANCES

COUNTRY	LEVEL	GAMES	GOALS
	Full	0	0
	B	0	0
	U-21	0	0
	Youth	0	0

NAME:	Keith Rowland
CLUB:	West Ham
BORN:	Portadown, 1/9/71
DEBUT v:	Darlington, 17/8/91
SUBSTITUTED:	6
BOOKINGS:	10
SENDINGS OFF:	0
OWN GOALS:	0
DOMESTIC PENS:	0
HAT-TRICKS:	0
STRIKE RATE (%):	1.54
EVER PRESENT:	–

LEAGUE CLUBS	YEARS	APPS	GOALS	FEE
West Ham	93-95	35	0	£110,000
Coventry	93	2	0	Loan
Bournemouth	89-93	72	2	Trainee

OVERALL RECORD

COMPETITION	APPS	GOALS	(PENS)	SUBS
League	92	2	0	17
FA Cup	13	0	0	0
League Cup	8	0	0	0
Europe	0	0	–	–
Scottish	0	0	–	–
Other	5	0	–	–

HONOURS

None

INTERNATIONAL APPEARANCES

COUNTRY	LEVEL	GAMES	GOALS
N. Ireland	Full	1	0
	B	1	0
	U-21	0	0
	Youth	0	0

NAME:	Vinny Samways
CLUB:	Everton
BORN:	Bethnal Green, 27/10/68
DEBUT v:	Nottm Forest, 2/5/87
SUBSTITUTED:	40
BOOKINGS:	17
SENDINGS OFF:	1
OWN GOALS:	0
DOMESTIC PENS:	0
HAT-TRICKS:	0
STRIKE RATE (%):	7.57
EVER PRESENT:	–

LEAGUE CLUBS	YEARS	APPS	GOALS	FEE
Everton	94-95	19	1	£2.2m
Tottenham	85-94	183	11	Appr

OVERALL RECORD

COMPETITION	APPS	GOALS	(PENS)	SUBS
League	169	12	0	33
FA Cup	15	2	0	1
League Cup	29	5	0	4
Europe	7	0	–	–
Scottish	0	0	–	–
Other	2	0	–	–

HONOURS

FA Cup 90-91, Charity Shield medal 91

INTERNATIONAL APPEARANCES

COUNTRY	LEVEL	GAMES	GOALS
England	Full	0	0
	B	0	0
	U-21	5	0
	Youth	10	0

NAME:	Scott Sellars
CLUB:	Newcastle
BORN:	Sheffield, 27/11/65
DEBUT v:	Shrewsbury, 7/5/83
SUBSTITUTED:	36
BOOKINGS:	7
SENDINGS OFF:	0
OWN GOALS:	1
DOMESTIC PENS:	3
HAT-TRICKS:	0
STRIKE RATE (%):	15.49
EVER PRESENT:	88-89

LEAGUE CLUBS	YEARS	APPS	GOALS	FEE
Newcastle	93-95	55	6	£700,000
Leeds	92-93	7	0	£720,000
Blackburn	86-92	202	35	£20,000
Leeds	83-86	76	12	Appr

OVERALL RECORD

COMPETITION	APPS	GOALS	(PENS)	SUBS
League	326	53	3	14
FA Cup	18	1	0	0
League Cup	21	5	0	2
Europe	5	1	–	–
Scottish	0	0	–	–
Other	22	3	–	–

HONOURS

First Division Championship 92-93, PFA Team Award Div 2. 90, 92

INTERNATIONAL APPEARANCES

COUNTRY	LEVEL	GAMES	GOALS
England	Full	0	0
	B	0	0
	U-21	2	0
	Youth	0	0

NAME:	Ian Selley
CLUB:	Arsenal
BORN:	Chertsey, 14/6/74
DEBUT v:	Blackburn, 12/9/92
SUBSTITUTED:	4
BOOKINGS:	11
SENDINGS OFF:	0
OWN GOALS:	0
DOMESTIC PENS:	0
HAT-TRICKS:	0
STRIKE RATE (%):	–
EVER PRESENT:	–

LEAGUE CLUBS	YEARS	APPS	GOALS	FEE
Arsenal	92-95	40	0	Trainee

OVERALL RECORD

COMPETITION	APPS	GOALS	(PENS)	SUBS
League	35	0	0	5
FA Cup	3	0	0	0
League Cup	5	0	0	1
Europe	8	2	–	–
Scottish	0	0	–	–
Other	2	0	–	–

HONOURS

FA Cup 92-93, League Cup 92-93, European Cup Winners' Cup 93-94

INTERNATIONAL APPEARANCES

COUNTRY	LEVEL	GAMES	GOALS
England	Full	0	0
	B	0	0
	U-21	3	0
	Youth	2	0

NAME:	Lee Sharpe
CLUB:	Manchester Utd
BORN:	Halesowen, 27/5/71
DEBUT v:	Exeter, 3/10/87
SUBSTITUTED:	34
BOOKINGS:	9
SENDINGS OFF:	0
OWN GOALS:	0
DOMESTIC PENS:	1
HAT-TRICKS:	1
STRIKE RATE (%):	14.09
EVER PRESENT:	–

LEAGUE CLUBS	YEARS	APPS	GOALS	FEE
Manchester Utd	88-95	162	18	£185,000
Torquay	87-88	14	3	Trainee

OVERALL RECORD

COMPETITION	APPS	GOALS	(PENS)	SUBS
League	148	21	1	28
FA Cup	18	1	0	5
League Cup	13	9	0	8
Europe	15	3	–	–
Scottish	0	0	–	–
Other	8	0	–	–

HONOURS

League Championship 92-93, 93-94, FA Cup 93-94, FA Cup r/u 94-95, League Cup 91-92, League Cup r/u 90-91, 93-94, Charity Shield medal 94, European Cup Winners' Cup 90-91, PFA Young Player of the Year 90-91

INTERNATIONAL APPEARANCES

COUNTRY	LEVEL	GAMES	GOALS
England	Full	8	0
	B	1	0
	U-21	8	0
	Youth	0	0

NAME:	Paul Sheerin
CLUB:	Southampton
BORN:	Edinburgh, 28/8/74
DEBUT v:	Berwick, 8/8/92
SUBSTITUTED:	0
BOOKINGS:	0
SENDINGS OFF:	0
OWN GOALS:	0
DOMESTIC PENS:	0
HAT-TRICKS:	0
STRIKE RATE (%):	–
EVER PRESENT:	–

LEAGUE CLUBS	YEARS	APPS	GOALS	FEE
Southampton	92-95	0	0	£60,000
Alloa	92	9	0	–
From: Whitehall Welfare				

OVERALL RECORD

COMPETITION	APPS	GOALS	(PENS)	SUBS
League	0	0	0	0
FA Cup	0	0	0	0
League Cup	0	0	0	0
Europe	0	0	–	–
Scottish	12	0	–	–

HONOURS

None

INTERNATIONAL APPEARANCES

COUNTRY	LEVEL	GAMES	GOALS
	Full	0	0
	B	0	0
	U-21	0	0
	Youth	0	0

NAME:	John Sheridan
CLUB:	Sheffield Wed
BORN:	Manchester, 1/10/64
DEBUT v:	Middlesbrough, 20/11/82
SUBSTITUTED:	39
BOOKINGS:	19
SENDINGS OFF:	0
OWN GOALS:	1
DOMESTIC PENS:	31
HAT-TRICKS:	0
STRIKE RATE (%):	17.19
EVER PRESENT:	84-85, 90-91

LEAGUE CLUBS	YEARS	APPS	GOALS	FEE
Sheffield Wed	89-95	181	25	£500,000
Nottm Forest	89	0	0	£650,000
Leeds	82-89	227	47	–

OVERALL RECORD

COMPETITION	APPS	GOALS	(PENS)	SUBS
League	399	72	28	9
FA Cup	28	4	2	2
League Cup	39	6	1	0
Europe	1	1	–	–
Scottish	0	0	–	–
Other	14	2	–	–

HONOURS

FA Cup r/u 92-93, League Cup 90-91, League Cup r/u 92-93

INTERNATIONAL APPEARANCES

COUNTRY	LEVEL	GAMES	GOALS
Eire	Full	31	4
	B	0	0
	U-21	3	0
	Youth	0	0

NAME:	Tim Sherwood
CLUB:	Blackburn
BORN:	St Albans, 6/2/69
DEBUT v:	Sheffield Wed, 12/9/87
SUBSTITUTED:	18
BOOKINGS:	21
SENDINGS OFF:	1
OWN GOALS:	0
DOMESTIC PENS:	0
HAT-TRICKS:	0
STRIKE RATE (%):	9.09
EVER PRESENT:	–

LEAGUE CLUBS	YEARS	APPS	GOALS	FEE
Blackburn	92-95	126	11	£500,000
Norwich	89-92	71	10	£175,000
Watford	87-89	30	2	Trainee

OVERALL RECORD

COMPETITION	APPS	GOALS	(PENS)	SUBS
League	208	23	0	19
FA Cup	21	1	0	1
League Cup	25	1	0	1
Europe	2	0	–	–
Scottish	0	0	–	–
Other	13	2	–	–

HONOURS

League Championship 94-95, Charity Shield medal 94, PFA Team Award Premier League 95

INTERNATIONAL APPEARANCES

COUNTRY	LEVEL	GAMES	GOALS
England	Full	1	0
	B	1	0
	U-21	4	0
	Youth	0	0

Fitzroy Simpson

NAME:	Fitzroy Simpson
CLUB:	Manchester City
BORN:	Bradford-On-Avon, 26/2/70
DEBUT v:	Shrewsbury, 3/12/88
SUBSTITUTED:	27
BOOKINGS:	24
SENDINGS OFF:	0
OWN GOALS:	0
DOMESTIC PENS:	0
HAT-TRICKS:	0
STRIKE RATE (%):	7.14
EVER PRESENT:	–

LEAGUE CLUBS	YEARS	APPS	GOALS	FEE
Manchester City	92-95	71	5	£500,000
Bristol City	94	3	0	Loan
Swindon	88-92	105	9	Trainee

OVERALL RECORD

COMPETITION	APPS	GOALS	(PENS)	SUBS
League	139	14	0	40
FA Cup	6	0	0	2
League Cup	20	1	0	3
Europe	0	0	–	–
Scottish	0	0	–	–
Other	5	0	–	–

HONOURS

None

INTERNATIONAL APPEARANCES

COUNTRY	LEVEL	GAMES	GOALS
	Full	0	0
	B	0	0
	U-21	0	0
	Youth	0	0

Trevor Sinclair

NAME:	Trevor Sinclair
CLUB:	Q.P.R.
BORN:	Dulwich, 2/3/73
DEBUT v:	Wigan, 19/8/89
SUBSTITUTED:	17
BOOKINGS:	9
SENDINGS OFF:	1
OWN GOALS:	0
DOMESTIC PENS:	0
HAT-TRICKS:	0
STRIKE RATE (%):	12.38
EVER PRESENT:	–

LEAGUE CLUBS	YEARS	APPS	GOALS	FEE
Q.P.R.	93-95	66	8	£600,000
Blackpool	89-93	112	15	Trainee

OVERALL RECORD

COMPETITION	APPS	GOALS	(PENS)	SUBS
League	148	23	0	31
FA Cup	8	0	0	1
League Cup	14	2	0	0
Europe	0	0	–	–
Scottish	0	0	–	–
Other	13	1	–	–

HONOURS

None

INTERNATIONAL APPEARANCES

COUNTRY	LEVEL	GAMES	GOALS
England	Full	0	0
	B	0	0
	U-21	6	3
	Youth	1	0

Andy Sinton

NAME:	Andy Sinton
CLUB:	Sheffield Wed
BORN:	Newcastle, 19/3/66
DEBUT v:	Wolves, 2/11/82
SUBSTITUTED:	36
BOOKINGS:	9
SENDINGS OFF:	0
OWN GOALS:	0
DOMESTIC PENS:	12
HAT-TRICKS:	1
STRIKE RATE (%):	14.01
EVER PRESENT:	85-86, 86-87, 87-88 89-90, 90-91

LEAGUE CLUBS	YEARS	APPS	GOALS	FEE
Sheffield Wed	93-95	50	3	£2.6m
Q.P.R.	89-93	160	22	£350,000
Brentford	85-89	149	28	£25,000
Cambridge	82-85	93	13	Appr

OVERALL RECORD

COMPETITION	APPS	GOALS	(PENS)	SUBS
League	446	66	12	6
FA Cup	31	3	0	0
League Cup	38	4	0	0
Europe	0	0	–	–
Scottish	0	0	–	–
Other	19	4	–	–

HONOURS

None

INTERNATIONAL APPEARANCES

COUNTRY	LEVEL	GAMES	GOALS
England	Full	12	0
	B	4	0
	U-21	0	0
	Youth	0	0

NAME:	Robbie Slater
CLUB:	Blackburn
BORN:	Liverpool, 22/11/64
DEBUT v:	Southampton, 20/8/94
SUBSTITUTED:	3
BOOKINGS:	3
SENDINGS OFF:	0
OWN GOALS:	0
DOMESTIC PENS:	0
HAT-TRICKS:	0
STRIKE RATE (%):	–
EVER PRESENT:	–

LEAGUE CLUBS	YEARS	APPS	GOALS	FEE
Blackburn	94-95	18	0	£300,000
From: Lens				

OVERALL RECORD

COMPETITION	APPS	GOALS	(PENS)	SUBS
League	12	0	0	6
FA Cup	1	0	0	0
League Cup	1	0	0	0
Europe	1	0	–	–
Scottish	0	0	–	–
Other	1	0	–	–

HONOURS

League Championship 94-95, Charity Shield medal 94, Belgian Cup 86-87, 87-88

INTERNATIONAL APPEARANCES

COUNTRY	LEVEL	GAMES	GOALS
Australia	Full	Record not available	
	B		
	U-21		
	Youth		

NAME:	Richard Sneekes
CLUB:	Bolton
BORN:	Amsterdam, 30/10/68
DEBUT v:	Grimsby, 13/8/94
SUBSTITUTED:	6
BOOKINGS:	5
SENDINGS OFF:	0
OWN GOALS:	0
DOMESTIC PENS:	0
HAT-TRICKS:	0
STRIKE RATE (%):	17.02
EVER PRESENT:	–

LEAGUE CLUBS	YEARS	APPS	GOALS	FEE
Bolton	94-95	38	6	£200,000
From: Fortuna Sittard				

OVERALL RECORD

COMPETITION	APPS	GOALS	(PENS)	SUBS
League	37	6	0	1
FA Cup	1	1	0	0
League Cup	7	1	0	1
Europe	0	0	–	–
Scottish	0	0	–	–

HONOURS

League Cup r/u 94-95

INTERNATIONAL APPEARANCES

COUNTRY	LEVEL	GAMES	GOALS
	Full	0	0
	B	0	0
	U-21	0	0
	Youth	0	0

NAME:	Gareth Southgate
CLUB:	Aston Villa
BORN:	Watford 3/9/70
DEBUT v:	Liverpool 23/4/91
SUBSTITUTED:	4
BOOKINGS:	11
SENDINGS OFF:	0
OWN GOALS:	0
DOMESTIC PENS:	0
HAT-TRICKS:	0
STRIKE RATE (%):	11.89
EVER PRESENT:	93-94, 94-95

LEAGUE CLUBS	YEARS	APPS	GOALS	FEE
AstonVilla	95	0	0	£2.5m
Crystal Palace	89-95	152	15	Trainee

OVERALL RECORD

COMPETITION	APPS	GOALS	(PENS)	SUBS
League	148	15	0	4
FA Cup	9	0	0	0
League Cup	23	7	0	1
Europe	0	0	–	–
Scottish	0	0	–	–
Other	6	0	–	–

HONOURS

First Division Championship 93-94

INTERNATIONAL APPEARANCES

COUNTRY	LEVEL	GAMES	GOALS
	Full	0	0
	B	0	0
	U-21	0	0
	Youth	0	0

NAME:	Nigel Spackman
CLUB:	Chelsea
BORN:	Romsey, 2/12/60
DEBUT v:	York, 16/8/80
SUBSTITUTED:	19
BOOKINGS:	3
SENDINGS OFF:	0
OWN GOALS:	1
DOMESTIC PENS:	7
HAT-TRICKS:	0
STRIKE RATE (%):	5.57
EVER PRESENT:	84-85

LEAGUE CLUBS	YEARS	APPS	GOALS	FEE
Chelsea	92-95	50	0	£485,000
Rangers	89-92	100	1	£500,000
Q.P.R.	89	29	1	£500,000
Liverpool	87-89	51	0	£400,000
Chelsea	83-87	141	12	£40,000
Bournemouth	80-83	119	0	–
From: Andover				

OVERALL RECORD

COMPETITION	APPS	GOALS	(PENS)	SUBS
League	369	23	7	21
FA Cup	26	2	0	0
League Cup	39	1	0	2
Europe	12	0	–	–
Scottish	117	3	–	–
Other	17	3	–	–

HONOURS

League Championship 87-88, Division Two Championship 83-84, FA Cup r/u 87-88, Scottish Premier League 89-90, 90-91, 91-92, Scottish Cup 91-92, Scottish League Cup r/u 90-91

INTERNATIONAL APPEARANCES

COUNTRY	LEVEL	GAMES	GOALS
	Full	0	0
	B	0	0
	U-21	0	0
	Youth	0	0

NAME:	Gary Speed
CLUB:	Leeds
BORN:	Hawarden, 8/9/69
DEBUT v:	Oldham, 6/5/89
SUBSTITUTED:	14
BOOKINGS:	18
SENDINGS OFF:	0
OWN GOALS:	0
DOMESTIC PENS:	0
HAT-TRICKS:	0
STRIKE RATE (%):	19.29
EVER PRESENT:	90-91

LEAGUE CLUBS	YEARS	APPS	GOALS	FEE
Leeds	88-95	219	37	Trainee

OVERALL RECORD

COMPETITION	APPS	GOALS	(PENS)	SUBS
League	202	37	0	17
FA Cup	16	4	0	0
League Cup	18	8	0	1
Europe	5	1	–	–
Scottish	0	0	–	–
Other	9	1	–	–

HONOURS

League Championship 91-92, Division Two Championship 89-90, Charity Shield medal 92, PFA Team Award Premier League 93

INTERNATIONAL APPEARANCES

COUNTRY	LEVEL	GAMES	GOALS
Wales	Full	31	1
	B	0	0
	U-21	3	2
	Youth	0	0

NAME:	Philip Stamp
CLUB:	Middlesbrough
BORN:	Middlesbrough, 12/12/75
DEBUT v:	Watford, 10/10/93
SUBSTITUTED:	2
BOOKINGS:	0
SENDINGS OFF:	0
OWN GOALS:	0
DOMESTIC PENS:	0
HAT-TRICKS:	0
STRIKE RATE (%):	–
EVER PRESENT:	–

LEAGUE CLUBS	YEARS	APPS	GOALS	FEE
Middlesbrough	93-95	13	0	Trainee

OVERALL RECORD

COMPETITION	APPS	GOALS	(PENS)	SUBS
League	9	0	0	4
FA Cup	1	0	0	0
League Cup	2	0	0	0
Europe	0	0	–	–
Scottish	0	0	–	–
Other	6	0	–	–

HONOURS

None

INTERNATIONAL APPEARANCES

COUNTRY	LEVEL	GAMES	GOALS
England	Full	0	0
	B	0	0
	U-21	0	0
	Youth	4	0

NAME:	Paul Stewart
CLUB:	Liverpool
BORN:	Manchester, 7/10/64
DEBUT v:	Rochdale, 10/2/82
SUBSTITUTED:	28
BOOKINGS:	24
SENDINGS OFF:	3
OWN GOALS:	0
DOMESTIC PENS:	14
HAT-TRICKS:	4
STRIKE RATE (%):	25.92
EVER PRESENT:	–

LEAGUE CLUBS	YEARS	APPS	GOALS	FEE
Liverpool	92-95	32	1	£2.3m
Burnley	95	6	0	Loan
Wolverhampton	94	8	2	Loan
Crystal Palace	94	18	3	Loan
Tottenham	88-92	131	28	£1.7m
Manchester City	87-88	51	27	£200,000
Blackpool	81-87	201	56	Appr

OVERALL RECORD

COMPETITION	APPS	GOALS	(PENS)	SUBS
League	422	117	14	25
FA Cup	24	5	0	0
League Cup	46	12	0	0
Europe	10	2	–	–
Scottish	0	0	–	–
Other	13	2	–	–

INTERNATIONAL APPEARANCES

COUNTRY	LEVEL	GAMES	GOALS
England	Full	3	0
	B	5	1
	U-21	1	1
	Youth	2	0

HONOURS

First Division Championship 93-94, FA Cup 90-91, Charity Shield medal 91, 92, PFA Team Award Div 2. 88

NAME:	Steve Stone
CLUB:	Nottm Forest
BORN:	Gateshead, 20/8/71
DEBUT v:	West Ham, 2/5/92
SUBSTITUTED:	7
BOOKINGS:	9
SENDINGS OFF:	0
OWN GOALS:	0
DOMESTIC PENS:	0
HAT-TRICKS:	0
STRIKE RATE (%):	9.57
EVER PRESENT:	93-94

LEAGUE CLUBS	YEARS	APPS	GOALS	FEE
Nottm Forest	89-95	100	11	Trainee

OVERALL RECORD

COMPETITION	APPS	GOALS	(PENS)	SUBS
League	98	11	0	2
FA Cup	5	0	0	0
League Cup	9	0	0	1
Europe	0	0	–	–
Scottish	0	0	–	–
Other	2	0	–	–

HONOURS

None

INTERNATIONAL APPEARANCES

COUNTRY	LEVEL	GAMES	GOALS
	Full	0	0
	B	0	0
	U-21	0	0
	Youth	0	0

NAME:	Gordon Strachan
CLUB:	Coventry
BORN:	Edinburgh, 9/2/57
DEBUT v:	Hearts, 23/4/75
SUBSTITUTED:	45
BOOKINGS:	7
SENDINGS OFF:	1
OWN GOALS:	0
DOMESTIC PENS:	26
HAT-TRICKS:	2
STRIKE RATE (%):	18.18
EVER PRESENT:	89-90

LEAGUE CLUBS	YEARS	APPS	GOALS	FEE
Coventry	95	5	0	Free
Leeds	89-95	197	37	£300,000
Manchester Utd	84-89	160	33	£500,000
Aberdeen	77-84	171	53	£50,000
Dundee	74-77	69	13	Appr

OVERALL RECORD

COMPETITION	APPS	GOALS	(PENS)	SUBS
League	348	70	25	14
FA Cup	35	4	1	0
League Cup	31	4	0	1
Europe	42	11	–	–
Scottish	341	97	–	–
Other	20	3	–	–

INTERNATIONAL APPEARANCES

COUNTRY	LEVEL	GAMES	GOALS
Scotland	Full	50	5
	B	1	1
	U-21	0	0
	Youth	0	0

HONOURS

League Championship 91-92, Division Two Championship 89-90, FA Cup 84-85, Charity Shield medal 92, European Cup Winners' Cup 82-83, Footballer of the Year 90-91, Scottish Premier League 79-80, 83-84, Scottish FA Cup 81-82, 82-83, 83-84, Scottish League Cup r/u 78-79, 79-80, Scottish Footballer of the Year 80, PFA Team Awards: Div 2. 90, Div 1. 91

NAME:	Graham Stuart
CLUB:	Everton
BORN:	Tooting, 24/10/70
DEBUT v:	Crystal Palace, 16/4/90
SUBSTITUTED:	23
BOOKINGS:	8
SENDINGS OFF:	0
OWN GOALS:	0
DOMESTIC PENS:	1
HAT-TRICKS:	0
STRIKE RATE (%):	14.94
EVER PRESENT:	–

LEAGUE CLUBS	YEARS	APPS	GOALS	FEE
Everton	93-95	58	6	£650,000
Chelsea	89-93	87	14	Appr

OVERALL RECORD

COMPETITION	APPS	GOALS	(PENS)	SUBS
League	116	20	1	29
FA Cup	9	3	0	5
League Cup	15	3	0	0
Europe	0	0	–	–
Scottish	0	0	–	–
Other	6	1	–	–

HONOURS

FA Cup 94-95

INTERNATIONAL APPEARANCES

COUNTRY	LEVEL	GAMES	GOALS
England	Full	0	0
	B	0	0
	U-21	5	2
	Youth	5	1

NAME:	Nicky Summerbee
CLUB:	Manchester City
BORN:	Altrincham, 26/8/71
DEBUT v:	Wolves, 3/9/89
SUBSTITUTED:	10
BOOKINGS:	16
SENDINGS OFF:	1
OWN GOALS:	1
DOMESTIC PENS:	0
HAT-TRICKS:	0
STRIKE RATE (%):	6.74
EVER PRESENT:	–

LEAGUE CLUBS	YEARS	APPS	GOALS	FEE
Manchester City	94-95	41	1	£1.5m
Swindon	89-94	112	6	Trainee

OVERALL RECORD

COMPETITION	APPS	GOALS	(PENS)	SUBS
League	128	7	0	25
FA Cup	5	0	0	4
League Cup	15	5	0	1
Europe	0	0	–	–
Scottish	0	0	–	–
Other	7	1	–	–

HONOURS

None

INTERNATIONAL APPEARANCES

COUNTRY	LEVEL	GAMES	GOALS
England	Full	0	0
	B	0	0
	U-21	3	1
	Youth	0	0

NAME:	Steven Talboys
CLUB:	Wimbledon
BORN:	Bristol, 18/9/66
DEBUT v:	Norwich, 5/12/92
SUBSTITUTED:	4
BOOKINGS:	2
SENDINGS OFF:	0
OWN GOALS:	0
DOMESTIC PENS:	0
HAT-TRICKS:	0
STRIKE RATE (%):	–
EVER PRESENT:	–

LEAGUE CLUBS	YEARS	APPS	GOALS	FEE
Wimbledon	92-95	21	1	£10,000
From: Gloucester City				

OVERALL RECORD

COMPETITION	APPS	GOALS	(PENS)	SUBS
League	16	1	0	5
FA Cup	2	1	0	1
League Cup	2	0	0	1
Europe	0	0	–	–
Scottish	0	0	–	–

HONOURS

None

INTERNATIONAL APPEARANCES

COUNTRY	LEVEL	GAMES	GOALS
	Full	0	0
	B	0	0
	U-21	0	0
	Youth	0	0

NAME:	Ian Taylor
CLUB:	Aston Villa
BORN:	Birmingham, 4/6/68
DEBUT v:	Fulham, 15/8/92
SUBSTITUTED:	8
BOOKINGS:	13
SENDINGS OFF:	1
OWN GOALS:	0
DOMESTIC PENS:	0
HAT-TRICKS:	0
STRIKE RATE (%):	24.44
EVER PRESENT:	–

LEAGUE CLUBS	YEARS	APPS	GOALS	FEE
Aston Villa	94-95	22	1	£1.25m
Sheffield Wed	94	14	1	£1.17m
Port Vale	92-94	83	27	£15,000
From: Moor Green				

OVERALL RECORD

COMPETITION	APPS	GOALS	(PENS)	SUBS
League	114	29	0	5
FA Cup	8	1	0	0
League Cup	6	3	0	2
Europe	0	0	–	–
Scottish	0	0	–	–
Other	13	4	–	–

HONOURS

PFA Team Awards Div 2. 93, 94

INTERNATIONAL APPEARANCES

COUNTRY	LEVEL	GAMES	GOALS
	Full	0	0
	B	0	0
	U-21	0	0
	Youth	0	0

NAME:	Michael Thomas
CLUB:	Liverpool
BORN:	Lambeth, 24/8/67
DEBUT v:	Reading, 1/1/87
SUBSTITUTED:	10
BOOKINGS:	5
SENDINGS OFF:	0
OWN GOALS:	0
DOMESTIC PENS:	3
HAT-TRICKS:	1
STRIKE RATE (%):	13.14
EVER PRESENT:	–

LEAGUE CLUBS	YEARS	APPS	GOALS	FEE
Liverpool	91-95	54	4	£1.5m
Portsmouth	86	3	0	Loan
Arsenal	84-91	163	24	Appr

OVERALL RECORD

COMPETITION	APPS	GOALS	(PENS)	SUBS
League	191	28	2	29
FA Cup	23	3	0	4
League Cup	23	5	1	4
Europe	4	0	–	–
Scottish	0	0	–	–
Other	14	1	–	–

HONOURS

League Championship 88-89, 90-91, FA Cup 91-92, League Cup 86-87, 94-95, League Cup r/u 87-88, Charity Shield medal 89, 91

INTERNATIONAL APPEARANCES

COUNTRY	LEVEL	GAMES	GOALS
England	Full	2	0
	B	6	0
	U-21	12	3
	Youth	22	0

NAME:	Scott Thomas
CLUB:	Manchester City
BORN:	Bury, 30/10/74
DEBUT v:	Nottm Forest, 6/5/95
SUBSTITUTED:	0
BOOKINGS:	0
SENDINGS OFF:	0
OWN GOALS:	0
DOMESTIC PENS:	0
HAT-TRICKS:	0
STRIKE RATE (%):	–
EVER PRESENT:	–

LEAGUE CLUBS	YEARS	APPS	GOALS	FEE
Manchester City	92-95	2	0	Trainee

OVERALL RECORD

COMPETITION	APPS	GOALS	(PENS)	SUBS
League	0	0	0	2
FA Cup	0	0	0	0
League Cup	0	0	0	0
Europe	0	0	–	–
Scottish	0	0	–	–

HONOURS

None

INTERNATIONAL APPEARANCES

COUNTRY	LEVEL	GAMES	GOALS
	Full	0	0
	B	0	0
	U-21	0	0
	Youth	0	0

NAME:	Alan Thompson
CLUB:	Bolton
BORN:	Newcastle, 22/12/73
DEBUT v:	Swindon, 2/11/91
SUBSTITUTED:	15
BOOKINGS:	11
SENDINGS OFF:	1
OWN GOALS:	0
DOMESTIC PENS:	1
HAT-TRICKS:	0
STRIKE RATE (%):	17.53
EVER PRESENT:	–

LEAGUE CLUBS	YEARS	APPS	GOALS	FEE
Bolton	93-95	64	14	£250,000
Newcastle	91-93	16	0	Trainee

OVERALL RECORD

COMPETITION	APPS	GOALS	(PENS)	SUBS
League	66	14	1	14
FA Cup	4	1	0	1
League Cup	11	2	0	1
Europe	0	0	–	–
Scottish	0	0	–	–
Other	11	1	–	–

HONOURS

League Cup r/u 94-95

INTERNATIONAL APPEARANCES

COUNTRY	LEVEL	GAMES	GOALS
England	Full	0	0
	B	0	0
	U-21	1	0
	Youth	11	2

NAME:	Ben Thornley
CLUB:	Manchester Utd
BORN:	Bury, 21/4/75
DEBUT v:	West Ham, 26/2/94
SUBSTITUTED:	0
BOOKINGS:	0
SENDINGS OFF:	0
OWN GOALS:	0
DOMESTIC PENS:	0
HAT-TRICKS:	0
STRIKE RATE (%):	–
EVER PRESENT:	–

LEAGUE CLUBS	YEARS	APPS	GOALS	FEE
Manchester Utd	93-95	1	0	Trainee

OVERALL RECORD

COMPETITION	APPS	GOALS	(PENS)	SUBS
League	0	0	0	1
FA Cup	0	0	0	0
League Cup	0	0	0	0
Europe	0	0	–	–
Scottish	0	0	–	–

HONOURS

FA Youth Cup 91-92, FA Youth Cup r/u 92-93

INTERNATIONAL APPEARANCES

COUNTRY	LEVEL	GAMES	GOALS
	Full	0	0
	B	0	0
	U-21	0	0
	Youth	0	0

NAME:	Francis Tierney
CLUB:	Liverpool
BORN:	Liverpool, 10/9/75
DEBUT v:	Barnet, 8/5/93
SUBSTITUTED:	3
BOOKINGS:	0
SENDINGS OFF:	0
OWN GOALS:	0
DOMESTIC PENS:	0
HAT-TRICKS:	0
STRIKE RATE (%):	–
EVER PRESENT:	–

LEAGUE CLUBS	YEARS	APPS	GOALS	FEE
Liverpool	95	0	0	£700,000
Crewe	92-95	29	5	Trainee

OVERALL RECORD

COMPETITION	APPS	GOALS	(PENS)	SUBS
League	17	5	0	12
FA Cup	0	0	0	2
League Cup	2	0	0	0
Europe	0	0	–	–
Scottish	0	0	–	–
Others	3	2	–	–

HONOURS

None

INTERNATIONAL APPEARANCES

COUNTRY	LEVEL	GAMES	GOALS
	Full	0	0
	B	0	0
	U-21	0	0
	Youth	0	0

NAME:	Mark Tinkler
CLUB:	Leeds
BORN:	Bishop Auckland, 24/10/74
DEBUT v:	Sheffield Utd, 6/4/93
SUBSTITUTED:	1
BOOKINGS:	0
SENDINGS OFF:	0
OWN GOALS:	0
DOMESTIC PENS:	0
HAT-TRICKS:	0
STRIKE RATE (%):	–
EVER PRESENT:	–

LEAGUE CLUBS	YEARS	APPS	GOALS	FEE
Leeds	91-95	13	0	Trainee

OVERALL RECORD

COMPETITION	APPS	GOALS	(PENS)	SUBS
League	8	0	0	5
FA Cup	0	0	0	0
League Cup	0	0	0	0
Europe	0	0	–	–
Scottish	0	0	–	–

HONOURS

FA Youth Cup 92-93

INTERNATIONAL APPEARANCES

COUNTRY	LEVEL	GAMES	GOALS
England	Full	0	0
	B	0	0
	U-21	0	0
	Youth	7	1

NAME:	Andy Townsend
CLUB:	Aston Villa
BORN:	Maidstone, 23/7/63
DEBUT v:	Aston Villa, 20/4/85
SUBSTITUTED:	24
BOOKINGS:	25
SENDINGS OFF:	3
OWN GOALS:	0
DOMESTIC PENS:	2
HAT-TRICKS:	0
STRIKE RATE (%):	9.90
EVER PRESENT:	–

LEAGUE CLUBS	YEARS	APPS	GOALS	FEE
Aston Villa	93-95	64	4	£2m
Chelsea	90-93	110	12	£1.2m
Norwich	88-90	71	8	£300,000
Southampton	85-88	83	5	£35,000
From: Weymouth				

OVERALL RECORD

COMPETITION	APPS	GOALS	(PENS)	SUBS
League	317	29	2	11
FA Cup	24	2	0	3
League Cup	37	8	0	2
Europe	8	1	–	–
Scottish	0	0	–	–
Other	12	0	–	–

HONOURS

League Cup 93-94, PFA Team Award Div 1. 89, 91, 92

INTERNATIONAL APPEARANCES

COUNTRY	LEVEL	GAMES	GOALS
Eire	Full	54	5
	B	1	0
	U-21	0	0
	Youth	0	0

NAME:	Andy Turner
CLUB:	Tottenham
BORN:	Woolwich, 23/3/75
DEBUT v:	Southamton, 15/8/92
SUBSTITUTED:	8
BOOKINGS:	0
SENDINGS OFF:	0
OWN GOALS:	0
DOMESTIC PENS:	0
HAT-TRICKS:	0
STRIKE RATE (%):	–
EVER PRESENT:	–

LEAGUE CLUBS	YEARS	APPS	GOALS	FEE
Tottenham	92-95	21	3	Trainee
Doncaster	94	4	1	Loan
Wycombe	94	4	0	Loan

OVERALL RECORD

COMPETITION	APPS	GOALS	(PENS)	SUBS
League	16	4	0	13
FA Cup	0	0	0	1
League Cup	0	1	0	2
Europe	0	0	–	–
Scottish	0	0	–	–

HONOURS

None

INTERNATIONAL APPEARANCES

COUNTRY	LEVEL	GAMES	GOALS
Eire	Full	0	0
	B	0	0
	U-21	3	0
	Youth	1	0

NAME:	Chris Waddle
CLUB:	Sheffield Wed
BORN:	Hepworth, 14/12/60
DEBUT v:	Shrewsbury, 22/10/80
SUBSTITUTED:	33
BOOKINGS:	3
SENDINGS OFF:	0
OWN GOALS:	0
DOMESTIC PENS:	0
HAT-TRICKS:	1
STRIKE RATE (%):	22.48
EVER PRESENT:	81-82, 83-84, 88-89

LEAGUE CLUBS	YEARS	APPS	GOALS	FEE
Sheffield Wed	92-95	77	8	£1m
From: Marseilles				
Tottenham	85-89	138	33	£590,000
Newcastle	80-85	170	46	£1,000
From: Tow Law Town				

OVERALL RECORD

COMPETITION	APPS	GOALS	(PENS)	SUBS
League	377	87	0	8
FA Cup	37	12	0	1
League Cup	44	6	0	0
Europe	23	4	–	–
Scottish	0	0	–	–
Other	124	23	–	–

INTERNATIONAL APPEARANCES

COUNTRY	LEVEL	GAMES	GOALS
England	Full	62	6
	B	0	0
	U-21	1	0
	Youth	0	0

HONOURS

FA Cup r/u 86-87, 92-3, League Cup r/u 92-93, Footballer of the Year 92-93, PFA Team Award Div 1. 89, French Championship 89-90, 90-91, 91-92, French Cup 91-92

NAME:	Mark Walters
CLUB:	Liverpool
BORN:	Birmingham, 2/6/64
DEBUT v:	Leeds, 28/4/82
SUBSTITUTED:	32
BOOKINGS:	13
SENDINGS OFF:	0
OWN GOALS:	0
DOMESTIC PENS:	5
HAT-TRICKS:	2
STRIKE RATE (%):	19.83
EVER PRESENT:	–

LEAGUE CLUBS	YEARS	APPS	GOALS	FEE
Liverpool	91-95	93	14	£1.25m
Wolverhampton	94	11	3	Loan
Stoke	94	9	2	Loan
Rangers	88-91	106	32	£500,000
Aston Villa	81-88	181	39	Appr

OVERALL RECORD

COMPETITION	APPS	GOALS	(PENS)	SUBS
League	246	58	5	48
FA Cup	17	1	0	4
League Cup	30	10	0	3
Europe	22	4	–	–
Scottish	133	49	–	–
Other	8	1	–	–

INTERNATIONAL APPEARANCES

COUNTRY	LEVEL	GAMES	GOALS
England	Full	1	0
	B	1	0
	U-21	9	1
	Youth	10	4

HONOURS

League Cup 94-95, Charity Shield medal 92, Scottish Premier League 88-89, 89-90, 90-91, Scottish FA Cup r/u 88-89, Scottish League Cup 88-89, 90-91, Scottish League Cup r/u 89-90

NAME:	Kevin Watson
CLUB:	Tottenham
BORN:	Hackney, 3/1/74
DEBUT v:	Sheffield Wed, 27/9/92
SUBSTITUTED:	6
BOOKINGS:	1
SENDINGS OFF:	0
OWN GOALS:	0
DOMESTIC PENS:	0
HAT-TRICKS:	0
STRIKE RATE (%):	–
EVER PRESENT:	–

LEAGUE CLUBS	YEARS	APPS	GOALS	FEE
Tottenham	92-95	5	0	Trainee
Barnet	95	13	0	Loan
Bristol City	94	2	0	Loan
Brentford	93	3	0	Loan

OVERALL RECORD

COMPETITION	APPS	GOALS	(PENS)	SUBS
League	20	0	0	3
FA Cup	0	0	0	1
League Cup	1	1	0	1
Europe	0	0	–	–
Scottish	0	0	–	–

HONOURS

None

INTERNATIONAL APPEARANCES

COUNTRY	LEVEL	GAMES	GOALS
England	Full	0	0
	B	0	0
	U-21	0	0
	Youth	1	0

NAME:	Steve Watson
CLUB:	Newcastle
BORN:	North Shields, 1/4/74
DEBUT v:	Wolves, 10/11/90
SUBSTITUTED:	10
BOOKINGS:	6
SENDINGS OFF:	0
OWN GOALS:	0
DOMESTIC PENS:	0
HAT-TRICKS:	0
STRIKE RATE (%):	5.47
EVER PRESENT:	–

LEAGUE CLUBS	YEARS	APPS	GOALS	FEE
Newcastle	90-95	112	7	Trainee

OVERALL RECORD

COMPETITION	APPS	GOALS	(PENS)	SUBS
League	96	7	0	16
FA Cup	7	0	0	2
League Cup	6	0	0	1
Europe	3	1	–	–
Scottish	0	0	–	–
Other	3	0	–	–

HONOURS

None

INTERNATIONAL APPEARANCES

COUNTRY	LEVEL	GAMES	GOALS
England	Full	0	0
	B	0	0
	U-21	10	1
	Youth	13	0

NAME:	Neil Webb
CLUB:	Nottm Forest
BORN:	Reading, 30/7/63
DEBUT v:	Mansfield, 16/2/80
SUBSTITUTED:	26
BOOKINGS:	3
SENDINGS OFF:	0
OWN GOALS:	0
DOMESTIC PENS:	6
HAT-TRICKS:	2
STRIKE RATE (%):	23.80
EVER PRESENT:	87-88

LEAGUE CLUBS	YEARS	APPS	GOALS	FEE
Nottm Forest	92-95	30	3	£800,000
Swindon	94	6	0	Loan
Manchester Utd	89-92	75	8	£1.5m
Nottm Forest	85-89	146	47	£250,000
Portsmouth	82-85	123	34	£83,000
Reading	80-82	72	22	Appr

OVERALL RECORD

COMPETITION	APPS	GOALS	(PENS)	SUBS
League	435	114	6	17
FA Cup	36	6	0	1
League Cup	48	9	0	5
Europe	10	1	–	–
Scottish	0	0	–	–
Other	11	3	–	–

HONOURS

Division Three Championship 82-83, FA Cup 89-90, League Cup 88-89 League Cup r/u 90-91, PFA Team Awards Div 3. 82, 83

INTERNATIONAL APPEARANCES

COUNTRY	LEVEL	GAMES	GOALS
England	Full	26	4
	B	6	0
	U-21	2	0
	Youth	10	4

NAME:	Peter Whiston
CLUB:	Southampton
BORN:	Widnes, 4/1/68
DEBUT v:	Oxford, 6/5/89
SUBSTITUTED:	14
BOOKINGS:	16
SENDINGS OFF:	2
OWN GOALS:	0
DOMESTIC PENS:	0
HAT-TRICKS:	0
STRIKE RATE (%):	5.59
EVER PRESENT:	–

LEAGUE CLUBS	YEARS	APPS	GOALS	FEE
Southampton	94-95	1	0	£30,000
Exeter	91-94	86	7	£25,000
Torquay	90-91	40	1	Free
Plymouth	87-90	10	0	
From: Widnes				

OVERALL RECORD

COMPETITION	APPS	GOALS	(PENS)	SUBS
League	129	8	0	8
FA Cup	12	0	0	0
League Cup	12	1	0	0
Europe	0	0	–	–
Scottish	0	0	–	–
Other	17	1	–	–

HONOURS

None

INTERNATIONAL APPEARANCES

COUNTRY	LEVEL	GAMES	GOALS
	Full	0	0
	B	0	0
	U-21	0	0
	Youth	0	0

NAME: Jason Wilcox
CLUB: Blackburn
BORN: Bolton, 15/7/71
DEBUT v: Swindon, 16/4/90
SUBSTITUTED: 23
BOOKINGS: 19
SENDINGS OFF: 2
OWN GOALS: 0
DOMESTIC PENS: 0
HAT-TRICKS: 0
STRIKE RATE (%): 12.00
EVER PRESENT: –

LEAGUE CLUBS	YEARS	APPS	GOALS	FEE
Blackburn	89-95	150	19	Trainee

OVERALL RECORD

COMPETITION	APPS	GOALS	(PENS)	SUBS
League	138	19	0	12
FA Cup	10	1	0	0
League Cup	14	1	0	1
Europe	2	0	–	–
Scottish	0	0	–	–
Other	3	0	–	–

HONOURS

League Championship 94-95, Charity Shield medal 94

INTERNATIONAL APPEARANCES

COUNTRY	LEVEL	GAMES	GOALS
England	Full	0	0
	B	1	0
	U-21	0	0
	Youth	0	0

NAME: Ray Wilkins
CLUB: Q.P.R.
BORN: Hillingdon, 14/9/56
DEBUT v: Norwich, 26/10/73
SUBSTITUTED: 24
BOOKINGS: 6
SENDINGS OFF: 0
OWN GOALS: 0
DOMESTIC PENS: 4
HAT-TRICKS: 0
STRIKE RATE (%): 9.38
EVER PRESENT: 75-76, 76-77, 81-82, 83-84, 90-91

LEAGUE CLUBS	YEARS	APPS	GOALS	FEE
Q.P.R.	94-95	2	0	£80,000
Crystal Palace	94	1	0	Free
Q.P.R.	89-94	154	7	Free
Rangers	87-89	70	2	£250,000
From: Paris St Germain				
Manchester Utd	79-84	160	7	£825,000
Chelsea	73-79	179	30	Appr

OVERALL RECORD

COMPETITION	APPS	GOALS	(PENS)	SUBS
League	489	44	3	7
FA Cup	33	5	0	1
League Cup	33	4	1	2
Europe	21	2	–	–
Scottish	96	2	–	–
Other	12	0	–	–

HONOURS

FA Cup 82-83, League Cup r/u 82-83, Charity Shield medal 83, Scottish Premier League 88-89, 89-90, Scottish FA Cup 88-89, Scottish FA Cup r/u 89-90, PFA Team Award Div 2. 77

INTERNATIONAL APPEARANCES

COUNTRY	LEVEL	GAMES	GOALS
England	Full	80	1
	B	2	0
	U-21	2	0
	Youth	4	0

NAME: Michael Williams
CLUB: Sheffield Wed
BORN: Bradford, 21/11/69
DEBUT v: Bury, 19/12/92
SUBSTITUTED: 3
BOOKINGS: 4
SENDINGS OFF: 0
OWN GOALS: 0
DOMESTIC PENS: 0
HAT-TRICKS: 0
STRIKE RATE (%): –
EVER PRESENT: –

LEAGUE CLUBS	YEARS	APPS	GOALS	FEE
Sheffield Wed	91-95	16	1	–
Halifax	92-93	9	1	Loan

OVERALL RECORD

COMPETITION	APPS	GOALS	(PENS)	SUBS
League	23	2	0	2
FA Cup	0	0	0	0
League Cup	1	0	0	1
Europe	0	0	–	–
Scottish	0	0	–	–
Other	1	0	–	–

HONOURS

None

INTERNATIONAL APPEARANCES

COUNTRY	LEVEL	GAMES	GOALS
	Full	0	0
	B	0	0
	U-21	0	0
	Youth	0	0

NAME:	Paul Williams
CLUB:	Coventry
BORN:	Leicester, 11/9/69
DEBUT v:	Torquay, 19/8/89
SUBSTITUTED:	8
BOOKINGS:	3
SENDINGS OFF:	1
OWN GOALS:	0
DOMESTIC PENS:	0
HAT-TRICKS:	0
STRIKE RATE (%):	3.67
EVER PRESENT:	–

LEAGUE CLUBS	YEARS	APPS	GOALS	FEE
Coventry	93-95	14	0	£150,000
Huddersfield	94-95	9	0	Loan
West Brom	93	5	0	Loan
Stockport	89-93	70	4	Free
Leicester	88-89	0	0	Trainee

OVERALL RECORD

COMPETITION	APPS	GOALS	(PENS)	SUBS
League	83	4	0	15
FA Cup	7	0	0	0
League Cup	3	0	0	1
Europe	0	0	–	–
Scottish	0	0	–	–
Other	12	1	–	–

HONOURS

None

INTERNATIONAL APPEARANCES

COUNTRY	LEVEL	GAMES	GOALS
	Full	0	0
	B	0	0
	U-21	0	0
	Youth	0	0

NAME:	Dennis Wise
CLUB:	Chelsea
BORN:	Kensington, 15/12/66
DEBUT v:	Cardiff, 11/5/85
SUBSTITUTED:	21
BOOKINGS:	37
SENDINGS OFF:	3
OWN GOALS:	0
DOMESTIC PENS:	14
HAT-TRICKS:	0
STRIKE RATE (%):	20.82
EVER PRESENT:	–

LEAGUE CLUBS	YEARS	APPS	GOALS	FEE
Chelsea	90-95	151	33	£1.6m
Wimbledon	85-90	135	26	Free
Southampton	84-85	0	0	Appr

OVERALL RECORD

COMPETITION	APPS	GOALS	(PENS)	SUBS
League	276	59	12	10
FA Cup	22	6	0	0
League Cup	33	6	2	0
Europe	5	1	–	–
Scottish	0	0	–	–
Other	14	2	–	–

HONOURS

FA Cup 87-88, FA Cup r/u 93-94, Charity Shield medal 88

INTERNATIONAL APPEARANCES

COUNTRY	LEVEL	GAMES	GOALS
England	Full	8	1
	B	3	1
	U-21	1	0
	Youth	0	0

NAME:	Ian Woan
CLUB:	Nottm Forest
BORN:	Heswall, 14/12/67
DEBUT v:	Norwich, 2/1/91
SUBSTITUTED:	15
BOOKINGS:	14
SENDINGS OFF:	0
OWN GOALS:	0
DOMESTIC PENS:	0
HAT-TRICKS:	0
STRIKE RATE (%):	15.86
EVER PRESENT:	–

LEAGUE CLUBS	YEARS	APPS	GOALS	FEE
Nottm Forest From: Runcorn	90-95	122	21	£80,000

OVERALL RECORD

COMPETITION	APPS	GOALS	(PENS)	SUBS
League	114	21	0	8
FA Cup	10	1	0	1
League Cup	10	1	0	2
Europe	0	0	–	–
Scottish	0	0	–	–
Other	6	2	–	–

HONOURS

FA Cup r/u 90-91

INTERNATIONAL APPEARANCES

COUNTRY	LEVEL	GAMES	GOALS
	Full	0	0
	B	0	0
	U-21	0	0
	Youth	0	0

INTRODUCTION – FORWARDS

Alan Shearer confirmed himself as the king of strikers by blasting 34 Premiership goals and winning the prestigious SHOOT/Adidas Golden Shoe award for 1995. The measure of Shearer's dominance was that he ended a dramatic and triumphant season no fewer than nine goals clear of his nearest rival, Liverpool's Robbie Fowler. In doing so, Shearer underlined his position as the most complete centre-forward in the country, arguably the best since Jimmy Greaves - the ultimate of tributes.

Some people thought that Kenny Dalglish had lost the plot when he paid a then British record £3.3m to Southampton for Shearer in the summer of 1992. But a hundred goals in just three seasons provides conclusive evidence of the fact that Dalglish's bold move was one of the best transfers he'll ever conduct as a manager. There's little doubt that when Shearer eventually moves on – more than likely to Italy next season - he'll become the most expensive British player of all time, valued at something in the region of £12m.

And it's incredible to think that the England striker had to overcome a career threatening, Gazza-type injury to elevate himself to superstar status. His all-round ability has made him the most respected striker in the game and, when you weigh up the standard of the opposition, that is a truly exalted position. Robbie Fowler, Stan Collymore, Les Ferdinand and Andy Cole all tried but failed to stay in the slipstream of the Shearer express, but the Blackburn man left them all standing.

A shin splint problem, coupled with the pressure of his record-busting £7m transfer to Manchester United, made it difficult for Cole to maintain his early season scoring form. He did manage five in a game for United, in the 9-0 win over relegated Ipswich, but Cole still ended the season 13 goals behind Shearer. But now that the former Arsenal forward has settled at Old Trafford – and that he'll be given the chance to strike up an Entente Cordial with Eric Cantona – he's sure to be pushing Shearer all the way for the coveted Golden Shoe this season.

Liverpool youngster Fowler, too, will have his sights set on the prestigious award after alerting the Premiership of his prolific powers in only his first full season. Fowler has clearly learned a lot from his master marksman Ian Rush who has taken something of a back seat on the scoring front with the emergence of the sorcerer's apprentice. The Young Player of the Year, Liverpool born and bred, plundered 25 Premiership goals alone as the Reds celebrated a return to the good old days with a Wembley triumph over Bolton in the Coca Cola Cup.

And for the 95-96 campaign Fowler will be joined by former Nottingham Forest striker Stan Collymore. It's remarkable to think that just three years ago Crystal Palace packed Collymore off to Southend for a fee of just £300,000, and yet now he's an England international worth £8.5m.

In London it's been all change for the men 'up front'. QPR have packed Les Ferdinand off to Newcastle to join forces with Frenchman David Ginola, placing faith in the talented young pairing of Dichio and Gallen – a partnership that fared well for the club at junior levels. While in North London Arsenal have put their faith in Dennis Bergkamp after his nightmare spell in Milan, and Spurs have paid £4.5m to relegated Crystal Palace for Chris Armstrong.

With all this striking talent in the Premiership, clean-sheets will be rare in 95-96.

NAME:	Bradley Allen
CLUB:	Q.P.R.
BORN:	Harold Wood, 13/9/71
DEBUT v:	Wimbledon, 14/1/89
SUBSTITUTED:	8
BOOKINGS:	4
SENDINGS OFF:	0
OWN GOALS:	0
DOMESTIC PENS:	0
HAT-TRICKS:	2
STRIKE RATE (%):	36.14
EVER PRESENT:	–

LEAGUE CLUBS	YEARS	APPS	GOALS	FEE
Q.P.R.	88-95	73	26	Appr

OVERALL RECORD

COMPETITION	APPS	GOALS	(PENS)	SUBS
League	51	26	0	22
FA Cup	1	0	0	2
League Cup	5	4	0	2
Europe	0	0	–	–
Scotland	0	0	–	–
Other	1	0	–	–

HONOURS

None

INTERNATIONAL APPEARANCES

COUNTRY	LEVEL	GAMES	GOALS
England	Full	0	0
	B	0	0
	U-21	8	2
	Youth	9	1

NAME:	Malcolm Allen
CLUB:	Newcastle
BORN:	Dioniolen, 21/3/67
DEBUT v:	West Ham, 16/11/85
SUBSTITUTED:	28
BOOKINGS:	11
SENDINGS OFF:	1
OWN GOALS:	0
DOMESTIC PENS:	8
HAT-TRICKS:	1
STRIKE RATE (%):	28.922
EVER PRESENT:	–

LEAGUE CLUBS	YEARS	APPS	GOALS	FEE
Newcastle	93-95	10	5	£300,000
Millwall	90-93	81	24	£400,000
Norwich	88-90	35	8	£175,000
Aston Villa	87	4	0	Loan
Watford	85-88	39	5	Appr

OVERALL RECORD

COMPETITION	APPS	GOALS	(PENS)	SUBS
League	124	42	6	45
FA Cup	11	13	1	9
League Cup	11	4	1	4
Europe	0	0	–	–
Scotland	0	0	–	–
Other	4	0	–	–

HONOURS

FA Youth Cup r/u 83-84

INTERNATIONAL HONOURS

COUNTRY	LEVEL	GAMES	GOALS
Wales	Full	14	3
	B	1	0
	U-21	0	0
	Youth	0	0

NAME:	Daniel Amokachi
CLUB:	Everton
BORN:	Nigeria, 30/12/72
DEBUT v:	Blackburn, 10/9/94
SUBSTITUTED:	4
BOOKINGS:	3
SENDINGS OFF:	0
OWN GOALS:	0
DOMESTIC PENS:	0
HAT-TRICKS:	0
STRIKE RATE (%):	27.272
EVER PRESENT:	–

LEAGUE CLUBS	YEARS	APPS	GOALS	FEE
Everton	94-95	18	4	£2.5m
From: Bruges				

OVERALL RECORD

COMPETITION	APPS	GOALS	(PENS)	SUBS
League	17	4	0	1
FA Cup	0	2	0	2
League Cup	2	0	0	0
Europe	0	0	–	–
Scotland	0	0	–	–

HONOURS

FA Cup 94-95, Belgian Cup r/u 93-94

INTERNATIONAL HONOURS

COUNTRY	LEVEL	GAMES	GOALS
Nigeria	Full	22	2
	B	0	0
	U-21	0	0
	Youth	0	0

NAME:	Chris Armstrong
CLUB:	Tottenham
BORN:	Newcastle, 19/6/71
DEBUT v:	Hartlepool, 4/11/94
SUBSTITUTED:	14
BOOKINGS:	22
SENDINGS OFF:	1
OWN GOALS:	0
DOMESTIC PENS:	0
HAT-TRICKS:	1
STRIKE RATE (%):	33.33
EVER PRESENT:	–

LEAGUE CLUBS	YEARS	APPS	GOALS	FEE
Tottenham	95	0	0	£4.5m
Crystal Palace	92-95	118	46	£1m
Millwall	91-92	28	5	£50,000
Wrexham	89-91	60	13	Free

OVERALL RECORD

COMPETITION	APPS	GOALS	(PENS)	SUBS
League	169	64	0	37
FA Cup	8	5	0	2
League Cup	13	8	0	2
Europe	3	0	–	–
Scotland	0	0	–	–
Other	6	4	–	–

HONOURS

First Division Championship 93-94, PFA Team Award Div 1. 94

INTERNATIONAL APPEARANCES

COUNTRY	LEVEL	GAMES	GOALS
England	Full	0	0
	B	1	0
	U-21	0	0
	Youth	0	0

NAME:	Dalian Atkinson
CLUB:	Aston Villa
BORN:	Shrewsbury, 21/3/68
DEBUT v:	Newcastle, 15/3/86
SUBSTITUTED:	20
BOOKINGS:	6
SENDINGS OFF:	0
OWN GOALS:	0
DOMESTIC PENS:	0
HAT-TRICKS:	2
STRIKE RATE (%):	32.09
EVER PRESENT:	89-90

LEAGUE CLUBS	YEARS	APPS	GOALS	FEE
Aston Villa	91-95	87	23	£1.6m
From: Real Sociedad				
Sheffield Wed	89-90	38	10	£450,000
Ipswich	85-89	60	18	Appr

OVERALL RECORD

COMPETITION	APPS	GOALS	(PENS)	SUBS
League	166	51	0	19
FA Cup	6	1	0	0
League Cup	23	17	0	1
Europe	11	2	–	–
Scotland	0	0	–	–
Other	6	2	–	–

HONOURS

League Cup 93-94

INTERNATIONAL APPEARANCES

COUNTRY	LEVEL	GAMES	GOALS
England	Full	0	0
	B	1	0
	U-21	0	0
	Youth	0	0

NAME:	Stuart Barlow
CLUB:	Everton
BORN:	Liverpool, 16/7/68
DEBUT v:	Wimbledon, 10/4/91
SUBSTITUTED:	8
BOOKINGS:	2
SENDINGS OFF:	1
OWN GOALS:	0
DOMESTIC PENS:	0
HAT-TRICKS:	0
STRIKE RATE (%):	15.854
EVER PRESENT:	–

LEAGUE CLUBS	YEARS	APPS	GOALS	FEE
Everton	90-95	68	10	£10,000

OVERALL RECORD

COMPETITION	APPS	GOALS	(PENS)	SUBS
League	24	10	0	44
FA Cup	4	2	0	3
League Cup	3	1	0	4
Europe	0	0	–	–
Scotland	0	0	–	–
Other	1	0	–	–

HONOURS

None

INTERNATIONAL APPEARANCES

COUNTRY	LEVEL	GAMES	GOALS
	Full	0	0
	B	0	0
	U-21	0	0
	Youth	0	0

NAME:	Nick Barmby
CLUB:	Tottenham
BORN:	Hull, 11/2/74
DEBUT v:	Sheffield Wed, 27/9/92
SUBSTITUTED:	24
BOOKINGS:	1
SENDINGS OFF:	0
OWN GOALS:	0
DOMESTIC PENS:	1
HAT-TRICKS:	0
STRIKE RATE (%):	25.00
EVER PRESENT:	–

LEAGUE CLUBS	YEARS	APPS	GOALS	FEE
Tottenham	91-95	87	20	Trainee

OVERALL RECORD

COMPETITION	APPS	GOALS	(PENS)	SUBS
League	81	20	1	6
FA Cup	12	5	0	1
League Cup	7	2	0	1
Europe	0	0	–	–
Scotland	0	0	–	–
Other	2	0	0	0

HONOURS

None

INTERNATIONAL APPEARANCES

COUNTRY	LEVEL	GAMES	GOALS
England	Full	2	0
	B	1	0
	U-21	4	0
	Youth	8	0

NAME:	Peter Beardsley
CLUB:	Newcastle
BORN:	Newcastle, 18/1/61
DEBUT v:	Blackburn, 21/8/79
SUBSTITUTED:	27
BOOKINGS:	4
SENDINGS OFF:	0
OWN GOALS:	0
DOMESTIC PENS:	30
HAT-TRICKS:	5
STRIKE RATE (%):	33.91
EVER PRESENT:	85-86, 91-92

LEAGUE CLUBS	YEARS	APPS	GOALS	FEE
Newcastle	93-95	69	33	£1.5m
Everton	91-93	81	25	£1m
Liverpool	87-91	131	46	£1.9m
Newcastle	83-87	147	61	£150,000
From: Vancouver				
Manchester Utd	82-83	0	0	£300,000
From: Vancouver				
Carlisle	79-82	102	22	Appr

OVERALL RECORD

COMPETITION	APPS	GOALS	(PENS)	SUBS
League	509	187	27	23
FA Cup	53	21	3	3
League Cup	44	7	0	2
Europe	4	2	–	–
Other	11	2	–	–

HONOURS

League Championship 87-88, 89-90, FA Cup 88-89, FA Cup r/u 87-88, PFA Team Awards: Div 1. 87, 88, 89; Premier League 94

INTERNATIONAL APPEARANCES

COUNTRY	LEVEL	GAMES	GOALS
England	Full	57	8
	B	3	0
	U-21	0	0
	Youth	0	0

NAME:	Frank Bennett
CLUB:	Southampton
BORN:	Birmingham, 3/1/69
DEBUT v:	Everton, 14/8/93
SUBSTITUTED:	0
BOOKINGS:	0
SENDINGS OFF:	0
OWN GOALS:	0
DOMESTIC PENS:	0
HAT-TRICKS:	0
STRIKE RATE (%):	–
EVER PRESENT:	–

LEAGUE CLUBS	YEARS	APPS	GOALS	FEE
Southampton	92-95	8	1	£5,000
From: Halesowen				

OVERALL RECORD

COMPETITION	APPS	GOALS	(PENS)	SUBS
League	0	1	0	8
FA Cup	0	0	0	1
League Cup	1	0	0	1
Europe	0	0	–	–
Scotland	0	0	–	–

HONOURS

None

INTERNATIONAL APPEARANCES

COUNTRY	LEVEL	GAMES	GOALS
	Full	0	0
	B	0	0
	U-21	0	0
	Youth	0	0

Dennis Bergkamp

NAME:	Dennis Bergkamp
CLUB:	Arsenal
BORN:	Holland, 10/5/69
DEBUT v:	–
SUBSTITUTED:	0
BOOKINGS:	0
SENDINGS OFF:	0
OWN GOALS:	0
DOMESTIC PENS:	0
HAT-TRICKS:	0
STRIKE RATE (%):	–
EVER PRESENT:	–

LEAGUE CLUBS	YEARS	APPS	GOALS	FEE
Arsenal	95-	0	0	£7.5m
From: Inter Milan				

OVERALL RECORD

COMPETITION	APPS	GOALS	(PENS)	SUBS
League	0	0	0	0
FA Cup	0	0	0	0
League Cup	0	0	0	0
Europe	38	17	–	–
Scotland	0	0	–	–
Other	236	114	–	–

HONOURS

European Cup Winners' Cup r/u 87-88, UEFA Cup 91-92, 93-94, Dutch League Championship 89-90, Dutch Cup 92-93, Dutch Footballer of the Year 92

INTERNATIONAL APPEARANCES

COUNTRY	LEVEL	GAMES	GOALS
Holland	Full	39	23
	B		
	U-21		
	Youth		

Gary Blissett

NAME:	Gary Blissett
CLUB:	Wimbledon
BORN:	Manchester, 29/6/64
DEBUT v:	Rochdale, 27/8/83
SUBSTITUTED:	41
BOOKINGS:	6
SENDINGS OFF:	1
OWN GOALS:	0
DOMESTIC PENS:	19
HAT-TRICKS:	0
STRIKE RATE (%):	32.18
EVER PRESENT:	92-93

LEAGUE CLUBS	YEARS	APPS	GOALS	FEE
Wimbledon	93-95	25	3	£350,000
Brentford	87-93	233	79	£60,000
Crewe	83-87	122	39	Free

OVERALL RECORD

COMPETITION	APPS	GOALS	(PENS)	SUBS
League	342	120	19	38
FA Cup	19	7	0	2
League Cup	26	12	0	5
Europe	0	0	–	–
Scotland	0	0	–	–
Other	32	14	–	–

HONOURS

Division Three Championship 91-92

INTERNATIONAL APPEARANCES

COUNTRY	LEVEL	GAMES	GOALS
	Full	0	0
	B	0	0
	U-21	0	0
	Youth	0	0

Jeroen Boere

NAME:	Jeroen Boere
CLUB:	West Ham
BORN:	Arnhem, 18/11/67
DEBUT v:	Newcastle, 25/9/93
SUBSTITUTED:	6
BOOKINGS:	4
SENDINGS OFF:	1
OWN GOALS:	0
DOMESTIC PENS:	0
HAT-TRICKS:	0
STRIKE RATE (%):	–
EVER PRESENT:	–

LEAGUE CLUBS	YEARS	APPS	GOALS	FEE
West Ham	94-95	24	6	£250,000
West Brom	94	5	0	Loan
Portsmouth	94	6	0	Loan
From: Go Ahead Eagles				

OVERALL RECORD

COMPETITION	APPS	GOALS	(PENS)	SUBS
League	25	6	0	10
FA Cup	2	0	0	0
League Cup	1	0	0	0
Europe	0	0	–	–
Scotland	0	0	–	–

HONOURS

None

INTERNATIONAL APPEARANCES

COUNTRY	LEVEL	GAMES	GOALS
Holland	Full	0	0
	B	2	0
	U-21	0	0
	Youth	0	0

NAME:	Mark Bright
CLUB:	Sheffield Wed
BORN:	Stoke, 6/6/62
DEBUT v:	York City, 1/5/82
SUBSTITUTED:	21
BOOKINGS:	20
SENDINGS OFF:	0
OWN GOALS:	0
DOMESTIC PENS:	4
HAT-TRICKS:	2
STRIKE RATE (%):	37.24
EVER PRESENT:	88-89, 91-92

LEAGUE CLUBS	YEARS	APPS	GOALS	FEE
Sheffield Wed	92-95	106	41	£1.375m
Crystal Palace	86-92	227	92	£75,000
Leicester	84-86	42	6	£33,000
Port Vale	81-84	29	10	Appr

OVERALL RECORD

COMPETITION	APPS	GOALS	(PENS)	SUBS
League	365	149	4	39
FA Cup	27	10	0	2
League Cup	43	19	0	2
Europe	0	0	–	–
Scotland	0	0	–	–
Other	25	9	–	–

HONOURS

FA Cup r/u 89-90, 92-93, League Cup r/u 92-93, PFA Team Award Div 2. 88

INTERNATIONAL APPEARANCES

COUNTRY	LEVEL	GAMES	GOALS
	Full	0	0
	B	0	0
	U-21	0	0
	Youth	0	0

NAME:	Marvin Bryan
CLUB:	Q.P.R.
BORN:	Paddington, 2/8/75
DEBUT v:	Northampton, 10/12/94
SUBSTITUTED:	2
BOOKINGS:	0
SENDINGS OFF:	0
OWN GOALS:	0
DOMESTIC PENS:	0
HAT-TRICKS:	0
STRIKE RATE (%):	–
EVER PRESENT:	–

LEAGUE CLUBS	YEARS	APPS	GOALS	FEE
Q.P.R.	92-95	0	0	Trainee
Doncaster	94-95	5	1	Loan

OVERALL RECORD

COMPETITION	APPS	GOALS	(PENS)	SUBS
League	5	1	0	0
FA Cup	0	0	0	0
League Cup	0	0	0	0
Europe	0	0	–	–
Scotland	0	0	–	–

HONOURS

None

INTERNATIONAL APPEARANCES

COUNTRY	LEVEL	GAMES	GOALS
	Full	0	0
	B	0	0
	U-21	0	0
	Youth	0	0

NAME:	Gary Bull
CLUB:	Nottm Forest
BORN:	Tipton, 12/6/66
DEBUT v:	Darlington, 1/4/88
SUBSTITUTED:	11
BOOKINGS:	4
SENDINGS OFF:	1
OWN GOALS:	0
DOMESTIC PENS:	9
HAT-TRICKS:	0
STRIKE RATE (%):	37.67
EVER PRESENT:	91-92

LEAGUE CLUBS	YEARS	APPS	GOALS	FEE
Nottm Forest	93-95	13	1	Free
Birmingham	94	10	6	Loan
Barnet	89-93	83	37	£2,000
Cambridge	88-89	19	4	Free
Southampton	86-88	0	0	Appr

OVERALL RECORD

COMPETITION	APPS	GOALS	(PENS)	SUBS
League	109	48	7	15
FA Cup	11	3	0	4
League Cup	6	4	2	1
Europe	0	0	–	–
Scotland	0	0	–	–
Other	12	3	–	–

HONOURS

GMV Championship 90-91, PFA Team Awards: Div 4. 92; Div 3. 93

INTERNATIONAL APPEARANCES

COUNTRY	LEVEL	GAMES	GOALS
	Full	0	0
	B	0	0
	U-21	0	0
	Youth	0	0

NAME:	Kevin Campbell
CLUB:	Nottingham Forest
BORN:	Lambeth, 4/2/70
DEBUT v:	Everton, 7/5/88
SUBSTITUTED:	12
BOOKINGS:	3
SENDINGS OFF:	0
OWN GOALS:	0
DOMESTIC PENS:	0
HAT-TRICKS:	2
STRIKE RATE (%):	28.81
EVER PRESENT:	–

LEAGUE CLUBS	YEARS	APPS	GOALS	FEE
Nottingham Forest	95-	0	0	£2m
Arsenal	88-95	166	46	Trainee
Leicester	89	11	5	Loan
Leyton Orient	89	16	9	Loan

OVERALL RECORD

COMPETITION	APPS	GOALS	(PENS)	SUBS
League	152	60	0	41
FA Cup	13	2	0	6
League Cup	15	6	0	9
Europe	15	6	–	–
Scotland	0	0	–	–
Other	9	1	–	–

HONOURS

League Championship 90-91, FA Cup 92-93, FA Youth Cup 87-88, League Cup 92-93, Charity Shield medal 91, 93, European Cup Winners' Cup 93-94

INTERNATIONAL APPEARANCES

COUNTRY	LEVEL	GAMES	GOALS
England	Full	0	0
	B	1	0
	U-21	4	1
	Youth	0	0

NAME:	Eric Cantona
CLUB:	Manchester Utd
BORN:	Paris, 24/5/66
DEBUT v:	Oldham, 8/2/92
SUBSTITUTED:	7
BOOKINGS:	17
SENDINGS OFF:	4
OWN GOALS:	0
DOMESTIC PENS:	8
HAT-TRICKS:	1
STRIKE RATE (%):	46.15
EVER PRESENT:	–

LEAGUE CLUBS	YEARS	APPS	GOALS	FEE
Manchester Utd	92-95	76	39	£1.2m
Leeds	92	28	9	£900,000
From: Nimes				

OVERALL RECORD

COMPETITION	APPS	GOALS	(PENS)	SUBS
League	93	48	6	11
FA Cup	7	5	2	0
League Cup	6	1	0	0
Europe	16	6	–	–
Other	187	58	–	–

HONOURS

League Championship 91-92, 92-93, 93-94, FA Cup 93-94, League Cup r/u 93-94, Charity Shield medal 92, 93, 94, PFA Player of the Year 93-94, PFA Team Award Premier League 94, French Championship 89-90, French Cup 88-89, 89-90

INTERNATIONAL APPEARANCES

COUNTRY	LEVEL	GAMES	GOALS
France	Full	44	18
	B	0	0
	U-21	0	0
	Youth	0	0

NAME:	Andy Clarke
CLUB:	Wimbledon
BORN:	Islington, 22/7/67
DEBUT v:	Norwich, 2/3/91
SUBSTITUTED:	19
BOOKINGS:	6
SENDINGS OFF:	1
OWN GOALS:	0
DOMESTIC PENS:	0
HAT-TRICKS:	0
STRIKE RATE (%):	12.34
EVER PRESENT:	–

LEAGUE CLUBS	YEARS	APPS	GOALS	FEE
Wimbledon	91-95	126	14	£250,000
From: Barnet				

OVERALL RECORD

COMPETITION	APPS	GOALS	(PENS)	SUBS
League	60	14	0	66
FA Cup	13	3	0	1
League Cup	9	2	0	5
Europe	0	0	–	–
Scotland	0	0	–	–

HONOURS

GMV Champions 90-91

INTERNATIONAL APPEARANCES

COUNTRY	LEVEL	GAMES	GOALS
	Full	0	0
	B	0	0
	U-21	0	0
	Youth	0	0

NAME:	Andrew Cole
CLUB:	Manchester Utd
BORN:	Nottingham, 15/10/71
DEBUT v:	Sheffield Utd, 29/12/90
SUBSTITUTED:	5
BOOKINGS:	16
SENDINGS OFF:	0
OWN GOALS:	0
DOMESTIC PENS:	0
HAT-TRICKS:	8
STRIKE RATE (%):	65.61
EVER PRESENT:	–

LEAGUE CLUBS	YEARS	APPS	GOALS	FEE
Manchester Utd	95	18	12	£7m
Newcastle	93-95	69	55	£1.75m
Bristol City	92-93	41	20	£500,000
Fulham	91	13	3	Loan
Arsenal	89-92	1	0	Appr

OVERALL RECORD

COMPETITION	APPS	GOALS	(PENS)	SUBS
League	139	90	0	3
FA Cup	5	1	0	0
League Cup	10	12	0	0
Europe	3	4	–	–
Scotland	0	0	–	–
Other	8	2	–	–

HONOURS

First Division Championship 92-93, Charity Shield medal 91, PFA Young Player of the Year 93-94

INTERNATIONAL APPEARANCES

COUNTRY	LEVEL	GAMES	GOALS
England	Full	1	0
	B	2	1
	U-21	8	3
	Youth	20	6

NAME:	Stan Collymore
CLUB:	Liverpool
BORN:	Stone, 22/1/71
DEBUT v:	Q.P.R., 16/2/91
SUBSTITUTED:	7
BOOKINGS:	12
SENDINGS OFF:	1
OWN GOALS:	1
DOMESTIC PENS:	1
HAT-TRICKS:	1
STRIKE RATE (%):	50.00
EVER PRESENT:	–

LEAGUE CLUBS	YEARS	APPS	GOALS	FEE
Liverpool	95-	0	0	£8.5m
Nottm Forest	93-95	65	40	£2m
Southend	92-93	30	15	£100,000
Crystal Palace	91-92	20	1	£100,000
From: Stafford Rangers				

OVERALL RECORD

COMPETITION	APPS	GOALS	(PENS)	SUBS
League	98	56	1	17
FA Cup	7	4	0	0
League Cup	11	8	0	3
Europe	0	0	–	–
Scotland	0	0	–	–
Other	2	1	–	–

HONOURS

PFA Team Award Div 1. 94

INTERNATIONAL APPEARANCES

COUNTRY	LEVEL	GAMES	GOALS
England	Full	2	0
	B	0	0
	U-21	0	0
	Youth	0	0

NAME:	Tony Cottee
CLUB:	West Ham
BORN:	West Ham, 11/7/65
DEBUT v:	Tottenham, 1/1/83
SUBSTITUTED:	33
BOOKINGS:	10
SENDINGS OFF:	1
OWN GOALS:	0
DOMESTIC PENS:	11
HAT-TRICKS:	11
STRIKE RATE (%):	42.20
EVER PRESENT:	85-86, 86-87, 87-88

LEAGUE CLUBS	YEARS	APPS	GOALS	FEE
West Ham	94-95	31	13	£1.1m
Everton	88-94	184	72	£2.05m
West Ham	82-88	212	92	Appr

OVERALL RECORD

COMPETITION	APPS	GOALS	(PENS)	SUBS
League	395	177	9	32
FA Cup	41	16	0	6
League Cup	41	26	2	4
Europe	0	0	–	–
Scotland	0	0	–	–
Other	14	3	–	–

HONOURS

FA Cup r/u 88-89, PFA Young Player of the Year 86

INTERNATIONAL APPEARANCES

COUNTRY	LEVEL	GAMES	GOALS
England	Full	7	0
	B	0	0
	U-21	9	2
	Youth	4	4

NAME:	Owen Coyle
CLUB:	Bolton
BORN:	Glasgow, 14/7/66
DEBUT v:	Ayr, 19/2/86
SUBSTITUTED:	10
BOOKINGS:	1
SENDINGS OFF:	0
OWN GOALS:	0
DOMESTIC PENS:	0
HAT-TRICKS:	0
STRIKE RATE (%):	28.57
EVER PRESENT:	–

LEAGUE CLUBS	YEARS	APPS	GOALS	FEE
Bolton	93-95	49	12	£250,000
Airdrie	90-93	123	50	£175,000
Clydebank	88-90	63	33	Undisclosed
Dumbarton	86-88	103	36	

OVERALL RECORD

COMPETITION	APPS	GOALS	(PENS)	SUBS
League	33	12	0	16
FA Cup	8	5	0	0
League Cup	5	1	0	1
Europe	2	0	–	–
Scotland	321	123	–	–
Other	10	5	–	–

HONOURS

Scottish First Division Championship 90-91, Scottish FA Cup r/u 91-92

INTERNATIONAL APPEARANCES

COUNTRY	LEVEL	GAMES	GOALS
Eire	Full	1	0
	B	2	0
	U-21	1	0
	Youth	0	0

NAME:	Brian Deane
CLUB:	Leeds
BORN:	Leeds, 7/2/68
DEBUT v:	Swansea, 4/2/86
SUBSTITUTED:	19
BOOKINGS:	26
SENDINGS OFF:	0
OWN GOALS:	1
DOMESTIC PENS:	2
HAT-TRICKS:	3
STRIKE RATE (%):	35.44
EVER PRESENT:	90-91

LEAGUE CLUBS	YEARS	APPS	GOALS	FEE
Leeds	93-95	76	20	£2.7m
Sheffield Utd	88-93	197	83	£30,000
Doncaster	85-88	66	12	Appr

OVERALL RECORD

COMPETITION	APPS	GOALS	(PENS)	SUBS
League	330	115	2	9
FA Cup	31	14	0	2
League Cup	22	11	0	1
Europe	0	0	–	–
Scotland	0	0	–	–
Other	5	2	–	–

HONOURS

None

INTERNATIONAL APPEARANCES

COUNTRY	LEVEL	GAMES	GOALS
England	Full	3	0
	B	3	0
	U-21	0	0
	Youth	0	0

NAME:	Daniele Dichio
CLUB:	Q.P.R.
BORN:	London, 19/10/74
DEBUT v:	Bristol Rovers, 26/3/94
SUBSTITUTED:	1
BOOKINGS:	1
SENDINGS OFF:	0
OWN GOALS:	0
DOMESTIC PENS:	0
HAT-TRICKS:	0
STRIKE RATE (%):	–
EVER PRESENT:	–

LEAGUE CLUBS	YEARS	APPS	GOALS	FEE
Q.P.R.	93-95	9	3	Trainee
Barnet	94	9	2	Loan

OVERALL RECORD

COMPETITION	APPS	GOALS	(PENS)	SUBS
League	13	5	0	5
FA Cup	1	0	0	0
League Cup	1	0	0	0
Europe	0	0	–	–
Scotland	0	0	–	–

HONOURS

None

INTERNATIONAL APPEARANCES

COUNTRY	LEVEL	GAMES	GOALS
	Full	0	0
	B	0	0
	U-21	0	0
	Youth	0	0

NAME:	Paul Dickov
CLUB:	Arsenal
BORN:	Livingston, 1/11/72
DEBUT v:	Southampton, 20/3/93
SUBSTITUTED:	4
BOOKINGS:	3
SENDINGS OFF:	0
OWN GOALS:	0
DOMESTIC PENS:	0
HAT-TRICKS:	0
STRIKE RATE (%):	27.50
EVER PRESENT:	–

LEAGUE CLUBS	YEARS	APPS	GOALS	FEE
Arsenal	90-95	13	2	Trainee
Brighton	94	8	5	Loan
Luton	93	15	1	Loan

OVERALL RECORD

COMPETITION	APPS	GOALS	(PENS)	SUBS
League	21	8	0	15
FA Cup	0	0	0	0
League Cup	2	3	0	2
Europe	0	0	–	–
Scotland	0	0	–	–

HONOURS

None

INTERNATIONAL APPEARANCES

COUNTRY	LEVEL	GAMES	GOALS
Scotland	Full	0	0
	B	0	0
	U-21	5	0
	Youth	0	0

NAME:	O'Neill Donaldson
CLUB:	Sheffield Wed
BORN:	Birmingham, 24/11/69
DEBUT v:	Hartlepool, 23/11/91
SUBSTITUTED:	9
BOOKINGS:	1
SENDINGS OFF:	0
OWN GOALS:	0
DOMESTIC PENS:	0
HAT-TRICKS:	0
STRIKE RATE (%):	29.55
EVER PRESENT:	–

LEAGUE CLUBS	YEARS	APPS	GOALS	FEE
Sheffield Wed	95	1	0	£50,000
Mansfield	94-95	4	6	Loan
Doncaster	94	8	2	Free
Shrewsbury	91-94	28	4	Free

OVERALL RECORD

COMPETITION	APPS	GOALS	(PENS)	SUBS
League	26	12	0	15
FA Cup	1	1	0	0
League Cup	2	0	0	0
Europe	0	0	–	–
Scotland	0	0	–	–
Other	3	0	–	–

HONOURS

None

INTERNATIONAL APPEARANCES

COUNTRY	LEVEL	GAMES	GOALS
	Full	0	0
	B	0	0
	U-21	0	0
	Youth	0	0

NAME:	Dion Dublin
CLUB:	Coventry
BORN:	Leicester, 22/4/69
DEBUT v:	Wrexham, 16/12/88
SUBSTITUTED:	18
BOOKINGS:	18
SENDINGS OFF:	1
OWN GOALS:	0
DOMESTIC PENS:	2
HAT-TRICKS:	1
STRIKE RATE (%):	36.67
EVER PRESENT:	89-90, 90-91

LEAGUE CLUBS	YEARS	APPS	GOALS	FEE
Coventry	94-95	31	13	£2m
Manchester Utd	92-94	12	2	£1m
Cambridge	88-92	156	53	Free
Norwich	88	0	0	Appr

OVERALL RECORD

COMPETITION	APPS	GOALS	(PENS)	SUBS
League	168	68	2	31
FA Cup	26	12	0	0
League Cup	12	8	0	3
Europe	1	0	–	–
Scotland	0	0	–	–
Other	15	5	–	–

HONOURS

Division Three Championship 90-91, Charity Shield medal 94

INTERNATIONAL APPEARANCES

COUNTRY	LEVEL	GAMES	GOALS
	Full	0	0
	B	0	0
	U-21	0	0
	Youth	0	0

Efan Ekoku

NAME:	Efan Ekoku
CLUB:	Wimbledon
BORN:	Manchester, 8/6/67
DEBUT v:	Brentford, 25/8/90
SUBSTITUTED:	18
BOOKINGS:	14
SENDINGS OFF:	0
OWN GOALS:	0
DOMESTIC PENS:	0
HAT-TRICKS:	1
STRIKE RATE (%):	34.29
EVER PRESENT:	–

LEAGUE CLUBS	YEARS	APPS	GOALS	FEE
Wimbledon	94-95	24	9	£1m
Norwich	93-94	37	15	£500,000
Bournemouth	90-93	62	21	£100,000
From: Sutton United				

OVERALL RECORD

COMPETITION	APPS	GOALS	(PENS)	SUBS
League	93	45	0	30
FA Cup	9	2	0	3
League Cup	3	1	0	2
Europe	3	1	–	–
Scotland	0	0	–	–
Other	4	1	–	–

HONOURS

None

INTERNATIONAL APPEARANCES

COUNTRY	LEVEL	GAMES	GOALS
Nigeria	Full	5	0
	B	0	0
	U-21	0	0
	Youth	0	0

David Farrell

NAME:	David Farrell
CLUB:	Aston Villa
BORN:	Birmingham, 11/11/71
DEBUT v:	Oldham, 24/10/92
SUBSTITUTED:	4
BOOKINGS:	0
SENDINGS OFF:	0
OWN GOALS:	0
DOMESTIC PENS:	0
HAT-TRICKS:	0
STRIKE RATE (%):	–
EVER PRESENT:	–

LEAGUE CLUBS	YEARS	APPS	GOALS	FEE
Aston Villa	92-95	5	0	£45,000
Scunthorpe	93	5	1	Loan

OVERALL RECORD

COMPETITION	APPS	GOALS	(PENS)	SUBS
League	8	1	0	2
FA Cup	0	0	0	0
League Cup	2	0	0	0
Europe	0	0	–	–
Scotland	0	0	–	–
Other	2	0	–	–

HONOURS

None

INTERNATIONAL APPEARANCES

COUNTRY	LEVEL	GAMES	GOALS
	Full	0	0
	B	0	0
	U-21	0	0
	Youth	0	0

John Fashanu

NAME:	John Fashanu
CLUB:	Aston Villa
BORN:	Kensington, 18/9/62
DEBUT v:	Shrewsbury, 17/10/81
SUBSTITUTED:	42
BOOKINGS:	22
SENDINGS OFF:	2
OWN GOALS:	1
DOMESTIC PENS:	19
HAT-TRICKS:	1
STRIKE RATE (%):	35.16
EVER PRESENT:	–

LEAGUE CLUBS	YEARS	APPS	GOALS	FEE
Aston Villa	94-95	13	3	£1.35m
Wimbledon	86-94	277	107	£125,000
Millwall	84-86	50	12	£55,000
Lincoln	83-84	36	11	Free
Crystal Palace	83	1	0	Loan
Norwich	79-83	7	1	Appr

OVERALL RECORD

COMPETITION	APPS	GOALS	(PENS)	SUBS
League	371	134	15	13
FA Cup	40	15	1	1
League Cup	28	11	3	2
Europe	1	0	–	–
Scotland	0	0	–	–
Other	8	3	–	–

HONOURS

FA Cup 87-88, Charity Shield medal 88

INTERNATIONAL APPEARANCES

COUNTRY	LEVEL	GAMES	GOALS
England	Full	2	0
	B	0	0
	U-21	0	0
	Youth	0	0

NAME: Graham Fenton
CLUB: Aston Villa
BORN: Wallsend, 22/5/74
DEBUT v: Leicester, 12/1/94
SUBSTITUTED: 6
BOOKINGS: 6
SENDINGS OFF: 0
OWN GOALS: 0
DOMESTIC PENS: 0
HAT-TRICKS: 0
STRIKE RATE (%): 14.63
EVER PRESENT: –

LEAGUE CLUBS	YEARS	APPS	GOALS	FEE
Aston Villa	92-95	29	3	Trainee
West Brom	94	7	3	Loan

OVERALL RECORD

COMPETITION	APPS	GOALS	(PENS)	SUBS
League	23	6	0	13
FA Cup	0	0	0	0
League Cup	2	0	0	3
Europe	0	0	–	–
Scotland	0	0	–	–

HONOURS

League Cup 93-94

INTERNATIONAL APPEARANCES

COUNTRY	LEVEL	GAMES	GOALS
England	Full	0	0
	B	0	0
	U-21	1	0
	Youth	0	0

NAME: Les Ferdinand
CLUB: Newcastle
BORN: Acton, 18/12/66
DEBUT v: Coventry, 20/4/87
SUBSTITUTED: 30
BOOKINGS: 23
SENDINGS OFF: 2
OWN GOALS: 1
DOMESTIC PENS: 0
HAT-TRICKS: 2
STRIKE RATE (%): 49.46
EVER PRESENT: –

LEAGUE CLUBS	YEARS	APPS	GOALS	FEE
Newcastle	95-	0	0	£6m
Q.P.R.	87-95	163	82	£15,000
From: Hayes				
Brentford	88	3	0	Loan

OVERALL RECORD

COMPETITION	APPS	GOALS	(PENS)	SUBS
League	155	82	0	11
FA Cup	6	3	0	1
League Cup	11	7	0	2
Europe	0	0	–	–
Scotland	0	0	–	–
Other	33	22	–	–

HONOURS

Turkish Cup 88-89

INTERNATIONAL APPEARANCES

COUNTRY	LEVEL	GAMES	GOALS
England	Full	6	3
	B	0	0
	U-21	0	0
	Youth	0	0

NAME: Duncan Ferguson
CLUB: Everton
BORN: Stirling, 27/12/71
DEBUT v: Rangers, 10/11/90
SUBSTITUTED: 1
BOOKINGS: 23
SENDINGS OFF: 3
OWN GOALS: 0
DOMESTIC PENS: 0
HAT-TRICKS: 0
STRIKE RATE (%): –
EVER PRESENT: –

LEAGUE CLUBS	YEARS	APPS	GOALS	FEE
Everton	94-95	23	7	£4m
Rangers	93-94	14	2	£4m
Dundee Utd	90-93	77	28	

OVERALL RECORD

COMPETITION	APPS	GOALS	(PENS)	SUBS
League	22	7	0	1
FA Cup	3	1	0	1
League Cup	1	0	0	0
Europe	1	0	–	–
Scotland	114	42	–	–

HONOURS

Scottish FA Cup r/u 90-91, 93-94, FA Cup 94-95

INTERNATIONAL APPEARANCES

COUNTRY	LEVEL	GAMES	GOALS
Scotland	Full	5	0
	B	0	0
	U-21	7	1
	Youth	0	0

Aage Jan Fjortoft

NAME:	Aage Jan Fjortoft
CLUB:	Middlesbrough
BORN:	Norway, 10/1/67
DEBUT v:	Sheffield Utd, 14/8/93
SUBSTITUTED:	9
BOOKINGS:	11
SENDINGS OFF:	0
OWN GOALS:	0
DOMESTIC PENS:	2
HAT-TRICKS:	2
STRIKE RATE (%):	43.01
EVER PRESENT:	–

LEAGUE CLUBS	YEARS	APPS	GOALS	FEE
Middlesbrough	95	8	3	£1.3m
Swindon	93-95	72	28	£500,000
From: Rapid Vienna				

OVERALL RECORD

COMPETITION	APPS	GOALS	(PENS)	SUBS
League	70	31	2	10
FA Cup	3	2	0	1
League Cup	9	7	0	0
Europe	0	0	–	–
Scotland	0	0	–	–
Other	2	0	–	–

HONOURS

PFA Team Award Div 1. 95, Austrian Cup r/u 92-93

INTERNATIONAL APPEARANCES

COUNTRY	LEVEL	GAMES	GOALS
Norway	Full	57	19
	B	0	0
	U-21	0	0
	Youth	0	0

Robert Fleck

NAME:	Robert Fleck
CLUB:	Chelsea
BORN:	Glasgow, 11/8/65
DEBUT v:	Clyde, 2/1/84
SUBSTITUTED:	36
BOOKINGS:	3
SENDINGS OFF:	2
OWN GOALS:	0
DOMESTIC PENS:	7
HAT-TRICKS:	0
STRIKE RATE (%):	28.45
EVER PRESENT:	–

LEAGUE CLUBS	YEARS	APPS	GOALS	FEE
Chelsea	92-95	40	3	£2.1m
Bristol City	95	10	1	Loan
Bolton	94	7	1	Loan
Norwich	87-92	143	40	£580,000
Partick	83	2	0	Loan
Rangers	83-87	85	29	Appr

OVERALL RECORD

COMPETITION	APPS	GOALS	(PENS)	SUBS
League	181	45	4	19
FA Cup	17	11	1	2
League Cup	20	12	2	0
Europe	7	3	–	–
Scotland	97	31	–	–
Other	8	4	–	–

HONOURS

Scottish Premier League 86-87, Scottish League Cup 86-87, 87-88, Scottish PFA Young Player of the Year 86-87

INTERNATIONAL APPEARANCES

COUNTRY	LEVEL	GAMES	GOALS
Scotland	Full	4	0
	B	1	0
	U-21	6	1
	Youth	0	0

Jamie Forrester

NAME:	Jamie Forrester
CLUB:	Leeds
BORN:	Bradford, 1/11/74
DEBUT v:	Nottm Forest, 21/3/93
SUBSTITUTED:	5
BOOKINGS:	0
SENDINGS OFF:	0
OWN GOALS:	0
DOMESTIC PENS:	0
HAT-TRICKS:	0
STRIKE RATE (%):	–
EVER PRESENT:	–

LEAGUE CLUBS	YEARS	APPS	GOALS	FEE
Leeds	92-95	9	0	£60,000
Grimsby	95	8	1	Loan
Southend	94	5	0	Loan

OVERALL RECORD

COMPETITION	APPS	GOALS	(PENS)	SUBS
League	17	1	0	5
FA Cup	1	2	0	0
League Cup	0	0	0	0
Europe	0	0	–	–
Scotland	0	0	–	–

HONOURS

FA Youth Cup 92-93

INTERNATIONAL APPEARANCES

COUNTRY	LEVEL	GAMES	GOALS
England	Full	0	0
	B	0	0
	U-21	0	0
	Youth	4	1

NAME:	Robbie Fowler
CLUB:	Liverpool
BORN:	Liverpool, 9/4/75
DEBUT v:	Chelsea, 25/9/93
SUBSTITUTED:	7
BOOKINGS:	4
SENDINGS OFF:	0
OWN GOALS:	0
DOMESTIC PENS:	3
HAT-TRICKS:	3
STRIKE RATE (%):	53.85
EVER PRESENT:	94-95

LEAGUE CLUBS	YEARS	APPS	GOALS	FEE
Liverpool	92-95	70	38	Trainee

OVERALL RECORD

COMPETITION	APPS	GOALS	(PENS)	SUBS
League	69	38	3	1
FA Cup	8	2	0	0
League Cup	13	9	0	0
Europe	0	0	–	–
Scotland	0	0	–	–

HONOURS

League Cup 94-95, PFA Young Player of the Year 94-95

INTERNATIONAL APPEARANCES

COUNTRY	LEVEL	GAMES	GOALS
England	Full	0	0
	B	1	1
	U-21	6	2
	Youth	6	8

NAME:	Chris Freestone
CLUB:	Middlesbrough
BORN:	Nottingham, 4/9/71
DEBUT v:	Tranmere, 7/5/95
SUBSTITUTED:	0
BOOKINGS:	0
SENDINGS OFF:	0
OWN GOALS:	0
DOMESTIC PENS:	0
HAT-TRICKS:	0
STRIKE RATE (%):	–
EVER PRESENT:	–

LEAGUE CLUBS	YEARS	APPS	GOALS	FEE
Middlesbrough	94-95	1	0	£10,000

OVERALL RECORD

COMPETITION	APPS	GOALS	(PENS)	SUBS
League	0	0	0	1
FA Cup	0	0	0	0
League Cup	0	0	0	0
Europe	0	0	–	–
Scotland	0	0	–	–

HONOURS

None

INTERNATIONAL APPEARANCES

COUNTRY	LEVEL	GAMES	GOALS
	Full	0	0
	B	0	0
	U-21	0	0
	Youth	0	0

NAME:	Paul Furlong
CLUB:	Chelsea
BORN:	Wood Green, 1/10/68
DEBUT v:	Manchester C, 17/8/91
SUBSTITUTED:	14
BOOKINGS:	27
SENDINGS OFF:	2
OWN GOALS:	0
DOMESTIC PENS:	1
HAT-TRICKS:	0
STRIKE RATE (%):	32.57
EVER PRESENT:	–

LEAGUE CLUBS	YEARS	APPS	GOALS	FEE
Chelsea	94-95	36	10	£2.3m
Watford	92-94	79	36	£250,000
Coventry	91-92	37	4	£130,000
From: Enfield				

OVERALL RECORD

COMPETITION	APPS	GOALS	(PENS)	SUBS
League	136	50	1	16
FA Cup	8	2	0	2
League Cup	13	5	0	0
Europe	7	3	–	–
Scotland	0	0	–	–
Other	6	1	–	–

HONOURS

None

INTERNATIONAL APPEARANCES

COUNTRY	LEVEL	GAMES	GOALS
	Full	0	0
	B	0	0
	U-21	0	0
	Youth	0	0

NAME:	Kevin Gallagher
CLUB:	Blackburn
BORN:	Clydebank, 23/11/66
DEBUT v:	Rangers, 14/12/85
SUBSTITUTED:	21
BOOKINGS:	13
SENDINGS OFF:	0
OWN GOALS:	0
DOMESTIC PENS:	0
HAT-TRICKS:	1
STRIKE RATE (%):	30.06
EVER PRESENT:	–

LEAGUE CLUBS	YEARS	APPS	GOALS	FEE
Blackburn	93-95	40	13	£1.5m
Coventry	90-93	100	28	£900,000
Dundee Utd	84-90	131	27	Appr

OVERALL RECORD

COMPETITION	APPS	GOALS	(PENS)	SUBS
League	136	41	0	4
FA Cup	8	1	0	0
League Cup	15	7	0	0
Europe	21	3	–	–
Scotland	167	37	–	–
Other	2	0	–	–

HONOURS

Scottish Cup r/u 86-87, 87-88, UEFA Cup r/u 86-87

INTERNATIONAL APPEARANCES

COUNTRY	LEVEL	GAMES	GOALS
Scotland	Full	19	2
	B	2	0
	U-21	7	2
	Youth	0	0

NAME:	Kevin Gallen
CLUB:	Q.P.R.
BORN:	Chiswick, 21/9/75
DEBUT v:	Man Utd, 20/8/94
SUBSTITUTED:	10
BOOKINGS:	5
SENDINGS OFF:	0
OWN GOALS:	0
DOMESTIC PENS:	0
HAT-TRICKS:	0
STRIKE RATE (%):	25.58
EVER PRESENT:	–

LEAGUE CLUBS	YEARS	APPS	GOALS	FEE
Q.P.R.	93-95	37	9	Trainee

OVERALL RECORD

COMPETITION	APPS	GOALS	(PENS)	SUBS
League	31	9	0	6
FA Cup	4	1	0	0
League Cup	1	1	0	1
Europe	0	0		
Scotland	0	0		

HONOURS

None

INTERNATIONAL APPEARANCES

COUNTRY	LEVEL	GAMES	GOALS
England	Full	0	0
	B	0	0
	U-21	3	0
	Youth	8	3

NAME:	Marcus Gayle
CLUB:	Wimbledon
BORN:	Hammersmith, 27/9/70
DEBUT v:	Preston, 22/10/88
SUBSTITUTED:	45
BOOKINGS:	3
SENDINGS OFF:	1
OWN GOALS:	0
DOMESTIC PENS:	0
HAT-TRICKS:	0
STRIKE RATE (%):	12.44
EVER PRESENT:	93-94

LEAGUE CLUBS	YEARS	APPS	GOALS	FEE
Wimbledon	94-95	33	2	£250,000
Brentford	89-94	157	21	Appr

OVERALL RECORD

COMPETITION	APPS	GOALS	(PENS)	SUBS
League	151	23	0	39
FA Cup	6	2	0	2
League Cup	8	1	0	3
Europe	0	0	–	–
Scotland	0	0	–	–
Other	21	2	–	–

HONOURS

Division Three Championship 91-92

INTERNATIONAL APPEARANCES

COUNTRY	LEVEL	GAMES	GOALS
England	Full	0	0
	B	0	0
	U-21	0	0
	Youth	1	0

NAME:	Jon Goodman
CLUB:	Wimbledon
BORN:	Walthamstow, 2/6/71
DEBUT v:	Leicester, 26/12/90
SUBSTITUTED:	30
BOOKINGS:	3
SENDINGS OFF:	0
OWN GOALS:	0
DOMESTIC PENS:	0
HAT-TRICKS:	1
STRIKE RATE (%):	28.47
EVER PRESENT:	–

LEAGUE CLUBS	YEARS	APPS	GOALS	FEE
Wimbledon	94-95	19	4	£600,000
Millwall	90-94	109	35	£50,000
From: Bromley				

OVERALL RECORD

COMPETITION	APPS	GOALS	(PENS)	SUBS
League	110	39	0	18
FA Cup	5	0	0	2
League Cup	5	2	0	4
Europe	0	0	–	–
Scotland	0	0	–	–
Other	3	0	–	–

INTERNATIONAL APPEARANCES

COUNTRY	LEVEL	GAMES	GOALS
	Full	0	0
	B	0	0
	U-21	0	0
	Youth	0	0

HONOURS

None

NAME:	Carl Griffiths
CLUB:	Manchester C
BORN:	Welshpool, 16/7/71
DEBUT v:	Oxford, 1/10/88
SUBSTITUTED:	29
BOOKINGS:	9
SENDINGS OFF:	1
OWN GOALS:	0
DOMESTIC PENS:	3
HAT-TRICKS:	1
STRIKE RATE (%):	34.81
EVER PRESENT:	92-93

LEAGUE CLUBS	YEARS	APPS	GOALS	FEE
Manchester C	93-95	18	4	£500,000
Shrewsbury	88-93	143	54	Trainee

OVERALL RECORD

COMPETITION	APPS	GOALS	(PENS)	SUBS
League	121	58	3	40
FA Cup	8	2	0	0
League Cup	7	3	0	5
Europe	0	0	–	–
Scotland	0	0	–	–
Other	11	3	–	–

HONOURS

PFA Team Award Div 3. 93

INTERNATIONAL APPEARANCES

COUNTRY	LEVEL	GAMES	GOALS
Wales	Full	0	0
	B	1	0
	U-21	2	0
	Youth	0	0

NAME:	Mick Harford
CLUB:	Wimbledon
BORN:	Sunderland, 12/2/59
DEBUT v:	Gillingham, 10/12/77
SUBSTITUTED:	19
BOOKINGS:	34
SENDINGS OFF:	0
OWN GOALS:	1
DOMESTIC PENS:	9
HAT-TRICKS:	8
STRIKE RATE (%):	34.87
EVER PRESENT:	–

LEAGUE CLUBS	YEARS	APPS	GOALS	FEE
Wimbledon	94-95	27	6	£50,000
Coventry	93-94	1	1	£200,000
Sunderland	93	11	2	£250,000
Chelsea	92-93	28	9	£300,000
Luton	91-92	29	12	£325,000
Derby	90-91	58	15	£450,000
Luton	84-90	139	57	£250,000
Birmingham	82-84	92	25	£100,000
Bristol City	81-82	30	11	£160,000
Newcastle	80-81	19	4	£180,000
Lincoln	77-80	115	41	Appr

OVERALL RECORD

COMPETITION	APPS	GOALS	(PENS)	SUBS
League	525	183	7	24
FA Cup	46	16	2	1
League Cup	54	28	0	1
Europe/Scotland	0	0	–	–
Other	7	3	–	–

INTERNATIONAL APPEARANCES

COUNTRY	LEVEL	GAMES	GOALS
England	Full	2	0
	B	1	0
	U-21	0	0
	Youth	0	0

HONOURS

League Cup 87-88, League Cup r/u 88-89

NAME:	John Hartson
CLUB:	Arsenal
BORN:	Swansea, 4/5/75
DEBUT v:	Nottm Forest, 28/8/93
SUBSTITUTED:	15
BOOKINGS:	11
SENDINGS OFF:	2
OWN GOALS:	0
DOMESTIC PENS:	0
HAT-TRICKS:	0
STRIKE RATE (%):	26.32
EVER PRESENT:	–

LEAGUE CLUBS	YEARS	APPS	GOALS	FEE
Arsenal	95	15	7	£2.5m
Luton	92-95	54	11	Trainee

OVERALL RECORD

COMPETITION	APPS	GOALS	(PENS)	SUBS
League	46	18	0	23
FA Cup	3	2	0	3
League Cup	0	0	0	1
Europe	5	1	–	–
Scotland	0	0	–	–
Other	2	0	–	–

HONOURS

European Cup Winners' Cup r/u 94-95

INTERNATIONAL APPEARANCES

COUNTRY	LEVEL	GAMES	GOALS
Wales	Full	3	0
	B	0	0
	U-21	3	3
	Youth	0	0

NAME:	John Hendrie
CLUB:	Middlesbrough
BORN:	Lennoxtown, 24/10/63
DEBUT v:	Tottenham, 5/12/81
SUBSTITUTED:	36
BOOKINGS:	13
SENDINGS OFF:	1
OWN GOALS:	0
DOMESTIC PENS:	0
HAT-TRICKS:	4
STRIKE RATE (%):	23.38
EVER PRESENT:	84-85, 85-86, 86-87

LEAGUE CLUBS	YEARS	APPS	GOALS	FEE
Middlesbrough	90-95	178	44	£550,000
Leeds	89-90	27	5	£600,000
Newcastle	88-89	34	4	£500,000
Bradford City	84-88	173	46	Free
Hereford	84	6	0	Loan
Coventry	81-84	21	2	Appr

OVERALL RECORD

COMPETITION	APPS	GOALS	(PENS)	SUBS
League	425	101	0	14
FA Cup	26	8	0	2
League Cup	42	10	0	0
Europe	0	0		
Scotland	0	0		
Other	22	7		

HONOURS

First Division Championship 94-95, Division Two
Championship 89-90, Division Three Championship 84-85,
PFA Team Awards: Div 2. 87, 88; Div 1. 95

INTERNATIONAL APPEARANCES

COUNTRY	LEVEL	GAMES	GOALS
Scotland	Full	0	0
	B	0	0
	U-21	0	0
	Youth	3	0

NAME:	Craig Hignett
CLUB:	Middlesbrough
BORN:	Prescot, 12/1/70
DEBUT v:	Wrexham, 8/10/88
SUBSTITUTED:	36
BOOKINGS:	16
SENDINGS OFF:	0
OWN GOALS:	0
DOMESTIC PENS:	7
HAT-TRICKS:	3
STRIKE RATE (%):	33.77
EVER PRESENT:	–

LEAGUE CLUBS	YEARS	APPS	GOALS	FEE
Middlesbrough	92-95	76	17	£500,000
Crewe	88-92	121	42	Free

OVERALL RECORD

COMPETITION	APPS	GOALS	(PENS)	SUBS
League	170	59	7	27
FA Cup	13	8	0	1
League Cup	15	10	0	2
Europe	0	0	–	–
Scotland	0	0	–	–
Other	15	4	–	–

HONOURS

First Division Championship 94-95

INTERNATIONAL APPEARANCES

COUNTRY	LEVEL	GAMES	GOALS
	Full	0	0
	B	0	0
	U-21	0	0
	Youth	0	0

NAME:	David Hirst
CLUB:	Sheffield Wed
BORN:	Cudworth, 7/12/67
DEBUT v:	Charlton, 17/8/85
SUBSTITUTED:	48
BOOKINGS:	8
SENDINGS OFF:	1
OWN GOALS:	0
DOMESTIC PENS:	2
HAT-TRICKS:	1
STRIKE RATE (%):	36.25
EVER PRESENT:	89-90

INTERNATIONAL APPEARANCES

COUNTRY	LEVEL	GAMES	GOALS
England	Full	3	1
	B	3	2
	U-21	7	1
	Youth	11	10

LEAGUE CLUBS	YEARS	APPS	GOALS	FEE
Sheffield Wed	86-95	233	87	£200,000
Barnsley	85-86	28	9	Appr

OVERALL RECORD

COMPETITION	APPS	GOALS	(PENS)	SUBS
League	235	96	2	26
FA Cup	11	6	0	5
League Cup	24	10	0	8
Europe	1	1	–	–
Scotland	0	0	–	–
Other	7	4	–	–

HONOURS

FA Cup r/u 92-93, League Cup 90-91, League Cup r/u 92-93, PFA Team Award Div 2. 91

NAME:	Dean Holdsworth
CLUB:	Wimbledon
BORN:	Walthamstow, 8/11/68
DEBUT v:	Luton, 12/12/87
SUBSTITUTED:	44
BOOKINGS:	20
SENDINGS OFF:	0
OWN GOALS:	0
DOMESTIC PENS:	7
HAT-TRICKS:	4
STRIKE RATE (%):	43.71
EVER PRESENT:	93-94

INTERNATIONAL APPEARANCES

COUNTRY	LEVEL	GAMES	GOALS
England	Full	0	0
	B	1	1
	U-21	0	0
	Youth	0	0

LEAGUE CLUBS	YEARS	APPS	GOALS	FEE
Wimbledon	92-95	105	43	£750,000
Brentford	89-92	110	53	£125,000
Brentford	88	7	1	Loan
Swansea	88	5	1	Loan
Port Vale	88	6	2	Loan
Carlisle	88	4	1	Loan
Watford	86-89	16	3	Appr

OVERALL RECORD

COMPETITION	APPS	GOALS	(PENS)	SUBS
League	226	104	7	27
FA Cup	12	10	0	2
League Cup	17	11	0	2
Europe	0	0	–	–
Scotland	0	0	–	–
Other	17	9	–	–

HONOURS

Division Three Championship 91-92, PFA Team Award Div 3. 92

NAME:	Mark Hughes
CLUB:	Chelsea
BORN:	Wrexham, 1/11/63
DEBUT v:	Southampton, 21/1/84
SUBSTITUTED:	23
BOOKINGS:	39
SENDINGS OFF:	4
OWN GOALS:	0
DOMESTIC PENS:	0
HAT-TRICKS:	3
STRIKE RATE (%):	35.51
EVER PRESENT:	88-89

LEAGUE CLUBS	YEARS	APPS	GOALS	FEE
Chelsea	95-	0	0	£1.5m
Manchester Utd	88-95	256	82	£1.5m
From: Barcelona				
Manchester Utd	80-86	89	37	Appr

OVERALL RECORD

COMPETITION	APPS	GOALS	(PENS)	SUBS
League	336	119	0	9
FA Cup	44	17	0	1
League Cup	37	16	0	1
Europe	29	8	–	–
Scotland	0	0	–	–
Other	10	1	–	–

HONOURS

League Championship 92-93, 93-94, FA Cup 84-85, 89-90, 93-94, FA Cup r/u 94-95, FA Youth Cup r/u 81-82, League Cup 91-92, League Cup r/u 90-91, 93-94, Charity Shield medal 85, 90, 93, 94, European Cup Winners' Cup 90-91, PFA Player of the Year 88-89, 90-91, PFA Young Player of the Year 84-85, PFA Team Awards: Div 1. 86, 89, 91, 92

INTERNATIONAL APPEARANCES

COUNTRY	LEVEL	GAMES	GOALS
Wales	Full	57	12
	B	0	0
	U-21	5	2
	Youth	0	0

NAME:	Mike Jeffrey
CLUB:	Newcastle
BORN:	Liverpool, 11/8/71
DEBUT v:	Wolves, 4/3/89
SUBSTITUTED:	6
BOOKINGS:	4
SENDINGS OFF:	0
OWN GOALS:	0
DOMESTIC PENS:	3
HAT-TRICKS:	0
STRIKE RATE (%):	22.67
EVER PRESENT:	–

LEAGUE CLUBS	YEARS	APPS	GOALS	FEE
Newcastle	93-95	2	0	£60,000
Doncaster	92-93	49	16	£20,000
Bolton	89-92	15	0	Trainee

OVERALL RECORD

COMPETITION	APPS	GOALS	(PENS)	SUBS
League	59	16	3	7
FA Cup	1	0	0	0
League Cup	6	1	0	2
Europe	2	0	–	–
Scotland	0	0	–	–
Other	6	1	–	–

HONOURS

None

INTERNATIONAL APPEARANCES

COUNTRY	LEVEL	GAMES	GOALS
	Full	0	0
	B	0	0
	U-21	0	0
	Youth	0	0

NAME:	Tommy Johnson
CLUB:	Aston Villa
BORN:	Newcastle, 15/1/71
DEBUT v:	Preston, 24/9/88
SUBSTITUTED:	62
BOOKINGS:	17
SENDINGS OFF:	0
OWN GOALS:	0
DOMESTIC PENS:	10
HAT-TRICKS:	2
STRIKE RATE (%):	34.62
EVER PRESENT:	–

LEAGUE CLUBS	YEARS	APPS	GOALS	FEE
Aston Villa	95	14	4	£1.75m
Derby	92-95	98	30	£1.3m
Notts County	89-92	118	47	Trainee

OVERALL RECORD

COMPETITION	APPS	GOALS	(PENS)	SUBS
League	202	81	8	28
FA Cup	8	2	0	3
League Cup	16	7	2	3
Europe	0	0	–	–
Scotland	0	0	–	–
Other	33	12	–	–

HONOURS

Anglo-Italian Cup r/u 92-93

INTERNATIONAL APPEARANCES

COUNTRY	LEVEL	GAMES	GOALS
England	Full	0	0
	B	0	0
	U-21	7	2
	Youth	0	0

NAME:	Lee Jones
CLUB:	Liverpool
BORN:	Wrexham, 29/5/73
DEBUT v:	Northampton, 9/11/90
SUBSTITUTED:	5
BOOKINGS:	1
SENDINGS OFF:	0
OWN GOALS:	0
DOMESTIC PENS:	0
HAT-TRICKS:	0
STRIKE RATE (%):	20.37
EVER PRESENT:	–

LEAGUE CLUBS	YEARS	APPS	GOALS	FEE
Liverpool	92-95	1	0	£300,000
Crewe	93-94	8	1	Loan
Wrexham	90-92	39	9	Appr

OVERALL RECORD

COMPETITION	APPS	GOALS	(PENS)	SUBS
League	32	10	0	16
FA Cup	1	1	0	2
League Cup	2	0	0	1
Europe	2	0	–	–
Scotland	0	0	–	–
Other	3	2	–	–

HONOURS

None

INTERNATIONAL APPEARANCES

COUNTRY	LEVEL	GAMES	GOALS
Wales	Full	0	0
	B	2	0
	U-21	11	9
	Youth	0	0

NAME:	Paul Kitson
CLUB:	Newcastle
BORN:	Peterlee, 9/1/71
DEBUT v:	West Brom, 9/9/89
SUBSTITUTED:	26
BOOKINGS:	9
SENDINGS OFF:	1
OWN GOALS:	0
DOMESTIC PENS:	0
HAT-TRICKS:	1
STRIKE RATE (%):	29.81
EVER PRESENT:	–

LEAGUE CLUBS	YEARS	APPS	GOALS	FEE
Newcastle	94-95	26	8	£2.25m
Derby	92-94	105	36	£1.3m
Leicester	88-92	50	6	Trainee

OVERALL RECORD

COMPETITION	APPS	GOALS	(PENS)	SUBS
League	168	50	0	13
FA Cup	10	5	0	2
League Cup	15	7	0	0
Europe	0	0	–	–
Scotland	0	0	–	–
Other	19	10	–	–

HONOURS

Anglo-Italian Cup r/u 92-93

INTERNATIONAL APPEARANCES

COUNTRY	LEVEL	GAMES	GOALS
England	Full	0	0
	B	1	0
	U-21	7	3
	Youth	4	0

NAME:	Chris Kiwomya
CLUB:	Arsenal
BORN:	Huddersfield, 2/12/69
DEBUT v:	Bradford, 24/9/88
SUBSTITUTED:	23
BOOKINGS:	11
SENDINGS OFF:	0
OWN GOALS:	0
DOMESTIC PENS:	0
HAT-TRICKS:	1
STRIKE RATE (%):	23.42
EVER PRESENT:	–

LEAGUE CLUBS	YEARS	APPS	GOALS	FEE
Arsenal	95	14	3	£1.25m
Ipswich	87-95	226	50	Appr

OVERALL RECORD

COMPETITION	APPS	GOALS	(PENS)	SUBS
League	203	53	0	37
FA Cup	14	2	0	0
League Cup	14	8	0	1
Europe	3	0	–	–
Scotland	0	0	–	–
Other	6	3	–	–

HONOURS

Division Two Championship 91-92, European Cup Winners' Cup r/u 94-95

INTERNATIONAL APPEARANCES

COUNTRY	LEVEL	GAMES	GOALS
	Full	0	0
	B	0	0
	U-21	0	0
	Youth	0	0

NAME:	Jason Lee
CLUB:	Nottm Forest
BORN:	Forest Gate, 9/5/71
DEBUT v:	Millwall, 9/12/89
SUBSTITUTED:	21
BOOKINGS:	24
SENDINGS OFF:	3
OWN GOALS:	0
DOMESTIC PENS:	1
HAT-TRICKS:	0
STRIKE RATE (%):	18.75
EVER PRESENT:	–

LEAGUE CLUBS	YEARS	APPS	GOALS	FEE
Nottm Forest	94-95	34	5	£100,000
Southend	93-94	18	3	£40,000
Lincoln	91-93	93	21	£35,000
Stockport	91	2	0	Loan
Charlton	89-91	1	0	Appr

OVERALL RECORD

COMPETITION	APPS	GOALS	(PENS)	SUBS
League	116	29	0	32
FA Cup	3	1	1	0
League Cup	7	0	0	2
Europe	0	0	–	–
Scotland	0	0	–	–
Other	14	3	–	–

HONOURS

None

INTERNATIONAL APPEARANCES

COUNTRY	LEVEL	GAMES	GOALS
	Full	0	0
	B	0	0
	U-21	0	0
	Youth	0	0

NAME:	John McGinlay
CLUB:	Bolton
BORN:	Inverness, 8/4/64
DEBUT v:	Walsall, 25/2/89
SUBSTITUTED:	45
BOOKINGS:	15
SENDINGS OFF:	0
OWN GOALS:	0
DOMESTIC PENS:	15
HAT-TRICKS:	4
STRIKE RATE (%):	44.65
EVER PRESENT:	–

LEAGUE CLUBS	YEARS	APPS	GOALS	FEE
Bolton	92-95	110	58	£125,000
Millwall	91-92	34	10	£80,000
Bury	90-91	25	9	£175,000
Shrewsbury	89-90	60	27	£10,000
From: Elgin City				

OVERALL RECORD

COMPETITION	APPS	GOALS	(PENS)	SUBS
League	205	104	11	24
FA Cup	23	12	3	0
League Cup	17	5	1	2
Europe	0	0	–	–
Scotland	4	1	–	–
Other	18	11	–	–

HONOURS

League Cup r/u 94-95

INTERNATIONAL APPEARANCES

COUNTRY	LEVEL	GAMES	GOALS
Scotland	Full	6	2
	B	0	0
	U-21	0	0
	Youth	0	0

NAME:	Neil Maddison
CLUB:	Southampton
BORN:	Darlington, 2/10/69
DEBUT v:	Tottenham, 25/10/88
SUBSTITUTED:	11
BOOKINGS:	5
SENDINGS OFF:	0
OWN GOALS:	1
DOMESTIC PENS:	0
HAT-TRICKS:	0
STRIKE RATE (%):	11.56
EVER PRESENT:	–

LEAGUE CLUBS	YEARS	APPS	GOALS	FEE
Southampton	88-95	130	17	Trainee

OVERALL RECORD

COMPETITION	APPS	GOALS	(PENS)	SUBS
League	117	17	0	13
FA Cup	7	0	0	3
League Cup	5	0	0	2
Europe	0	0	–	–
Scotland	0	0	–	–
Other	1	0	–	–

HONOURS

None

INTERNATIONAL APPEARANCES

COUNTRY	LEVEL	GAMES	GOALS
	Full	0	0
	B	0	0
	U-21	0	0
	Youth	0	0

NAME:	Philomen Masinga
CLUB:	Leeds
BORN:	Johanesburg, 28/6/69
DEBUT v:	West Ham, 20/8/94
SUBSTITUTED:	8
BOOKINGS:	2
SENDINGS OFF:	0
OWN GOALS:	0
DOMESTIC PENS:	0
HAT-TRICKS:	1
STRIKE RATE (%):	–
EVER PRESENT:	–

LEAGUE CLUBS	YEARS	APPS	GOALS	FEE
Leeds	94-95	22	5	£275,000
From: Sundowns				

OVERALL RECORD

COMPETITION	APPS	GOALS	(PENS)	SUBS
League	15	5	0	7
FA Cup	2	4	0	2
League Cup	1	0	0	0
Europe	0	0	–	–
Scotland	0	0	–	–

HONOURS

None

INTERNATIONAL APPEARANCES

COUNTRY	LEVEL	GAMES	GOALS
South Africa	Full	17	8
	B	0	0
	U-21	0	0
	Youth	0	0

NAME:	Craig Maskell
CLUB:	Southampton
BORN:	Aldershot, 10/4/68
DEBUT v:	Birmingham, 19/4/86
SUBSTITUTED:	25
BOOKINGS:	2
SENDINGS OFF:	1
OWN GOALS:	0
DOMESTIC PENS:	14
HAT-TRICKS:	4
STRIKE RATE (%):	38.91
EVER PRESENT:	88-89

LEAGUE CLUBS	YEARS	APPS	GOALS	FEE
Southampton	94-95	16	1	£350,000
Swindon	92-94	47	21	£225,000
Reading	90-92	72	26	£250,000
Huddersfield	88-90	87	43	£20,000
Southampton	86-88	6	1	Appr

OVERALL RECORD

COMPETITION	APPS	GOALS	(PENS)	SUBS
League	195	92	14	33
FA Cup	16	3	0	1
League Cup	11	5	0	1
Europe	0	0	–	–
Scotland	0	0	–	–
Other	13	8	–	–

INTERNATIONAL APPEARANCES

COUNTRY	LEVEL	GAMES	GOALS
England	Full	0	0
	B	1	2
	U-21	0	0
	Youth	0	0

HONOURS

None

NAME:	Trevor Morley
CLUB:	West Ham
BORN:	Nottingham, 20/3/61
DEBUT v:	Burnley, 17/8/85
SUBSTITUTED:	30
BOOKINGS:	17
SENDINGS OFF:	0
OWN GOALS:	0
DOMESTIC PENS:	5
HAT-TRICKS:	2
STRIKE RATE (%):	32.69
EVER PRESENT:	93-94

LEAGUE CLUBS	YEARS	APPS	GOALS	FEE
West Ham	89-95	178	57	£500,000
Manchester City	88-89	72	18	£175,000
Northampton	85-88	107	39	£20,000
From: Nuneaton				

OVERALL RECORD

COMPETITION	APPS	GOALS	(PENS)	SUBS
League	335	114	3	22
FA Cup	23	9	1	5
League Cup	27	12	1	1
Europe	0	0	–	–
Scotland	0	0	–	–
Other	15	1	–	–

INTERNATIONAL APPEARANCES

COUNTRY	LEVEL	GAMES	GOALS
	Full	0	0
	B	0	0
	U-21	0	0
	Youth	0	0

HONOURS

Division Four Championship 86-87, PFA Team Awards: Div 4. 87; Div 2. 91

NAME:	Peter Ndlovu
CLUB:	Coventry
BORN:	Bulawayo, 25/2/73
DEBUT v:	Q.P.R., 24/8/91
SUBSTITUTED:	5
BOOKINGS:	2
SENDINGS OFF:	0
OWN GOALS:	0
DOMESTIC PENS:	5
HAT-TRICKS:	1
STRIKE RATE (%):	25.00
EVER PRESENT:	–

LEAGUE CLUBS	YEARS	APPS	GOALS	FEE
Coventry	91-95	125	31	£10,000
From: Highlanders				

OVERALL RECORD

COMPETITION	APPS	GOALS	(PENS)	SUBS
League	104	31	5	21
FA Cup	5	2	0	0
League Cup	6	1	0	0
Europe	0	0	–	–
Scotland	0	0	–	–
Other	1	0	–	–

HONOURS

None

INTERNATIONAL APPEARANCES

COUNTRY	LEVEL	GAMES	GOALS
Zimbawbe	Full	29	11
	B	0	0
	U-21	0	0
	Youth	0	0

NAME: Mike Newell

NAME:	Mike Newell
CLUB:	Blackburn
BORN:	Liverpool, 27/1/65
DEBUT v:	Swindon, 8/10/83
SUBSTITUTED:	28
BOOKINGS:	16
SENDINGS OFF:	1
OWN GOALS:	2
DOMESTIC PENS:	4
HAT-TRICKS:	2
STRIKE RATE (%):	29.54
EVER PRESENT:	86-87

LEAGUE CLUBS	YEARS	APPS	GOALS	FEE
Blackburn	91-95	100	26	£1.1m
Everton	89-91	68	15	£1.1m
Leicester	87-89	81	21	£350,000
Luton	86-87	63	18	£40,000
Wigan	84-86	72	25	
Crewe	83-84	3	0	

OVERALL RECORD

COMPETITION	APPS	GOALS	(PENS)	SUBS
League	345	105	3	42
FA Cup	28	13	0	5
League Cup	32	17	1	5
Europe	0	0	–	–
Scotland	0	0	–	–
Other	18	7	–	–

HONOURS

None

INTERNATIONAL APPEARANCES

COUNTRY	LEVEL	GAMES	GOALS
England	Full	0	0
	B	3	1
	U-21	4	0
	Youth	0	0

NAME:	Mixu Paatelainen
CLUB:	Bolton
BORN:	Helsinki, 3/2/67
DEBUT v:	St. Mirren, 31/10/87
SUBSTITUTED:	2
BOOKINGS:	14
SENDINGS OFF:	1
OWN GOALS:	0
DOMESTIC PENS:	0
HAT-TRICKS:	0
STRIKE RATE (%):	27.59
EVER PRESENT:	–

LEAGUE CLUBS	YEARS	APPS	GOALS	FEE
Bolton	94-95	44	12	£300,000
Aberdeen	92-94	75	23	£200,000
Dundee Utd	87-92	133	33	£120,000
From: Valkeakosken Haka				

OVERALL RECORD

COMPETITION	APPS	GOALS	(PENS)	SUBS
League	43	12	0	1
FA Cup	1	0	0	0
League Cup	7	3	0	1
Europe	12	2	–	–
Scotland	248	73	–	–
Other	3	1	–	–

HONOURS

League Cup r/u 94-95, Scottish FA Cup r/u 87-88, 91-92, 92-93, Scottish League Cup r/u 92-93

INTERNATIONAL APPEARANCES

COUNTRY	LEVEL	GAMES	GOALS
Finland	Full	44	8
	B	0	0
	U-21	0	0
	Youth	0	0

NAME:	Gary Penrice
CLUB:	Q.P.R.
BORN:	Bristol, 23/3/64
DEBUT v:	Leyton Orient, 27/4/85
SUBSTITUTED:	24
BOOKINGS:	7
SENDINGS OFF:	0
OWN GOALS:	0
DOMESTIC PENS:	0
HAT-TRICKS:	1
STRIKE RATE (%):	28.53
EVER PRESENT:	87-88

LEAGUE CLUBS	YEARS	APPS	GOALS	FEE
Q.P.R.	91-95	80	20	£625,000
Aston Villa	91	20	1	£1m
Watford	89-91	43	17	£500,000
Bristol Rovers	84-89	188	53	Free

OVERALL RECORD

COMPETITION	APPS	GOALS	(PENS)	SUBS
League	297	91	0	34
FA Cup	17	9	0	2
League Cup	16	5	0	2
Europe	0	0	–	–
Scotland	0	0	–	–
Other	17	4	–	–

HONOURS

Division Three Championship 89-90

INTERNATIONAL APPEARANCES

COUNTRY	LEVEL	GAMES	GOALS
	Full	0	0
	B	0	0
	U-21	0	0
	Youth	0	0

NAME:	Mick Quinn
CLUB:	Coventry
BORN:	Liverpool, 2/5/62
DEBUT v:	Halifax, 12/4/80
SUBSTITUTED:	40
BOOKINGS:	12
SENDINGS OFF:	3
OWN GOALS:	0
DOMESTIC PENS:	22
HAT-TRICKS:	10
STRIKE RATE (%):	44.35
EVER PRESENT:	–

LEAGUE CLUBS	YEARS	APPS	GOALS	FEE
Coventry	92-95	64	25	£250,000
Watford	95	5	0	Loan
Plymouth	94	3	0	Loan
Newcastle	89-92	115	59	£680,000
Portsmouth	86-89	121	54	£150,000
Oldham	84-86	80	34	£50,000
Stockport	82-84	63	39	Free
Wigan	79-82	69	19	Free

OVERALL RECORD

COMPETITION	APPS	GOALS	(PENS)	SUBS
League	485	230	21	35
FA Cup	22	13	0	1
League Cup	29	12	1	3
Europe	0	0	–	–
Scotland	0	0	–	–
Other	13	9	–	–

HONOURS

PFA Team Award Div 2. 89, 90

INTERNATIONAL APPEARANCES

COUNTRY	LEVEL	GAMES	GOALS
	Full	0	0
	B	0	0
	U-21	0	0
	Youth	0	0

NAME:	Niall Quinn
CLUB:	Manchester City
BORN:	Dublin, 6/10/66
DEBUT v:	Liverpool, 14/12/85
SUBSTITUTED:	28
BOOKINGS:	17
SENDINGS OFF:	1
OWN GOALS:	0
DOMESTIC PENS:	0
HAT-TRICKS:	1
STRIKE RATE (%):	28.47
EVER PRESENT:	90-91

LEAGUE CLUBS	YEARS	APPS	GOALS	FEE
Manchester City	90-95	171	57	£800,000
Arsenal	83-90	67	14	Appr

OVERALL RECORD

COMPETITION	APPS	GOALS	(PENS)	SUBS
League	218	71	0	20
FA Cup	17	4	0	5
League Cup	31	9	0	4
Europe	0	0	–	–
Scotland	0	0	–	–
Other	5	2	–	–

HONOURS

League Cup 86-87, Charity Shield medal 89

INTERNATIONAL APPEARANCES

COUNTRY	LEVEL	GAMES	GOALS
Eire	Full	50	12
	B	2	3
	U-21	6	1
	Youth	0	0

NAME:	Paul Read
CLUB:	Arsenal
BORN:	Harlow, 25/9/73
DEBUT v:	Oxford, 4/3/95
SUBSTITUTED:	2
BOOKINGS:	0
SENDINGS OFF:	0
OWN GOALS:	0
DOMESTIC PENS:	0
HAT-TRICKS:	0
STRIKE RATE (%):	–
EVER PRESENT:	–

LEAGUE CLUBS	YEARS	APPS	GOALS	FEE
Arsenal	91-95	0	0	Trainee
Leyton Orient	95	11	0	Loan

OVERALL RECORD

COMPETITION	APPS	GOALS	(PENS)	SUBS
League	11	0	0	0
FA Cup	0	0	0	0
League Cup	0	0	0	0
Europe	0	0	–	–
Scotland	0	0	–	–

HONOURS

None

INTERNATIONAL APPEARANCES

COUNTRY	LEVEL	GAMES	GOALS
	Full	0	0
	B	0	0
	U-21	0	0
	Youth	0	0

NAME:	Paul Rideout
CLUB:	Everton
BORN:	Bournemouth, 14/8/64
DEBUT v:	Hull City, 29/11/80
SUBSTITUTED:	38
BOOKINGS:	6
SENDINGS OFF:	1
OWN GOALS:	0
DOMESTIC PENS:	10
HAT-TRICKS:	4
STRIKE RATE (%):	31.23
EVER PRESENT:	–

LEAGUE CLUBS	YEARS	APPS	GOALS	FEE
Everton	92-95	77	23	£500,000
Rangers	92	12	1	£500,000
Notts County	91-92	11	3	£250,000
Swindon	91	9	1	Loan
Southampton	88-91	75	19	£350,000
From: Bari				
Aston Villa	83-85	54	19	£200,000
Swindon	80-83	95	38	Appr

OVERALL RECORD

COMPETITION	APPS	GOALS	(PENS)	SUBS
League	289	103	9	32
FA Cup	21	4	0	3
League Cup	30	10	1	3
Europe	1	0	–	–
Scotland	15	1	–	–
Other	7	1	–	–

HONOURS

Scottish Premier League 91-92, FA Cup 94-95, PFA Team Award Div 4. 83

INTERNATIONAL APPEARANCES

COUNTRY	LEVEL	GAMES	GOALS
England	Full	0	0
	B	0	0
	U-21	5	1
	Youth	4	1

NAME:	Robert Rosario
CLUB:	Nottm Forest
BORN:	Hammersmith, 4/3/66
DEBUT v:	Watford, 7/4/84
SUBSTITUTED:	31
BOOKINGS:	15
SENDINGS OFF:	1
OWN GOALS:	0
DOMESTIC PENS:	0
HAT-TRICKS:	0
STRIKE RATE (%):	15.38
EVER PRESENT:	–

LEAGUE CLUBS	YEARS	APPS	GOALS	FEE
Nottm Forest	93-95	27	3	£400,000
Coventry	91-93	59	8	£600,000
Wolverhampton	85	2	1	Loan
Norwich	83-91	126	18	Appr

OVERALL RECORD

COMPETITION	APPS	GOALS	(PENS)	SUBS
League	196	30	0	18
FA Cup	16	3	0	1
League Cup	15	5	0	1
Europe	0	0	–	–
Scotland	0	0	–	–
Other	14	5	–	–

HONOURS

None

INTERNATIONAL APPEARANCES

COUNTRY	LEVEL	GAMES	GOALS
England	Full	0	0
	B	0	0
	U-21	4	0
	Youth	3	0

NAME:	Ronny Rosenthal
CLUB:	Tottenham
BORN:	Haifa, 11/10/63
DEBUT v:	Southampton, 31/3/90
SUBSTITUTED:	17
BOOKINGS:	6
SENDINGS OFF:	0
OWN GOALS:	0
DOMESTIC PENS:	0
HAT-TRICKS:	2
STRIKE RATE (%):	22.22
EVER PRESENT:	–

LEAGUE CLUBS	YEARS	APPS	GOALS	FEE
Tottenham	94-95	34	2	£250,000
Liverpool	90-94	74	21	£1m
From: Standard Leige				

OVERALL RECORD

COMPETITION	APPS	GOALS	(PENS)	SUBS
League	56	23	0	52
FA Cup	7	4	0	1
League Cup	3	1	0	7
Europe	13	2	–	–
Scotland	0	0	–	–
Other	258	93	–	–

HONOURS

Charity Shield medal 90, 92

INTERNATIONAL APPEARANCES

COUNTRY	LEVEL	GAMES	GOALS
Israel	Full	42	7
	B	0	0
	U-21	0	0
	Youth	0	0

NAME:	Uwe Rosler
CLUB:	Manchester City
BORN:	Attenburg, 15/11/68
DEBUT v:	Q.P.R., 5/3/94
SUBSTITUTED:	8
BOOKINGS:	8
SENDINGS OFF:	1
OWN GOALS:	0
DOMESTIC PENS:	0
HAT-TRICKS:	1
STRIKE RATE (%):	52.94
EVER PRESENT:	–

LEAGUE CLUBS	YEARS	APPS	GOALS	FEE
Manchester City	94-95	43	20	£750,000
From: Dynamo Dresden				

OVERALL RECORD

COMPETITION	APPS	GOALS	(PENS)	SUBS
League	41	20	0	2
FA Cup	4	5	0	0
League Cup	3	2	0	1
Europe	0	0	–	–
Scotland	0	0	–	–
Other	68	4	–	–

HONOURS

None

INTERNATIONAL APPEARANCES

COUNTRY	LEVEL	GAMES	GOALS
Germany	Full	0	0
	B	0	0
	U-21	0	0
	Youth	0	0

NAME:	Zeke Rowe
CLUB:	Chelsea
BORN:	Stoke Newington, 30/10/73
DEBUT v:	Bradford, 6/11/93
SUBSTITUTED:	1
BOOKINGS:	1
SENDINGS OFF:	1
OWN GOALS:	0
DOMESTIC PENS:	0
HAT-TRICKS:	0
STRIKE RATE (%):	–
EVER PRESENT:	–

LEAGUE CLUBS	YEARS	APPS	GOALS	FEE
Chelsea	91-95	0	0	Appr
Barnet	93-94	10	2	Loan

OVERALL RECORD

COMPETITION	APPS	GOALS	(PENS)	SUBS
League	9	2	0	1
FA Cup	2	1	0	0
League Cup	0	0	0	0
Europe	0	0	–	–
Scotland	0	0	–	–

HONOURS

None

INTERNATIONAL APPEARANCES

COUNTRY	LEVEL	GAMES	GOALS
	Full	0	0
	B	0	0
	U-21	0	0
	Youth	0	0

NAME:	Bryan Roy
CLUB:	Nottm Forest
BORN:	Amsterdam, 12/2/70
DEBUT v:	Ipswich, 20/8/94
SUBSTITUTED:	16
BOOKINGS:	7
SENDINGS OFF:	0
OWN GOALS:	0
DOMESTIC PENS:	0
HAT-TRICKS:	0
STRIKE RATE (%):	31.82
EVER PRESENT:	–

LEAGUE CLUBS	YEARS	APPS	GOALS	FEE
Nottm Forest	94-95	37	13	£2.5m
From: Foggia				

OVERALL RECORD

COMPETITION	APPS	GOALS	(PENS)	SUBS
League	37	13	0	0
FA Cup	3	0	0	0
League Cup	4	1	0	0
Europe	0	0	–	–
Scotland	0	0	–	–
Other	176	31	–	–

HONOURS

UEFA Cup 91-92

INTERNATIONAL APPEARANCES

COUNTRY	LEVEL	GAMES	GOALS
Holland	Full	29	8
	B	0	0
	U-21	0	0
	Youth	0	0

NAME:	Ian Rush
CLUB:	Liverpool
BORN:	St. Asaph, 20/10/61
DEBUT v:	Sheffield Wed, 28/4/79
SUBSTITUTED:	25
BOOKINGS:	13
SENDINGS OFF:	0
OWN GOALS:	0
DOMESTIC PENS:	3
HAT-TRICKS:	14
STRIKE RATE (%):	52.50
EVER PRESENT:	86-87, 93-94

INTERNATIONAL APPEARANCES

COUNTRY	LEVEL	GAMES	GOALS
Wales	Full	71	27
	B	0	0
	U-21	2	1
	Youth	0	0

LEAGUE CLUBS	YEARS	APPS	GOALS	FEE
Liverpool	88-95	225	85	£2.8m
From: Juventus				
Liverpool	80-87	224	139	£300,000
Chester	79-80	34	14	Appr

OVERALL RECORD

COMPETITION	APPS	GOALS	(PENS)	SUBS
League	470	238	2	13
FA Cup	60	41	0	2
League Cup	76	47	1	0
Europe	35	14		
Scotland	0	0		
Other	58	25		

HONOURS

League Championship 81-82, 82-83, 83-84, 85-86, 89-90, FA Cup 85-86, 88-89, 91-92, League Cup 80-81, 81-82, 82-83, 94-95, League Cup r/u 86-87, Charity Shield medal 82, 83, 84, 86, 88, 89, 92, European Cup 83-84, European Cup r/u 84-85, Golden Boot 83-84, Footballer of the Year 83-84, PFA Player of the Year 83-84, PFA Young Player of the Year 83, PFA Team Awards Div 1. 83, 84, 85, 87, 91

NAME:	Matthew Rush
CLUB:	West Ham
BORN:	Hackney, 6/8/71
DEBUT v:	Hull City, 6/10/90
SUBSTITUTED:	12
BOOKINGS:	7
SENDINGS OFF:	0
OWN GOALS:	0
DOMESTIC PENS:	0
HAT-TRICKS:	0
STRIKE RATE (%):	10.45
EVER PRESENT:	–

INTERNATIONAL APPEARANCES

COUNTRY	LEVEL	GAMES	GOALS
Eire	Full	0	0
	B	0	0
	U-21	4	0
	Youth	0	0

LEAGUE CLUBS	YEARS	APPS	GOALS	FEE
West Ham	90-95	48	5	Trainee
Swansea	93	4	1	Loan
Cambridge	93	10	0	Loan

OVERALL RECORD

COMPETITION	APPS	GOALS	(PENS)	SUBS
League	35	6	0	27
FA Cup	0	0	0	0
League Cup	5	1	0	0
Europe	0	0	–	–
Scotland	0	0	–	–
Other	3	1	–	–

HONOURS

None

NAME:	Dean Saunders
CLUB:	Aston Villa
BORN:	Swansea, 21/6/64
DEBUT v:	Charlton, 22/10/83
SUBSTITUTED:	25
BOOKINGS:	7
SENDINGS OFF:	0
OWN GOALS:	0
DOMESTIC PENS:	30
HAT-TRICKS:	3
STRIKE RATE (%):	35.17
EVER PRESENT:	85-86, 86-87, 89-90 90-91

INTERNATIONAL APPEARANCES

COUNTRY	LEVEL	GAMES	GOALS
Wales	Full	49	15
	B	0	0
	U-21	0	0
	Youth	0	0

LEAGUE CLUBS	YEARS	APPS	GOALS	FEE
Aston Villa	92-95	112	38	£2.3m
Liverpool	91-92	42	11	£2.9m
Derby	88-91	106	42	£1m
Oxford	87-88	59	22	£60,000
Brighton	85-87	72	20	Free
Cardiff	84	4	0	Loan
Swansea	82-85	49	12	Appr

OVERALL RECORD

COMPETITION	APPS	GOALS	(PENS)	SUBS
League	427	145	25	17
FA Cup	33	13	2	0
League Cup	47	27	3	2
Europe	14	10	–	–
Scotland	0	0	–	–
Other	15	7	–	–

HONOURS

FA Cup 91-92, League Cup 93-94, Charity Shield medal 92

NAME:	Paul Scholes
CLUB:	Manchester Utd
BORN:	Salford, 16/11/74
DEBUT v:	Ipswich, 24/9/94
SUBSTITUTED:	1
BOOKINGS:	1
SENDINGS OFF:	0
OWN GOALS:	0
DOMESTIC PENS:	0
HAT-TRICKS:	0
STRIKE RATE (%):	–
EVER PRESENT:	–

LEAGUE CLUBS	YEARS	APPS	GOALS	FEE
Manchester Utd	93-95	17	5	Appr

OVERALL RECORD

COMPETITION	APPS	GOALS	(PENS)	SUBS
League	6	5	0	11
FA Cup	1	0	0	2
League Cup	3	2	0	0
Europe	2	0	–	–
Scotland	0	0	–	–

HONOURS

FA Cup r/u 94-95, FA Youth Cup r/u 92-93

INTERNATIONAL APPEARANCES

COUNTRY	LEVEL	GAMES	GOALS
England	Full	0	0
	B	0	0
	U-21	0	0
	Youth	1	0

NAME:	Paul Shaw
CLUB:	Arsenal
BORN:	Burnham, 4/9/73
DEBUT v:	Nottm Forest, 3/12/94
SUBSTITUTED:	4
BOOKINGS:	1
SENDINGS OFF:	0
OWN GOALS:	0
DOMESTIC PENS:	0
HAT-TRICKS:	0
STRIKE RATE (%):	–
EVER PRESENT:	–

LEAGUE CLUBS	YEARS	APPS	GOALS	FEE
Arsenal	91-95	1	0	Trainee
Burnley	95	9	4	Loan

OVERALL RECORD

COMPETITION	APPS	GOALS	(PENS)	SUBS
League	8	4	0	2
FA Cup	0	0	0	0
League Cup	0	0	0	0
Europe	0	0	–	–
Scotland	0	0	–	–

HONOURS

None

INTERNATIONAL APPEARANCES

COUNTRY	LEVEL	GAMES	GOALS
England	Full	0	0
	B	0	0
	U-21	0	0
	Youth	1	0

NAME:	Alan Shearer
CLUB:	Blackburn
BORN:	Newcastle, 13/8/70
DEBUT v:	Chelsea, 26/3/88
SUBSTITUTED:	13
BOOKINGS:	22
SENDINGS OFF:	0
OWN GOALS:	0
DOMESTIC PENS:	10
HAT-TRICKS:	5
STRIKE RATE (%):	47.97
EVER PRESENT:	94-95

LEAGUE CLUBS	YEARS	APPS	GOALS	FEE
Blackburn	92-95	103	81	£3.6m
Southampton	87-92	118	23	Trainee

OVERALL RECORD

COMPETITION	APPS	GOALS	(PENS)	SUBS
League	202	104	8	19
FA Cup	17	6	1	3
League Cup	28	20	1	2
Europe	2	1	–	–
Scotland	0	0	–	–
Other	8	5	–	–

HONOURS

League Championship 94-95, Golden Boot 94-95, Footballer of the Year 93-94, PFA Player of the Year 94-95, PFA Team Awards: Div 1. 92; Premier League 93, 94, 95

INTERNATIONAL APPEARANCES

COUNTRY	LEVEL	GAMES	GOALS
England	Full	16	5
	B	1	0
	U-21	12	13
	Youth	5	1

NAME:	Teddy Sheringham	
CLUB:	Tottenham	
BORN:	Walthamstow, 2/4/66	
DEBUT v:	Brentford, 15/1/84	
SUBSTITUTED:	13	
BOOKINGS:	12	
SENDINGS OFF:	0	
OWN GOALS:	0	
DOMESTIC PENS:	18	
HAT-TRICKS:	9	
STRIKE RATE (%):	45.33	
EVER PRESENT:	86-87, 90-91, 94-95	

LEAGUE CLUBS	YEARS	APPS	GOALS	FEE
Tottenham	92-95	99	53	£2.1m
Nottm Forest	91-92	42	14	£2m
Aldershot	85	5	0	Loan
Millwall	84-91	220	93	Appr

OVERALL RECORD

COMPETITION	APPS	GOALS	(PENS)	SUBS
League	347	160	16	19
FA Cup	27	15	1	0
League Cup	34	19	1	1
Europe	0	0	–	–
Scotland	0	0	–	–
Other	20	8	–	–

HONOURS

Division Two Championship 87-88, League Cup r/u 91-92

INTERNATIONAL APPEARANCES

COUNTRY	LEVEL	GAMES	GOALS
England	Full	10	1
	B	0	0
	U-21	1	0
	Youth	11	5

NAME:	Neil Shipperley	
CLUB:	Southampton	
BORN:	Chatham, 30/10/74	
DEBUT v:	Southampton, 10/4/93	
SUBSTITUTED:	13	
BOOKINGS:	3	
SENDINGS OFF:	0	
OWN GOALS:	0	
DOMESTIC PENS:	0	
HAT-TRICKS:	0	
STRIKE RATE (%):	21.62	
EVER PRESENT:	–	

LEAGUE CLUBS	YEARS	APPS	GOALS	FEE
Southampton	95	19	4	£1.3m
Watford	94	5	1	Loan
Chelsea	92-95	37	7	Trainee

OVERALL RECORD

COMPETITION	APPS	GOALS	(PENS)	SUBS
League	49	12	0	12
FA Cup	7	3	0	0
League Cup	4	1	0	2
Europe	2	0	–	–
Scotland	0	0	–	–
Other	1	0	–	–

HONOURS

None

INTERNATIONAL APPEARANCES

COUNTRY	LEVEL	GAMES	GOALS
England	Full	0	0
	B	0	0
	U-21	3	2
	Youth	0	0

NAME:	Alan Smith	
CLUB:	Arsenal	
BORN:	Birmingham, 21/11/62	
DEBUT v:	Charlton, 28/8/82	
SUBSTITUTED:	29	
BOOKINGS:	1	
SENDINGS OFF:	0	
OWN GOALS:	0	
DOMESTIC PENS:	1	
HAT-TRICKS:	4	
STRIKE RATE (%):	35.16	
EVER PRESENT:	86-87, 89-90	

LEAGUE CLUBS	YEARS	APPS	GOALS	FEE
Arsenal	87-95	264	86	£800,000
Leicester	82-87	200	76	£22,000
From: Alvechurch				

OVERALL RECORD

COMPETITION	APPS	GOALS	(PENS)	SUBS
League	432	162	1	32
FA Cup	31	10	0	4
League Cup	45	20	0	2
Europe	17	7	–	–
Scotland	0	0	–	–
Other	13	4	–	–

HONOURS

League Championship 88-89, 90-91, FA Cup 92-93, League Cup r/u 87-88, Charity Shield medal 89, 91, European Cup Winners' Cup 93-94, Golden Boot 88-89, 90-91, PFA Team Award Div 1. 89

INTERNATIONAL APPEARANCES

COUNTRY	LEVEL	GAMES	GOALS
England	Full	13	2
	B	5	4
	U-21	0	0
	Youth	0	0

NAME:	John Spencer
CLUB:	Chelsea
BORN:	Glasgow, 11/9/70
DEBUT v:	Partick, 4/3/89
SUBSTITUTED:	12
BOOKINGS:	12
SENDINGS OFF:	1
OWN GOALS:	0
DOMESTIC PENS:	1
HAT-TRICKS:	0
STRIKE RATE (%):	28.74
EVER PRESENT:	–

LEAGUE CLUBS	YEARS	APPS	GOALS	FEE
Chelsea	92-95	70	22	£450,000
Greenock Morton	89	4	1	Loan
Rangers	87-92	13	2	Appr

OVERALL RECORD

COMPETITION	APPS	GOALS	(PENS)	SUBS
League	51	22	1	19
FA Cup	8	3	0	4
League Cup	1	0	0	4
Europe	7	2	–	–
Scotland	19	3	–	–
Other	1	0	–	–

HONOURS

FA Cup r/u 93-94

INTERNATIONAL APPEARANCES

COUNTRY	LEVEL	GAMES	GOALS
Scotland	Full	3	0
	B	0	0
	U-21	3	1
	Youth	0	0

NAME:	Mark Stein
CLUB:	Chelsea
BORN:	South Africa, 28/1/66
DEBUT v:	Everton, 7/4/84
SUBSTITUTED:	33
BOOKINGS:	16
SENDINGS OFF:	0
OWN GOALS:	0
DOMESTIC PENS:	9
HAT-TRICKS:	1
STRIKE RATE (%):	36.24
EVER PRESENT:	92-93

LEAGUE CLUBS	YEARS	APPS	GOALS	FEE
Chelsea	93-95	42	21	£2m
Stoke	91-93	94	50	£100,000
Oxford	89-91	82	18	£500,000
Q.P.R.	88-89	33	4	£300,000
Aldershot	86	2	1	Loan
Luton	84-88	54	19	Appr

OVERALL RECORD

COMPETITION	APPS	GOALS	(PENS)	SUBS
League	268	113	9	39
FA Cup	26	6	0	2
League Cup	20	10	0	1
Europe	3	2	–	–
Scotland	0	0	–	–
Other	27	11	–	–

HONOURS

Second Division Championship 92-93, FA Cup r/u 93-94, League Cup 87-88, League Cup r/u 88-89, PFA Team Award Div 2. 93

INTERNATIONAL APPEARANCES

COUNTRY	LEVEL	GAMES	GOALS
England	Full	0	0
	B	0	0
	U-21	0	0
	Youth	3	0

NAME:	Chris Sutton
CLUB:	Blackburn
BORN:	Nottingham, 10/3/73
DEBUT v:	Q.P.R., 4/5/91
SUBSTITUTED:	13
BOOKINGS:	16
SENDINGS OFF:	0
OWN GOALS:	0
DOMESTIC PENS:	1
HAT-TRICKS:	2
STRIKE RATE (%):	37.50
EVER PRESENT:	–

LEAGUE CLUBS	YEARS	APPS	GOALS	FEE
Blackburn	94-95	40	15	£5m
Norwich	91-94	102	35	Trainee

OVERALL RECORD

COMPETITION	APPS	GOALS	(PENS)	SUBS
League	129	50	1	13
FA Cup	12	7	0	0
League Cup	13	6	0	1
Europe	8	1	–	–
Scotland	0	0	–	–

HONOURS

League Championship 94-95, PFA Team Award Premier League 95

INTERNATIONAL APPEARANCES

COUNTRY	LEVEL	GAMES	GOALS
England	Full	0	0
	B	2	1
	U-21	13	1
	Youth	0	0

NAME:	Paul Tisdale
CLUB:	Southampton
BORN:	Malta, 14/1/73
DEBUT v:	Hereford, 13/2/93
SUBSTITUTED:	2
BOOKINGS:	0
SENDINGS OFF:	0
OWN GOALS:	0
DOMESTIC PENS:	0
HAT-TRICKS:	0
STRIKE RATE (%):	–
EVER PRESENT:	–

LEAGUE CLUBS	YEARS	APPS	GOALS	FEE
Southampton	91-95	7	0	Appr
Northampton	93	5	0	Loan

OVERALL RECORD

COMPETITION	APPS	GOALS	(PENS)	SUBS
League	5	0	0	7
FA Cup	0	0	0	1
League Cup	0	0	0	1
Europe	0	0	–	–
Scotland	0	0	–	–

HONOURS

None

INTERNATIONAL APPEARANCES

COUNTRY	LEVEL	GAMES	GOALS
	Full	0	0
	B	0	0
	U-21	0	0
	Youth	0	0

NAME:	Graeme Tomlinson
CLUB:	Manchester Utd
BORN:	Keighley, 10/12/75
DEBUT v:	York City, 30/10/93
SUBSTITUTED:	1
BOOKINGS:	0
SENDINGS OFF:	0
OWN GOALS:	0
DOMESTIC PENS:	0
HAT-TRICKS:	0
STRIKE RATE (%):	–
EVER PRESENT:	–

LEAGUE CLUBS	YEARS	APPS	GOALS	FEE
Manchester Utd	94-95	0	0	£70,000
Bradford	94	17	6	Trainee

OVERALL RECORD

COMPETITION	APPS	GOALS	(PENS)	SUBS
League	12	6	0	5
FA Cup	0	0	0	1
League Cup	0	0	0	0
Europe	0	0	–	–
Scotland	0	0	–	–

HONOURS

None

INTERNATIONAL APPEARANCES

COUNTRY	LEVEL	GAMES	GOALS
	Full	0	0
	B	0	0
	U-21	0	0
	Youth	0	0

NAME:	Rodney Wallace
CLUB:	Leeds
BORN:	Lewisham, 2/10/69
DEBUT v:	Newcastle, 26/9/87
SUBSTITUTED:	43
BOOKINGS:	15
SENDINGS OFF:	0
OWN GOALS:	0
DOMESTIC PENS:	0
HAT-TRICKS:	1
STRIKE RATE (%):	30.74
EVER PRESENT:	88-89, 89-90

LEAGUE CLUBS	YEARS	APPS	GOALS	FEE
Leeds	91-95	135	39	£1,6m
Southampton	87-91	128	44	Trainee

OVERALL RECORD

COMPETITION	APPS	GOALS	(PENS)	SUBS
League	240	83	0	23
FA Cup	15	3	0	4
League Cup	26	9	0	1
Europe	2	0	–	–
Scotland	0	0	–	–
Other	8	3	–	–

HONOURS

League Championship 91-92, Charity Shield medal 92

INTERNATIONAL APPEARANCES

COUNTRY	LEVEL	GAMES	GOALS
England	Full	0	0
	B	1	0
	U-21	11	2
	Youth	0	0

NAME:	Paul Walsh
CLUB:	Manchester City
BORN:	Plumstead, 1/10/62
DEBUT v:	Shrewsbury, 27/9/79
SUBSTITUTED:	69
BOOKINGS:	5
SENDINGS OFF:	1
OWN GOALS:	0
DOMESTIC PENS:	0
HAT-TRICKS:	8
STRIKE RATE (%):	25.47
EVER PRESENT:	–

INTERNATIONAL APPEARANCES

COUNTRY	LEVEL	GAMES	GOALS
England	Full	5	1
	B	0	0
	U-21	7	4
	Youth	10	5

LEAGUE CLUBS	YEARS	APPS	GOALS	FEE
Manchester City	94-95	49	16	£750,000
Portsmouth	92-94	73	13	£400,000
Q.P.R.	91	2	0	Loan
Tottenham	88-92	128	19	£500,000
Liverpool	84-88	77	25	£700,000
Luton	82-84	80	24	£400,000
Charlton	79-82	87	24	Appr

OVERALL RECORD

COMPETITION	APPS	GOALS	(PENS)	SUBS
League	430	121	0	66
FA Cup	24	8	0	6
League Cup	46	19	0	9
Europe	10	3	–	–
Scotland	0	0	–	–
Other	15	6	–	–

HONOURS

League Championship 85-86, FA Cup 90-91, League Cup r/u 86-87, Charity Shield medal 84, PFA Young Player of the Year 83-84, European Cup r/u 84-85, PFA Team Awards: Div 2. 82; Div 1. 86, 94

NAME:	Paul Warhurst
CLUB:	Blackburn
BORN:	Stockport, 26/9/69
DEBUT v:	Portsmouth, 29/10/88
SUBSTITUTED:	25
BOOKINGS:	16
SENDINGS OFF:	2
OWN GOALS:	0
DOMESTIC PENS:	0
HAT-TRICKS:	0
STRIKE RATE (%):	9.13
EVER PRESENT:	–

INTERNATIONAL APPEARANCES

COUNTRY	LEVEL	GAMES	GOALS
England	Full	0	0
	B	0	0
	U-21	7	0
	Youth	0	0

LEAGUE CLUBS	YEARS	APPS	GOALS	FEE
Blackburn	93-95	36	2	£1.75m
Sheffield Wed	91-93	66	6	£750,000
Oldham	88-91	67	2	£10,000
Manchester City	87-88	0	0	Trainee

OVERALL RECORD

COMPETITION	APPS	GOALS	(PENS)	SUBS
League	144	10	0	25
FA Cup	13	5	0	5
League Cup	21	4	0	0
Europe	5	3	–	–
Scotland	0	0	–	–
Other	3	0	–	–

HONOURS

League Championship 94-95, Division Two Championship 90-91, FA Cup r/u 92-93, League Cup r/u 89-90, 92-93

NAME:	Gordon Watson
CLUB:	Southampton
BORN:	Sidcup, 20/3/71
DEBUT v:	Derby, 19/8/89
SUBSTITUTED:	17
BOOKINGS:	8
SENDINGS OFF:	1
OWN GOALS:	0
DOMESTIC PENS:	0
HAT-TRICKS:	0
STRIKE RATE (%):	23.85
EVER PRESENT:	–

INTERNATIONAL APPEARANCES

COUNTRY	LEVEL	GAMES	GOALS
England	Full	0	0
	B	0	0
	U-21	2	1
	Youth	1	0

LEAGUE CLUBS	YEARS	APPS	GOALS	FEE
Southampton	95	12	3	£1.2m
Sheffield Wed	91-95	66	15	£250,000
Charlton	89-91	31	7	Trainee

OVERALL RECORD

COMPETITION	APPS	GOALS	(PENS)	SUBS
League	61	25	0	48
FA Cup	5	0	0	3
League Cup	8	6	0	5
Europe	3	1	–	–
Scotland	0	0	–	–
Other	3	0	–	–

HONOURS

None

NAME:	Roy Wegerle
CLUB:	Coventry
BORN:	South Africa, 19/3/64
DEBUT v:	Everton, 8/11/86
SUBSTITUTED:	43
BOOKINGS:	6
SENDINGS OFF:	1
OWN GOALS:	1
DOMESTIC PENS:	14
HAT-TRICKS:	0
STRIKE RATE (%):	26.83
EVER PRESENT:	–

LEAGUE CLUBS	YEARS	APPS	GOALS	FEE
Coventry	93-95	53	9	£1m
Blackburn	92-93	34	6	£1.2m
Q.P.R.	89-92	75	29	£1m
Luton	88-89	45	10	£75,000
Swindon	88	7	1	Loan
Chelsea	86-88	23	3	£100,000
From: Tampa Bay Rowdies				

OVERALL RECORD

COMPETITION	APPS	GOALS	(PENS)	SUBS
League	198	58	13	39
FA Cup	20	5	1	4
League Cup	23	14	0	3
Europe	0	0	–	–
Scotland	0	0	–	–
Other	7	0	–	–

HONOURS

League Cup r/u 88-89

INTERNATIONAL APPEARANCES

COUNTRY	LEVEL	GAMES	GOALS
U.S.A.	Full	20	1
	B	1	1
	U-21	0	0
	Youth	0	0

NAME:	Noel Whelan
CLUB:	Leeds
BORN:	Leeds, 30/12/74
DEBUT v:	Sheffield Wed, 4/5/93
SUBSTITUTED:	7
BOOKINGS:	6
SENDINGS OFF:	0
OWN GOALS:	0
DOMESTIC PENS:	0
HAT-TRICKS:	0
STRIKE RATE (%):	17.78
EVER PRESENT:	–

LEAGUE CLUBS	YEARS	APPS	GOALS	FEE
Leeds	93-95	40	7	Trainee

OVERALL RECORD

COMPETITION	APPS	GOALS	(PENS)	SUBS
League	25	7	0	15
FA Cup	2	0	0	0
League Cup	3	1	0	0
Europe	0	0	–	–
Scotland	0	0	–	–

HONOURS

FA Youth Cup 92-93

INTERNATIONAL APPEARANCES

COUNTRY	LEVEL	GAMES	GOALS
England	Full	0	0
	B	0	0
	U-21	2	1
	Youth	2	0

NAME:	David White
CLUB:	Leeds
BORN:	Manchester, 30/10/67
DEBUT v:	Luton, 27/9/86
SUBSTITUTED:	32
BOOKINGS:	14
SENDINGS OFF:	0
OWN GOALS:	0
DOMESTIC PENS:	0
HAT-TRICKS:	3
STRIKE RATE (%):	27.85
EVER PRESENT:	87-88, 90-91, 92-93

LEAGUE CLUBS	YEARS	APPS	GOALS	FEE
Leeds	93-95	38	8	£2m
Manchester City	85-93	285	80	Appr

OVERALL RECORD

COMPETITION	APPS	GOALS	(PENS)	SUBS
League	300	88	0	23
FA Cup	28	6	0	0
League Cup	24	11	0	2
Europe	0	0	–	–
Scotland	0	0	–	–
Other	9	2	–	–

HONOURS

None

INTERNATIONAL APPEARANCES

COUNTRY	LEVEL	GAMES	GOALS
England	Full	1	0
	B	2	0
	U-21	6	2
	Youth	4	0

Guy Whittingham

NAME:	Guy Whittingham
CLUB:	Sheffield Wed
BORN:	Evesham, 10/11/64
DEBUT v:	Stoke, 26/8/89
SUBSTITUTED:	29
BOOKINGS:	1
SENDINGS OFF:	0
OWN GOALS:	0
DOMESTIC PENS:	1
HAT-TRICKS:	7
STRIKE RATE (%):	49.80
EVER PRESENT:	89-90, 92-93

LEAGUE CLUBS	YEARS	APPS	GOALS	FEE
Sheffield Wed	94-95	21	9	£1m
Wolverhampton	94	13	8	Loan
Aston Villa	93-94	25	5	£1.2m
Portsmouth	89-93	161	88	

OVERALL RECORD

COMPETITION	APPS	GOALS	(PENS)	SUBS
League	196	110	1	24
FA Cup	14	10	0	1
League Cup	13	4	0	1
Europe	3	0	–	–
Scotland	0	0	–	–
Other	9	3	–	–

HONOURS

PFA Team Award Div 1. 93

INTERNATIONAL APPEARANCES

COUNTRY	LEVEL	GAMES	GOALS
	Full	0	0
	B	0	0
	U-21	0	0
	Youth	0	0

Paul Wilkinson

NAME:	Paul Wilkinson
CLUB:	Middlesbrough
BORN:	Louth, 30/10/64
DEBUT v:	Charlton, 22/1/83
SUBSTITUTED:	26
BOOKINGS:	22
SENDINGS OFF:	1
OWN GOALS:	1
DOMESTIC PENS:	3
HAT-TRICKS:	3
STRIKE RATE (%):	34.06
EVER PRESENT:	90-91, 91-92

LEAGUE CLUBS	YEARS	APPS	GOALS	FEE
Middlesbrough	91-95	161	50	£550,000
Watford	88-91	134	52	£300,000
Nottm Forest	87-88	34	5	£200,000
Everton	85-87	31	6	£250,000
Grimsby	82-85	71	27	Appr

OVERALL RECORD

COMPETITION	APPS	GOALS	(PENS)	SUBS
League	412	140	3	19
FA Cup	30	9	0	4
League Cup	36	22	0	1
Europe	0	0	–	–
Scotland	0	0	–	–
Other	23	8	–	–

HONOURS

League Championship 86-87, First Division Championship 94-95, Charity Shield medal 86, PFA Team Award Div 2. 85

INTERNATIONAL APPEARANCES

COUNTRY	LEVEL	GAMES	GOALS
England	Full	0	0
	B	0	0
	U-21	4	1
	Youth	0	0

John Williams

NAME:	John Williams
CLUB:	Coventry
BORN:	Birmingham, 11/5/68
DEBUT v:	Bolton, 24/8/91
SUBSTITUTED:	23
BOOKINGS:	10
SENDINGS OFF:	1
OWN GOALS:	0
DOMESTIC PENS:	0
HAT-TRICKS:	1
STRIKE RATE (%):	17.69
EVER PRESENT:	–

LEAGUE CLUBS	YEARS	APPS	GOALS	FEE
Coventry	92-95	80	11	£250,000
Swansea	95	7	2	Loan
Stoke	95	4	0	Loan
Notts County	94	5	2	Loan
Swansea	91-92	39	11	£6,000
From: Cradley Town				

OVERALL RECORD

COMPETITION	APPS	GOALS	(PENS)	SUBS
League	112	26	0	23
FA Cup	5	0	0	0
League Cup	6	0	0	1
Europe	0	0	–	–
Scotland	0	0	–	–
Other	1	0	–	–

HONOURS

None

INTERNATIONAL APPEARANCES

COUNTRY	LEVEL	GAMES	GOALS
	Full	0	0
	B	0	0
	U-21	0	0
	Youth	0	0

NAME:	Danny Williamson
CLUB:	West Ham
BORN:	London, 5/12/73
DEBUT v:	Lincoln, 9/10/93
SUBSTITUTED:	1
BOOKINGS:	1
SENDINGS OFF:	0
OWN GOALS:	0
DOMESTIC PENS:	0
HAT-TRICKS:	0
STRIKE RATE (%):	–
EVER PRESENT:	–

LEAGUE CLUBS	YEARS	APPS	GOALS	FEE
West Ham	92-95	7	1	Appr
Doncaster	93-94	10	1	Loan

OVERALL RECORD

COMPETITION	APPS	GOALS	(PENS)	SUBS
League	14	2	0	3
FA Cup	2	1	0	0
League Cup	0	0	0	0
Europe	0	0	–	–
Scotland	0	0	–	–

HONOURS

None

INTERNATIONAL APPEARANCES

COUNTRY	LEVEL	GAMES	GOALS
	Full	0	0
	B	0	0
	U-21	0	0
	Youth	0	0

NAME:	Ian Wright
CLUB:	Arsenal
BORN:	Woolwich, 3/11/63
DEBUT v:	Huddersfield, 31/8/85
SUBSTITUTED:	34
BOOKINGS:	43
SENDINGS OFF:	0
OWN GOALS:	0
DOMESTIC PENS:	14
HAT-TRICKS:	12
STRIKE RATE (%):	50.36
EVER PRESENT:	90-91

LEAGUE CLUBS	YEARS	APPS	GOALS	FEE
Arsenal	91-95	130	80	£2.5m
Crystal Palace	85-91	225	90	
From: Greenwich Borough				

OVERALL RECORD

COMPETITION	APPS	GOALS	(PENS)	SUBS
League	334	170	12	21
FA Cup	21	14	1	2
League Cup	37	25	1	0
Europe	16	12	–	–
Scotland	0	0	–	–
Other	26	17	–	–

HONOURS

FA Cup 92-93, FA Cup r/u 89-90, League Cup 92-93, Charity Shield medal 93, European Cup Winners' Cup 93-94, European Cup Winners' Cup r/u 94-5, Golden Boot 91-92, PFA Team Awards: Div 2. 89; Premier League 93

INTERNATIONAL APPEARANCES

COUNTRY	LEVEL	GAMES	GOALS
England	Full	20	5
	B	3	0
	U-21	0	0
	Youth	0	0

NAME:	Tommy Wright
CLUB:	Middlesbrough
BORN:	Dunfermline, 10/1/66
DEBUT v:	Fulham, 16/4/83
SUBSTITUTED:	45
BOOKINGS:	7
SENDINGS OFF:	0
OWN GOALS:	0
DOMESTIC PENS:	0
HAT-TRICKS:	1
STRIKE RATE (%):	20.05
EVER PRESENT:	84-85

LEAGUE CLUBS	YEARS	APPS	GOALS	FEE
Middlesbrough	92-95	53	5	£650,000
Leicester	89-92	129	22	£350,000
Oldham	86-89	112	23	£80,000
Leeds	83-86	81	24	Appr

OVERALL RECORD

COMPETITION	APPS	GOALS	(PENS)	SUBS
League	349	74	0	26
FA Cup	14	6	0	0
League Cup	20	3	0	5
Europe	0	0	–	–
Scotland	0	0	–	–
Other	20	7	–	–

HONOURS

None

INTERNATIONAL APPEARANCES

COUNTRY	LEVEL	GAMES	GOALS
Scotland	Full	0	0
	B	0	0
	U-21	3	0
	Youth	0	0

NAME:	Tony Yeboah
CLUB:	Leeds
BORN:	Ghana, 6/6/66
DEBUT v:	Q.P.R., 24/1/95
SUBSTITUTED:	3
BOOKINGS:	0
SENDINGS OFF:	0
OWN GOALS:	0
DOMESTIC PENS:	0
HAT-TRICKS:	1
STRIKE RATE (%):	–
EVER PRESENT:	–

LEAGUE CLUBS	YEARS	APPS	GOALS	FEE
Leeds	95	18	12	£3.5m
From: Eintract Frankfurt				

OVERALL RECORD

COMPETITION	APPS	GOALS	(PENS)	SUBS
League	16	12	0	2
FA Cup	0	0	0	0
League Cup	0	0	0	0
Europe	0	0	–	–
Scotland	0	0	–	–

HONOURS

None

INTERNATIONAL APPEARANCES

COUNTRY	LEVEL	GAMES	GOALS
Ghana	Full	25	5
	B	0	0
	U-21	0	0
	Youth	0	0

NAME:	Dwight Yorke
CLUB:	Aston Villa
BORN:	Tobago, 3/12/71
DEBUT v:	Crystal Palace, 24/3/90
SUBSTITUTED:	26
BOOKINGS:	4
SENDINGS OFF:	0
OWN GOALS:	0
DOMESTIC PENS:	0
HAT-TRICKS:	1
STRIKE RATE (%):	24.03
EVER PRESENT:	–

LEAGUE CLUBS	YEARS	APPS	GOALS	FEE
Aston Villa	89-95	128	27	£120,000
From: Tobago				

OVERALL RECORD

COMPETITION	APPS	GOALS	(PENS)	SUBS
League	92	27	0	36
FA Cup	13	7	0	2
League Cup	9	3	0	2
Europe	0	0	–	–
Scotland	0	0	–	–
Other	1	1	–	–

HONOURS

None

INTERNATIONAL APPEARANCES

COUNTRY	LEVEL	GAMES	GOALS
Trinidad & Tobago	Full	35	7
	B	0	0
	U-21	0	0
	Youth	0	0

Bartram, Vince – Arsenal

OPPONENTS	HOME APPS	HOME GC	AWAY APPS	AWAY GC	TOTAL APPS	TOTAL GC
Arsenal	0	0	0	0	0	0
Aston Villa	1	0	0	0	1	0
Blackburn Rovers	0	0	2	4	2	4
Bolton Wanderers	2	4	3	3	5	7
Chelsea	0	0	0	0	0	0
Coventry	0	0	0	0	0	0
Everton	0	0	0	0	0	0
Leeds Utd	1	3	0	0	1	3
Liverpool	0	0	0	0	0	0
Manchester City	0	0	1	1	1	1
Manchester Utd	0	0	1	3	1	3
Middlesbrough	0	0	1	2	1	2
Newcastle	0	0	1	1	1	1
Nottingham Forest	1	1	1	2	2	3
Q.P.R.	1	3	0	0	1	3
Sheffield Wednesday	0	0	0	0	0	0
Southampton	0	0	0	0	0	0
Tottenham	0	0	0	0	0	0
West Ham	1	1	0	0	1	1
Wimbledon	0	0	0	0	0	0

Beasant, David – Southampton

OPPONENTS	HOME APPS	HOME GC	AWAY APPS	AWAY GC	TOTAL APPS	TOTAL GC
Arsenal	8	10	4	10	12	20
Aston Villa	4	6	5	7	9	13
Blackburn Rovers	4	3	2	4	6	7
Bolton Wanderers	1	0	1	2	2	2
Chelsea	3	4	4	3	7	7
Coventry	7	8	5	8	12	16
Everton	7	9	8	14	15	23
Leeds Utd	3	7	6	13	9	20
Liverpool	5	13	6	12	11	25
Manchester City	6	6	6	10	12	16
Manchester Utd	5	3	7	11	12	14
Middlesbrough	4	1	2	3	6	4
Newcastle	2	1	4	3	6	4
Nottingham Forest	5	5	5	14	10	19
Q.P.R.	8	7	6	13	14	20
Sheffield Wednesday	5	2	5	6	10	8
Southampton	5	9	5	10	10	19
Tottenham	6	9	6	8	12	17
West Ham	5	5	5	10	10	15
Wimbledon	5	8	2	0	7	8

Beeney, Mark – Leeds United

OPPONENTS	HOME APPS	HOME GC	AWAY APPS	AWAY GC	TOTAL APPS	TOTAL GC
Arsenal	1	1	0	0	1	1
Aston Villa	0	0	1	1	1	1
Blackburn Rovers	1	3	2	3	3	6
Bolton Wanderers	1	2	1	0	2	2
Chelsea	0	0	1	1	1	1
Coventry	0	0	2	3	2	3
Everton	0	0	1	1	1	1
Leeds Utd	0	0	0	0	0	0
Liverpool	0	0	0	0	0	0
Manchester City	1	2	0	0	1	2
Manchester Utd	0	0	1	0	1	0
Middlesbrough	1	1	0	0	1	1
Newcastle	1	2	1	2	2	4
Nottingham Forest	0	0	0	0	0	0
Q.P.R.	1	1	0	0	1	1
Sheffield Wednesday	0	0	1	3	1	3
Southampton	0	0	1	0	1	0
Tottenham	0	0	1	1	1	1
West Ham	0	0	1	0	1	0
Wimbledon	1	0	0	0	1	0

Bosnich, Mark – Aston Villa

OPPONENTS	HOME APPS	HOME GC	AWAY APPS	AWAY GC	TOTAL APPS	TOTAL GC
Arsenal	1	4	2	1	3	5
Aston Villa	0	0	0	0	0	0
Blackburn Rovers	2	2	3	7	5	9
Bolton Wanderers	0	0	0	0	0	0
Chelsea	1	0	3	2	4	2
Coventry	2	0	2	0	4	0
Everton	2	1	1	2	3	3
Leeds Utd	1	0	2	3	3	3
Liverpool	2	1	2	5	4	6
Manchester City	3	2	2	4	5	6
Manchester Utd	0	0	2	4	2	4
Middlesbrough	0	0	0	0	0	0
Newcastle	0	0	1	3	1	3
Nottingham Forest	0	0	2	1	2	1
Q.P.R.	1	1	3	6	4	7
Sheffield Wednesday	3	3	1	1	4	4
Southampton	2	3	0	0	2	3
Tottenham	3	1	2	4	5	5
West Ham	2	3	2	2	4	5
Wimbledon	4	2	1	4	5	6

Branagan, Keith – Bolton Wanderers

OPPONENTS	HOME APPS	HOME GC	AWAY APPS	AWAY GC	TOTAL APPS	TOTAL GC
Arsenal	0	0	1	2	1	2
Aston Villa	0	0	1	1	1	1
Blackburn Rovers	0	0	1	1	1	1
Bolton Wanderers	0	0	2	2	2	2
Chelsea	1	3	0	0	1	3
Coventry	0	0	1	3	1	3
Everton	1	2	0	0	1	2
Leeds Utd	0	0	0	0	0	0
Liverpool	0	0	1	1	1	1
Manchester City	1	1	0	0	1	1
Manchester Utd	1	2	0	0	1	2
Middlesbrough	2	2	1	1	3	3
Newcastle	0	0	0	0	0	0
Nottingham Forest	1	3	1	3	2	6
Q.P.R.	1	2	0	0	1	2
Sheffield Wednesday	1	2	1	1	2	3
Southampton	0	0	0	0	0	0
Tottenham	1	1	0	0	1	1
West Ham	0	0	0	0	0	0
Wimbledon	1	0	0	0	1	0

Burridge, John – Manchester City

OPPONENTS	HOME APPS	HOME GC	AWAY APPS	AWAY GC	TOTAL APPS	TOTAL GC
Arsenal	4	5	5	9	9	14
Aston Villa	5	7	6	8	11	15
Blackburn Rovers	9	10	5	12	14	22
Bolton Wanderers	3	3	6	5	9	8
Chelsea	4	3	2	0	6	3
Coventry	2	2	5	9	7	11
Everton	5	3	7	12	12	15
Leeds Utd	6	3	6	4	12	7
Liverpool	5	6	5	9	10	15
Manchester City	3	1	4	6	7	7
Manchester Utd	4	5	6	11	10	16
Middlesbrough	9	10	11	16	20	26
Newcastle	7	4	4	6	11	10
Nottingham Forest	5	4	6	14	11	18
Q.P.R.	7	11	6	9	13	20
Sheffield Wednesday	7	7	7	7	14	14
Southampton	4	4	2	5	6	9
Tottenham	5	6	4	10	9	16
West Ham	8	5	7	8	15	13
Wimbledon	4	2	4	14	8	16

Coton, Tony – Manchester City

OPPONENTS	HOME		AWAY		TOTAL	
	APPS	GC	APPS	GC	APPS	GC
Arsenal	9	4	11	13	20	17
Aston Villa	6	5	9	15	15	20
Blackburn Rovers	4	7	5	9	9	16
Bolton Wanderers	0	0	0	0	0	0
Chelsea	7	12	9	12	16	24
Coventry	9	8	9	14	18	22
Everton	10	13	10	17	20	30
Leeds Utd	8	7	8	15	16	22
Liverpool	11	16	8	18	19	34
Manchester City	4	5	3	3	7	8
Manchester Utd	8	11	8	12	16	23
Middlesbrough	2	1	2	3	4	4
Newcastle	5	4	5	10	10	14
Nottingham Forest	9	9	8	14	17	23
Q.P.R.	6	6	8	15	14	21
Sheffield Wednesday	8	13	6	7	14	20
Southampton	10	13	10	14	20	27
Tottenham	9	8	11	19	20	27
West Ham	10	7	7	13	17	20
Wimbledon	7	6	7	9	14	15

Crossley, Mark – Nottingham Forest

OPPONENTS	HOME		AWAY		TOTAL	
	APPS	GC	APPS	GC	APPS	GC
Arsenal	4	7	2	2	6	9
Aston Villa	4	5	5	8	9	13
Blackburn Rovers	2	5	2	7	4	12
Bolton Wanderers	1	2	0	0	1	2
Chelsea	4	2	4	1	8	3
Coventry	4	1	4	2	8	3
Everton	5	4	4	5	9	9
Leeds Utd	4	4	4	6	8	10
Liverpool	5	4	5	7	10	11
Manchester City	3	5	5	10	8	15
Manchester Utd	4	4	5	5	9	9
Middlesbrough	2	1	1	2	3	3
Newcastle	1	0	2	3	3	3
Nottingham Forest	0	0	0	0	0	0
Q.P.R.	4	3	4	6	8	9
Sheffield Wednesday	2	3	3	5	5	8
Southampton	4	6	4	5	8	11
Tottenham	3	7	4	5	7	12
West Ham	2	3	2	5	4	8
Wimbledon	4	5	2	5	6	10

Davison, Aidan – Bolton Wanderers

OPPONENTS	HOME		AWAY		TOTAL	
	APPS	GC	APPS	GC	APPS	GC
Arsenal	0	0	0	0	0	0
Aston Villa	0	0	0	0	0	0
Blackburn Rovers	1	3	1	2	2	5
Bolton Wanderers	0	0	0	0	0	0
Chelsea	0	0	0	0	0	0
Coventry	0	0	0	0	0	0
Everton	0	0	0	0	0	0
Leeds Utd	0	0	0	0	0	0
Liverpool	0	0	0	0	0	0
Manchester City	0	0	0	0	0	0
Manchester Utd	0	0	0	0	0	0
Middlesbrough	2	1	1	1	3	2
Newcastle	1	1	1	0	2	1
Nottingham Forest	0	0	1	3	1	3
Q.P.R.	0	0	0	0	0	0
Sheffield Wednesday	0	0	0	0	0	0
Southampton	0	0	0	0	0	0
Tottenham	0	0	0	0	0	0
West Ham	0	0	0	0	0	0
Wimbledon	0	0	0	0	0	0

Dibble, Andy – Manchester City

OPPONENTS	HOME APPS	HOME GC	AWAY APPS	AWAY GC	TOTAL APPS	TOTAL GC
Arsenal	3	5	0	0	3	5
Aston Villa	3	5	3	4	6	9
Blackburn Rovers	2	3	2	2	4	5
Bolton Wanderers	1	2	0	0	1	2
Chelsea	6	10	4	5	10	15
Coventry	2	0	0	0	2	0
Everton	2	2	2	2	4	4
Leeds Utd	2	1	2	2	4	3
Liverpool	2	6	4	8	6	14
Manchester City	1	1	1	2	2	3
Manchester Utd	1	3	4	5	5	8
Middlesbrough	1	1	1	2	2	3
Newcastle	4	5	3	5	7	10
Nottingham Forest	4	8	3	5	7	13
Q.P.R.	2	2	5	5	7	7
Sheffield Wednesday	3	5	4	10	7	15
Southampton	2	3	4	4	6	7
Tottenham	1	2	3	7	4	9
West Ham	0	0	2	3	2	3
Wimbledon	2	1	1	3	3	4

Dykstra, Sieb – Q.P.R.

OPPONENTS	HOME APPS	HOME GC	AWAY APPS	AWAY GC	TOTAL APPS	TOTAL GC
Arsenal	0	0	0	0	0	0
Aston Villa	1	0	0	0	1	0
Blackburn Rovers	0	0	1	4	1	4
Bolton Wanderers	0	0	0	0	0	0
Chelsea	0	0	0	0	0	0
Coventry	0	0	0	0	0	0
Everton	0	0	0	0	0	0
Leeds Utd	1	2	0	0	1	2
Liverpool	1	1	0	0	1	1
Manchester City	0	0	0	0	0	0
Manchester Utd	1	3	0	0	1	3
Middlesbrough	0	0	0	0	0	0
Newcastle	0	0	1	2	1	2
Nottingham Forest	0	0	0	0	0	0
Q.P.R.	0	0	0	0	0	0
Sheffield Wednesday	0	0	1	0	1	0
Southampton	1	2	0	0	1	2
Tottenham	0	0	0	0	0	0
West Ham	1	1	0	0	1	1
Wimbledon	0	0	0	0	0	0

Filan, John – Coventry

OPPONENTS	HOME APPS	HOME GC	AWAY APPS	AWAY GC	TOTAL APPS	TOTAL GC
Arsenal	0	0	0	0	0	0
Aston Villa	0	0	0	0	0	0
Blackburn Rovers	0	0	0	0	0	0
Bolton Wanderers	0	0	0	0	0	0
Chelsea	0	0	0	0	0	0
Coventry	0	0	0	0	0	0
Everton	1	0	0	0	1	0
Leeds Utd	0	0	0	0	0	0
Liverpool	0	0	0	0	0	0
Manchester City	0	0	0	0	0	0
Manchester Utd	0	0	0	0	0	0
Middlesbrough	0	0	0	0	0	0
Newcastle	1	3	0	0	1	3
Nottingham Forest	0	0	0	0	0	0
Q.P.R.	0	0	0	0	0	0
Sheffield Wednesday	0	0	0	0	0	0
Southampton	0	0	0	0	0	0
Tottenham	0	0	1	1	1	1
West Ham	0	0	1	2	1	2
Wimbledon	0	0	0	0	0	0

Flowers, Tim – Blackburn

OPPONENTS	HOME		AWAY		TOTAL	
	APPS	GC	APPS	GC	APPS	GC
Arsenal	7	12	7	17	14	29
Aston Villa	6	4	7	8	13	12
Blackburn Rovers	2	4	1	0	3	4
Bolton Wanderers	2	2	1	4	3	6
Chelsea	6	7	6	6	12	13
Coventry	7	4	8	12	15	16
Everton	7	12	6	9	13	21
Leeds Utd	7	11	6	15	13	26
Liverpool	6	5	6	13	12	18
Manchester City	7	9	6	10	13	19
Manchester Utd	7	12	7	15	14	27
Middlesbrough	2	1	2	3	4	4
Newcastle	3	1	3	6	6	7
Nottingham Forest	6	5	6	10	12	15
Q.P.R.	8	12	6	9	14	21
Sheffield Wednesday	5	7	5	8	10	15
Southampton	2	2	2	4	4	6
Tottenham	5	4	6	11	11	15
West Ham	3	2	3	3	6	5
Wimbledon	6	8	7	8	13	16

Gould, Jon – Coventry urn

OPPONENTS	HOME		AWAY		TOTAL	
	APPS	GC	APPS	GC	APPS	GC
Arsenal	0	0	1	0	1	0
Aston Villa	2	0	1	0	3	0
Blackburn Rovers	1	0	0	0	1	0
Bolton Wanderers	0	0	0	0	0	0
Chelsea	0	0	2	3	2	3
Coventry	0	0	0	0	0	0
Everton	0	0	0	0	0	0
Leeds Utd	1	3	1	3	2	6
Liverpool	2	1	2	6	4	7
Manchester City	0	0	1	1	1	1
Manchester Utd	2	4	1	5	3	9
Middlesbrough	0	0	0	0	0	0
Newcastle	1	1	0	0	1	1
Nottingham Forest	0	0	0	0	0	0
Q.P.R.	0	0	1	5	1	5
Sheffield Wednesday	0	0	0	0	0	0
Southampton	2	1	1	0	3	1
Tottenham	0	0	0	0	0	0
West Ham	1	1	0	0	1	1
Wimbledon	0	0	0	0	0	0

Grobbelaar, Bruce – Southampton

OPPONENTS	HOME		AWAY		TOTAL	
	APPS	GC	APPS	GC	APPS	GC
Arsenal	11	6	10	12	21	18
Aston Villa	11	11	12	13	23	24
Blackburn Rovers	2	2	1	3	3	5
Bolton Wanderers	0	0	0	0	0	0
Chelsea	8	9	7	13	15	22
Coventry	10	2	12	10	22	12
Everton	10	7	12	12	22	19
Leeds Utd	5	3	4	3	9	6
Liverpool	1	2	1	3	2	5
Manchester City	8	13	9	8	17	21
Manchester Utd	12	14	10	11	22	25
Middlesbrough	2	4	2	0	4	4
Newcastle	5	3	6	12	11	15
Nottingham Forest	12	6	8	9	20	15
Q.P.R.	9	6	10	10	19	16
Sheffield Wednesday	9	8	7	8	16	16
Southampton	12	10	9	20	21	30
Tottenham	13	12	13	17	26	29
West Ham	9	3	7	8	16	11
Wimbledon	8	15	7	5	15	20

Kevin Hitchcock – Chelsea

OPPONENTS	HOME APPS	HOME GC	AWAY APPS	AWAY GC	TOTAL APPS	TOTAL GC
Arsenal	1	1	2	5	3	6
Aston Villa	2	1	0	0	2	1
Blackburn Rovers	1	2	2	4	3	6
Bolton Wanderers	1	2	1	0	2	2
Chelsea	0	0	0	0	0	0
Coventry	1	2	1	1	2	3
Everton	0	0	1	0	1	0
Leeds Utd	3	4	1	4	4	8
Liverpool	3	3	2	4	5	7
Manchester City	2	7	2	1	4	8
Manchester Utd	2	4	2	1	4	5
Middlesbrough	1	1	2	1	3	2
Newcastle	1	1	0	0	1	1
Nottingham Forest	2	0	2	4	4	4
Q.P.R.	0	0	1	1	1	1
Sheffield Wednesday	1	3	1	3	2	6
Southampton	3	3	1	1	4	4
Tottenham	1	0	2	2	3	2
West Ham	0	0	3	5	3	5
Wimbledon	0	0	5	6	5	6

Hooper, Mike – Newcastle

OPPONENTS	HOME APPS	HOME GC	AWAY APPS	AWAY GC	TOTAL APPS	TOTAL GC
Arsenal	2	1	3	7	5	8
Aston Villa	2	2	1	0	3	2
Blackburn Rovers	1	1	0	0	1	1
Bolton Wanderers	0	0	0	0	0	0
Chelsea	1	2	2	4	3	6
Coventry	2	1	2	6	4	7
Everton	3	2	3	4	6	6
Leeds Utd	1	1	1	4	2	5
Liverpool	1	0	0	0	1	0
Manchester City	3	1	0	0	3	1
Manchester Utd	2	1	2	3	4	4
Middlesbrough	2	1	1	6	3	7
Newcastle	2	6	1	0	3	6
Nottingham Forest	0	0	2	3	2	3
Q.P.R.	2	5	4	4	6	9
Sheffield Wednesday	1	4	2	2	3	6
Southampton	1	2	4	6	5	8
Tottenham	1	1	1	2	2	3
West Ham	1	0	2	2	3	2
Wimbledon	2	1	1	4	3	5

James, David – Liverpool

OPPONENTS	HOME APPS	HOME GC	AWAY APPS	AWAY GC	TOTAL APPS	TOTAL GC
Arsenal	2	2	3	1	5	3
Aston Villa	1	2	3	8	4	10
Blackburn Rovers	3	5	5	10	8	15
Bolton Wanderers	0	0	0	0	0	0
Chelsea	3	3	2	0	5	3
Coventry	3	3	1	1	4	4
Everton	3	1	1	2	4	3
Leeds Utd	2	1	3	3	5	4
Liverpool	0	0	0	0	0	0
Manchester City	1	0	2	3	3	3
Manchester Utd	2	2	2	3	4	5
Middlesbrough	2	5	3	3	5	8
Newcastle	3	4	3	4	6	8
Nottingham Forest	2	0	2	2	4	2
Q.P.R.	2	1	1	2	3	3
Sheffield Wednesday	2	3	3	4	5	7
Southampton	2	2	2	2	4	4
Tottenham	1	1	2	2	3	3
West Ham	2	1	3	5	5	6
Wimbledon	1	0	3	3	4	3

Judge, Alan – Chelsea

OPPONENTS	HOME APPS	GC	AWAY APPS	GC	TOTAL APPS	GC
Arsenal	1	0	1	0	2	0
Aston Villa	1	1	1	1	2	2
Blackburn Rovers	1	1	0	0	1	1
Bolton Wanderers	0	0	0	0	0	0
Chelsea	2	5	1	1	3	6
Coventry	1	1	0	0	1	1
Everton	2	1	1	3	3	4
Leeds Utd	1	2	1	2	2	4
Liverpool	0	0	0	0	0	0
Manchester City	1	0	2	2	3	2
Manchester Utd	2	5	0	0	2	5
Middlesbrough	0	0	0	0	0	0
Newcastle	3	3	2	5	5	8
Nottingham Forest	1	2	1	5	2	7
Q.P.R.	1	3	2	6	3	9
Sheffield Wednesday	1	0	3	11	4	11
Southampton	1	0	1	1	2	1
Tottenham	1	0	0	0	1	0
West Ham	1	0	3	7	4	7
Wimbledon	0	0	0	0	0	

Kearton, Jason – Everton

OPPONENTS	HOME APPS	GC	AWAY APPS	GC	TOTAL APPS	GC
Arsenal	0	0	0	0	0	0
Aston Villa	0	0	2	2	2	2
Blackburn Rovers	0	0	0	0	0	0
Bolton Wanderers	2	1	0	0	2	1
Chelsea	0	0	0	0	0	0
Coventry	0	0	0	0	0	0
Everton	0	0	0	0	0	0
Leeds Utd	0	0	0	0	0	0
Liverpool	0	0	0	0	0	0
Manchester City	0	0	1	1	1	1
Manchester Utd	0	0	0	0	0	0
Middlesbrough	0	0	0	0	0	0
Newcastle	0	0	0	0	0	0
Nottingham Forest	0	0	0	0	0	0
Q.P.R.	0	0	1	2	1	2
Sheffield Wednesday	0	0	1	1	1	1
Southampton	0	0	0	0	0	0
Tottenham	0	0	0	0	0	0
West Ham	0	0	0	0	0	0
Wimbledon	0	0	0	0	0	0

Key, Lance – Sheffield Wednesday

OPPONENTS	HOME APPS	GC	AWAY APPS	GC	TOTAL APPS	GC
Arsenal	0	0	0	0	0	0
Aston Villa	0	0	0	0	0	0
Blackburn Rovers	0	0	0	0	0	0
Bolton Wanderers	0	0	0	0	0	0
Chelsea	0	0	1	0	1	0
Coventry	0	0	0	0	0	0
Everton	0	0	0	0	0	0
Leeds Utd	0	0	0	0	0	0
Liverpool	0	0	0	0	0	0
Manchester City	0	0	0	0	0	0
Manchester Utd	0	0	0	0	0	0
Middlesbrough	0	0	0	0	0	0
Newcastle	0	0	0	0	0	0
Nottingham Forest	1	3	0	0	1	3
Q.P.R.	0	0	0	0	0	0
Sheffield Wednesday	0	0	0	0	0	0
Southampton	0	0	0	0	0	0
Tottenham	0	0	0	0	0	0
West Ham	0	0	0	0	0	0
Wimbledon	0	0	0	0	0	0

Kharine, Dmitri – Chelsea

OPPONENTS	HOME		AWAY		TOTAL	
	APPS	GC	APPS	GC	APPS	GC
Arsenal	2	2	2	4	4	6
Aston Villa	2	1	2	4	4	5
Blackburn Rovers	2	4	1	2	3	6
Bolton Wanderers	0	0	0	0	0	0
Chelsea	0	0	0	0	0	0
Coventry	2	3	2	3	4	6
Everton	2	3	2	7	4	10
Leeds Utd	1	1	1	2	2	3
Liverpool	2	0	1	2	3	2
Manchester City	2	0	1	2	3	2
Manchester Utd	2	3	1	0	3	3
Middlesbrough	0	0	0	0	0	0
Newcastle	1	0	2	4	3	4
Nottingham Forest	1	2	1	0	2	2
Q.P.R.	2	0	2	2	4	2
Sheffield Wednesday	3	3	2	4	5	7
Southampton	2	2	2	4	4	6
Tottenham	2	4	2	1	4	5
West Ham	2	2	2	2	4	4
Wimbledon	3	3	1	1	4	4

Lukic, John – Leeds

OPPONENTS	HOME		AWAY		TOTAL	
	APPS	GC	APPS	GC	APPS	GC
Arsenal	6	9	8	7	14	16
Aston Villa	11	12	11	6	22	18
Blackburn Rovers	3	4	3	4	6	8
Bolton Wanderers	2	3	0	0	2	3
Chelsea	9	11	11	8	20	19
Coventry	14	4	11	15	25	19
Everton	12	4	13	26	25	30
Leeds Utd	0	0	0	0	0	0
Liverpool	12	16	14	24	26	40
Manchester City	9	3	10	18	19	21
Manchester Utd	14	10	13	17	27	27
Middlesbrough	6	2	6	7	12	9
Newcastle	7	4	6	4	13	8
Nottingham Forest	13	15	12	18	25	33
Q.P.R.	10	8	10	16	20	24
Sheffield Wednesday	10	7	9	14	19	21
Southampton	14	19	13	19	27	38
Tottenham	15	11	13	18	28	29
West Ham	9	7	6	6	15	13
Wimbledon	8	6	9	8	17	14

Margetson, Martyn – Manchester City

OPPONENTS	HOME		AWAY		TOTAL	
	APPS	GC	APPS	GC	APPS	GC
Arsenal	0	0	0	0	0	0
Aston Villa	0	0	0	0	0	0
Blackburn Rovers	0	0	0	0	0	0
Bolton Wanderers	0	0	0	0	0	0
Chelsea	0	0	0	0	0	0
Coventry	0	0	0	0	0	0
Everton	0	0	1	0	1	0
Leeds Utd	1	3	0	0	1	3
Liverpool	0	0	0	0	0	0
Manchester City	0	0	0	0	0	0
Manchester Utd	0	0	1	1	1	1
Middlesbrough	0	0	0	0	0	0
Newcastle	0	0	0	0	0	0
Nottingham Forest	0	0	0	0	0	0
Q.P.R.	0	0	0	0	0	0
Sheffield Wednesday	0	0	0	0	0	0
Southampton	1	1	0	0	1	1
Tottenham	0	0	0	0	0	0
West Ham	0	0	0	0	0	0
Wimbledon	0	0	0	0	0	0

Miklosko, Ludek – West Ham

OPPONENTS	HOME APPS	HOME GC	AWAY APPS	AWAY GC	TOTAL APPS	TOTAL GC
Arsenal	3	4	3	0	6	4
Aston Villa	3	1	3	6	6	7
Blackburn Rovers	4	3	3	7	7	10
Bolton Wanderers	0	0	0	0	0	0
Chelsea	3	3	3	5	6	8
Coventry	3	4	3	4	6	8
Everton	2	3	3	5	5	8
Leeds Utd	3	4	4	6	7	10
Liverpool	3	2	3	3	6	5
Manchester City	3	1	3	5	6	6
Manchester Utd	3	5	3	6	6	11
Middlesbrough	1	0	2	0	3	0
Newcastle	4	8	5	9	9	17
Nottingham Forest	2	1	2	3	4	4
Q.P.R.	3	6	2	2	5	8
Sheffield Wednesday	4	5	3	9	7	14
Southampton	3	4	2	1	5	5
Tottenham	3	6	3	7	6	13
West Ham	0	0	0	0	0	0
Wimbledon	3	3	3	4	6	7

Miller, Alan – Middlesbrough

OPPONENTS	HOME APPS	HOME GC	AWAY APPS	AWAY GC	TOTAL APPS	TOTAL GC
Arsenal	0	0	0	0	0	0
Aston Villa	0	0	0	0	0	0
Blackburn Rovers	0	0	0	0	0	0
Bolton Wanderers	1	0	2	2	3	2
Chelsea	1	1	0	0	1	1
Coventry	0	0	0	0	0	0
Everton	0	0	0	0	0	0
Leeds Utd	0	0	2	3	2	3
Liverpool	0	0	0	0	0	0
Manchester City	0	0	0	0	0	0
Manchester Utd	0	0	0	0	0	0
Middlesbrough	0	0	0	0	0	0
Newcastle	0	0	0	0	0	0
Nottingham Forest	0	0	0	0	0	0
Q.P.R.	1	1	0	0	1	1
Sheffield Wednesday	1	1	0	0	1	1
Southampton	0	0	0	0	0	0
Tottenham	1	3	0	0	1	3
West Ham	0	0	0	0	0	0
Wimbledon	0	0	0	0	0	0

Mimms, Bobby – Blackburn

OPPONENTS	HOME APPS	HOME GC	AWAY APPS	AWAY GC	TOTAL APPS	TOTAL GC
Arsenal	4	5	4	2	8	7
Aston Villa	1	0	2	2	3	2
Blackburn Rovers	2	1	0	0	2	1
Bolton Wanderers	2	2	1	2	3	4
Chelsea	2	1	2	1	4	2
Coventry	2	6	3	1	5	7
Everton	2	4	2	3	4	7
Leeds Utd	2	0	5	11	7	11
Liverpool	1	1	4	4	5	5
Manchester City	1	0	3	4	4	4
Manchester Utd	4	4	3	3	7	7
Middlesbrough	4	4	3	4	7	8
Newcastle	3	1	5	5	8	6
Nottingham Forest	4	5	3	1	7	6
Q.P.R.	4	2	3	5	7	7
Sheffield Wednesday	5	5	5	5	10	10
Southampton	3	3	2	1	5	4
Tottenham	3	2	3	6	6	8
West Ham	3	4	1	0	4	4
Wimbledon	3	3	4	6	7	9

Ogrizovic, Steve – Coventry City

OPPONENTS	HOME APPS	HOME GC	AWAY APPS	AWAY GC	TOTAL APPS	TOTAL GC
Arsenal	10	11	9	22	19	33
Aston Villa	8	10	8	12	16	22
Blackburn Rovers	5	4	5	10	10	14
Bolton Wanderers	1	0	1	1	2	1
Chelsea	12	16	10	17	22	33
Coventry	0	0	0	0	0	0
Everton	10	12	10	17	20	29
Leeds Utd	7	7	5	9	12	16
Liverpool	9	17	9	20	18	37
Manchester City	9	12	8	11	17	23
Manchester Utd	9	14	10	15	19	29
Middlesbrough	4	7	4	7	8	14
Newcastle	8	11	9	18	17	28
Nottingham Forest	10	15	10	21	20	36
Q.P.R.	12	12	11	19	23	31
Sheffield Wednesday	11	7	12	15	23	22
Southampton	9	12	9	17	18	29
Tottenham	11	15	8	14	19	29
West Ham	7	7	8	10	15	17
Wimbledon	9	11	7	9	16	20

Pressman, Kevin – Sheffield Wednesday

OPPONENTS	HOME APPS	HOME GC	AWAY APPS	AWAY GC	TOTAL APPS	TOTAL GC
Arsenal	4	5	2	1	6	6
Aston Villa	4	4	1	1	5	5
Blackburn Rovers	2	3	2	3	4	6
Bolton Wanderers	0	0	0	0	0	0
Chelsea	3	2	1	1	4	3
Coventry	4	3	1	1	5	4
Everton	2	1	2	1	4	2
Leeds Utd	2	4	1	2	3	6
Liverpool	4	8	2	6	6	14
Manchester City	3	2	2	4	5	6
Manchester Utd	2	5	1	0	3	5
Middlesbrough	0	0	0	0	0	0
Newcastle	4	5	1	2	5	7
Nottingham Forest	1	7	3	5	4	12
Q.P.R.	3	3	5	10	8	13
Sheffield Wednesday	0	0	0	0	0	0
Southampton	2	3	3	4	5	7
Tottenham	2	4	2	4	4	8
West Ham	4	2	2	0	6	2
Wimbledon	2	3	3	3	5	6

Roberts, Tony – Q.P.R.

OPPONENTS	HOME APPS	HOME GC	AWAY APPS	AWAY GC	TOTAL APPS	TOTAL GC
Arsenal	4	5	3	4	7	9
Aston Villa	1	1	4	10	5	11
Blackburn Rovers	2	4	1	1	3	5
Bolton Wanderers	0	0	0	0	0	0
Chelsea	5	4	2	3	7	7
Coventry	3	4	2	3	5	7
Everton	3	6	2	5	5	11
Leeds Utd	0	0	2	5	2	5
Liverpool	2	4	2	2	4	6
Manchester City	2	3	3	7	5	10
Manchester Utd	1	3	2	5	3	8
Middlesbrough	0	0	1	0	1	0
Newcastle	2	2	0	0	2	2
Nottingham Forest	2	4	3	5	5	9
Q.P.R.	0	0	0	0	0	0
Sheffield Wednesday	2	3	3	6	5	9
Southampton	2	2	1	2	3	4
Tottenham	2	1	4	7	6	8
West Ham	1	0	2	0	3	0
Wimbledon	3	4	3	4	6	8

Schmeichel, Peter – Manchester Utd

OPPONENTS	HOME APPS	HOME GC	AWAY APPS	AWAY GC	TOTAL APPS	TOTAL GC
Arsenal	4	1	3	3	7	4
Aston Villa	4	2	3	2	7	4
Blackburn Rovers	3	2	3	4	6	6
Bolton Wanderers	0	0	0	0	0	0
Chelsea	3	1	3	3	6	4
Coventry	2	0	4	2	6	2
Everton	4	3	4	1	8	4
Leeds Utd	4	1	4	3	8	4
Liverpool	4	2	4	8	8	10
Manchester City	4	2	4	3	8	5
Manchester Utd	0	0	0	0	0	0
Middlesbrough	1	0	1	1	2	1
Newcastle	2	1	2	2	4	3
Nottingham Forest	2	2	3	2	5	4
Q.P.R.	4	5	3	3	7	8
Sheffield Wednesday	4	2	4	9	8	11
Southampton	3	1	3	1	6	2
Tottenham	4	3	4	2	8	5
West Ham	3	1	3	4	6	5
Wimbledon	4	2	4	3	8	5

Sealey, Les – West Ham

OPPONENTS	HOME APPS	HOME GC	AWAY APPS	AWAY GC	TOTAL APPS	TOTAL GC
Arsenal	10	10	12	24	22	34
Aston Villa	11	9	8	13	19	22
Blackburn Rovers	0	0	0	0	0	0
Bolton Wanderers	2	3	1	0	3	3
Chelsea	4	5	5	10	9	15
Coventry	6	6	7	12	13	18
Everton	12	12	11	15	23	27
Leeds Utd	5	6	2	3	7	9
Liverpool	9	4	9	28	18	32
Manchester City	7	6	9	19	16	25
Manchester Utd	10	18	9	11	19	29
Middlesbrough	4	1	4	3	8	4
Newcastle	5	3	3	7	8	10
Nottingham Forest	10	18	8	14	18	32
Q.P.R.	7	1	10	14	17	15
Sheffield Wednesday	6	4	5	6	11	10
Southampton	9	8	11	23	20	31
Tottenham	10	14	8	13	18	27
West Ham	8	10	7	11	15	21
Wimbledon	4	3	5	9	9	12

Seaman, David – Arsenal

OPPONENTS	HOME APPS	HOME GC	AWAY APPS	AWAY GC	TOTAL APPS	TOTAL GC
Arsenal	5	5	3	5	8	10
Aston Villa	8	4	9	8	17	12
Blackburn Rovers	4	3	3	4	7	7
Bolton Wanderers	0	0	0	0	0	0
Chelsea	8	9	8	12	16	21
Coventry	9	11	10	10	19	21
Everton	10	6	9	15	19	21
Leeds Utd	5	2	6	10	11	12
Liverpool	10	11	10	20	20	31
Manchester City	8	3	9	7	17	10
Manchester Utd	10	13	9	6	19	19
Middlesbrough	3	3	3	2	6	5
Newcastle	6	7	4	6	10	13
Nottingham Forest	8	8	8	13	16	21
Q.P.R.	4	1	6	8	10	9
Sheffield Wednesday	8	7	6	13	14	20
Southampton	10	13	11	11	21	24
Tottenham	9	5	10	12	19	17
West Ham	3	4	7	3	10	7
Wimbledon	10	15	11	11	21	26

Segers, Hans – Wimbledon

OPPONENTS	HOME APPS	HOME GC	AWAY APPS	AWAY GC	TOTAL APPS	TOTAL GC
Arsenal	7	15	7	7	14	22
Aston Villa	10	14	7	10	17	24
Blackburn Rovers	3	5	3	5	6	10
Bolton Wanderers	0	0	0	0	0	0
Chelsea	6	5	8	15	14	20
Coventry	7	5	9	8	16	13
Everton	9	8	7	13	16	21
Leeds Utd	5	1	5	17	10	18
Liverpool	7	8	9	15	16	23
Manchester City	5	3	6	5	11	8
Manchester Utd	10	19	8	11	18	30
Middlesbrough	2	1	1	2	3	3
Newcastle	4	4	5	11	9	15
Nottingham Forest	6	7	6	10	12	17
Q.P.R.	9	7	7	11	16	18
Sheffield Wednesday	8	8	4	6	12	14
Southampton	9	11	6	7	15	18
Tottenham	8	13	9	16	17	23
West Ham	4	4	4	6	8	10
Wimbledon	1	2	0	0	1	2

Shilton, Peter – Bolton Wanderers

OPPONENTS	HOME APPS	HOME GC	AWAY APPS	AWAY GC	TOTAL APPS	TOTAL GC
Arsenal	20	20	19	27	39	47
Aston Villa	16	11	15	21	31	32
Blackburn Rovers	4	7	3	7	7	14
Bolton Wanderers	5	6	5	6	10	12
Chelsea	14	17	10	16	24	33
Coventry	21	15	21	24	42	39
Everton	20	22	17	31	37	53
Leeds Utd	12	10	13	22	25	32
Liverpool	22	28	20	41	42	69
Manchester City	18	12	16	20	34	32
Manchester Utd	20	18	19	27	39	45
Middlesbrough	11	9	13	14	24	23
Newcastle	14	7	14	12	28	19
Nottingham Forest	11	16	12	14	23	30
Q.P.R.	17	6	16	18	33	24
Sheffield Wednesday	7	9	9	14	16	23
Southampton	15	10	14	15	29	25
Tottenham	19	17	19	33	38	50
West Ham	14	17	17	30	31	47
Wimbledon	5	6	5	12	10	18

Southall, Neville – Everton

OPPONENTS	HOME APPS	HOME GC	AWAY APPS	AWAY GC	TOTAL APPS	TOTAL GC
Arsenal	12	11	11	17	23	28
Aston Villa	13	11	10	12	23	29
Blackburn Rovers	3	6	3	7	6	13
Bolton Wanderers	0	0	0	0	0	0
Chelsea	9	17	10	14	19	31
Coventry	13	11	12	18	25	29
Everton	0	0	0	0	0	0
Leeds Utd	6	5	5	9	11	14
Liverpool	14	20	12	20	26	40
Manchester City	9	7	8	10	17	17
Manchester Utd	12	12	13	11	25	23
Middlesbrough	3	3	2	4	5	7
Newcastle	6	2	6	9	12	11
Nottingham Forest	11	5	10	13	21	18
Q.P.R.	11	15	11	16	22	31
Sheffield Wednesday	9	10	9	13	18	23
Southampton	12	6	12	18	24	24
Tottenham	13	13	10	20	23	33
West Ham	8	3	9	5	17	8
Wimbledon	10	8	8	13	18	21

Spink, Nigel – Aston Villa

OPPONENTS	HOME APPS	HOME GC	AWAY APPS	AWAY GC	TOTAL APPS	TOTAL GC
Arsenal	11	22	7	11	18	33
Aston Villa	0	0	0	0	0	0
Blackburn Rovers	2	1	1	3	3	4
Bolton Wanderers	0	0	0	0	0	0
Chelsea	6	6	6	12	12	18
Coventry	8	4	9	16	17	20
Everton	8	6	6	10	14	16
Leeds Utd	4	3	5	7	9	10
Liverpool	9	11	9	15	18	26
Manchester City	6	10	6	8	12	18
Manchester Utd	9	18	7	15	16	33
Middlesbrough	3	3	3	7	6	10
Newcastle	6	7	3	8	9	15
Nottingham Forest	8	9	9	18	17	27
Q.P.R.	9	12	3	4	12	16
Sheffield Wednesday	3	1	7	9	10	10
Southampton	7	7	11	23	18	30
Tottenham	7	5	7	11	14	16
West Ham	2	1	6	13	8	14
Wimbledon	4	6	5	5	9	11

Srnicek, Pavel – Newcastle

OPPONENTS	HOME APPS	HOME GC	AWAY APPS	AWAY GC	TOTAL APPS	TOTAL GC
Arsenal	2	0	1	2	3	2
Aston Villa	2	2	1	0	3	2
Blackburn Rovers	2	2	2	2	4	4
Bolton Wanderers	0	0	0	0	0	0
Chelsea	1	0	1	1	2	1
Coventry	2	0	2	2	4	2
Everton	1	0	0	0	1	0
Leeds Utd	1	2	2	1	3	3
Liverpool	1	1	2	2	3	3
Manchester City	1	0	2	2	3	2
Manchester Utd	1	1	2	3	3	4
Middlesbrough	0	0	1	3	1	3
Newcastle	0	0	0	0	0	0
Nottingham Forest	1	1	1	0	2	1
Q.P.R.	1	1	0	0	1	1
Sheffield Wednesday	2	1	2	0	4	1
Southampton	1	1	1	3	2	4
Tottenham	2	4	1	4	3	8
West Ham	1	0	4	4	5	4
Wimbledon	1	1	1	3	2	4

Sullivan, Neil – Wimbledon

OPPONENTS	HOME APPS	HOME GC	AWAY APPS	AWAY GC	TOTAL APPS	TOTAL GC
Arsenal	0	0	1	0	1	0
Aston Villa	0	0	1	1	1	1
Blackburn Rovers	0	0	0	0	0	0
Bolton Wanderers	0	0	0	0	0	0
Chelsea	1	1	0	0	1	1
Coventry	0	0	0	0	0	0
Everton	0	0	1	0	1	0
Leeds Utd	0	0	0	0	0	0
Liverpool	1	0	0	0	1	0
Manchester City	1	0	0	0	1	0
Manchester Utd	0	0	0	0	0	0
Middlesbrough	0	0	0	0	0	0
Newcastle	0	0	0	0	0	0
Nottingham Forest	1	2	0	0	1	2
Q.P.R.	0	0	1	1	1	1
Sheffield Wednesday	0	0	1	0	1	0
Southampton	2	3	1	2	3	5
Tottenham	0	0	0	0	0	0
West Ham	0	0	1	3	1	3
Wimbledon	0	0	0	0	0	0

Thorstvedt, Erik – Tottenham

OPPONENTS	HOME APPS	HOME GC	AWAY APPS	AWAY GC	TOTAL APPS	TOTAL GC
Arsenal	5	3	4	4	9	7
Aston Villa	4	3	4	6	8	9
Blackburn Rovers	0	0	2	1	2	1
Bolton Wanderers	0	0	0	0	0	0
Chelsea	5	11	4	7	9	18
Coventry	4	5	5	5	9	10
Everton	4	7	4	7	8	14
Leeds Utd	4	4	4	8	8	12
Liverpool	6	10	4	6	10	16
Manchester City	5	4	4	3	9	7
Manchester Utd	2	3	4	8	6	11
Middlesbrough	0	0	1	2	1	2
Newcastle	1	2	1	0	2	2
Nottingham Forest	4	6	4	4	8	10
Q.P.R.	4	6	4	5	8	11
Sheffield Wednesday	4	4	3	3	7	7
Southampton	4	3	5	7	9	10
Tottenham	0	0	0	0	0	0
West Ham	2	1	2	3	4	4
Wimbledon	3	4	5	9	8	13

Walker, Ian – Tottenham

OPPONENTS	HOME APPS	HOME GC	AWAY APPS	AWAY GC	TOTAL APPS	TOTAL GC
Arsenal	1	0	2	2	3	2
Aston Villa	3	10	2	1	5	11
Blackburn Rovers	3	5	1	2	4	7
Bolton Wanderers	0	0	0	0	0	0
Chelsea	1	0	2	5	3	5
Coventry	2	5	2	1	4	6
Everton	3	5	2	0	5	5
Leeds Utd	1	1	1	1	2	2
Liverpool	1	0	2	7	3	7
Manchester City	1	1	2	6	3	7
Manchester Utd	4	5	2	3	6	8
Middlesbrough	1	2	1	3	2	5
Newcastle	1	2	1	3	2	5
Nottingham Forest	1	4	2	3	3	7
Q.P.R.	2	1	3	7	5	8
Sheffield Wednesday	2	4	2	5	4	9
Southampton	2	4	2	4	4	8
Tottenham	0	0	0	0	0	0
West Ham	2	4	2	3	4	7
Wimbledon	3	5	3	5	6	10

Walsh, Gary – Manchester Utd

OPPONENTS	HOME APPS	HOME GC	AWAY APPS	AWAY GC	TOTAL APPS	TOTAL GC
Arsenal	1	0	2	3	3	3
Aston Villa	1	1	2	4	3	5
Blackburn Rovers	1	2	0	0	1	2
Bolton Wanderers	0	0	0	0	0	0
Chelsea	2	2	1	2	3	4
Coventry	2	0	3	1	5	1
Everton	0	0	1	2	1	2
Leeds Utd	0	0	0	0	0	0
Liverpool	2	1	1	0	3	1
Manchester City	1	0	0	0	1	0
Manchester Utd	0	0	0	0	0	0
Middlesbrough	0	0	0	0	0	0
Newcastle	1	2	1	2	2	4
Nottingham Forest	3	4	0	0	3	4
Q.P.R.	0	0	2	3	2	3
Sheffield Wednesday	0	0	2	5	2	5
Southampton	1	0	0	0	1	0
Tottenham	1	0	1	4	2	4
West Ham	0	0	3	3	3	3
Wimbledon	2	2	1	2	3	4

Woods, Chris – Sheffield Wednesday

OPPONENTS	HOME APPS	GC	AWAY APPS	GC	TOTAL APPS	GC
Arsenal	5	5	4	13	9	18
Aston Villa	4	8	5	8	9	16
Blackburn Rovers	3	0	6	11	9	11
Bolton Wanderers	2	1	2	1	4	2
Chelsea	3	6	6	4	9	10
Coventry	4	5	6	7	10	12
Everton	5	6	5	3	10	9
Leeds Utd	3	7	4	4	7	11
Liverpool	5	5	5	9	10	14
Manchester City	4	6	3	4	7	10
Manchester Utd	5	11	7	12	12	23
Middlesbrough	3	3	2	2	5	5
Newcastle	5	4	3	7	8	11
Nottingham Forest	4	6	5	8	9	14
Q.P.R.	4	5	4	7	8	12
Sheffield Wednesday	3	4	4	2	7	6
Southampton	4	3	6	9	10	12
Tottenham	4	3	6	7	10	10
West Ham	4	2	6	6	10	8
Wimbledon	3	3	3	5	6	8

Wright, Tommy – Nottingham Forest

OPPONENTS	HOME APPS	GC	AWAY APPS	GC	TOTAL APPS	GC
Arsenal	0	0	0	0	0	0
Aston Villa	0	0	1	3	1	3
Blackburn Rovers	1	0	2	5	3	5
Bolton Wanderers	0	0	1	4	1	4
Chelsea	0	0	0	0	0	0
Coventry	0	0	2	2	2	2
Everton	0	0	0	0	0	0
Leeds Utd	1	2	0	0	1	2
Liverpool	1	2	0	0	1	2
Manchester City	0	0	0	0	0	0
Manchester Utd	0	0	1	2	1	2
Middlesbrough	2	1	1	1	3	2
Newcastle	0	0	0	0	0	0
Nottingham Forest	0	0	0	0	0	0
Q.P.R.	1	2	0	0	1	2
Sheffield Wednesday	1	2	0	0	1	2
Southampton	0	0	0	0	0	0
Tottenham	0	0	0	0	0	0
West Ham	2	2	0	0	2	2
Wimbledon	0	0	0	0	0	0

Allen, Bradley – Q.P.R.

OPPONENTS	HOME APPS	HOME GOALS	AWAY APPS	AWAY GOALS	TOTAL APPS	TOTAL GOALS
Arsenal	1	0	3	1	4	1
Aston Villa	3	2	3	0	6	2
Blackburn Rovers	2	0	0	0	2	0
Bolton Wanderers	0	0	0	0	0	0
Chelsea	1	1	1	1	2	2
Coventry	2	2	0	0	2	2
Everton	1	0	2	3	3	3
Leeds Utd	3	1	1	0	4	1
Liverpool	1	0	2	0	3	0
Manchester City	2	0	1	0	3	0
Manchester Utd	2	1	1	1	3	2
Middlesbrough	0	0	1	0	1	0
Newcastle	0	0	1	1	1	1
Nottingham Forest	1	0	3	2	4	2
Q.P.R.	0	0	0	0	0	0
Sheffield Wednesday	1	2	2	0	3	2
Southampton	0	0	3	0	3	0
Tottenham	2	0	2	0	4	0
West Ham	1	0	2	2	3	2
Wimbledon	1	0	2	1	3	1

Allen, Malcolm – Newcastle

OPPONENTS	HOME APPS	HOME GOALS	AWAY APPS	AWAY GOALS	TOTAL APPS	TOTAL GOALS
Arsenal	3	1	3	3	6	4
Aston Villa	2	0	3	0	5	0
Blackburn Rovers	0	0	2	0	2	0
Bolton Wanderers	0	0	0	0	0	0
Chelsea	0	0	1	0	1	0
Coventry	1	0	1	0	2	0
Everton	3	1	1	1	4	2
Leeds Utd	0	0	0	0	0	0
Liverpool	3	0	2	0	5	0
Manchester City	0	0	1	0	1	0
Manchester Utd	2	1	0	0	2	1
Middlesbrough	2	0	2	0	4	0
Newcastle	3	0	4	2	7	2
Nottingham Forest	3	0	3	0	6	0
Q.P.R.	1	1	2	0	3	1
Sheffield Wednesday	4	1	0	0	4	1
Southampton	1	0	3	1	4	1
Tottenham	2	0	2	0	4	0
West Ham	4	1	5	1	9	2
Wimbledon	1	0	3	2	4	2

Armstrong, Chris – Tottenham

OPPONENTS	HOME APPS	HOME GOALS	AWAY APPS	AWAY GOALS	TOTAL APPS	TOTAL GOALS
Arsenal	2	0	2	0	4	0
Aston Villa	2	0	2	0	4	1
Blackburn Rovers	1	0	3	2	4	2
Bolton Wanderers	1	0	1	0	2	0
Chelsea	2	1	1	0	3	1
Coventry	1	0	2	3	3	0
Everton	2	0	2	2	4	2
Leeds Utd	2	0	2	1	4	1
Liverpool	2	2	2	0	4	2
Manchester City	2	1	2	0	4	0
Manchester Utd	3	0	2	0	5	0
Middlesbrough	2	1	3	1	5	2
Newcastle	2	0	1	1	3	1
Nottingham Forest	3	1	3	0	6	1
Q.P.R.	1	0	2	1	3	1
Sheffield Wednesday	1	1	2	1	3	2
Southampton	2	0	2	0	4	0
Tottenham	2	1	1	0	3	1
West Ham	1	1	1	0	2	1
Wimbledon	2	0	1	0	3	0

Atkinson, Dalian – Aston Villa

OPPONENTS	HOME APPS	HOME GOALS	AWAY APPS	AWAY GOALS	TOTAL APPS	TOTAL GOALS
Arsenal	3	0	3	0	6	0
Aston Villa	1	1	1	0	2	1
Blackburn Rovers	2	0	4	0	6	0
Bolton Wanderers	0	0	0	0	0	0
Chelsea	3	2	4	0	7	2
Coventry	3	0	1	1	4	1
Everton	1	1	4	0	5	1
Leeds Utd	4	1	4	0	8	1
Liverpool	2	2	4	2	6	4
Manchester City	3	0	4	0	7	0
Manchester Utd	4	3	2	0	6	3
Middlesbrough	1	3	1	1	2	4
Newcastle	1	0	2	0	3	0
Nottingham Forest	1	0	2	0	3	0
Q.P.R.	3	4	4	0	7	4
Sheffield Wednesday	2	1	1	0	3	1
Southampton	3	1	2	1	5	2
Tottenham	2	1	4	1	6	2
West Ham	1	2	2	0	3	2
Wimbledon	2	0	4	1	6	1

Bailey, Dennis – Q.P.R.

OPPONENTS	HOME APPS	HOME GOALS	AWAY APPS	AWAY GOALS	TOTAL APPS	TOTAL GOALS
Arsenal	1	0	1	1	2	1
Aston Villa	1	0	0	0	1	0
Blackburn Rovers	0	0	0	0	0	0
Bolton Wanderers	1	1	1	0	2	1
Chelsea	0	0	0	0	0	0
Coventry	1	0	1	0	2	0
Everton	1	1	1	0	2	1
Leeds Utd	0	0	0	0	0	0
Liverpool	1	0	1	0	2	0
Manchester City	0	0	1	2	1	2
Manchester Utd	0	0	1	3	1	3
Middlesbrough	1	1	0	0	1	1
Newcastle	0	0	1	0	1	0
Nottingham Forest	1	0	0	0	1	0
Q.P.R.	0	0	0	0	0	0
Sheffield Wednesday	1	0	1	1	2	1
Southampton	1	0	0	0	1	0
Tottenham	0	0	0	0	0	0
West Ham	1	0	0	0	1	0
Wimbledon	1	0	1	1	2	1

Barmby, Nick – Tottenham

OPPONENTS	HOME APPS	HOME GOALS	AWAY APPS	AWAY GOALS	TOTAL APPS	TOTAL GOALS
Arsenal	1	0	1	0	2	0
Aston Villa	3	0	1	0	4	0
Blackburn Rovers	2	1	2	0	4	1
Bolton Wanderers	0	0	1	0	1	0
Chelsea	2	0	1	0	3	0
Coventry	2	0	2	1	4	1
Everton	1	0	2	0	3	0
Leeds Utd	2	0	1	0	3	0
Liverpool	3	0	1	0	4	0
Manchester City	1	0	2	0	3	0
Manchester Utd	2	0	3	1	5	1
Middlesbrough	1	1	1	0	2	1
Newcastle	2	0	2	1	4	1
Nottingham Forest	1	1	2	1	3	2
Q.P.R.	3	1	3	0	6	1
Sheffield Wednesday	3	1	3	1	6	2
Southampton	3	1	2	0	5	1
Tottenham	0	0	0	0	0	0
West Ham	2	1	2	0	4	1
Wimbledon	2	1	2	1	4	2

Barnes, John – Liverpool

OPPONENTS	HOME APPS	HOME GOALS	AWAY APPS	AWAY GOALS	TOTAL APPS	TOTAL GOALS
Arsenal	10	2	13	6	23	8
Aston Villa	11	4	10	1	21	5
Blackburn Rovers	3	1	4	1	7	2
Bolton Wanderers	1	0	1	0	2	0
Chelsea	9	1	8	2	17	3
Coventry	11	1	9	6	20	7
Everton	12	4	10	2	22	6
Leeds Utd	4	2	3	2	7	4
Liverpool	5	1	5	1	10	2
Manchester City	8	3	6	1	14	4
Manchester Utd	11	1	11	3	22	4
Middlesbrough	1	0	2	0	3	0
Newcastle	7	2	7	0	14	2
Nottingham Forest	11	2	10	0	21	2
Q.P.R.	10	4	10	7	20	11
Sheffield Wednesday	6	4	10	2	16	6
Southampton	10	1	11	3	21	4
Tottenham	9	3	10	2	19	5
West Ham	9	2	8	2	17	4
Wimbledon	5	3	8	2	13	5

Beardsley, Peter – Newcastle

OPPONENTS	HOME APPS	HOME GOALS	AWAY APPS	AWAY GOALS	TOTAL APPS	TOTAL GOALS
Arsenal	11	4	9	2	20	6
Aston Villa	10	8	8	2	18	10
Blackburn Rovers	4	0	4	0	8	0
Bolton Wanderers	0	0	0	0	0	0
Chelsea	8	1	11	3	19	4
Coventry	9	6	8	3	17	9
Everton	8	5	7	3	15	8
Leeds Utd	5	0	3	0	8	0
Liverpool	7	1	7	1	14	2
Manchester City	8	4	9	4	17	8
Manchester Utd	10	5	9	1	19	6
Middlesbrough	3	3	2	1	5	4
Newcastle	2	0	2	0	4	0
Nottingham Forest	9	3	8	2	17	5
Q.P.R.	9	2	10	1	19	3
Sheffield Wednesday	10	4	12	4	22	8
Southampton	9	2	11	4	20	6
Tottenham	10	5	10	8	20	13
West Ham	7	2	6	1	13	3
Wimbledon	7	3	8	5	15	8

Blissett, Gary – Wimbledon

OPPONENTS	HOME APPS	HOME GOALS	AWAY APPS	AWAY GOALS	TOTAL APPS	TOTAL GOALS
Arsenal	0	0	0	0	0	0
Aston Villa	0	0	0	0	0	0
Blackburn Rovers	0	0	1	0	1	0
Bolton Wanderers	0	0	0	0	0	0
Chelsea	0	0	1	0	1	0
Coventry	0	0	2	0	2	0
Everton	0	0	0	0	0	0
Leeds Utd	1	0	2	0	3	0
Liverpool	1	0	1	0	2	0
Manchester City	0	0	1	0	1	0
Manchester Utd	0	0	0	0	0	0
Middlesbrough	0	0	0	0	0	0
Newcastle	2	2	2	0	4	2
Nottingham Forest	0	0	0	0	0	0
Q.P.R.	1	0	2	0	3	0
Sheffield Wednesday	2	0	1	1	3	1
Southampton	0	0	1	0	1	0
Tottenham	1	0	0	0	1	0
West Ham	1	0	1	0	2	0
Wimbledon	0	0	0	0	0	0

Bright, Mark – Sheffield Wednesday

OPPONENTS	HOME APPS	HOME GOALS	AWAY APPS	AWAY GOALS	TOTAL APPS	TOTAL GOALS
Arsenal	7	3	7	0	14	3
Aston Villa	8	3	7	0	15	3
Blackburn Rovers	7	3	5	1	12	4
Bolton Wanderers	0	0	1	0	1	0
Chelsea	6	1	7	1	13	2
Coventry	4	3	6	1	10	4
Everton	6	5	5	3	11	8
Leeds Utd	7	4	6	0	13	4
Liverpool	7	2	6	0	13	2
Manchester City	7	1	9	3	16	4
Manchester Utd	6	1	7	3	13	4
Middlesbrough	2	2	2	1	4	3
Newcastle	3	0	2	0	5	0
Nottingham Forest	5	1	3	0	8	1
Q.P.R.	7	4	6	2	13	6
Sheffield Wednesday	5	2	3	1	8	3
Southampton	7	1	6	1	13	2
Tottenham	7	4	7	4	14	8
West Ham	5	1	5	2	10	3
Wimbledon	7	4	5	1	12	5

Bull, Gary – Nottingham Forest

OPPONENTS	HOME APPS	HOME GOALS	AWAY APPS	AWAY GOALS	TOTAL APPS	TOTAL GOALS
Arsenal	0	0	0	0	0	0
Aston Villa	0	0	0	0	0	0
Blackburn Rovers	0	0	0	0	0	0
Bolton Wanderers	2	1	0	0	2	1
Chelsea	0	0	0	0	0	0
Coventry	0	0	0	0	0	0
Everton	0	0	0	0	0	0
Leeds Utd	0	0	0	0	0	0
Liverpool	0	0	0	0	0	0
Manchester City	0	0	0	0	0	0
Manchester Utd	0	0	0	0	0	0
Middlesbrough	0	0	1	0	1	0
Newcastle	0	0	0	0	0	0
Nottingham Forest	0	0	0	0	0	0
Q.P.R.	0	0	0	0	0	0
Sheffield Wednesday	0	0	0	0	0	0
Southampton	0	0	0	0	0	0
Tottenham	0	0	0	0	0	0
West Ham	0	0	0	0	0	0
Wimbledon	0	0	0	0	0	0

Campbell, Kevin – Nottingham Forest

OPPONENTS	HOME APPS	HOME GOALS	AWAY APPS	AWAY GOALS	TOTAL APPS	TOTAL GOALS
Arsenal	0	0	0	0	0	0
Aston Villa	6	2	2	0	8	2
Blackburn Rovers	3	0	3	2	6	2
Bolton Wanderers	0	0	0	0	0	0
Chelsea	6	2	3	0	9	2
Coventry	5	1	5	2	10	3
Everton	5	0	4	0	9	0
Leeds Utd	6	2	4	1	10	3
Liverpool	4	0	4	0	8	0
Manchester City	5	2	4	0	9	2
Manchester Utd	3	0	3	0	6	0
Middlesbrough	1	0	1	0	2	0
Newcastle	1	0	1	1	2	1
Nottingham Forest	4	2	3	0	7	2
Q.P.R.	5	0	3	1	8	1
Sheffield Wednesday	4	2	3	0	7	2
Southampton	4	1	5	1	9	2
Tottenham	2	1	4	0	6	1
West Ham	2	0	2	0	4	0
Wimbledon	3	0	4	0	7	3

Cantona, Eric – Manchester Utd

OPPONENTS	HOME APPS	HOME GOALS	AWAY APPS	AWAY GOALS	TOTAL APPS	TOTAL GOALS
Arsenal	2	1	3	0	5	1
Aston Villa	4	2	2	0	6	2
Blackburn Rovers	3	1	1	1	4	2
Bolton Wanderers	0	0	0	0	0	0
Chelsea	3	2	3	2	5	4
Coventry	5	2	2	1	7	3
Everton	4	0	1	0	5	0
Leeds Utd	1	0	3	1	4	1
Liverpool	3	0	2	0	5	0
Manchester City	3	3	4	3	7	6
Manchester Utd	0	0	1	0	1	0
Middlesbrough	1	1	1	1	2	2
Newcastle	1	0	2	0	3	0
Nottingham Forest	1	1	0	0	1	1
Q.P.R.	1	1	2	1	3	2
Sheffield Wednesday	2	2	2	1	4	3
Southampton	2	0	2	1	4	1
Tottenham	3	4	2	0	5	4
West Ham	3	2	1	0	4	2
Wimbledon	4	2	1	0	5	2

Clough, Nigel – Liverpool

OPPONENTS	HOME APPS	HOME GOALS	AWAY APPS	AWAY GOALS	TOTAL APPS	TOTAL GOALS
Arsenal	9	2	9	2	18	4
Aston Villa	7	3	8	1	15	4
Blackburn Rovers	2	1	2	0	5	1
Bolton Wanderers	0	0	0	0	0	0
Chelsea	7	2	7	3	14	5
Coventry	8	2	9	1	17	3
Everton	8	2	7	1	15	3
Leeds Utd	4	3	3	1	7	4
Liverpool	8	2	8	0	16	2
Manchester City	7	0	7	2	14	2
Manchester Utd	9	3	9	1	18	4
Middlesbrough	2	0	2	1	4	1
Newcastle	3	1	6	1	9	2
Nottingham Forest	0	0	0	0	0	0
Q.P.R.	8	4	8	3	16	7
Sheffield Wednesday	7	3	7	2	14	5
Southampton	6	3	9	4	15	7
Tottenham	9	4	10	5	19	9
West Ham	5	1	7	5	12	6
Wimbledon	8	2	7	2	15	4

Cole, Andrew – Manchester Utd

OPPONENTS	HOME APPS	HOME GOALS	AWAY APPS	AWAY GOALS	TOTAL APPS	TOTAL GOALS
Arsenal	2	1	2	0	4	1
Aston Villa	2	2	2	2	4	4
Blackburn Rovers	3	0	0	0	3	0
Bolton Wanderers	0	0	1	1	1	1
Chelsea	3	2	1	0	4	2
Coventry	2	4	3	2	5	6
Everton	1	0	2	1	3	1
Leeds Utd	2	1	2	1	4	2
Liverpool	2	3	2	1	4	4
Manchester City	2	2	2	1	4	3
Manchester Utd	1	1	1	1	2	2
Middlesbrough	1	1	0	0	1	1
Newcastle	1	0	0	0	1	0
Nottingham Forest	0	0	0	0	0	0
Q.P.R.	1	0	1	0	2	0
Sheffield Wednesday	3	3	1	1	4	4
Southampton	3	4	1	1	4	5
Tottenham	2	0	2	0	4	0
West Ham	2	2	3	1	5	3
Wimbledon	1	1	1	0	2	1

Collymore, Stan – Liverpool

OPPONENTS	HOME APPS	HOME GOALS	AWAY APPS	AWAY GOALS	TOTAL APPS	TOTAL GOALS
Arsenal	1	0	1	0	2	0
Aston Villa	3	1	1	0	4	1
Blackburn Rovers	0	0	1	0	1	0
Bolton Wanderers	1	1	1	2	2	3
Chelsea	1	0	1	2	2	2
Coventry	1	1	1	0	2	1
Everton	3	1	1	0	4	1
Leeds Utd	2	1	1	0	3	1
Liverpool	1	1	1	0	2	1
Manchester City	2	1	1	1	3	2
Manchester Utd	2	1	1	1	3	2
Middlesbrough	1	1	0	0	1	1
Newcastle	2	0	1	0	3	0
Nottingham Forest	0	0	0	0	0	0
Q.P.R.	3	2	1	0	4	2
Sheffield Wednesday	1	0	2	2	3	2
Southampton	3	1	2	1	5	2
Tottenham	2	0	1	0	3	0
West Ham	3	1	2	0	5	1
Wimbledon	1	1	2	0	3	1

Cottee, Tony – West Ham

OPPONENTS	HOME APPS	HOME GOALS	AWAY APPS	AWAY GOALS	TOTAL APPS	TOTAL GOALS
Arsenal	10	5	12	1	22	6
Aston Villa	10	5	10	1	20	6
Blackburn Rovers	2	1	3	3	5	4
Bolton Wanderers	0	0	0	0	0	0
Chelsea	7	6	8	3	15	9
Coventry	11	3	11	9	22	12
Everton	6	2	6	1	12	3
Leeds Utd	3	3	5	0	8	3
Liverpool	7	3	12	0	19	3
Manchester City	6	4	7	1	13	5
Manchester Utd	9	2	11	0	20	2
Middlesbrough	1	1	2	1	3	2
Newcastle	6	3	7	1	13	4
Nottingham Forest	11	8	9	2	20	10
Q.P.R.	9	5	11	8	20	13
Sheffield Wednesday	7	1	10	4	17	5
Southampton	11	8	10	2	21	10
Tottenham	12	8	11	4	23	12
West Ham	3	1	3	1	6	2
Wimbledon	7	4	8	4	15	8

Coyle, Owen – Bolton

OPPONENTS	HOME APPS	HOME GOALS	AWAY APPS	AWAY GOALS	TOTAL APPS	TOTAL GOALS
Arsenal	0	0	0	0	0	0
Aston Villa	0	0	0	0	0	0
Blackburn Rovers	0	0	0	0	0	0
Bolton Wanderers	0	0	0	0	0	0
Chelsea	0	0	0	0	0	0
Coventry	0	0	0	0	0	0
Everton	0	0	0	0	0	0
Leeds Utd	0	0	0	0	0	0
Liverpool	0	0	0	0	0	0
Manchester City	0	0	0	0	0	0
Manchester Utd	0	0	0	0	0	0
Middlesbrough	1	0	1	0	2	0
Newcastle	0	0	0	0	0	0
Nottingham Forest	1	0	1	0	2	0
Q.P.R.	0	0	0	0	0	0
Sheffield Wednesday	0	0	0	0	0	0
Southampton	0	0	0	0	0	0
Tottenham	0	0	0	0	0	0
West Ham	0	0	0	0	0	0
Wimbledon	0	0	0	0	0	0

Deane, Brian – Leeds

OPPONENTS	HOME APPS	HOME GOALS	AWAY APPS	AWAY GOALS	TOTAL APPS	TOTAL GOALS
Arsenal	4	0	5	1	9	1
Aston Villa	5	2	5	1	10	3
Blackburn Rovers	4	2	4	0	8	2
Bolton Wanderers	1	0	2	0	3	0
Chelsea	3	1	4	2	7	3
Coventry	5	0	3	1	8	1
Everton	2	0	5	0	7	0
Leeds Utd	4	1	3	0	7	1
Liverpool	4	3	5	3	9	6
Manchester City	5	4	4	1	9	5
Manchester Utd	5	5	4	0	9	5
Middlesbrough	3	1	2	0	5	1
Newcastle	2	1	3	0	5	1
Nottingham Forest	3	1	4	1	7	2
Q.P.R.	5	2	5	4	10	6
Sheffield Wednesday	4	1	4	1	8	2
Southampton	4	1	5	1	9	2
Tottenham	5	5	5	2	10	7
West Ham	4	1	4	1	8	2
Wimbledon	4	0	5	1	9	1

Dickov, Paul – Arsenal

OPPONENTS	HOME APPS	HOME GOALS	AWAY APPS	AWAY GOALS	TOTAL APPS	TOTAL GOALS
Arsenal	0	0	0	0	0	0
Aston Villa	1	0	0	0	1	0
Blackburn Rovers	1	0	0	0	1	0
Bolton Wanderers	0	0	0	0	0	0
Chelsea	0	0	1	0	1	0
Coventry	0	0	0	0	0	0
Everton	0	0	0	0	0	0
Leeds Utd	0	0	0	0	0	0
Liverpool	0	0	0	0	0	0
Manchester City	1	0	0	0	1	0
Manchester Utd	1	0	0	0	1	0
Middlesbrough	0	0	0	0	0	0
Newcastle	0	0	0	0	0	0
Nottingham Forest	0	0	0	0	0	0
Q.P.R.	0	0	0	0	0	0
Sheffield Wednesday	1	0	0	0	1	0
Southampton	1	0	1	0	2	0
Tottenham	1	1	0	0	1	1
West Ham	1	0	0	0	1	0
Wimbledon	0	0	0	0	0	0

Dublin, Dion – Coventry

OPPONENTS	HOME APPS	HOME GOALS	AWAY APPS	AWAY GOALS	TOTAL APPS	TOTAL GOALS
Arsenal	1	0	1	0	2	0
Aston Villa	0	0	1	0	1	0
Blackburn Rovers	2	1	1	0	3	1
Bolton Wanderers	1	0	1	1	2	1
Chelsea	2	0	1	1	3	1
Coventry	1	0	0	0	1	0
Everton	2	0	1	1	3	1
Leeds Utd	1	1	0	0	1	1
Liverpool	0	0	1	0	1	0
Manchester City	1	1	1	0	2	1
Manchester Utd	1	0	1	0	2	0
Middlesbrough	1	0	1	1	2	1
Newcastle	1	0	1	0	2	0
Nottingham Forest	0	0	2	0	2	0
Q.P.R.	1	0	1	1	2	1
Sheffield Wednesday	1	1	0	0	1	1
Southampton	1	0	2	1	3	1
Tottenham	0	0	1	1	1	1
West Ham	1	0	2	0	3	0
Wimbledon	0	0	1	0	1	0

Ekoku, Efan – Wimbledon

OPPONENTS	HOME APPS	HOME GOALS	AWAY APPS	AWAY GOALS	TOTAL APPS	TOTAL GOALS
Arsenal	2	1	0	0	2	1
Aston Villa	2	0	1	0	3	0
Blackburn Rovers	3	0	1	1	4	1
Bolton Wanderers	0	0	2	1	2	1
Chelsea	1	1	2	1	3	2
Coventry	2	0	0	0	2	0
Everton	1	0	2	4	3	4
Leeds Utd	2	1	2	1	4	2
Liverpool	3	0	2	0	5	0
Manchester City	0	0	2	0	2	0
Manchester Utd	2	0	0	0	2	0
Middlesbrough	0	0	1	2	1	2
Newcastle	2	1	1	1	3	2
Nottingham Forest	1	0	1	0	2	0
Q.P.R.	1	2	1	0	2	2
Sheffield Wednesday	1	0	1	1	2	1
Southampton	1	0	2	0	3	0
Tottenham	0	0	3	4	3	4
West Ham	2	0	1	0	3	0
Wimbledon	1	0	1	1	2	1

Fashanu, John – Aston Villa

OPPONENTS	HOME APPS	HOME GOALS	AWAY APPS	AWAY GOALS	TOTAL APPS	TOTAL GOALS
Arsenal	7	2	9	1	16	3
Aston Villa	7	4	7	4	14	8
Blackburn Rovers	3	1	4	1	7	2
Bolton Wanderers	2	0	3	0	5	0
Chelsea	4	2	5	2	9	4
Coventry	7	1	7	2	14	3
Everton	8	4	7	2	15	6
Leeds Utd	6	0	3	0	9	0
Liverpool	7	1	7	3	14	4
Manchester City	4	2	6	1	10	3
Manchester Utd	7	3	5	1	12	4
Middlesbrough	2	0	1	0	3	0
Newcastle	2	1	3	1	5	2
Nottingham Forest	6	5	7	3	13	8
Q.P.R.	6	4	6	5	12	9
Sheffield Wednesday	5	4	5	1	10	5
Southampton	8	3	7	1	15	4
Tottenham	7	4	6	2	13	6
West Ham	4	1	6	3	10	4
Wimbledon	2	0	2	0	4	0

Ferdinand, Les – Newcastle

OPPONENTS	HOME APPS	HOME GOALS	AWAY APPS	AWAY GOALS	TOTAL APPS	TOTAL GOALS
Arsenal	2	0	4	0	6	0
Aston Villa	2	1	5	2	7	3
Blackburn Rovers	2	1	3	0	5	1
Bolton Wanderers	0	0	0	0	0	0
Chelsea	3	3	4	0	7	3
Coventry	5	2	4	1	9	3
Everton	3	2	4	5	7	7
Leeds Utd	4	4	5	1	9	5
Liverpool	3	1	6	3	9	4
Manchester City	5	3	3	2	8	5
Manchester Utd	5	3	3	0	8	3
Middlesbrough	1	1	1	1	2	2
Newcastle	2	2	2	1	4	3
Nottingham Forest	3	3	4	1	7	4
Q.P.R.	0	0	0	0	0	0
Sheffield Wednesday	3	3	6	1	9	4
Southampton	4	4	4	3	8	7
Tottenham	4	3	4	0	8	3
West Ham	3	1	3	2	6	3
Wimbledon	5	1	4	2	9	3

Ferguson, Duncan – Everton

OPPONENTS	HOME APPS	HOME GOALS	AWAY APPS	AWAY GOALS	TOTAL APPS	TOTAL GOALS
Arsenal	1	0	1	0	2	0
Aston Villa	0	0	1	0	1	0
Blackburn Rovers	0	0	0	0	0	0
Bolton Wanderers	0	0	0	0	0	0
Chelsea	0	0	1	0	1	0
Coventry	1	0	1	0	2	0
Everton	0	0	0	0	0	0
Leeds Utd	1	1	1	0	2	1
Liverpool	1	1	1	0	2	1
Manchester City	1	0	0	0	1	0
Manchester Utd	1	1	0	0	1	1
Middlesbrough	0	0	0	0	0	0
Newcastle	0	0	0	0	0	0
Nottingham Forest	0	0	1	0	1	0
Q.P.R.	0	0	0	0	0	0
Sheffield Wednesday	1	1	1	0	2	1
Southampton	0	0	0	0	0	0
Tottenham	0	0	0	0	0	0
West Ham	1	0	1	0	2	0
Wimbledon	0	0	1	0	1	0

Fjortoft, Jan – Middlesbrough

OPPONENTS	HOME APPS	HOME GOALS	AWAY APPS	AWAY GOALS	TOTAL APPS	TOTAL GOALS
Arsenal	1	0	1	0	2	0
Aston Villa	1	0	1	0	2	0
Blackburn Rovers	1	0	1	1	2	1
Bolton Wanderers	0	0	1	0	1	0
Chelsea	1	0	1	0	2	0
Coventry	1	3	0	0	1	3
Everton	1	0	1	0	2	0
Leeds Utd	1	0	1	0	2	0
Liverpool	1	0	1	0	2	0
Manchester City	1	0	1	1	2	1
Manchester Utd	1	1	1	0	2	1
Middlesbrough	1	1	1	1	2	2
Newcastle	1	0	1	0	2	0
Nottingham Forest	0	0	0	0	0	0
Q.P.R.	0	0	1	1	1	1
Sheffield Wednesday	1	0	1	0	2	0
Southampton	0	0	1	0	1	0
Tottenham	1	1	1	0	2	1
West Ham	1	1	1	0	2	1
Wimbledon	1	0	1	0	2	0

Fleck, Robert – Chelsea

OPPONENTS	HOME APPS	HOME GOALS	AWAY APPS	AWAY GOALS	TOTAL APPS	TOTAL GOALS
Arsenal	4	0	5	0	9	0
Aston Villa	3	1	5	1	8	2
Blackburn Rovers	2	0	1	0	3	0
Bolton Wanderers	0	0	0	0	0	0
Chelsea	3	1	3	2	6	3
Coventry	5	2	4	1	9	3
Everton	4	0	5	1	9	1
Leeds Utd	4	0	2	0	6	0
Liverpool	5	2	5	0	10	2
Manchester City	4	0	4	2	8	2
Manchester Utd	4	3	3	1	7	4
Middlesbrough	2	0	3	2	5	2
Newcastle	1	0	2	3	3	3
Nottingham Forest	5	2	5	0	10	2
Q.P.R.	5	0	4	0	9	0
Sheffield Wednesday	3	1	4	2	7	3
Southampton	4	3	5	0	9	3
Tottenham	3	1	5	1	8	2
West Ham	2	0	1	0	3	0
Wimbledon	3	1	5	0	8	1

Fowler, Robbie – Liverpool

OPPONENTS	HOME APPS	HOME GOALS	AWAY APPS	AWAY GOALS	TOTAL APPS	TOTAL GOALS
Arsenal	2	3	2	1	4	4
Aston Villa	2	3	2	1	4	4
Blackburn Rovers	1	0	1	1	2	1
Bolton Wanderers	0	0	0	0	0	0
Chelsea	2	2	2	0	4	2
Coventry	1	0	1	0	2	0
Everton	2	1	1	0	3	1
Leeds Utd	1	0	1	1	2	1
Liverpool	0	0	0	0	0	0
Manchester City	1	1	2	0	3	1
Manchester Utd	2	0	2	0	4	0
Middlesbrough	0	0	0	0	0	0
Newcastle	2	1	2	0	4	1
Nottingham Forest	1	1	1	1	2	2
Q.P.R.	2	0	1	0	3	0
Sheffield Wednesday	1	0	2	1	3	1
Southampton	2	4	1	1	3	5
Tottenham	1	1	2	2	3	3
West Ham	2	0	2	1	4	1
Wimbledon	2	2	2	0	4	2

Furlong, Paul – Chelsea

OPPONENTS	HOME APPS	HOME GOALS	AWAY APPS	AWAY GOALS	TOTAL APPS	TOTAL GOALS
Arsenal	2	1	2	0	4	1
Aston Villa	2	0	2	0	4	0
Blackburn Rovers	1	0	1	0	2	0
Bolton Wanderers	0	0	1	0	1	0
Chelsea	1	0	1	0	2	0
Coventry	0	0	1	0	1	0
Everton	2	0	2	2	4	2
Leeds Utd	2	0	2	0	4	0
Liverpool	1	0	1	0	2	0
Manchester City	2	0	2	0	4	0
Manchester Utd	2	0	2	0	4	0
Middlesbrough	1	1	1	1	2	2
Newcastle	2	1	2	1	4	2
Nottingham Forest	2	0	1	0	3	0
Q.P.R.	1	0	2	0	3	0
Sheffield Wednesday	2	0	1	0	3	0
Southampton	2	0	2	1	4	1
Tottenham	2	0	1	0	3	0
West Ham	2	1	3	1	5	2
Wimbledon	2	1	2	0	4	1

Gallagher, Kevin – Blackburn Rovers

OPPONENTS	HOME APPS	HOME GOALS	AWAY APPS	AWAY GOALS	TOTAL APPS	TOTAL GOALS
Arsenal	3	1	3	1	6	2
Aston Villa	3	1	2	1	5	2
Blackburn Rovers	1	0	0	0	1	0
Bolton Wanderers	0	0	0	0	0	0
Chelsea	4	0	2	1	6	1
Coventry	1	0	0	0	1	0
Everton	4	1	1	0	5	1
Leeds Utd	3	1	4	1	7	2
Liverpool	5	2	3	0	8	2
Manchester City	3	2	4	1	7	3
Manchester Utd	2	1	6	2	8	3
Middlesbrough	0	0	0	0	0	0
Newcastle	1	0	1	0	2	0
Nottingham Forest	3	0	4	1	7	1
Q.P.R.	3	1	2	0	5	1
Sheffield Wednesday	3	0	2	1	5	1
Southampton	3	1	4	0	7	1
Tottenham	4	1	4	2	8	3
West Ham	2	0	1	1	3	1
Wimbledon	3	0	2	0	5	0

Gallen, Kevin – QPR

OPPONENTS	HOME APPS	HOME GOALS	AWAY APPS	AWAY GOALS	TOTAL APPS	TOTAL GOALS
Arsenal	1	1	1	1	2	2
Aston Villa	1	0	1	0	2	0
Blackburn Rovers	1	0	1	0	2	0
Bolton Wanderers	0	0	0	0	0	0
Chelsea	1	1	1	0	2	1
Coventry	1	0	1	0	2	0
Everton	1	1	0	0	1	1
Leeds Utd	1	1	1	0	2	1
Liverpool	1	0	1	0	2	0
Manchester City	1	0	1	0	2	0
Manchester Utd	1	0	1	0	2	0
Middlesbrough	0	0	0	0	0	0
Newcastle	1	0	1	0	2	0
Nottingham Forest	1	0	0	0	1	0
Q.P.R.	0	0	0	0	0	0
Sheffield Wednesday	1	1	1	0	2	1
Southampton	1	1	1	0	2	1
Tottenham	0	0	0	0	0	0
West Ham	1	0	1	0	2	0
Wimbledon	1	0	1	0	2	0

Goodman, Jon – Wimbledon

OPPONENTS	HOME APPS	HOME GOALS	AWAY APPS	AWAY GOALS	TOTAL APPS	TOTAL GOALS
Arsenal	0	0	1	0	1	0
Aston Villa	0	0	1	0	1	0
Blackburn Rovers	1	0	0	0	1	0
Bolton Wanderers	1	0	2	0	3	0
Chelsea	1	1	0	0	1	1
Coventry	1	0	0	0	1	0
Everton	0	0	1	0	1	0
Leeds Utd	1	0	0	0	1	0
Liverpool	1	0	0	0	1	0
Manchester City	1	0	0	0	1	0
Manchester Utd	1	0	0	0	1	0
Middlesbrough	1	1	1	0	2	1
Newcastle	3	0	3	0	6	0
Nottingham Forest	1	0	1	1	2	1
Q.P.R.	1	0	0	0	1	0
Sheffield Wednesday	0	0	2	0	2	0
Southampton	1	0	0	0	1	0
Tottenham	0	0	0	0	0	0
West Ham	1	0	1	1	2	1
Wimbledon	0	0	0	0	0	0

Griffiths, Carl – Manchester City

OPPONENTS	HOME APPS	HOME GOALS	AWAY APPS	AWAY GOALS	TOTAL APPS	TOTAL GOALS
Arsenal	1	0	0	0	1	0
Aston Villa	0	0	0	0	0	0
Blackburn Rovers	1	0	1	0	2	0
Bolton Wanderers	2	0	2	0	4	0
Chelsea	0	0	2	0	2	0
Coventry	0	0	1	0	1	0
Everton	1	1	0	0	1	1
Leeds Utd	1	2	3	3	4	5
Liverpool	0	0	1	1	1	1
Manchester City	0	0	1	2	1	2
Manchester Utd	0	0	0	0	0	0
Middlesbrough	0	0	0	0	0	0
Newcastle	0	0	0	0	0	0
Nottingham Forest	0	0	0	0	0	0
Q.P.R.	0	0	1	0	1	0
Sheffield Wednesday	0	0	0	0	0	0
Southampton	1	0	0	0	1	0
Tottenham	1	0	0	0	1	0
West Ham	1	0	1	0	2	0
Wimbledon	0	0	0	0	0	0

Harford, Mick – Wimbledon

OPPONENTS	HOME APPS	HOME GOALS	AWAY APPS	AWAY GOALS	TOTAL APPS	TOTAL GOALS
Arsenal	11	3	6	1	17	4
Aston Villa	8	1	8	1	16	2
Blackburn Rovers	5	0	3	0	8	0
Bolton Wanderers	0	0	0	0	0	0
Chelsea	8	2	4	1	12	3
Coventry	8	3	12	2	20	5
Everton	11	3	10	1	21	4
Leeds Utd	5	0	3	2	8	2
Liverpool	8	1	11	3	19	4
Manchester City	6	1	6	2	12	3
Manchester Utd	9	5	7	0	16	5
Middlesbrough	2	1	1	0	3	1
Newcastle	3	3	6	1	9	4
Nottingham Forest	10	3	8	1	18	4
Q.P.R.	10	4	8	2	18	6
Sheffield Wednesday	9	3	7	3	16	6
Southampton	4	3	10	3	14	6
Tottenham	9	3	7	4	16	7
West Ham	7	4	6	1	13	5
Wimbledon	6	0	4	1	10	1

Hartson, John – Arsenal

OPPONENTS	HOME APPS	HOME GOALS	AWAY APPS	AWAY GOALS	TOTAL APPS	TOTAL GOALS
Arsenal	0	0	0	0	0	0
Aston Villa	0	0	1	2	1	2
Blackburn Rovers	0	0	1	0	1	0
Bolton Wanderers	2	0	1	0	3	0
Chelsea	0	0	1	1	1	1
Coventry	0	0	1	1	1	1
Everton	1	0	0	0	1	0
Leeds Utd	0	0	0	0	0	0
Liverpool	1	0	0	0	1	0
Manchester City	0	0	0	0	0	0
Manchester Utd	0	0	0	0	0	0
Middlesbrough	2	1	1	0	3	1
Newcastle	0	0	1	0	1	0
Nottingham Forest	1	1	0	0	1	1
Q.P.R.	0	0	1	0	1	0
Sheffield Wednesday	0	0	1	0	1	0
Southampton	1	1	0	0	1	1
Tottenham	1	0	0	0	1	0
West Ham	0	0	0	0	0	0
Wimbledon	1	0	0	0	1	0

Hignett, Craig – Middlesbrough

OPPONENTS	HOME APPS	HOME GOALS	AWAY APPS	AWAY GOALS	TOTAL APPS	TOTAL GOALS
Arsenal	1	0	1	0	2	0
Aston Villa	0	0	1	1	1	1
Blackburn Rovers	1	0	0	0	1	0
Bolton Wanderers	3	0	2	0	5	0
Chelsea	1	0	1	0	2	0
Coventry	1	0	0	0	1	0
Everton	1	0	1	2	2	2
Leeds Utd	0	0	1	0	1	0
Liverpool	1	0	0	0	1	0
Manchester City	0	0	0	0	0	0
Manchester Utd	0	0	0	0	0	0
Middlesbrough	0	0	0	0	0	0
Newcastle	0	0	0	0	0	0
Nottingham Forest	1	0	0	0	1	0
Q.P.R.	1	0	0	0	1	0
Sheffield Wednesday	0	0	1	0	1	0
Southampton	0	0	0	0	0	0
Tottenham	1	0	0	0	1	0
West Ham	0	0	0	0	0	0
Wimbledon	0	0	0	0	0	0

Hirst, David – Sheffield Wednesday

OPPONENTS	HOME		AWAY		TOTAL	
	APPS	GOALS	APPS	GOALS	APPS	GOALS
Arsenal	6	2	4	1	10	3
Aston Villa	4	2	4	1	8	3
Blackburn Rovers	2	0	2	2	4	2
Bolton Wanderers	0	0	0	0	0	0
Chelsea	3	4	3	0	6	4
Coventry	4	1	4	1	8	2
Everton	4	1	5	1	9	2
Leeds Utd	3	2	3	1	6	3
Liverpool	4	2	5	0	9	2
Manchester City	4	2	2	1	6	3
Manchester Utd	7	5	4	1	11	6
Middlesbrough	4	0	2	1	6	1
Newcastle	3	2	2	1	5	3
Nottingham Forest	5	3	6	1	11	4
Q.P.R.	5	3	5	1	10	4
Sheffield Wednesday	0	0	0	0	0	0
Southampton	5	1	4	2	9	3
Tottenham	6	3	5	2	11	5
West Ham	4	2	5	1	9	3
Wimbledon	5	1	5	0	10	1

Holdsworth, Dean – Wimbledon

OPPONENTS	HOME		AWAY		TOTAL	
	APPS	GOALS	APPS	GOALS	APPS	GOALS
Arsenal	4	0	4	1	8	1
Aston Villa	2	1	3	1	5	2
Blackburn Rovers	4	1	3	1	7	2
Bolton Wanderers	3	4	2	1	5	5
Chelsea	2	0	2	1	4	1
Coventry	3	2	3	2	6	4
Everton	2	0	3	1	5	1
Leeds Utd	2	1	2	0	4	1
Liverpool	2	0	2	0	4	0
Manchester City	3	0	3	0	6	0
Manchester Utd	3	1	2	0	5	1
Middlesbrough	1	1	1	0	2	1
Newcastle	1	1	2	0	3	1
Nottingham Forest	2	2	1	0	3	2
Q.P.R.	3	1	1	0	4	1
Sheffield Wednesday	2	0	3	1	5	1
Southampton	3	1	2	2	5	3
Tottenham	3	1	2	1	5	2
West Ham	2	1	2	0	4	1
Wimbledon	0	0	0	0	0	0

Hughes, Mark – Chelsea

OPPONENTS	HOME		AWAY		TOTAL	
	APPS	GOALS	APPS	GOALS	APPS	GOALS
Arsenal	10	3	9	3	19	6
Aston Villa	8	7	8	1	16	8
Blackburn Rovers	2	0	3	1	5	1
Bolton Wanderers	0	0	0	0	0	0
Chelsea	8	3	7	4	15	7
Coventry	8	6	9	3	17	9
Everton	8	1	10	1	18	2
Leeds Utd	4	0	5	0	9	0
Liverpool	9	3	8	1	17	4
Manchester City	7	2	6	2	13	4
Manchester Utd	0	0	0	0	0	0
Middlesbrough	2	0	2	0	4	0
Newcastle	5	2	5	3	10	5
Nottingham Forest	7	2	7	2	14	4
Q.P.R.	7	3	6	0	13	3
Sheffield Wednesday	8	3	7	2	15	5
Southampton	10	4	8	1	18	5
Tottenham	9	3	10	4	19	7
West Ham	6	2	6	2	12	4
Wimbledon	6	1	7	3	13	4

Johnson, Tommy – Aston Villa

OPPONENTS	HOME APPS	HOME GOALS	AWAY APPS	AWAY GOALS	TOTAL APPS	TOTAL GOALS
Arsenal	2	0	1	0	3	0
Aston Villa	1	0	1	0	2	0
Blackburn Rovers	2	3	0	0	2	3
Bolton Wanderers	2	1	1	0	3	1
Chelsea	1	1	2	1	3	2
Coventry	1	0	1	0	2	0
Everton	0	0	1	0	1	0
Leeds Utd	1	1	1	0	2	1
Liverpool	1	1	0	0	1	1
Manchester City	1	0	0	0	1	0
Manchester Utd	1	1	2	0	3	1
Middlesbrough	2	1	2	0	4	1
Newcastle	2	0	3	1	5	1
Nottingham Forest	1	0	2	0	3	0
Q.P.R.	2	0	1	0	3	0
Sheffield Wednesday	2	2	1	0	3	2
Southampton	1	0	1	0	2	0
Tottenham	1	0	1	0	2	0
West Ham	4	0	3	0	7	0
Wimbledon	2	3	1	0	3	3

Kitson, Paul – Newcastle

OPPONENTS	HOME APPS	HOME GOALS	AWAY APPS	AWAY GOALS	TOTAL APPS	TOTAL GOALS
Arsenal	1	0	0	0	1	0
Aston Villa	1	0	1	0	2	0
Blackburn Rovers	2	1	0	0	2	1
Bolton Wanderers	1	0	1	0	2	0
Chelsea	0	0	1	0	1	0
Coventry	0	0	1	0	1	0
Everton	0	0	1	0	1	0
Leeds Utd	1	0	1	0	2	0
Liverpool	0	0	1	0	1	0
Manchester City	1	0	0	0	1	0
Manchester Utd	1	1	0	0	1	1
Middlesbrough	2	0	2	0	4	0
Newcastle	2	1	2	0	4	1
Nottingham Forest	2	0	2	0	4	0
Q.P.R.	1	1	1	0	2	1
Sheffield Wednesday	1	0	1	0	2	0
Southampton	0	0	1	1	1	1
Tottenham	0	0	0	0	0	0
West Ham	3	1	1	0	4	1
Wimbledon	1	1	1	1	2	2

Le Tissier, Matt – Southampton

OPPONENTS	HOME APPS	HOME GOALS	AWAY APPS	AWAY GOALS	TOTAL APPS	TOTAL GOALS
Arsenal	7	1	6	2	13	3
Aston Villa	7	6	6	4	13	10
Blackburn Rovers	3	2	3	2	6	4
Bolton Wanderers	0	0	0	0	0	0
Chelsea	8	0	6	4	14	4
Coventry	8	2	6	1	14	3
Everton	6	0	6	1	12	1
Leeds Utd	5	0	4	0	9	0
Liverpool	6	5	7	2	13	7
Manchester City	7	2	5	1	12	3
Manchester Utd	7	0	9	2	16	2
Middlesbrough	2	1	2	1	4	2
Newcastle	4	2	4	3	8	5
Nottingham Forest	6	2	6	3	12	5
Q.P.R.	7	3	9	4	16	7
Sheffield Wednesday	8	3	6	2	14	5
Southampton	0	0	0	0	0	0
Tottenham	7	4	6	2	13	6
West Ham	6	1	3	2	9	3
Wimbledon	7	4	7	6	14	10

McClair, Brian – Manchester Utd

OPPONENTS	HOME APPS	HOME GOALS	AWAY APPS	AWAY GOALS	TOTAL APPS	TOTAL GOALS
Arsenal	7	1	8	2	15	3
Aston Villa	6	0	6	0	12	0
Blackburn Rovers	3	0	3	0	6	0
Bolton Wanderers	0	0	0	0	0	0
Chelsea	7	1	7	3	14	4
Coventry	8	1	7	1	15	2
Everton	7	2	8	2	15	4
Leeds Utd	5	0	4	0	9	0
Liverpool	7	2	8	1	15	3
Manchester City	5	0	5	2	10	2
Manchester Utd	0	0	0	0	0	0
Middlesbrough	2	0	2	0	4	0
Newcastle	4	2	4	0	8	2
Nottingham Forest	7	1	6	0	13	1
Q.P.R.	7	3	7	0	14	3
Sheffield Wednesday	7	3	6	8	13	11
Southampton	7	3	8	0	15	3
Tottenham	8	4	8	3	16	7
West Ham	4	0	5	2	9	2
Wimbledon	6	5	8	0	14	5

McGinlay, John – Bolton

OPPONENTS	HOME APPS	HOME GOALS	AWAY APPS	AWAY GOALS	TOTAL APPS	TOTAL GOALS
Arsenal	0	0	0	0	0	0
Aston Villa	0	0	0	0	0	0
Blackburn Rovers	0	0	1	0	1	0
Bolton Wanderers	2	1	2	4	4	5
Chelsea	1	1	0	0	1	1
Coventry	0	0	0	0	0	0
Everton	0	0	0	0	0	0
Leeds Utd	1	0	0	0	1	0
Liverpool	0	0	0	0	0	0
Manchester City	1	0	0	0	1	0
Manchester Utd	0	0	0	0	0	0
Middlesbrough	3	4	2	1	5	5
Newcastle	0	0	1	0	1	0
Nottingham Forest	0	0	1	0	1	0
Q.P.R.	0	0	0	0	0	0
Sheffield Wednesday	0	0	0	0	0	0
Southampton	0	0	0	0	0	0
Tottenham	0	0	0	0	0	0
West Ham	0	0	0	0	0	0
Wimbledon	0	0	0	0	0	0

Maskell, Craig – Southampton

OPPONENTS	HOME APPS	HOME GOALS	AWAY APPS	AWAY GOALS	TOTAL APPS	TOTAL GOALS
Arsenal	2	0	0	0	2	0
Aston Villa	1	0	0	0	1	0
Blackburn Rovers	1	0	1	0	2	0
Bolton Wanderers	4	1	4	2	8	3
Chelsea	1	0	1	0	2	0
Coventry	1	0	1	0	2	0
Everton	1	0	0	0	1	0
Leeds Utd	0	0	1	0	1	0
Liverpool	2	1	1	0	3	1
Manchester City	1	0	0	0	1	0
Manchester Utd	0	0	2	0	2	0
Middlesbrough	0	0	0	0	0	0
Newcastle	0	0	1	0	1	0
Nottingham Forest	1	0	0	0	1	0
Q.P.R.	0	0	1	0	1	0
Sheffield Wednesday	1	0	2	2	3	2
Southampton	1	0	1	1	2	1
Tottenham	1	0	2	1	3	1
West Ham	1	0	1	1	2	1
Wimbledon	2	0	1	0	3	0

Merson, Paul – Arsenal

OPPONENTS	HOME APPS	HOME GOALS	AWAY APPS	AWAY GOALS	TOTAL APPS	TOTAL GOALS
Arsenal	0	0	0	0	0	0
Aston Villa	6	0	5	0	11	0
Blackburn Rovers	3	1	2	0	5	1
Bolton Wanderers	0	0	1	0	1	0
Chelsea	3	2	7	0	10	2
Coventry	7	0	7	1	14	1
Everton	6	1	6	3	12	4
Leeds Utd	4	2	4	0	8	2
Liverpool	7	3	6	1	13	4
Manchester City	6	2	5	1	11	3
Manchester Utd	6	2	7	0	13	2
Middlesbrough	2	2	1	0	3	2
Newcastle	3	0	2	0	5	0
Nottingham Forest	6	1	5	2	11	3
Q.P.R.	5	2	8	3	13	5
Sheffield Wednesday	6	5	6	2	12	7
Southampton	6	3	6	1	12	4
Tottenham	5	1	5	0	10	1
West Ham	4	0	4	0	8	0
Wimbledon	7	3	7	3	14	6

Morley, Trevor – West Ham

OPPONENTS	HOME APPS	HOME GOALS	AWAY APPS	AWAY GOALS	TOTAL APPS	TOTAL GOALS
Arsenal	2	0	3	1	5	1
Aston Villa	3	0	2	0	5	0
Blackburn Rovers	3	0	4	1	7	1
Bolton Wanderers	0	0	0	0	0	0
Chelsea	4	1	4	0	8	1
Coventry	3	1	3	0	6	1
Everton	2	0	2	0	4	0
Leeds Utd	4	0	3	1	7	1
Liverpool	3	0	2	0	5	0
Manchester City	2	0	3	0	5	0
Manchester Utd	3	2	1	0	4	2
Middlesbrough	1	0	3	0	4	0
Newcastle	3	0	4	1	7	1
Nottingham Forest	0	0	1	0	1	0
Q.P.R.	3	0	2	0	5	0
Sheffield Wednesday	1	0	3	0	4	0
Southampton	3	0	3	1	6	1
Tottenham	3	0	1	2	4	2
West Ham	0	0	0	0	0	0
Wimbledon	2	1	3	0	5	1

Ndlovu, Peter – Coventry

OPPONENTS	HOME APPS	HOME GOALS	AWAY APPS	AWAY GOALS	TOTAL APPS	TOTAL GOALS
Arsenal	3	0	4	1	7	1
Aston Villa	3	1	3	0	6	1
Blackburn Rovers	2	0	2	1	4	1
Bolton Wanderers	0	0	0	0	0	0
Chelsea	4	0	2	2	6	2
Coventry	0	0	0	0	0	0
Everton	4	0	3	1	7	1
Leeds Utd	1	1	4	1	5	2
Liverpool	2	0	3	3	5	3
Manchester City	3	1	3	0	6	1
Manchester Utd	2	1	3	0	5	1
Middlesbrough	0	0	1	1	1	1
Newcastle	2	1	1	0	3	1
Nottingham Forest	1	0	3	0	4	0
Q.P.R.	3	0	3	1	6	1
Sheffield Wednesday	4	2	3	2	7	4
Southampton	2	0	3	0	5	0
Tottenham	2	1	3	2	5	3
West Ham	3	1	3	0	6	1
Wimbledon	2	1	3	1	5	2

Newell, Mike – Blackburn

OPPONENTS	HOME APPS	HOME GOALS	AWAY APPS	AWAY GOALS	TOTAL APPS	TOTAL GOALS
Arsenal	7	1	3	1	10	2
Aston Villa	7	4	4	1	11	5
Blackburn Rovers	2	1	2	1	4	2
Bolton Wanderers	1	0	2	1	3	1
Chelsea	6	3	8	3	14	6
Coventry	6	2	6	0	12	2
Everton	3	2	3	2	6	4
Leeds Utd	4	0	4	0	8	0
Liverpool	5	5	5	2	10	7
Manchester City	6	1	8	4	14	5
Manchester Utd	6	1	6	1	12	2
Middlesbrough	2	1	2	0	4	1
Newcastle	2	0	3	0	5	0
Nottingham Forest	4	0	4	2	8	2
Q.P.R.	5	1	7	1	12	2
Sheffield Wednesday	5	0	5	1	10	1
Southampton	6	1	6	2	12	3
Tottenham	7	3	4	2	11	5
West Ham	4	0	2	0	6	0
Wimbledon	4	0	6	0	10	0

Paatelainen, Mixu – Bolton

OPPONENTS	HOME APPS	HOME GOALS	AWAY APPS	AWAY GOALS	TOTAL APPS	TOTAL GOALS
Arsenal	0	0	0	0	0	0
Aston Villa	0	0	0	0	0	0
Blackburn Rovers	0	0	0	0	0	0
Bolton Wanderers	0	0	0	0	0	0
Chelsea	0	0	0	0	0	0
Coventry	0	0	0	0	0	0
Everton	0	0	0	0	0	0
Leeds Utd	0	0	0	0	0	0
Liverpool	0	0	0	0	0	0
Manchester City	0	0	0	0	0	0
Manchester Utd	0	0	0	0	0	0
Middlesbrough	1	1	1	0	2	1
Newcastle	0	0	0	0	0	0
Nottingham Forest	0	0	0	0	0	0
Q.P.R.	0	0	0	0	0	0
Sheffield Wednesday	0	0	0	0	0	0
Southampton	0	0	0	0	0	0
Tottenham	0	0	0	0	0	0
West Ham	0	0	0	0	0	0
Wimbledon	0	0	0	0	0	0

Penrice, Gary – Q.P.R.

OPPONENTS	HOME APPS	HOME GOALS	AWAY APPS	AWAY GOALS	TOTAL APPS	TOTAL GOALS
Arsenal	5	2	2	0	7	2
Aston Villa	3	2	0	0	3	2
Blackburn Rovers	1	1	1	0	2	1
Bolton Wanderers	1	0	3	1	4	1
Chelsea	1	0	5	0	6	0
Coventry	1	2	4	2	5	4
Everton	3	1	2	0	5	1
Leeds Utd	2	0	4	1	6	1
Liverpool	1	0	1	0	2	0
Manchester City	3	1	3	0	6	1
Manchester Utd	2	0	2	0	4	0
Middlesbrough	2	1	3	0	5	1
Newcastle	2	1	0	0	2	1
Nottingham Forest	2	0	1	0	3	0
Q.P.R.	0	0	1	0	1	0
Sheffield Wednesday	2	1	2	0	4	1
Southampton	1	1	3	0	4	1
Tottenham	4	2	0	0	4	2
West Ham	3	1	3	0	6	1
Wimbledon	3	1	2	0	5	1

Quinn, Mick – Coventry

OPPONENTS	HOME APPS	HOME GOALS	AWAY APPS	AWAY GOALS	TOTAL APPS	TOTAL GOALS
Arsenal	2	1	1	3	3	4
Aston Villa	2	2	2	0	4	2
Blackburn Rovers	7	1	9	3	16	4
Bolton Wanderers	0	0	0	0	0	0
Chelsea	3	1	4	2	7	3
Coventry	1	0	1	0	2	0
Everton	3	2	1	0	4	2
Leeds Utd	7	6	5	1	12	7
Liverpool	3	2	3	0	6	2
Manchester City	5	4	3	0	8	4
Manchester Utd	3	0	2	1	5	1
Middlesbrough	3	1	8	5	11	6
Newcastle	2	1	2	0	4	1
Nottingham Forest	3	0	1	0	4	0
Q.P.R.	1	0	3	0	4	0
Sheffield Wednesday	2	0	4	0	6	0
Southampton	3	1	3	2	6	3
Tottenham	1	0	2	0	3	0
West Ham	3	1	3	0	6	1
Wimbledon	9	1	4	1	13	2

Quinn, Niall – Manchester City

OPPONENTS	HOME APPS	HOME GOALS	AWAY APPS	AWAY GOALS	TOTAL APPS	TOTAL GOALS
Arsenal	4	0	5	0	9	0
Aston Villa	4	1	6	1	10	2
Blackburn Rovers	3	1	2	0	5	1
Bolton Wanderers	0	0	0	0	0	0
Chelsea	5	1	7	0	12	1
Coventry	4	1	5	2	9	3
Everton	8	2	6	2	14	4
Leeds Utd	4	1	4	1	8	2
Liverpool	7	1	6	2	13	3
Manchester City	1	1	1	0	2	1
Manchester Utd	7	4	6	1	13	5
Middlesbrough	0	0	1	0	1	0
Newcastle	3	0	1	0	4	0
Nottingham Forest	7	4	5	2	12	6
Q.P.R.	8	5	5	0	13	5
Sheffield Wednesday	5	3	2	1	7	4
Southampton	6	1	4	3	10	4
Tottenham	5	1	7	2	12	3
West Ham	2	0	3	0	5	0
Wimbledon	5	0	6	1	11	1

Rideout, Paul – Everton

OPPONENTS	HOME APPS	HOME GOALS	AWAY APPS	AWAY GOALS	TOTAL APPS	TOTAL GOALS
Arsenal	4	0	6	0	10	0
Aston Villa	5	1	5	1	10	2
Blackburn Rovers	0	0	2	0	2	0
Bolton Wanderers	0	0	0	0	0	0
Chelsea	4	3	4	1	8	4
Coventry	2	0	4	3	6	3
Everton	2	0	5	1	7	1
Leeds Utd	2	2	3	1	5	3
Liverpool	7	2	6	1	13	3
Manchester City	4	1	2	0	6	1
Manchester Utd	4	1	4	1	8	2
Middlesbrough	2	1	1	0	3	1
Newcastle	2	3	2	0	4	3
Nottingham Forest	4	1	6	2	10	3
Q.P.R.	6	4	5	0	11	4
Sheffield Wednesday	5	1	3	1	8	2
Southampton	2	1	3	0	5	1
Tottenham	6	0	4	3	10	3
West Ham	5	3	5	2	10	5
Wimbledon	5	0	4	2	9	2

Rosler, Uwe – Manchester City

OPPONENTS	HOME APPS	HOME GOALS	AWAY APPS	AWAY GOALS	TOTAL APPS	TOTAL GOALS
Arsenal	1	0	1	0	2	0
Aston Villa	2	3	1	1	3	4
Blackburn Rovers	1	0	1	1	2	1
Bolton Wanderers	0	0	0	0	0	0
Chelsea	2	1	1	0	3	1
Coventry	1	0	0	0	1	0
Everton	1	2	1	0	2	2
Leeds Utd	0	0	0	0	0	0
Liverpool	1	0	1	0	2	0
Manchester City	0	0	0	0	0	0
Manchester Utd	1	0	1	0	2	0
Middlesbrough	0	0	0	0	0	0
Newcastle	2	0	1	0	3	0
Nottingham Forest	0	0	0	0	0	0
Q.P.R.	1	0	1	0	2	0
Sheffield Wednesday	1	2	2	1	3	3
Southampton	0	0	2	0	2	0
Tottenham	0	0	1	1	1	1
West Ham	1	1	1	0	2	1
Wimbledon	2	1	1	0	3	1

Roy, Brian – Nottm Forest

OPPONENTS	HOME APPS	HOME GOALS	AWAY APPS	AWAY GOALS	TOTAL APPS	TOTAL GOALS
Arsenal	1	1	0	0	1	1
Aston Villa	1	0	1	0	2	0
Blackburn Rovers	1	0	1	0	2	0
Bolton Wanderers	0	0	0	0	0	0
Chelsea	1	0	1	0	2	0
Coventry	1	0	0	0	1	0
Everton	1	0	1	0	2	0
Leeds Utd	1	2	1	0	2	2
Liverpool	1	0	1	0	2	0
Manchester City	1	0	0	0	1	0
Manchester Utd	1	0	1	0	2	0
Middlesbrough	0	0	0	0	0	0
Newcastle	1	0	0	0	1	0
Nottingham Forest	0	0	0	0	0	0
Q.P.R.	1	1	1	0	2	1
Sheffield Wednesday	1	1	1	2	2	3
Southampton	1	2	1	0	2	2
Tottenham	1	0	1	2	2	2
West Ham	1	0	1	0	2	0
Wimbledon	1	0	0	0	1	0

Rush, Ian – Liverpool

OPPONENTS	HOME APPS	HOME GOALS	AWAY APPS	AWAY GOALS	TOTAL APPS	TOTAL GOALS
Arsenal	10	3	10	2	20	5
Aston Villa	9	2	11	6	20	8
Blackburn Rovers	2	0	4	1	6	1
Bolton Wanderers	0	0	0	0	0	0
Chelsea	8	5	9	3	17	8
Coventry	13	12	10	3	23	15
Everton	11	5	11	8	22	13
Leeds Utd	5	4	6	1	11	5
Liverpool	0	0	0	0	0	0
Manchester City	9	5	8	6	17	11
Manchester Utd	12	2	11	1	23	3
Middlesbrough	2	2	3	1	5	3
Newcastle	5	2	6	4	11	6
Nottingham Forest	11	3	13	7	24	10
Q.P.R.	9	7	10	3	19	10
Sheffield Wednesday	9	5	8	1	17	6
Southampton	12	7	10	3	22	10
Tottenham	11	4	10	4	21	8
West Ham	8	5	8	3	16	8
Wimbledon	7	2	5	2	12	4

Saunders, Dean – Aston Villa

OPPONENTS	HOME APPS	HOME GOALS	AWAY APPS	AWAY GOALS	TOTAL APPS	TOTAL GOALS
Arsenal	8	1	8	2	16	3
Aston Villa	4	1	4	1	8	2
Blackburn Rovers	7	1	5	1	12	2
Bolton Wanderers	1	0	1	0	2	0
Chelsea	7	5	7	2	14	7
Coventry	8	1	9	1	17	2
Everton	7	4	7	1	14	5
Leeds Utd	6	0	10	0	16	0
Liverpool	8	3	7	1	15	4
Manchester City	7	5	7	1	14	6
Manchester Utd	8	2	9	1	17	3
Middlesbrough	3	2	3	2	6	4
Newcastle	3	1	4	0	7	1
Nottingham Forest	7	1	6	1	13	2
Q.P.R.	7	5	8	2	15	7
Sheffield Wednesday	8	4	5	2	13	6
Southampton	7	4	8	2	15	6
Tottenham	8	5	9	5	17	10
West Ham	5	2	4	0	9	2
Wimbledon	10	8	9	4	19	12

Shearer, Alan – Blackburn

OPPONENTS	HOME APPS	HOME GOALS	AWAY APPS	AWAY GOALS	TOTAL APPS	TOTAL GOALS
Arsenal	7	6	6	0	13	6
Aston Villa	4	4	5	2	9	6
Blackburn Rovers	0	0	0	0	0	0
Bolton Wanderers	0	0	0	0	0	0
Chelsea	5	4	6	1	11	5
Coventry	5	2	7	2	12	4
Everton	6	7	3	1	9	8
Leeds Utd	5	5	4	4	9	9
Liverpool	6	1	4	2	10	3
Manchester City	6	2	4	1	10	3
Manchester Utd	6	2	5	0	11	2
Middlesbrough	0	0	2	0	2	0
Newcastle	3	1	2	2	5	3
Nottingham Forest	4	2	3	1	7	3
Q.P.R.	5	6	6	2	11	8
Sheffield Wednesday	4	2	6	1	10	3
Southampton	2	4	3	1	5	5
Tottenham	7	3	5	1	12	4
West Ham	4	3	3	0	7	3
Wimbledon	5	2	6	3	11	5

Sheringham, Teddy – Tottenham

OPPONENTS	HOME APPS	HOME GOALS	AWAY APPS	AWAY GOALS	TOTAL APPS	TOTAL GOALS
Arsenal	6	2	5	1	11	3
Aston Villa	5	3	7	0	12	3
Blackburn Rovers	5	3	6	1	11	4
Bolton Wanderers	0	0	0	0	0	0
Chelsea	5	2	4	2	9	4
Coventry	4	3	6	2	10	5
Everton	6	1	5	2	11	3
Leeds Utd	5	5	6	1	11	6
Liverpool	5	2	6	3	11	5
Manchester City	6	0	4	1	10	1
Manchester Utd	3	0	6	1	9	1
Middlesbrough	5	2	5	2	10	4
Newcastle	3	3	4	3	7	6
Nottingham Forest	4	1	4	2	8	3
Q.P.R.	6	3	4	4	10	7
Sheffield Wednesday	6	2	8	3	14	5
Southampton	5	3	4	3	9	6
Tottenham	2	0	2	0	4	0
West Ham	5	3	3	1	8	4
Wimbledon	6	0	5	2	11	2

Smith, Alan – Arsenal

OPPONENTS	HOME APPS	HOME GOALS	AWAY APPS	AWAY GOALS	TOTAL APPS	TOTAL GOALS
Arsenal	4	1	4	0	8	1
Aston Villa	8	5	10	3	18	8
Blackburn Rovers	4	0	2	1	6	1
Bolton Wanderers	1	0	1	0	2	0
Chelsea	10	1	8	3	18	4
Coventry	11	4	10	0	21	4
Everton	9	2	11	2	20	4
Leeds Utd	4	0	5	3	9	3
Liverpool	10	2	10	6	20	8
Manchester City	8	3	7	3	15	6
Manchester Utd	11	5	9	0	20	5
Middlesbrough	3	0	3	0	6	0
Newcastle	6	2	7	3	13	5
Nottingham Forest	10	2	10	7	20	9
Q.P.R.	12	3	12	2	24	5
Sheffield Wednesday	11	6	8	3	19	9
Southampton	9	6	10	1	19	7
Tottenham	11	2	10	2	21	4
West Ham	7	2	9	2	16	4
Wimbledon	8	2	8	5	16	7

Spencer, John – Chelsea

OPPONENTS	HOME APPS	HOME GOALS	AWAY APPS	AWAY GOALS	TOTAL APPS	TOTAL GOALS
Arsenal	1	0	1	0	2	0
Aston Villa	3	0	1	0	4	0
Blackburn Rovers	2	1	0	0	2	1
Bolton Wanderers	0	0	0	0	0	0
Chelsea	0	0	0	0	0	0
Coventry	2	2	2	1	4	3
Everton	2	1	0	0	2	1
Leeds Utd	1	1	2	2	3	3
Liverpool	1	0	1	1	2	1
Manchester City	2	1	1	0	3	1
Manchester Utd	1	1	3	0	4	1
Middlesbrough	1	1	0	0	1	1
Newcastle	2	0	2	0	4	0
Nottingham Forest	2	0	2	1	4	1
Q.P.R.	0	0	2	1	2	1
Sheffield Wednesday	2	1	1	1	3	2
Southampton	3	1	2	0	5	1
Tottenham	3	1	1	0	4	1
West Ham	2	0	2	0	4	0
Wimbledon	2	1	2	0	4	1

Stein, Mark – Chelsea

OPPONENTS	HOME APPS	HOME GOALS	AWAY APPS	AWAY GOALS	TOTAL APPS	TOTAL GOALS
Arsenal	5	1	3	1	8	2
Aston Villa	3	2	2	0	5	2
Blackburn Rovers	2	0	2	1	4	1
Bolton Wanderers	2	0	3	2	5	2
Chelsea	1	1	1	0	2	1
Coventry	0	0	3	1	3	1
Everton	5	2	5	3	10	5
Leeds Utd	2	0	2	1	4	1
Liverpool	2	0	0	0	2	0
Manchester City	2	0	2	2	4	2
Manchester Utd	3	0	6	0	9	0
Middlesbrough	3	1	3	0	6	1
Newcastle	5	3	4	1	9	4
Nottingham Forest	3	3	4	2	7	5
Q.P.R.	4	0	2	1	6	1
Sheffield Wednesday	4	0	3	1	7	1
Southampton	3	0	2	1	5	1
Tottenham	3	2	1	0	4	2
West Ham	2	1	6	3	8	4
Wimbledon	2	0	4	1	6	1

Stewart, Paul – Liverpool

OPPONENTS	HOME APPS	HOME GOALS	AWAY APPS	AWAY GOALS	TOTAL APPS	TOTAL GOALS
Arsenal	4	2	5	0	9	2
Aston Villa	2	0	4	0	6	0
Blackburn Rovers	1	0	0	0	1	0
Bolton Wanderers	3	1	2	1	5	2
Chelsea	4	0	4	0	8	0
Coventry	5	2	5	1	10	3
Everton	4	2	7	0	11	2
Leeds Utd	3	0	4	0	7	0
Liverpool	4	1	2	1	6	2
Manchester City	2	0	4	0	6	0
Manchester Utd	5	0	4	0	9	0
Middlesbrough	2	0	3	3	5	3
Newcastle	2	0	1	0	3	0
Nottingham Forest	5	1	6	1	11	2
Q.P.R.	4	0	4	0	8	0
Sheffield Wednesday	2	2	5	1	7	3
Southampton	8	2	3	0	11	2
Tottenham	3	0	3	0	6	0
West Ham	3	1	3	0	6	1
Wimbledon	5	1	4	1	9	2

Sutton, Chris – Blackburn

OPPONENTS	HOME APPS	HOME GOALS	AWAY APPS	AWAY GOALS	TOTAL APPS	TOTAL GOALS
Arsenal	4	0	4	0	8	0
Aston Villa	4	2	5	0	9	2
Blackburn Rovers	2	2	2	2	4	4
Bolton Wanderers	0	0	0	0	0	0
Chelsea	4	0	3	2	7	2
Coventry	4	5	4	0	8	5
Everton	4	1	3	3	7	4
Leeds Utd	3	4	3	1	6	5
Liverpool	4	4	4	0	8	4
Manchester City	2	0	4	0	6	0
Manchester Utd	4	0	3	1	7	1
Middlesbrough	1	0	1	0	2	0
Newcastle	2	0	1	0	3	0
Nottingham Forest	2	0	3	2	5	2
Q.P.R.	5	2	3	2	8	4
Sheffield Wednesday	3	1	2	1	5	2
Southampton	4	2	2	1	6	3
Tottenham	3	1	4	1	7	2
West Ham	2	0	3	2	5	2
Wimbledon	2	0	3	0	5	0

Wallace, Rod – Leeds

OPPONENTS	HOME APPS	HOME GOALS	AWAY APPS	AWAY GOALS	TOTAL APPS	TOTAL GOALS
Arsenal	8	1	7	1	15	2
Aston Villa	5	2	6	2	11	4
Blackburn Rovers	3	1	0	0	3	1
Bolton Wanderers	0	0	0	0	0	0
Chelsea	6	6	5	0	11	6
Coventry	8	5	6	7	14	12
Everton	5	1	7	1	12	2
Leeds Utd	1	0	1	0	2	0
Liverpool	6	2	8	3	14	5
Manchester City	6	2	5	0	11	2
Manchester Utd	6	1	6	1	12	2
Middlesbrough	2	0	2	1	4	1
Newcastle	2	0	3	1	5	1
Nottingham Forest	6	2	6	2	12	4
Q.P.R.	6	2	7	3	13	5
Sheffield Wednesday	6	1	6	3	12	4
Southampton	4	0	3	2	7	2
Tottenham	8	4	7	1	15	5
West Ham	4	0	4	2	8	2
Wimbledon	7	1	6	0	13	1

Walsh, Paul – Manchester City

OPPONENTS	HOME APPS	HOME GOALS	AWAY APPS	AWAY GOALS	TOTAL APPS	TOTAL GOALS
Arsenal	7	2	11	0	18	2
Aston Villa	9	1	8	2	17	3
Blackburn Rovers	1	1	2	1	3	2
Bolton Wanderers	2	1	1	0	3	1
Chelsea	7	1	5	2	12	3
Coventry	6	0	8	3	14	3
Everton	6	5	7	1	13	6
Leeds Utd	2	0	1	0	3	0
Liverpool	7	1	8	0	15	1
Manchester City	2	1	6	0	8	1
Manchester Utd	7	1	8	1	15	2
Middlesbrough	2	0	1	0	3	0
Newcastle	8	4	3	0	11	4
Nottingham Forest	10	1	8	0	18	1
Q.P.R.	9	0	11	2	20	2
Sheffield Wednesday	8	4	8	1	16	5
Southampton	5	2	8	0	13	2
Tottenham	4	3	5	0	9	3
West Ham	9	3	7	6	16	9
Wimbledon	4	1	4	0	8	1

Wegerle, Roy – Coventry

OPPONENTS	HOME APPS	HOME GOALS	AWAY APPS	AWAY GOALS	TOTAL APPS	TOTAL GOALS
Arsenal	7	2	6	1	13	3
Aston Villa	6	1	4	1	10	2
Blackburn Rovers	1	0	1	0	2	0
Bolton Wanderers	0	0	0	0	0	0
Chelsea	4	1	3	0	7	1
Coventry	5	1	4	0	9	1
Everton	5	2	6	1	11	3
Leeds Utd	3	1	1	2	4	3
Liverpool	4	0	4	2	8	2
Manchester City	2	0	6	3	8	3
Manchester Utd	7	0	4	1	11	1
Middlesbrough	1	0	2	0	3	0
Newcastle	4	0	3	0	7	0
Nottingham Forest	6	1	3	1	9	2
Q.P.R.	2	1	3	0	5	1
Sheffield Wednesday	4	0	6	0	10	0
Southampton	7	2	6	1	13	3
Tottenham	7	0	6	2	13	2
West Ham	4	2	2	0	6	2
Wimbledon	6	2	5	1	11	3

White, David – Leeds

OPPONENTS	HOME APPS	HOME GOALS	AWAY APPS	AWAY GOALS	TOTAL APPS	TOTAL GOALS
Arsenal	5	2	6	1	11	3
Aston Villa	5	1	8	5	13	6
Blackburn Rovers	3	1	6	0	9	1
Bolton Wanderers	0	0	0	0	0	0
Chelsea	7	1	8	1	15	2
Coventry	5	2	5	1	10	3
Everton	8	2	6	1	14	3
Leeds Utd	6	3	6	0	12	3
Liverpool	8	3	4	2	12	5
Manchester City	0	0	1	0	1	0
Manchester Utd	7	2	5	0	12	2
Middlesbrough	2	0	2	0	4	0
Newcastle	3	0	2	0	5	0
Nottingham Forest	5	0	6	1	11	1
Q.P.R.	7	3	6	2	13	5
Sheffield Wednesday	6	1	4	0	10	1
Southampton	7	1	4	1	11	2
Tottenham	6	2	4	0	10	2
West Ham	3	1	3	0	6	1
Wimbledon	5	1	6	1	11	2

Whittingham, Guy – Sheffield Wed

OPPONENTS	HOME APPS	HOME GOALS	AWAY APPS	AWAY GOALS	TOTAL APPS	TOTAL GOALS
Arsenal	1	0	1	1	2	1
Aston Villa	1	0	0	0	1	0
Blackburn Rovers	3	2	4	0	7	2
Bolton Wanderers	0	0	1	2	1	2
Chelsea	1	0	1	0	2	0
Coventry	2	2	1	0	3	2
Everton	2	0	2	3	4	3
Leeds Utd	1	2	1	0	2	2
Liverpool	1	0	2	1	3	1
Manchester City	1	0	1	1	2	1
Manchester Utd	1	0	2	0	3	0
Middlesbrough	3	2	3	0	6	2
Newcastle	6	1	2	1	8	2
Nottingham Forest	2	0	0	0	2	0
Q.P.R.	0	0	0	0	0	0
Sheffield Wednesday	2	1	1	1	3	2
Southampton	2	0	1	0	3	0
Tottenham	1	0	0	0	1	0
West Ham	3	0	4	1	7	1
Wimbledon	2	0	0	0	2	0

Wilkinson Paul – Middlesbrough

OPPONENTS	HOME APPS	HOME GOALS	AWAY APPS	AWAY GOALS	TOTAL APPS	TOTAL GOALS
Arsenal	3	0	1	0	4	0
Aston Villa	2	0	1	0	3	0
Blackburn Rovers	7	1	6	3	13	4
Bolton Wanderers	2	1	1	0	3	1
Chelsea	4	1	4	2	8	3
Coventry	2	1	3	2	5	3
Everton	2	1	1	0	3	1
Leeds Utd	4	4	5	1	9	5
Liverpool	4	1	2	0	6	1
Manchester City	3	1	6	0	9	1
Manchester Utd	3	0	4	1	7	1
Middlesbrough	5	2	4	1	9	3
Newcastle	4	2	6	2	10	4
Nottingham Forest	2	0	3	0	5	0
Q.P.R.	2	1	2	0	4	1
Sheffield Wednesday	4	5	6	0	10	5
Southampton	1	1	4	3	5	4
Tottenham	3	1	3	1	6	2
West Ham	2	0	4	0	6	0
Wimbledon	0	0	3	0	3	0

Wright, Ian – Arsenal

OPPONENTS	HOME APPS	HOME GOALS	AWAY APPS	AWAY GOALS	TOTAL APPS	TOTAL GOALS
Arsenal	2	0	2	0	4	0
Aston Villa	5	2	6	6	11	8
Blackburn Rovers	6	3	6	2	12	5
Bolton Wanderers	0	0	0	0	0	0
Chelsea	7	7	4	1	11	8
Coventry	5	3	6	2	11	5
Everton	6	9	3	0	9	9
Leeds Utd	8	2	7	2	15	4
Liverpool	5	2	6	1	11	3
Manchester City	6	2	7	2	13	4
Manchester Utd	6	2	6	0	12	2
Middlesbrough	3	2	2	1	5	3
Newcastle	2	2	2	0	4	2
Nottingham Forest	4	2	2	0	6	2
Q.P.R.	4	0	6	2	10	2
Sheffield Wednesday	3	2	3	1	6	3
Southampton	4	3	5	8	9	11
Tottenham	5	3	6	2	11	5
West Ham	4	1	3	3	7	4
Wimbledon	8	2	6	9	14	11

LEADING SCORERS
PLAYERS WHO HAVE SCORED MORE THAN 99 LEAGUE, FA CUP AND LEAGUE CUP GOALS

			Goals
1	Ian Rush	Liverpool	326
2	Mick Quinn	Coventry	255
3	Mick Harford	Wimbledon	227
4	Tony Cottee	West Ham	219
5	Peter Beardsley	Newcastle	215
6	Ian Wright	Arsenal	209
7	Teddy Sheringham	Tottenham	194
8	Alan Smith	Arsenal	192
9	Dean Saunders	Aston Villa	185
10	John Barnes	Liverpool	179
11	Mark Bright	Sheffield Wednesday	178
12	Paul Wilkinson	Middlesbrough	171
13	John Fashanu	Aston Villa	160
14	Mark Hughes	Chelsea	152
15	Paul Walsh	Manchester City	148
16	Matt Le Tissier	Southampton	147
17	Brian Deane	Leeds	140
18	Gary Blissett	Wimbledon	139
19	Nigel Clough	Liverpool	137
20	Trevor Morley	West Ham	135
	Mike Newell	Blackburn	135
22	Paul Stewart	Liverpool	134
23	Bryan Robson	Middlesbrough	133
24	Alan Shearer	Blackburn	130
25	Mark Stein	Chelsea	129
	Neil Webb	Nottm Forest	129
27	Dean Holdsworth	Wimbledon	125
28	Guy Whittingham	Sheffield Wednesday	124
29	John McGinlay	Bolton	121
30	Robbie Earle	Wimbledon	119
	John Hendrie	Middlesbrough	119
32	Brian McClair	Manchester Utd	118
33	Paul Rideout	Everton	117
34	David Hirst	Sheffield Wednesday	112
	Glenn Hoddle	Chelsea	112
36	Garry Penrice	Q.P.R.	105
	Chris Waddle	Sheffield Wednesday	105
38	Andy Cole	Manchester Utd	103
39	Steve Bruce	Manchester Utd	101
40	Craig Maskell	Southampton	100

UP FOR THE CUP
PLAYERS WHO HAVE SCORED 20 GOALS IN THE LEAGUE CUP & FA CUP

1	Ian Rush	Liverpool	88
2	Mick Harford	Wimbledon	44
3	Tony Cottee	West Ham	42
4	Dean Saunders	Aston Villa	40
5	Ian Wright	Arsenal	39
6	John Barnes	Liverpool	37
7	Teddy Sheringham	Tottenham	34
8	Mark Hughes	Chelsea	33
	Brian McClair	Manchester Utd	33
10	Paul Wilkinson	Middlesbrough	31
11	Nigel Clough	Liverpool	30
	Mike Newell	Blackburn	30
	Alan Smith	Arsenal	30
14	Matt Le Tissier	Southampton	29
	Mark Bright	Sheffield Wednesday	29
16	Peter Beardsley	Newcastle	28
17	Paul Walsh	Manchester City	27
18	Alan Shearer	Blackburn	26
	John Fashanu	Wimbledon	26
20	Brian Deane	Leeds Utd	25
	Mick Quinn	Coventry	25
22	Robert Fleck	Chelsea	23
23	Steve Bruce	Manchester Utd	22
	Glenn Hoddle	Chelsea	22
25	Dean Holdsworth	Wimbledon	21
	Trevor Morley	West Ham	21
27	Dion Dublin	Coventry	20

SPOT ON
CAREER PENALTIES BY PREMIERSHIP PLAYERS IN THE LEAGUE, FA CUP & LEAGUE CUP

1	Jan Molby	39	Liverpool
2	Matt Le Tissier	31	Southampton
3	John Sheridan	31	Sheffield Wednesday
4	Dean Saunders	30	Aston Villa
5	Glenn Hoddle	28	Chelsea
6	Peter Beardsley	27	Newcastle
7	Gordon Strachan	26	Coventry
8	Julian Dicks	25	West Ham
9	Stuart Pearce	22	Nottingham Forest
	Mick Quinn	22	Coventry
11	Nigel Clough	20	Liverpool
	Alan Kimble	20	Wimbledon
	Gary Mcallister	20	Leeds
	Alan Shearer	20	Blackburn

BAD BOYS
PREMIERSHIP PLAYERS WITH THE MOST BOOKINGS AND SENDINGS-OFF OVER THE LAST FIVE COMPLETE SEASONS IN LEAGUE, FA CUP, LEAGUE CUP AND INTERNATIONAL MATCHES

			B'kings	S-Offs	Points
1	Vinny Jones	Wimbledon	53	6	189
2	Neil Ruddock	Liverpool	42	4	146
3	Mark Hughes	Chelsea	39	4	137
4	Ian Wright	Arsenal	43	0	129
5	David Burrows	Coventry	42	0	126
	Dennis Wise	Chelsea	37	3	126
7	Julian Dicks	West Ham	36	3	123
8	Collin Cooper	Nottm Forest	36	2	118
9	Roy Keane	Manchester Utd	35	1	110
	Martin Allen	West Ham	33	2	109
11	Francis Benali	Southampton	31	2	103
12	Mick Harford	Wimbledon	34	0	102
13	Matt Le Tissier	Southampton	32	1	101
14	Tony Adams	Arsenal	30	2	100
	Carlton Palmer	Sheffield Wednesday	30	2	100
16	Frank Sinclair	Chelsea	29	2	97
17	Graham Le Saux	Blackburn	30	1	95
18	Barry Horne	Everton	26	3	93
	Andy Thorne	Wimbledon	26	3	93
20	Andy Pearce	Sheffield Wednesday	29	1	92
	Alan Reeves	Wimbledon	29	1	92
22	Paul Furlong	Chelsea	27	2	91
	Kevin Scott	Tottenham	27	2	91
24	Andy Townsend	Aston Villa	25	3	90
25	Martin Keown	Arsenal	24	3	87
	Jason Lee	Nottm Forest	24	3	87
	Paul Stewart	Liverpool	24	3	87
28	Jamie Pollock	Middlesbrough	27	1	86
	Nigel Winterburn	Arsenal	27	1	86
30	Alan McDonald	Q.P.R.	27	1	86
31	Duncan Ferguson	Everton	23	3	84
	John Pemberton	Leeds Utd	28	0	84
33	Ken Monkou	Southampton	24	2	82
34	Tim Breaker	West Ham	23	2	79
	Les Ferdinand	Q.P.R.	23	2	79
36	Brian Deane	Leeds Utd	26	0	78
	John Ebbrell	Everton	26	0	78
38	Stuart Pearce	Nottm Forest	24	1	77
39	David Batty	Blackburn	25	0	75
	Alan Kernighan	Manchester City	25	0	75

(NB 3 points are awarded for each booking and 5 for each sending-off)

ALWAYS THERE
PREMIERSHIP PLAYERS WITH THE MOST EVER-PRESENT SEASONS

8	Dave Beasant	Southampton
	John Lukic	Leeds Utd
	Peter Shilton	Bolton
7	Steve Ogrizovic	Coventry
6	Bruce Grobbelaar	Southampton
	Neville Southall	Everton
5	Earl Barrett	Everton
	Collin Calderwood	Tottenham
	Andy Sinton	Sheffield Wednesday
	Ray Wilkins	Q.P.R.
	Chris Woods	Sheffield Wednesday
4	Steve Bruce	Manchester Utd
	Robbie Earle	Wimbledon
	Gary McAllister	Leeds Utd
	Brian McClair	Manchester Utd
	Ludek Miklosko	West Ham
	Gary Pallister	Manchester Utd
	David Phillips	Nottm Forest
	Dean Saunders	Aston Villa
3	John Burridge	Manchester City
	Nigel Clough	Liverpool
	Tony Cottee	West Ham
	Lee Dixon	Arsenal
	John Hendrie	Middlesbrough
	Barry Horne	Everton
	Dave Seaman	Arsenal
	Teddy Sheringham	Tottenham
	Chris Waddle	Sheffield Wednesday
	David White	Leeds
	Nigel Winterburn	Arsenal

THE VETERANS
PREMIER LEAGUE PLAYERS WITH 500+ LEAGUE, FA CUP AND LEAGUE CUP APPEARANCES

		Apps	*Present Club*
1	Peter Shilton	1181	Bolton
2	John Burridge	786	Manchester City
3	Steve Bruce	751	Manchester Utd
4	Viv Anderson	722	Middlesborough
5	David O'Leary	708	Leeds
6	Bryan Robson	681	Middlesbrough
7	Gary Mabbutt	679	Tottenham
8	Neville Southall	671	Everton
9	Mick Harford	651	Coventry
10	John Lukic	649	Leeds Utd
11	Bruce Grobbelaar	638	Southampton
12	Peter Beardsley	634	Newcastle
13	Dave Watson	628	Everton
14	Paul Allen	627	Southampton
15	Ian Rush	621	Liverpool
16	Dave Beasant	612	Southampton
17	David Seaman	599	Arsenal
18	Steve Ogrizovic	598	Coventry
19	John Barnes	590	Liverpool
20	Tony Coton	588	Manchester City
21	Paul Walsh	581	Manchester City
22	Glenn Hoddle	577	Chelsea
23	David Phillips	576	Nottm Forest
24	Mick Quinn	575	Coventry
25	Ray Wilkins	565	Q.P.R.
26	Alvin Martin	564	West Ham
27	Brian Borrows	563	Coventry
28	Colin Calderwood	558	Tottenham
29	Alan Smith	546	Arsenal
30	Neil Webb	542	Nottm Forest
31	Nigel Worthington	532	Leeds
32	Les Sealey	529	West Ham
33	Nigel Winterburn	527	Arsenal
34	Dean Saunders	526	Aston Villa
35	Dennis Irwin	525	Manchester Utd
36	Andy Sinton	521	Sheffield Wednesday
37	Tony Cottee	519	West Ham
38	Lee Dixon	518	Arsenal
	Ian Holloway	518	Q.P.R.
40	Paul Stewart	517	Liverpool
41	Andy Linighan	514	Arsenal
42	John Hendrie	509	Middlesbrough
43	David Bardsley	508	Q.P.R.
44	Keith Curle	503	Manchester City
45	Paul Wilkinson	502	Middlesbrough

SUPER-SUBS
PREMIERSHIP PLAYERS WITH THE MOST SUBSTITUTE LEAGUE APPEARANCES

			Number of sub apps
1	Paul Walsh	Manchester City	81
2	Andy Clarke	Wimbledon	72
3	Ronny Rosenthal	Tottenham	60
4	Malcolm Allen	Newcastle	59
5	Alan Kernighan	Manchester City	58
6	Kevin Campbell	Arsenal	56
	Gordon Watson	Southampton	56
	Mark Walters	Liverpool	56
9	Micky Hazard	Tottenham	55
10	Mike Newell	Blackburn	53
11	Stuart Barlow	Everton	52
12	Leigh Jenkinson	Coventry	51
	Clayton Blackmore	Middlesbrough	51
14	Scott Green	Bolton	48
15	Roy Wegerle	Coventry	47
16	Peter Beagrie	Manchester City	45
	Gary Blissett	Wimbledon	45
	Carl Griffiths	Manchester City	45
	Stuart Ripley	Blackburn	45
	Fitzroy Simpson	Manchester City	45
21	Mark Atkins	Blackburn	44
	Marcus Gayle	Wimbledon	44
	Paul Merson	Arsenal	44
24	Mark Bright	Sheffield Wednesday	43
25	Tony Cottee	Everton	42
	Mark Stein	Chelsea	42
27	Martin Allen	West Ham	41
	Chris Armstrong	Tottenham	41
	David Howells	Tottenham	41
	David O'leary	Leeds	41
	Lee Sharpe	Manchester Utd	41
32	Chris Bart-Williams	Sheffield Wednesday	40
	Dwight Yorke	Aston Villa	40

PULLED OFF AGAIN
PREMIERSHIP PLAYERS SUBSTITUTED MOST OFTEN FROM LEAGUE GAMES

			Number of times subbed
1	David Rocastle	Chelsea	75
2	Paul Merson	Arsenal	69
	Paul Walsh	Manchester City	69
4	Stuart Ripley	Blackburn	65
5	Tommy Johnson	Aston Villa	62
6	Micky Hazzard	Tottenham	56
7	Mattie Holmes	West Ham	49
8	David Hirst	Sheffield Wednesday	48
9	Anders Limpar	Everton	47
10	Marcus Gayle	Wimbledon	45
	John McGinlay	Bolton	45
	Gordon Strachan	Coventry	45
	Tommy Wright	Middlesbrough	45
14	Dean Holdsworth	Wimbledon	44
15	Rod Wallace	Leeds	43
	Roy Wegerle	Coventry	43
17	David Howells	Tottenham	42
	John Fashanu	Aston Villa	42
	Robbie Mustoe	Middlesbrough	42
20	Gary Blissett	Wimbledon	41
	Paul Cook	Coventry	41
22	Matt Le Tissier	Southampton	40
	Mick Quinn	Coventry	40
	Vinny Samways	Everton	40

HAT-TRICK HEROES
THE COMPLETE RECORDS OF THE PREMIERSHIP'S MOST FREQUENT TRIPLE SCORERS

IAN RUSH, LIVERPOOL, 14 HAT-TRICKS
26.1.82 v Notts County, 6.11.82 v Everton (4), 13.11.82 v Coventry, 1.1.83 v Notts
Couny, 29.10.83 v Luton (5), 20.1.84 v Aston Villa, 7.5.84 v Coventry (4), 10.3.85 v
Barnsley (FAC), 22.3.86 v Oxford, 14.2.87 v Leicester, 9.1.90 v Swansea (FAC)
9.10.90 v Crewe (LC), 27.10.93 v Ipswich (LC), 30.11.94 v Blackburn (LC)

IAN WRIGHT, ARSENAL, 12
3.11.87 v Plymouth, 13.5.89 v Birmingham, 25.9.90 v Southend (LC), 4.5.91 v
Wimbledon, 10.9.91 v Southampton, 21.12.91 v Everton (4), 2.5.92 v Southampton
2.1.93 v Yeovil (FAC), 21.9.93 v Huddersfield (LC), 5.3.94 v Ipswich, 19.3.94 v
Southampton, 15.4.95 v Ipswich

TONY COTTEE, WEST HAM, 11
25.10.83 v Bury (4) (LC), 6.3.85 v Wimbledon (FAC), 13.9.86 v Q.P.R., 7.10.86 v Preston, 24.1.87 v Coventry, 27.8.88 v Newcastle, 25.9.90 v Wrexham (LC), 5.10.91 v Tottenham, 21.8.93 v Sheffield Utd, 15.1.94 v Swindon, 17.12.94 v Manchester City

MICK QUINN, COVENTRY, 10
8.10.80 v Doncaster, 10.12.82 v Crewe, 1.1.83 v Halifax, 30.9.83 v Crewe, 11.5.85 v Carlisle, 21.10.86 v Derby, 19.8.89 v Leeds (4), 21.10.89 v Brighton, 1.12.90 v Leicester, 14.8.93 v Arsenal

TEDDY SHERINGHAM, TOTTENHAM, 9
13.12.86 v Huddersfield 26.12.87 v West Brom, 6.10.90 v West Brom, 28.2.91 v Plymouth (4), 10.4.91 v Charlton, 27.4.91 v Bristol City, 5.2.92 v Crystal Palace (LC) 20.2.93 v Leeds, 3.12.94 v Newcastle

ANDY COLE, MANCHESTER UTD, 8
25.8.92 v Cardiff (LC), 7.4.93 v Barnsley, 9.5.93 v Leicester, 22.9.93 v Notts County (LC), 5.10.93 v Notts County (LC), 21.11.93 v Liverpool, 23.2.94 v Coventry, 4.3.95 v Ipswich (5)

MICK HARFORD, WIMBLEDON, 8
29.2.80 v Wigan, 9.8.80 v Hull City (LC), 12.11.80 v Torquay, 25.10.83 v Derby (LC) 1.1.86 v Leicester, 26.4.86 v Watford, 6.10.87 v Wigan (LC), 31.10.90 v Sunderland (LC)

PAUL WALSH, MANCHESTER CITY, 8
12.8.80 v Brentford (LC), 4.9.82 v Notts County, 4.1.83 v West Ham, 23.4.83 v Swansea, 10.12.83 v Stoke, 29.10.85 v Brighton (LC), 1.11.86 v Norwich, 20.10.91 v Sheffield Utd

MATT LE TISSIER, SOUTHAMPTON, 7
7.3.87 v Leicester, 27.2.90 v Norwich, 17.3.90 v Wimbledon, 8.5.93 v Oldham 12.2.94 v Liverpool, 9.4.94 v Norwich, 5.10.94 v Huddersfield (4) (LC)

GUY WHITTINGHAM, SHEFFIELD WEDNESDAY, 7
30.12.89 v Oldham, 26.1.91 v Bournemouth (4) (FAC), 14.3.92 v Millwall , 15.8.92 v Bristol City (LC), 3.10.92 v Luton, 26.12.92 v Bristol Rovers, 6.4.93 v Peterborough

PETER BEARDSLEY, NEWCASTLE, 5
29.10.83 v Manchester City, 1.1.85 v Sunderland, 16.9.90 v Manchester Utd, 21.9.91 Coventry, 30.10.93 Wimbledon

ALAN SHEARER, BLACKBURN, 5
9.4.88 v Arsenal, 23.10.93 v Leeds, 26.11.94 v Q.P.R., 2.1.95 v West Ham, 28.1.95, Ipswich

JOHN HENDRIE, MIDDLESBROUGH, 4
13.2.88 v Oldham, 5.12.92 v Blackburn, 8.5.94 v Charlton, 17.12.94 v Burnley

DEAN HOLDSWORTH, WIMBLEDON, 4
6.1.90 v Rotherham, 17.8.91 v Leyton Orient, 6.1.94 v Scunthorpe (FAC), 26.4.94 v Oldham

JOHN MCGINLAY, BOLTON WANDERERS, 4
7.4.90 v Huddersfield, 19.3.91 v Bolton, 5.3.94 v Charlton, 23.4.94 v Middlesbrough

CRAIG MASKELL, SOUTHAMPTON, 4
1.4.89 v Bury, 17.3.90 v Cardiff (4), 29.1.92 v Carlisle, 10.3.92 v Darlington

PAUL RIDEOUT, EVERTON, 4
27.4.82 v Chester, 22.1.83 v Rochdale, 22.12.84 v Newcastle, 21.9.93 v Lincoln (LC)

ALAN SMITH, ARSENAL, 4
10.12.83 v Wolverhampton, 29.8.87 v Portsmouth, 27.8.88 v Wimbledon, 6.5.91 v Manchester Utd

PAUL STEWART, LIVERPOOL, 4
24.3.84 v Chester, 28.2.87 v Port Vale, 7.11.87 v Huddersfield, 29.4.89 v Millwall

JOHN BARNES, LIVERPOOL, 3
25.9.84 v Cardiff (LC), 5.5.90 v Coventry, 6.1.92 v Crewe (FAC)

BRIAN DEANE, LEEDS, 3
17.9.88 v Chester, 16.1.93 v Ipswich, 12.1.93 v Burnley (FAC)

ROBBIE FOWLER, LIVERPOOL, 3
5.10.93 v Fulham (5) (LC), 30.10.93 v Southampton, 28.8.94 v Arsenal

CRAIG HIGNETT, MIDDLESBROUGH, 3
30.4.91 v Rotherham, 14.11.92 v Wrexham (4) (FAC), 21.9.93 v Brighton (4) (LC)

MARK HUGHES, CHELSEA, 3
23.3.85 v Aston Villa, 16.9.89 v Millwall, 23.1.91 v Southampton

DEAN SAUNDERS, ASTON VILLA, 3
4.10.89 v Cambridge (LC), 2.3.91 v Newcastle, 12.2.94 v Swindon

DAVID WHITE, LEEDS, 3
7.11.87 v Huddersfield, 23.4.91 v Aston Villa (4), 2.5.92 v Oldham

PAUL WILKINSON, MIDDLESBROUGH, 3
7.10.86 v Newport (LC), 13.4.91 v Wolverhampton, 27.9.94 v Scarborough (LC)

TOP OF THE CHARTS

PREMIERSHIP PLAYERS WHO HAVE FINISHED AS THE SEASON'S TOP SCORERS IN A LEAGUE/DIVISION

	League/Division	Season
Tony Yeboah	Bundesliga	92-93
Mick Quinn	Football League	89-90
Guy Whittingham	Football League	92-93
Ian Wright	Football League	91-92
Ian Rush	Division 1	83-84
Alan Smith	Division 1	88-89
Alan Smith	Division 1	90-91
Ian Wright	Division 1	91-92
Teddy Sheringham	Premier	92-93
Andy Cole	Premier	93-94
Alan Shearer	Premier	94-95
Guy Whittingham	Division 1	92-93
John McGinlay	Division 1	93-94
Mick Quinn	Division 2	86-87
Mick Quinn	Division 2	89-90
Teddy Sheringham	Division 2	90-91
Carl Griffiths	Division 3	92-93
Dean Holdsworth	Division 3	91-92
Gary Bull	G.M.V.C. League	92-93
Brian McClair	Scottish Premier	86-87
Denis Bergkamp	Dutch Division 1	90-91
Denis Bergkamp	Dutch Division 1	91-92
Denis Bergkamp	Dutch Division 1	92-93